LORDSHIP AND ARCHITE

Lordship and Architecture

in Medieval and Renaissance Scotland

edited by

Richard D. Oram and Geoffrey P. Stell

RCAHMS

First published in Great Britain in 2005 by
John Donald (Publisher) an imprint of Birlinn Ltd
West Newington House
10 West Newington Road
Edinburgh EH9 1QS

www.birlinn.co.uk

ISBN 10: 0 85976 628 4
ISBN 13: 978 0 85976 628 9

We gratefully acknowedge the support of the following bodies:
The Scotland Inheritance Fund
The Russell Trust
The Binks Trust
The Convention of the Baronage of Scotland
The Royal Commission on the Ancient and Historical Monuments of Scotland

British Library Cataloguing in Publication Data
A catalogue record is available on request from the British Library

Typeset by Carnegie Publishing Ltd, Chatsworth Road, Lancaster
Printed and bound by Bell & Bain Ltd, Glasgow

Contents

Acknowledgements   vii
Contributors   viii
List of Illustrations   ix
List of Abbreviations   xvi

Foreword   xix
RICHARD D. ORAM *and* GEOFFREY P. STELL

1. Prelatical Builders: A Preliminary Study, *c.* 1124–*c.* 1500   I
    RICHARD D. ORAM

2. Adapting Tradition?: The Earldom of Strathearn, 1114–1296   26
    FIONA J. WATSON

3. The Brus Lordship of Annandale, 1124–1296   45
    PETER CORSER

4. The Comyns to 1300   61
    ALAN YOUNG

5. The Heirs of Somerled   85
    IAN FISHER

6. Domestic Architecture in the Lordship of the Isles   97
    DAVID H. CALDWELL *and* NIGEL A. RUCKLEY

7. 'Pillars of the Community': Clan Campbell and Architectural
    Patronage in the Fifteenth Century   123
    STEPHEN I. BOARDMAN

8. The Black Douglases, 1369–1455   161
    CHRISTINE A. MCGLADDERY

LORDSHIP AND
ARCHITECTURE
IN MEDIEVAL
AND
RENAISSANCE
SCOTLAND

❧

9. The Sinclairs in the Late Middle Ages 189
BARBARA E. CRAWFORD

10. The Maxwells of Caerlaverock 205
ALASTAIR M. T. MAXWELL-IRVING

11. The Homes and the East March 231
MAUREEN M. MEIKLE

12. The Gordons and the North-East, 1452–1640 251
HARRY GORDON SLADE

13. The Mackenzies 273
JEAN MUNRO

14. Court and Courtier Architecture, 1424–1660 293
AONGHUS McKECHNIE

Index

Acknowledgements

The publisher and editors wish to record their gratitude, above all, to all their fellow contributors, who have patiently waited a long time to see this project reach publication. A material debt of gratitude is also owed to The Convention of the Baronage of Scotland, which has generously contributed to the costs of producing and reproducing the illustrations, and to the Royal Commission on the Ancient and Historical Monuments of Scotland (RCAHMS) for supplying the bulk of the illustrations and for hosting a number of seminars under the auspices of the Baronial Research Group (BARG) of The Colloquium for Scottish Medieval and Renaissance Studies. We are also much indebted to the Society of Antiquaries of Scotland for their collaboration in the presentation of a one-day conference on this theme in May 1997, an event which helped significantly to foster wider interest in the subject and in the completion of the book. The hard work of Alison Sandison of the Cartographic Unit, Department of Geography, University of Aberdeen, in standardising and producing the maps, is gratefully acknowledged.

Contributors

RICHARD ORAM is a Senior Lecturer in History at the University of Stirling.

GEOFFREY STELL was formerly Head of Architecture at RCAHMS, Edinburgh.

FIONA WATSON is a Senior Lecturer in History at the University of Stirling.

PETER CORSER was formerly an Archaeological Field Investigator with RCAHMS, Edinburgh.

ALAN YOUNG was formerly Principal Lecturer in History at the University College of Ripon and York St John, Edinburgh.

IAN FISHER was formerly Head of Thematic Architectural Survey at RCAHMS, Edinburgh.

DAVID CALDWELL is Keeper of History & Applied Art at the National Museums of Scotland, Edinburgh.

NIGEL RUCKLEY was formerly Geoarchaeology Co-ordinator at the British Geological Survey (Scotland), Edinburgh.

STEPHEN BOARDMAN is a Lecturer in Scottish History at the University of Edinburgh.

CHRISTINE MCGLADDERY is an Honorary Lecturer in Scottish History at the University of St Andrews.

BARBARA CRAWFORD was formerly Lecturer in Medieval History at the University of St Andrews.

ALASTAIR MAXWELL-IRVING is an independent scholar.

MAUREEN MEIKLE is a Senior Lecturer in History at the University of Sunderland.

HARRY GORDON SLADE is an independent scholar.

JEAN MUNRO is an independent scholar.

AONGHUS MCKECHNIE is a Principal Inspector of Historic Buildings with Historic Scotland, Edinburgh.

List of Illustrations

1.1 Map: prelatical builders xx
1.2 St Andrews Castle, Fife: from John Slezer, *Theatrum Scotiae* 4
1.3 St Andrews Castle, Fife: aerial view 6
1.4 Spynie Palace, Moray: aerial view 7
1.5 Spynie Palace, Moray: view from south-east 8
1.6 Glasgow, Bishop's Palace: from *Swan's Views of Glasgow* (1828) 17
1.7 Crossraguel Abbey, Ayrshire: aerial view 20
1.8 Arbroath Abbey, Angus: gatehouse range, from Grose's
Antiquities (1790) 21
1.9 Carnassarie Castle, Argyll: south elevation 22

2.1 Map: earldom of Strathearn properties mentioned in text 26
2.2 Dunknock, Perthshire: aerial view 33
2.3 Muthill Old Parish Church, Perthshire: view from south-east 39

3.1 Map: Brus lordship of Annandale 44
3.2 Timber castles: comparative plans (sheet 1) 46
3.3 Timber castles: comparative plans (sheet 2) 47
3.4 Lochmaben, Dumfriesshire: vertical aerial view 49
3.5 Torthorwald Castle, Dumfriesshire: aerial view 50
3.6 Garpol Water, motte-and-bailey, Dumfriesshire: aerial view 52
3.7 Tinwald, motte-and-bailey and parish church, Dumfriesshire:
aerial view 53
3.8 Auchen Castle, Dumfriesshire: aerial view 54

4.1 Map: Comyn properties mentioned in the text 60
4.2 Lochindorb Castle, Moray: general view 64
4.3 Inverlochy Castle, Inverness-shire: view by Bouquet, 1849 65
4.4 Balvenie Castle, Moray: aerial view 66
4.5 Inchmahome Priory, Perthshire: aerial view 68
4.6 Blair Atholl Castle, Perthshire: aerial view 70
4.7 Deer Abbey, Aberdeenshire: aerial view 71
4.8 Tarset Castle, Northumberland: aerial view 76

5.1 Map: heirs of Somerled 84

LORDSHIP AND
ARCHITECTURE
IN MEDIEVAL
AND
RENAISSANCE
SCOTLAND

❧

5.2   The heirs of Somerled: genealogical tree   86
5.3   Iona Nunnery, Argyll: church from south-east   88
5.4   Castle Sween, Argyll: view from south-west   89
5.5   Dunstaffnage Castle, Argyll: view from north-east   90
5.6   Cairnburgh Mor Castle, Argyll: view from north-east   91
5.7   Mingary Castle, Argyll: aerial view   92

6.1   Map: Lordship of the Isles   96
6.2   Skipness Castle, Argyll: view from north-west   101
6.3   Dunstaffnage Chapel, Argyll: exterior of south wall, 1972   102
6.4   Ardtornish Castle, Argyll: from south   105
6.5   Aros Castle, Argyll: view from south-east   115

7.1   Map: Campbell properties mentioned in the text   122
7.2   Innis Chonnell Castle, Argyll: general view   125
7.3   Dunoon Castle, Argyll: general view from west   126
7.4   Detail of effigy of Margaret Stewart, Lady Campbell   129
7.5   Detail of effigy of Sir Duncan Campbell   129
7.6   Carrick Castle, Argyll: view from south-east   141

8.1   Map: the Black Douglases   160
8.2   Bothwell Castle, Lanarkshire: aerial view   162
8.3   Bothwell Castle, Lanarkshire: 'Douglas Tower'   163
8.4   Threave Castle, Stewartry of Kirkcudbright: aerial view   165
8.5   Lincluden College, Dumfries: chancel showing monument to
         Margaret, Countess of Douglas, c.1880   167
8.6   Newark Castle, Selkirkshire: general view   173
8.7   Darnaway Castle, Moray: roof over great hall   183

9.1   Map: Sinclair properties mentioned in the text   188
9.2   Roslin Castle and Chapel, Midlothian: general view, c.1880   190
9.3   Roslin Chapel, Midlothian: eastern aisle by R. W. Billings   191
9.4   Roslin Castle, Midlothian: view from north-west (from
         MacGibbon and Ross, Castellated and Domestic Architecture,
         volume 1 (1887), 368, Fig. 318)
9.5   Ravenscraig Castle, Fife: aerial view   197
9.6   Ravenscraig Castle, Fife: from north-west   198
9.7   Castle Sinclair Girnigoe, Caithness: general view, c.1908   200
9.8   Castle Sinclair Girnigoe, Caithness: aerial view   201

10.1 Map: Maxwell properties mentioned in the text   204
10.2 Caerlaverock Castle, Dumfriesshire: view from north-west   206
10.3 Caerlaverock Castle, Dumfriesshire: Nithsdale Apartments   208
10.4 Mearns Castle, Renfrewshire: view from south-east   209

10.5 Hills Tower, Stewartry of Kirkcudbright: view from north   213

10.6 Kirkconnell House and Tower, Stewartry of Kirkcudbright: view from east   216

10.7 Kirkconnell House and Tower, Stewartry of Kirkcudbright: ground-floor plan   217

10.8 Hoddom Castle, Dumfriesshire: view from south   219

10.9 Hoddom Castle, Dumfriesshire: ground- and first-floor plans   220

10.10 Terregles 'Queir', Stewartry of Kirkcudbright: view from south-east   221

10.11 Fourmerkland Tower, Dumfriesshire: view from south   225

11.1 Map: Home properties mentioned in the text   232

11.2 Cowdenknowes, Berwickshire: view *c.*1845   235

11.3 Huttonhall, Berwickshire: general view   237

11.4 Huttonhall, Berwickshire: general view showing ruinous tower, *c.*1880   239

11.5 Huttonhall, Berwickshire: ground- and first-floor plans, *c.*1892   240

11.6 Huttonhall, Berwickshire: dining room, 1915   241

11.7 Home Castle, Berwickshire: aerial view   242

11.8 Home Castle, Berwickshire: detail of Saxton's map of Northumberland, 1570   243

11.9 Duns Castle, Berwickshire: 1790s   244

11.10 Fast Castle, Berwickshire: aerial view of headland and castle   246

12.1 Map: Gordon properties mentioned in the text   250

12.2 Drumminor (Castle Forbes), Aberdeenshire: floor-plans   253

12.3 Huntly Castle, Aberdeenshire: south front by R.W. Billings   254

12.4 Huntly Castle, Aberdeenshire: principal doorway by R.W. Billings   255

12.5 Huntly Castle, Aberdeenshire: from north-east.   256

12.6 Terpersie Castle, Aberdeenshire: view from south-west by R.W. Billings   258

12.7 Midmar Castle, Aberdeenshire: reconstruction of south front as in *c.*1609   261

12.8 The Bog (Gordon Castle), Moray: from John Slezer, *Theatrum Scotiae*   263

12.9 The Bog (Gordon Castle), Moray: sketch reconstruction of first-floor plan   265

12.10 Cluny Castle, Aberdeenshire: reconstruction of view from south-west   267

13.1 Map: Mackenzie properties mentioned in the text   274

13.2 Mackenzie of Kintail: genealogical table   275

LORDSHIP AND
ARCHITECTURE
IN MEDIEVAL
AND
RENAISSANCE
SCOTLAND

𓏪

13.3 Tarbat House (Old), Ross and Cromarty   284

13.4 Castle Leod, Ross and Cromarty: view from south-east   285

13.5 Beauly Priory, Inverness-shire: view from south-west.   287

13.6 Eilean Donan Castle, Ross and Cromarty: general view,
     late nineteenth century   288

14.1 Map: properties mentioned in the text   292

14.2 Linlithgow Palace, West Lothian: general view of east front   295

14.3 Restalrig, St Triduana's Chapel, Edinburgh: interior   298

14.4 Stirling Castle: Forework   300

14.5 Stirling Castle, Palace: sculpture on north quarter   301

14.6 Falkland Palace, Fife: general view of courtyard from
     north-west   303

14.7 Mar's Wark, Stirling: principal façade   307

14.8 Eyemouth Fort, Berwickshire: aerial view   309

14.9 Culross Abbey House, Fife: general view   313

14.10 Barcaldine Castle, Argyll: general view   315

14.11 Argyll Lodging, Stirling: general view   316

14.12 Dunbar Monument, Dunbar Parish Church, East Lothian   321

List of Abbreviations

Aberdeen-Banff Ill.	*Illustrations of the Topography and Antiquities of the Shires of Aberdeen and Banff* (Spalding Club, 1847–69).
Aberdeen Registrum	*Registrum Episcopatus Aberdonensis* (Spalding and Maitland Clubs, 1845).
Acts of the Lords of the Isles	*The Acts of the Lords of the Isles 1336–1493*, eds. J. Munro and R. W. Munro (Scottish History Society, 1986).
ADC	*The Acts of the Lords of Council in Civil Causes*, eds. T. Thomson and others (Edinburgh, 1839 and 1918–).
ADCP	*Acts of the Lords of Council in Public Affairs 1501–1554: Selections from Acta Dominorum Concilii*, ed. R. K. Hannay (Edinburgh, 1932).
APS	*The Acts of the Parliaments of Scotland*, eds. T. Thomson and C. Innes (Edinburgh, 1814–75).
Anderson, *Scottish Annals*	*Scottish Annals from English Chronicles* AD *500 to 1286*, ed. A. O. Anderson (London, 1908).
Anderson, *Early Sources*	*Early Sources of Scottish History* AD *500 to 1286*, ed. A. O. Anderson (Edinburgh, 1922).
Arbroath Liber	*Liber S. Thome de Aberbrothoc* (Bannatyne Club, 1848–56).
AT	*Argyll Transcripts, made by 10th Duke of Argyll* (Argyll MSS, Inveraray; photostat copies of entries to 1600 in Department of Scottish History, University of Glasgow).
Barbour, *Bruce*	John Barbour, *The Bruce*, ed. A. A. M. Duncan (Edinburgh, 1997).
Boece, *Vitae*	*Hectoris Boetii Murthlacensium et Aberdonensium Episcoporum Vitae* (New Spalding Club, 1894).
Buchanan, *History*	G. Buchanan, *The History of Scotland*, trans. J. Aikman (Glasgow and Edinburgh, 1827–9).
Cal. Border Papers	Calendar of Papers and Letters relating to the affairs of the Borders of England and Scotland, ed. J. Bain (Edinburgh, 1894–6).
Cambuskenneth Registrum	*Registrum Monasterii Sancte Marie de Cambuskenneth* (Grampian Club, 1872).

LORDSHIP AND
ARCHITECTURE
IN MEDIEVAL
AND
RENAISSANCE
SCOTLAND

✣

Cawdor Bk.	*The Book of the Thanes of Cawdor* (Spalding Club, 1859).
CDS	*Calendar of Documents Relating to Scotland*, eds. J. Bain and others (Edinburgh, 1881–1985).
Chron. Auchinleck	The Auchinleck Chronicle, in C. A. McGladdery, *James II* (Edinburgh, 1990), Appendix 2.
Chron. Bower (Watt)	Walter Bower, *Scotichronicon*, eds. D. E. R. Watt and others (Aberdeen, 1987–97).
Chron. Fordun	*Johannis de Fordun, Chronica Gentis Scotorum*, ed. W. F. Skene (Edinburgh, 1871–2).
Chron. Melrose	*Chronica de Mailros* (Bannatyne Club, 1835).
Chron. Pluscarden	*Liber Pluscardensis*, ed. F. J. H. Skene (Edinburgh, 1870–80).
Chron. Wyntoun (Laing)	*Androw of Wyntoun, The Orygynale Cronykil of Scotland*, ed. D. Laing (Edinburgh, 1872–9).
Coldstream Chartulary	*Chartulary of the Cistercian Priory of Coldstream* (Grampian Club, 1879).
Coupar Angus Chrs.	*Charters of the Abbey of Coupar Angus*, ed. D. E. Easson (Scottish History Society, 1947).
Cowan, *Parishes*	I. B. Cowan, *The Parishes of Medieval Scotland* (Scottish Record Society, xciii, 1967).
Cowan and Easson, *Religious Houses*	I. B. Cowan and D. E. Easson, *Medieval Religious Houses: Scotland* (London, 1976).
CPL	*Calendar of Entries in the Papal Registers Relating to Great Britain and Ireland: Papal Letters*, eds. W. H. Bliss and others (London, 1893); 1378–94, ed. C. Burns (Scottish History Society, 1976); 1394–1419, ed. F. McGurk (Scottish History Society, 1976).
CPP	*Calendar of Entries in the Papal Registers Relating to Great Britain and Ireland: Petitions to the Pope*, ed. W. H. Bliss (London, 1896).
Crossraguel Chrs.	*Charters of the Abbey of Crossraguel* (Archaeological and Historical Collections relating to Ayrshire and Galloway, 1886).
CSP Scot.	*Calendar of the State Papers relating to Scotland and Mary, Queen of Scots 1547–1603*, eds. J. Bain and others (Edinburgh, 1898–).
CSSR	*Calendar of Scottish Supplications to Rome*: i, 1418–22, eds. E. R. Lindsay and A. I. Cameron (Scottish History Society, 1934); ii, 1423–28, ed. A. I. Dunlop (Scottish History Society, 1956); iii, 1428–32, eds. A. I. Dunlop and I. B. Cowan (Scottish History Society, 1970); iv, 1433–47, eds. A. I. Dunlop and D. MacLauchlan (Glasgow, 1983).

DES	*Discovery and Excavation, Scotland.*
Diplom. Norv.	*Diplomatarium Norvegicum* (Kristiania, 1849–1919).
Dryburgh Liber	*Liber S.Marie de Dryburgh* (Bannatyne Club, 1847).
Dunfermline Registrum	*Registrum de Dunfermelyn* (Bannatyne Club, 1842).
ER	*The Exchequer Rolls of Scotland,* eds. J. Stuart and others (Edinburgh, 1878–1908).
Fraser, *Annandale*	W. Fraser, *The Annandale Family Book* (Edinburgh, 1894).
Fraser, *Buccleuch*	W. Fraser, *The Scotts of Buccleuch* (Edinburgh, 1878).
Fraser, *Caerlaverock*	W. Fraser, *The Book of Caerlaverock* (Edinburgh, 1873).
Fraser, *Cromartie*	W. Fraser, *The Earls of Cromartie* (Edinburgh, 1876).
Fraser, *Douglas*	W. Fraser, *The Douglas Book* (Edinburgh, 1885).
Fraser, *Elphinstone*	W. Fraser, *The Elphinstone Family Book* (Edinbugh, 1897).
Fraser, *Grant*	W. Fraser, *The Chiefs of Grant* (Edinburgh, 1883).
Fraser, *Lennox*	W. Fraser, *The Lennox* (Edinburgh, 1874).
Fraser, *Melville*	W. Fraser, *The Melvilles Earls of Melville and the Leslies Earls of Leven* (Edinburgh, 1890).
Fraser, *Menteith*	W. Fraser, *The Red Book of Menteith* (Edinburgh, 1880).
GAJ	*Glasgow Archaeological Journal.*
Glasgow Friars Munimenta	*Munimenta Fratrum Predicatorum de Glasgu* (Maitland Club, 1846).
Glasgow Registrum	*Registrum Episcopatus Glasguensis* (Bannatyne and Maitland Clubs, 1843).
Hamilton Papers	*The Hamilton Papers,* ed. J. Bain (Edinburgh, 1890–92).
Hary's Wallace	*Vita Nobilissimi Defensoris Scotie Wilelmi Wallace Militis,* ed. M. P. McDiarmid (Scottish Text Society, 1968).
Hay, *Sainteclaires*	*Genealogie of the Sainteclaires of Rosslyn,* ed. R. A. Hay (Edinburgh, 1835).
HBNC	*History of the Berwickshire Naturalists' Club.*
Highland Papers	*Highland Papers,* ed. J. R. N. McPhail (Scottish History Society, 1914–34).
HMC	*Reports of the Royal Commission on Historic Manuscripts* (London, 1870-).
Holyrood Liber	*Liber Cartarum Sancte Crucis* (Bannatyne Club, 1840).
Inchaffray Chrs.	*Charters, Bulls and other Documents relating to the Abbey of Inchaffray* (Scottish History Society, 1908).
Inchaffray Liber	*Liber Insule Missarum* (Bannatyne Club, 1847).
Inchcolm Chrs.	*Charters of the Abbey of Inchcolm,* eds. D. E. Easson and A. Macdonald (Scottish History Society, 1938).

LORDSHIP AND
ARCHITECTURE
IN MEDIEVAL
AND
RENAISSANCE
SCOTLAND

❧

James IV Letters	*The Letters of James the Fourth 1505–13*, eds. R. K. Hannay and R. L. Mackie (Scottish History Society, 1953).
James V Letters	*The Letters of James V*, eds. R. K. Hannay and D. Hay (Edinburgh, 1954).
Kelso Liber	*Liber S.Marie de Calchou* (Bannatyne Club, 1816).
L. & P., Hen. VIII	*Letters and Papers, Foreign and Domestic of Henry VIII*, eds. J. S. Brewer and others (London, 1864–1932).
Laing, *Seals*	H. Laing, *Descriptive Catalogue of Impressions from Ancient Scottish Seals* (Bannatyne and Maitland Clubs, 1850).
Lamont Papers	*An Inventory of Lamont Papers* (Scottish Records Society, 1914).
Lawrie, *ESC*	*Early Scottish Charters prior to 1153*, ed. A. C. Lawrie (Glasgow, 1905).
Lennox Cartularium	*Cartularium Comitatus de Levenax* (Maitland Club, 1833).
Lindores Chartulary	*Chartulary of the Abbey of Lindores* (Scottish History Society, 1903).
Macfarlane, *Genealogical Coll.*	*Genealogical Collections concerning Families in Scotland made by Walter Macfarlane* (Scottish History Society, 1900).
Macfarlane, *Geographical Coll.*	*Geographical Collections relating to Scotland made by Walter Macfarlane* (Scottish History Society, 1906–8).
MacGibbon and Ross, *Castellated and Domestic Architecture*	D. MacGibbon and T. Ross, *The Castellated and Domestic Architecture of Scotland* (Edinburgh, 1887–92).
MacGibbon and Ross, *Ecclesiastical Architecture*	D. MacGibbon and T. Ross, *The Ecclesiastical Architecture of Scotland* (Edinburgh, 1896–7).
Melrose Liber	*Liber Sancte Marie de Melros* (Bannatyne Club, 1837).
Moray Registrum	*Registrum Episcopatus Moraviensis* (Bannatyne Club, 1837).
Morton Registrum	*Registrum Honoris de Morton* (Bannatyne Club, 1853).
Myln, *Vitae*	A. Myln, *Vitae Dunkeldensis Ecclesiae Episcoporum* (Bannatyne Club, 1831).
NAS	National Archives of Scotland.
Newbattle Registrum	*Registrum S.Marie de Neubotle* (Bannatyne Club, 1849).
NLS	National Library of Scotland.
NRAS	National Register of Archives for Scotland.
NSA	*The New Statistical Account of Scotland* (Edinburgh, 1845).
OPS	*Origines Parochiales Scotiae* (Bannatyne Club, 1851–55).

Orkney Recs.	*Records of the Earldom of Orkney* (Scottish History Society, Edinburgh, 1914).
OSA	*The Statistical Account of Scotland* (Edinburgh, 1791–9).
Paisley Registrum	*Registrum Monasterii de Passelet* (Maitland Club, 1832).
Palgrave, *Docs. Hist. Scot.*	*Documents and Records Illustrative of the History of Scotland*, ed. F. Palgrave (London, 1837).
Panmure Registrum	*Registrum de Panmure*, ed. J. Stuart (Edinburgh, 1874).
Pinkerton, *History*	J. Pinkerton, *The History of Scotland from the Accession of the House of Stuart to that of Mary, with Appendixes of Original Papers* (London, 1797).
Pitscottie, *Historie*	R. Lindesay of Pitscottie, *The Historie and Cronicles of Scotland* (Scottish Text Society, 1899–1911).
PSAS	*Proceedings of the Society of Antiquaries of Scotland.*
RCAHMS	Royal Commision on the Ancient and Historical Monuments of Scotland.
RCAHMS, *Argyll*	*Argyll, An Inventory of the Monuments*: i, Kintyre (Edinburgh, 1971); ii, Lorn (Edinburgh, 1975); iii, Mull, Tiree, Coll and Northern Argyll (Edinburgh, 1980); iv, Iona (Edinburgh, 1982); v, Islay, Jura, Colonsay and Oronsay (Edinburgh, 1984); vii, Medieval and Later Monuments of Mid Argyll and Cowal (Edinburgh, 1992).
RCAHMS, *Berwickshire*	*Inventory of Ancient Monuments and Historical Constructions of the County of Berwick* (Edinburgh, 1915).
RCAHMS, *Dumfriesshire*	*Inventory of Monuments and Constructions in the County of Dumfries* (Edinburgh, 1920).
RCAHMS, *Eastern Dumfries*	*Eastern Dumfriesshire: An Archaeological Landscape* (Edinburgh, 1997).
RCAHMS, *Fife*	*Inventory of Ancient Monuments and Constructions in the Counties of Fife, Kinross and Clackmannan* (Edinburgh, 1933).
RCAHMS, *Lanarkshire*	*Inventory of Prehistoric and Roman Monuments of Lanarkshire* (Edinburgh, 1982).
RCAHMS, *Midlothian*	*Inventory of Monuments in Midlothian and West Lothian* (Edinburgh, 1929).
RCAHMS, *Peeblesshire*	*Inventory of Monuments of Peeblesshire* (Edinburgh, 1967).
RCAHMS, *Roxburghshire*	*Inventory of the Ancient Monuments and Historical Constructions of Roxburghshire* (Edinburgh, 1956).
Retours	*Retours Inquisitionum ad Capellam Domini Regis Retornatarium quae in Publicis Archivis Scotiae adhuc servantur, Abbreviatio* (Record Commission, 1811–16).

LORDSHIP AND
ARCHITECTURE
IN MEDIEVAL
AND
RENAISSANCE
SCOTLAND

᙭

RMS	*Registrum Magni Sigilli Regum Scotorum*, eds. J. M. Thomson and others (Edinburgh, 1882–1914).
RPC	*The Register of the Privy Council of Scotland*, eds. J. H. Burton and others (Edinburgh, 1877-).
RRS	*Regesta Regum Scotorum*: i, *The Acts of Malcolm IV*, ed. G. W. S. Barrow (Edinburgh, 1960); ii, *The Acts of William I*, eds. G. W. S. Barrow and W. W. Scott (Edinburgh, 1971); v, *The Acts of Robert I*, ed. A. A. M. Duncan (Edinburgh, 1988); vi, *The Acts of David II*, ed. B. Webster (Edinburgh, 1982).
RSCHS	*Records of the Scottish Church History Society.*
RSS	*Registrum Secreti Sigilli Regum Scotorum*, eds. M. Livingstone and others (Edinburgh, 1908-).
Rotuli Scotiae	*Rotuli Scotiae in Turri Londiniensi et in Domo Capitulari Westmonasteriensi Asservati*, eds. D. Macpherson and others (1814–19).
St Andrews Liber	*Liber Cartarum Prioratus Sancti Andree in Scotia* (Bannatyne Club, 1841).
Scone Liber	*Liber Ecclesie de Scon* (Bannatyne and Maitland Clubs, 1843).
Scots Peerage	*The Scots Peerage*, ed. Sir J. Balfour Paul (Edinburgh, 1904–14).
SHR	*Scottish Historical Review.*
SRS	Scottish Record Society.
Stevenson, *Documents*	*Documents Illustrative of the History of Scotland 1286–1306*, ed. J. Stevenson (Edinburgh, 1870).
STS	Scottish Text Society.
TA	*Accounts of the Lord High Treasurer of Scotland*, eds. T. Dickson and Sir J. Balfour Paul (Edinburgh, 1877–1916).
Taymouth Bk.	*The Black Book of Taymouth* (Bannatyne Club, 1855).
TDGNHAS	*Transactions of the Dumfriesshire and Galloway Natural History and Antiquarian Society.*
TGAS	*Transactions of the Glasgow Archaeological Society.*
TGSI	*Transactions of the Gaelic Society of Inverness.*
Theiner, *Monumenta*	*Vetera Monumenta Hibernorum et Scotorum Historiam Illustrantia*, ed. A. Theiner (Rome, 1864).
TRHS	*Transactions of the Royal Historical Society.*
TSES	*Transactions of the Scottish Ecclesiological Society.*
Watt, *Fasti*	*Fasti Ecclesie Scoticanae Medii Aevi ad annum 1638*, ed. D. E. R. Watt, 2nd draft (Scottish Record Society, 1969).

Foreword

Richard D. Oram and *Geoffrey P. Stell*

Castle studies in Scotland have had a long and distinguished history as a field of academic and antiquarian endeavour. From the monumental achievement of the Edinburgh-based architects David MacGibbon and Thomas Ross in their *Castellated and Domestic Architecture of Scotland* (5 vols., 1887–92), through W. Mackay Mackenzie's *The Medieval Castle in Scotland* (Edinburgh, 1927) and Stewart Cruden's *The Scottish Castle* (3rd edition, Edinburgh, 1981), to Joachim Zeune's exposition of the evolution and development of the tower-house tradition, Scotland's castles have been subjected to detailed architectural analysis and classification. The chief focus within this tradition has been largely on form and plan, with chronologically-based schemes of stylistic evolution hammering the structures into a rigid framework which charted a progression from early – and, therefore, by definition unsophisticated – fortifications of earth and timber, through stone castles of enclosure to the complex tower-houses of the sixteenth and seventeenth centuries. In effect, castles have been viewed as architectural artefacts, to be typologised and categorised as part of a morphological sequence. Defensive developments as chronological indicators have weighed heavily in these studies, with the consequence that castles have been projected primarily as fortifications, a projection aided by the stark and evidently uncompromisingly military character of many of the surviving structures.

More recently there has been a growing trend towards emphasis on the domestic aspects of Scotland's castles, partly as a consequence of the increasing amount of archaeological investigation of sites. Excavation in particular has served to demolish the notion of a supposed paranoid introversion and an anxiety for defence allegedly symptomatic of the prolonged traumas of the Wars of Independence and responsible for the stark towers which so characterise Scotland's late medieval castle-building tradition. Rather than isolated defence-driven monoliths, the towers have been revealed as the centrepieces of lightly-defended complexes of halls, accommodation blocks and domestic buildings. The fruits of this trend can be seen in Christopher Tabraham's *Scottish Castles and Fortifications* (HMSO, 1986) or *Scotland's Castles* (London, 1997), or in Peter Yeoman's

LORDSHIP AND
ARCHITECTURE
IN MEDIEVAL
AND
RENAISSANCE
SCOTLAND

꒰꒱

Medieval Scotland (London, 1995), where, although the chronological development of fortification still provides the central interpretative strand, great stress has been laid on their non-military, primarily residential, functions and the material aspects of the daily routines of castle life.

Alongside this approach stands a quite different tradition, where the focus is primarily on the social, economic and political function of the castle as a centre of lordship, on its structural symbolism and psychology. This can be traced in part from W. Mackay Mackenzie's family-based approach to castle research, where study of the families of patrons and builders was given equal weighting with structural analysis. It found an enthusiastic follower in W. Douglas Simpson. His considerable output of research into individual castles was founded on a synthetic approach which placed the buildings in a broad context: the economic, social and juris-dictional hub of a complex of landed properties and seigneurial rights; the residence and projection of the social and political aspirations of a family; and the physical manifestation of their lordship. His style reached maturity in *The Earldom of Mar* (Aberdeen, 1949), itself a development of the integrationist approach which he had earlier presented in his Rhind Lectures of 1941, published as *The Province of Mar* (Aberdeen, 1943). In the *Earldom of Mar*, through a synthesis of landscape studies, family and parish history, archaeology and architectural studies, he lifted castles such as Craig, Kildrummy and Midmar above the one-dimensional, fortress-fixated interpretations of his contemporaries to present them as dynamic organisms around which revolved the life of a wider political and economic community. Unfortunately, few scholars followed in the Simpson tradition, and the highly florid prose which was his trademark quickly dated much of his work and rendered it relatively unreadable to modern students. But this does not detract from the vitality and freshness of his ideas, which have provided one of the main inspirations for the approach taken in this collection of essays.

This present volume, the results of a second collaborative programme of research by members of the Baronial Research Group (the first resulting in a collection of *Essays on the Nobility of Medieval Scotland*, edited by K. J. Stringer (Edinburgh, 1985)), focuses on a collection of noble families and peer groups, each broadly representative of a period or a region, and examines the development and projection of their lordship and authority through their architectural patronage. Castles of some form generally lie at the core of these individual studies, but the essays are offered as part of a wider appraisal of the architecture of lordship or the physical projection of seigneurial powers to be seen also in patronage of the Church or in the symbol-laden monumental sculpture which commemorated the noble dead. A study of *Lordship and Architecture* embraces not only the tangible evidence for architectural styles and constructional techniques, but also the abstract ideals of lordly symbolism projected through the built environment. In their architecture, we are faced with the largest body of surviving and largely unread 'documentary' evidence for the activities and aspirations, motives and machinations of the governing elites of medieval Scotland.

It is fully acknowledged that, even in a collaborative venture such as this, only a selective sample of the broad theme can be presented within the covers of one book. The question of royal patronage, for example, the subject of other, parallel studies, has been deliberately omitted, but otherwise it is hoped that the case-studies presented here will be reasonably representative, and will help to stimulate further research along similar, integrated lines.

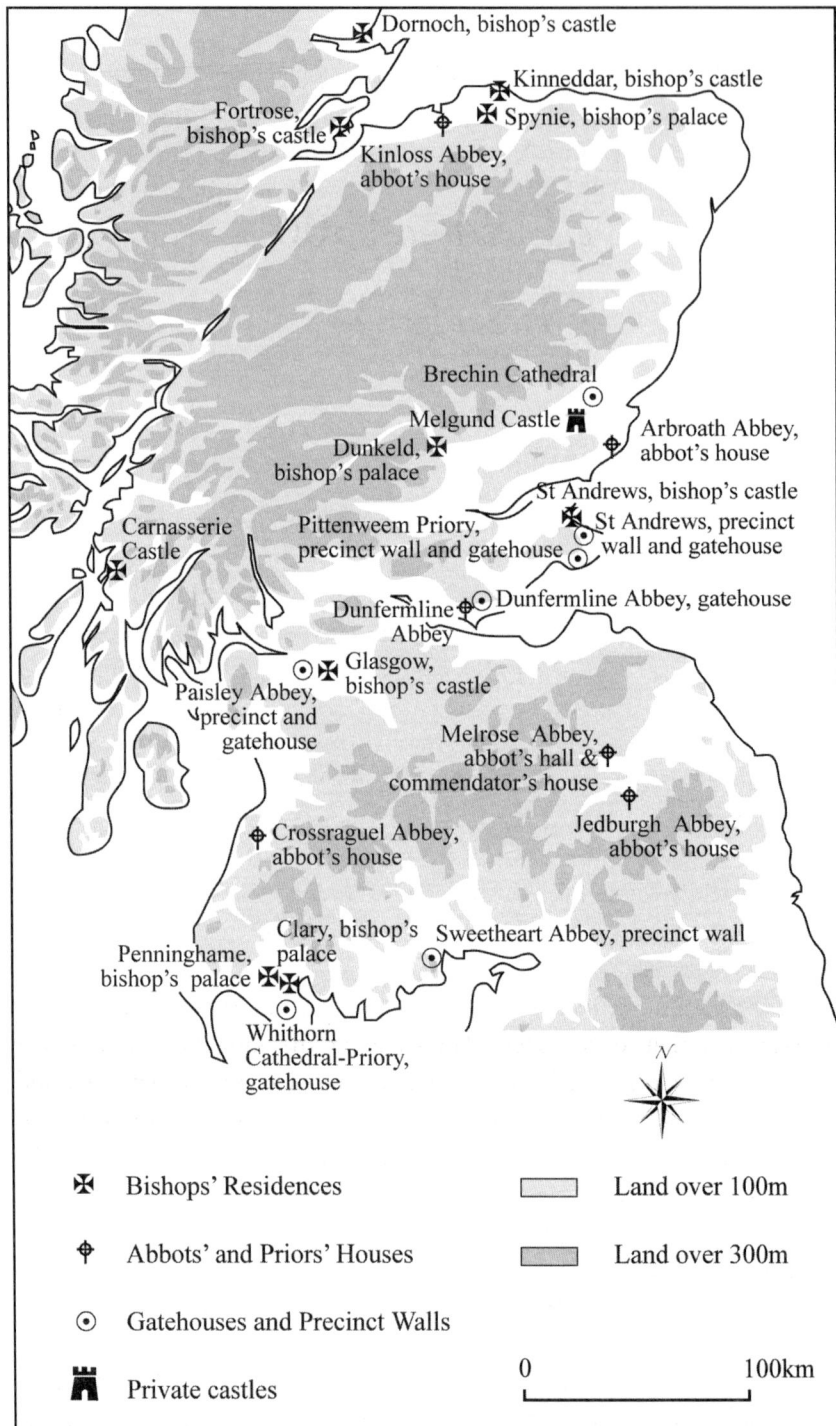

Dornoch, bishop's castle

Kinneddar, bishop's castle

Spynie, bishop's palace

Fortrose, bishop's castle

Kinloss Abbey, abbot's house

Brechin Cathedral

Melgund Castle

Arbroath Abbey, abbot's house

Dunkeld, bishop's palace

St Andrews, bishop's castle

Carnasserie Castle

Pittenweem Priory, precinct wall and gatehouse

St Andrews, precinct wall and gatehouse

Dunfermline Abbey, gatehouse

Dunfermline Abbey

Glasgow, bishop's castle

Paisley Abbey, precinct and gatehouse

Melrose Abbey, abbot's hall & commendator's house

Crossraguel Abbey, abbot's house

Jedburgh Abbey, abbot's house

Clary, bishop's palace

Sweetheart Abbey, precinct wall

Penninghame, bishop's palace

Whithorn Cathedral-Priory, gatehouse

N

✠ Bishops' Residences

☩ Abbots' and Priors' Houses

⊙ Gatehouses and Precinct Walls

♜ Private castles

Land over 100m

Land over 300m

0   100km

Figure 1.1
Prelatical builders.

Chapter 1

∂⅀

PRELATICAL BUILDERS: A PRELIMINARY STUDY, *c.*1124–*c.*1500 [1]

Richard D. Oram

INTRODUCTION

While aristocratic families climbed and plummeted, through failure of heirs or forfeiture, their prelatical counterparts enjoyed a continuity unbroken until the sixteenth century. This continuity arose from the corporate nature of the Church, a characteristic which ensured that property remained secure in its grasp, and which, for present purposes, permits a view of the developing status and concomitant socio-economic standing of a distinct segment of the wider nobility. This segment of the nobility had no requirement to assert its social credentials with each changing generation, nor, for the most part, to reflect shifting patterns of lordship in its use of monumental architecture. However, although not strictly a kin-based group, individual churchmen's building works often displayed the influence of the wider lay aristocracy from which they came: in their perspectives they tended to share the outlook and aspirations of the secular nobility.

The reorganisation of the Scottish Church in the early twelfth century profoundly reshaped the social landscape of the kingdom. In the first generation of reform, clerics who were appointed to major benefices, and who formed new monastic communities, were overwhelmingly non-native. As a consequence, they imported cultural attitudes and ideas of dramatically new forms, clearly evident in their architecture. Most senior clerics were of Frankish or Anglo-Norman aristocratic stock, and their social background is explicitly revealed in the residences which they built, carrying identical symbolic messages of power and lordship to those of their secular counterparts. As the higher clergy acquired greater temporal power as lords of substantial propertied estates – in effect lords of men – their residences more clearly reflected their worldly status and membership of the aristocratic

LORDSHIP AND
ARCHITECTURE
IN MEDIEVAL
AND
RENAISSANCE
SCOTLAND

❧

social elite, while monastic complexes and cathedral precincts were dressed in the symbolic architectural vocabulary of seigneurial power.

THE EPISCOPATE

In spite of historiographical recognition of the aristocratic background of the senior clergy of the Middle Ages, no study of their socio-political role has moved beyond examination of their tenurial or ministerial status to examine in any depth either their seigneurial function or the physical mechanisms through which they projected their social status. We can recognise that control of land – the temporalities of the see – gave the episcopate their political muscle in the Middle Ages, but generally choose to look at their cathedral-building work as a gauge of standing in the pecking-order of bishoprics, to the neglect of the castle-building which signalled their position in the hierarchy of nobility. Bishops were not simply pastors to their diocesan flock, but were territorial magnates vested with temporal powers which placed them towards the top of the hierarchy of regional secular authority.

Extensive episcopal landholding was an established phenomenon by the early twelfth century, as revealed by the *Inquest of David* into the possessions of the bishops of Glasgow.[2] Bishops, too, led the advance into the northern and western districts of mainland Scotland: the bishops of Moray, Ross and Caithness acted as royal agents in the colonial venture. Land accrued to their station as much in response to their prominent socio-political roles as by virtue of their spiritual office. The powers and privileges incumbent in extensive landholding became rights defended jealously by an increasingly secularised episcopate: the root of Bishop Bur of Moray's dispute with Alexander Stewart, Lord of Badenoch, in the 1380s, lay in conflicting claims of jurisdiction over men on episcopal lands in Strathspey.[3] Where the legal trappings of secular lordship were secured by the episcopate, we should also expect the physical manifestation of that lordship projected through construction of suitable settings for the active exercise of the lordly role. The role of such settings, albeit in a lay aristocratic rather than an episcopal context, is admirably summarised by Dr Keith Stringer[4] in his discussion of the position of Inverurie in the lordship of Garioch:

> It was the pivot of economic administration for the castle-area ... where revenues were received and kept in secure storage or sold. It was the lord's residence and judicial centre. All these functions were different aspects of the lordship imposed to dominate and exploit the territory subject to its influence. It was also a strong military base, and although

the administrative element rapidly subsumed the military, strategic considerations had been uppermost in determining its siting.

Such functions are characteristic of the exercise of lordship, irrespective of whether the holder of that lordship was a secular or ecclesiastical lord.

Little survives of structures which gave expression to such lordly status erected by the first generation of episcopal builders in the twelfth century. A rare example of an excavated twelfth-century bishop's residence in Scotland is at Glasgow,[5] where the earliest phase was a ditched earthen ringwork, 28m in diameter, entered across a timber bridge. A timber gatehouse defended the entrance, and any internal structures – hall, private chamber, chapel and domestic buildings – were probably likewise timber-built: no trace of these was found. Facing the west front of the cathedral, the ringwork lay on the axis of the stone church consecrated in 1136, but is probably attributable to Bishop Herbert (1147–64), formerly abbot of Kelso, or Enguerrand (1165–74), a secular clerk and chancellor to Malcolm IV prior to his election to the bishopric in 1164. Enguerrand's elevated administrative background in the household of a king who embraced the lordly symbolism of Frankish culture points to him rather than the monastic Herbert as builder of a residence which projected the secular authority of the bishop.

A second episcopal ringwork stands at Mains of Penninghame in Wigtownshire. This was the heart of one of the mensal estates of the bishops of Whithorn, a unit whose origins lie in the eighth century and which remained the location of the later medieval bishops' principal rural residence, the Clary, 1.5kms to the east.[6] The earthwork is a massive roughly triangular embanked enclosure, approximately 125m along each side. Its scale is in marked contrast to Glasgow and probably reflects differences in the function of the two. While Glasgow is most clearly residential, Penninghame was also the administrative focus of an agricultural estate – here the analogy with Inverurie is strongest – and probably contained the complex of domestic and store buildings attendant on that role.

Ringworks are characteristic of eleventh- and twelfth-century defensive engineering throughout Britain.[7] Their use in frontier contexts reveals them as more than symbolic statements of lordship: this was a recognised military tradition with no obvious social hierarchy amongst its builders. Examples at Auldearn, Tarradale and, possibly, Castlehill near Thurso, were royal strongholds; Glasgow was the work of a senior bishop; a group in Renfrewshire are associated with the Steward and his tenants.[8] Ringworks, clearly, were socially acceptable – and long-lived – settings for lordly power.[9] It is possible that their less overt militarism, in contrast to motte-and-bailey castles which functioned regularly as garrisoned strongpoints at

LORDSHIP AND
ARCHITECTURE
IN MEDIEVAL
AND
RENAISSANCE
SCOTLAND

❧

the advance edge of colonial plantations,[10] commended them to supposedly non-military episcopal builders. Their greatest attraction, however, was adaptability for administrative or residential functions. Where defence was secondary to administrative requirements, but where defences were a recognised adjunct of lordship, the cramped inconvenience of the motte could be abandoned in favour of the more spacious ringwork.

Structural symbolism as a statement of status, rather than practical defence, is evident in the later thirteenth-century development of the bishop's castle at Glasgow. This may be attributable to William de Bondington (1233–58), who remodelled the eastern limb of the cathedral. His role as chancellor (1231–47) and councillor of Alexander II provided the social spur for construction of a suitable visual expression of his status. The ringwork was largely maintained, improved by the replacement in stone of the earlier timber gatehouse, but construction of a stone hall required a breach to be made in the enclosure which cannot but have compromised its defensive capabilities.[11] Comfort, convenience, fashion and status all outweighed defence in Bondington's priorities.

Status and convenience lay behind the decision of Bishop Roger de Beaumont (1189–1202), younger son of Robert III de Beaumont, Earl of Leicester and a cousin of William the Lion, to erect a residence outwith the cathedral precinct at St Andrews. According to Wyntoun, Roger built a 'castell' on the site of the present fortification.[12] This thirteenth-century building was razed in 1337, but masonry of what is possibly a stone tower

Figure 1.2
St Andrews Castle,
Fife: from John Slezer,
Theatrum Scotiae
(c.1693, 1718 edn).
RCAHMS, C 370917

Rudera Arcis Sancti ANDREÆ. *The Ruins of the Castle of* St ANDREWS.

This plate & ye following Prospect of the City of St Andrews is Mostehumbly Inscrib'd to the RightHon.ble John Earl of Rothess & Lord Vice Admirall of North Britain & Governour of Sterling Castle

built by Bishop Roger has been identified within the present Fore Tower. No such early masonry has been firmly identified elsewhere within the enclosure, leading Stewart Cruden to speculate that the original work comprised, until the fourteenth century, '... a simple rectangular tower, perhaps with an adjacent courtyard defended by a palisade and ditch ...'[13] The surviving thirteenth-century masonry, however, incorporates the original gateway of the castle, and it should perhaps be considered that a stone gatehouse was, as at Glasgow, one of a group of high-status buildings within the earth and timber enclosure. Provision of an imposing stone entrance to the bishop's residence speaks strongly of the symbolic projection of episcopal authority through architecture, with the gatehouse being manifestly the most visual expression of seigneurial might.[14]

Strongly visual imagery is evident in the palace built at Spynie by the bishops of Moray in the fourteenth century. A residence existed there before about 1200, but excavation revealed little of its earthwork phase in the late twelfth century. After a mid-thirteenth century redevelopment, marked by fragments of a stone tower set into the rampart and a free-standing kitchen, Spynie was left derelict for much of the later thirteenth century, Bishop Archibald (1253–98) preferring the castle at Kinneddar, for which only tantalising fragments of evidence remain.[15] It was perhaps destroyed in 1307 during the earl of Ross's harrying of the lands of Bishop David Murray (1299–1326), an associate of the Bruce party and one of three bishops to attend Robert I's inauguration in 1306.[16] It is possible that reoccupation at Spynie commenced as early as *c.*1308–10, by which time the theatre of the Anglo-Scottish war had moved south, and the earl of Ross had submitted and agreed – under threat of excommunication – to make good the damage to the episcopal properties. Taking advantage of the destruction of Kinneddar, Murray opted to redevelop the more conveniently sited Spynie.

His work produced a roughly quadrangular courtyard castle, apparently with angle towers: a large cylindrical tower is indicated at the south-west by a circular vault incorporated in the base of the late fifteenth-century tower house which dominates the palace ruins. This tower probably accommodated Murray's apartments. Immediately adjacent to the north lay a two-storey block, with a hall, represented by two partially blocked traceried windows at first-floor level, over a range of cellars. North of this was the kitchen and further accommodation, probably for important household officials, in the so-called Kitchen Tower at the north-west angle.[17]

This arrangement, which both echoes thirteenth-century architectural traditions and heralds later fourteenth-century developments, encapsulated the prime requisites of aristocratic accommodation. In its planning it bears

Figure 1.3
St Andrews Castle,
Fife: aerial view.
RCAHMS F/7921

superficial similarities to the earlier thirteenth-century Kildrummy, architecturally the most sophisticated castle in the north-east.[18] It is possible
that Kildrummy's plan was perceived as satisfying the social requirements
of the bishop's lordly role: military in its fortified appearance, residential
in the private accommodation in the tower, public ceremonial and judicial
in the hall, and revenue storage in the ancillary blocks. The tower and
adjacent hall pairing, representing the military and jurisdictional facets of
lordly status, emerged in the second half of the fourteenth century as an
enduring characteristic of Scottish seigneurial architecture.

Figure 1.4
Spynie Palace, Moray:
aerial view.
RCAHMS, B 23617

A similar hybrid appeared at St Andrews before 1400. The occupation of St Andrews by an English garrison in 1336 saw the castle's capture and destruction in 1337, and it was not until the episcopate of Walter Traill (1385–1401) that rebuilding began.[19] Traill's castle was a roughly pentagonal enclosure with angle towers and a redeveloped Fore Tower. The latter had been enlarged during the English occupation of 1336–37, when a new gate with drawbridge was provided in a southern extension. Traill's reconstruction, however, saw the relocation of the gateway to the south-west curtain – its present position – and refurbishment of the Fore Tower as the four-storeyed private suite of the bishop, with a chapel at first-floor level in a range built against the inner face of the south-east curtain and abutting the east gable of the tower. The hall at Spynie was immediately adjacent to the bishop's tower; at St Andrews it occupied the east range of the courtyard and was served by kitchens accommodated in the north-east, or Kitchen Tower. The submerging of the Fore Tower in an enlarged

7

LORDSHIP AND
ARCHITECTURE
IN MEDIEVAL
AND
RENAISSANCE
SCOTLAND

⁂

south-west range in the sixteenth-century building operations of Cardinal David Beaton (1539–46) and Archbishop John Hamilton (1547–71) has obscured the significance of Traill's work. Here, at the principal residence of the greatest ecclesiastic in the land, he adopted the chief contemporary icon of lordship, the tower house, the first amongst the episcopate to embrace this fashion. This arrangement of tower and adjacent, or near-adjacent, hall block, as discussed by Christopher Tabraham, was the current architectural vogue in aristocratic planning, typified by the Douglas castles of Bothwell, Newark and Threave, and possibly also Darnaway where the timber ceiling of the hall has been re-dated to the later 1380s.[20]

The receptiveness of the episcopate to the architectural symbolism of lordship as expressed by the free-standing tower house, and to its obvious defensive merits, is apparent at Dunkeld. There, Bishop Robert de Cardeny (1398–1437) undertook the complete rebuilding of his palace. He had inherited a residence constructed, according to Alexander Myln in his *Lives of the Bishops of Dunkeld*, 'alpinatum more' and comprising '… great houses built upon the ground …'.[21] What Myln meant by that description

*Figure 1.5
Spynie Palace, Moray:
view from south-east,
c.1880.
RCAHMS, MO/912*

SPYNIE CASTLE, NEAR ELGIN. 1997. J.V.

is unclear, but there is nothing in the Latin to indicate a 'rambling structure' as is often suggested.[22] There are two key phrases in the Latin text: 'alpinatum more' and 'ex domibus magnis super terram constructis'. To Myln, the fact that the palace was 'alpinatum more' in the early 1400s was worthy of notice over a century later, and he did not take it for granted that his readership would understand what was meant by 'in the style of the Highlanders', providing a description in the second phrase. The emphasis in the sentence structure is on 'super terram constructis', which might mean upon the ground or upon the earth. This is open to wide interpretation. Possibly single-storeyed structures are meant; or buildings with no stone foundation, possibly with walls resting on sleeper beams; or possibly it refers to structures built on the earthen remains of the early medieval monastic enclosure. Whatever the case, Myln clearly saw it as significantly different from the late medieval building traditions of lowland Scotland. Following his nocturnal kidnapping from his chamber, Cardeny provided himself with more secure accommodation in the form of a tower house. His palace, still standing in the late seventeenth century when Slezer produced his panoramic view of Dunkeld, has been entirely demolished, but it was described by Myln in the early sixteenth century as being strongly fortified and standing amongst other buildings, which included a separate block with first-floor hall over vaulted cellarage.

Roughly contemporary with Cardeny's work at Dunkeld was the complete remodelling of the castle at Glasgow by Bishop John Cameron (1426–46), Chancellor to King James I. Here, the late thirteenth-century hall and earlier earthworks were levelled and replaced by a substantial tower house.[23] The scale of this building, a massive four-storeyed rectangle later enlarged into an L-plan structure, was in keeping with Cameron's status and pretensions. Its inspiration was almost certainly Threave, with which Cameron, formerly provost of Lincluden and secretary to Archibald Douglas, earl of Wigtown[24] – grandson of Threave's builder – would have been familiar. There is no indication of a separate hall block contemporary with Cameron's tower house, which contained a vaulted hall on its first floor – the level of the main entrance – and what appears to have been a more sophisticated timber-ceilinged hall on the floor above, but such a block may have been swept away in the redevelopment of the palace in the early sixteenth century.

Massive though Cameron's tower was, it was dwarfed by that begun at Spynie by David Stewart (1461–77) and completed by William Tulloch (1477–82).[25] It is a formidable structure, rising through four storeys and an attic over vaulted cellars, but its internal arrangements and generous fenestration indicate that comfort and convenience outweighed defence in its planning. Indeed, until Patrick Hepburn (1538–73) inserted wide-mouthed

9

LORDSHIP AND
ARCHITECTURE
IN MEDIEVAL
AND
RENAISSANCE
SCOTLAND

᷒

gunports for cannon in the basement of the tower, its defensive arrangements were restricted to the wall-head, where there was a parapet with rounds at each external angle, all carried on corbelled machicolations. Construction of the tower entailed demolition of the fourteenth-century hall, onto whose site the tower house impinges. Stewart's tower contained a fine hall at first-floor level, but this was part of his private accommodation and would not have fulfilled the public ceremonial role of the larger great hall. Such a hall was part of David Stewart's scheme, but it was probably Bishop Andrew Stewart (1482–1501), half-uncle of James III, who completed the plan with construction of a magnificent great hall at the north-east side of the courtyard.

The tower and hall at Spynie represent the monumental climax of this particular manifestation of lordly architecture. They were not quite the last essay in that tradition, Bishop Andrew Stewart of Caithness producing soon after 1501 a five-storey tower with adjoining hall range at Dornoch,[26] while at Fortrose the medieval palace was replaced c.1500 by a large rectangular tower house and adjacent domestic block.[27] It is possible, too, that Cardinal Beaton's castle at Melgund,[28] where tower house and hall are fused into one, represents a lingering tradition of what was required in a lordly residence, or more particularly the residence of a bishop, a possibility strengthened by the re-emergence of this integrated plan at Carnassarie, built in the 1560s for John Carsewell, Bishop of the Isles.[29] In secular tradition, while tower house building remained the most common expression of lordly status through architecture into the second half of the seventeenth century, the towers of the sixteenth and seventeenth centuries were self-contained units which incorporated halls within their mass. The changing social requirements of the greater nobility, and the emergence of new architectural forms with which to project the symbols of lordship, had superseded the formalised arrangement of public ceremonial hall and detached private suite.

ABBOTS AND PRIORS

By about 1200, the pioneering zeal which powered the monastic movement in the twelfth century had faded, taking with its passing the rules of strict personal asceticism of earlier generations. The change is most evident in the Crown's episcopal appointments, which shifted from promotion of heads of monasteries of the reformed orders in favour of clerks in royal service. Monasteries, too, experienced changed priorities concerning the skills and ability of their ruling heads. Whereas pastoral skills and spirituality had been important attributes in abbots in the heady days of twelfth-century revivalist enthusiasm, enforced evolution occasioned by the flow of propertied endowments from the pious faithful required new forms of expertise. Otherworldly spirituality was of little practical use in charting the intricacies of the commercial world. Gifts made monasteries substantial landholders and, consequently, lords of men. As great lords of what was a rapidly emerging political first estate, the heads of the major monasteries could expect to be courted and visited by their compeers amongst the secular nobility.

The physical manifestation of greater secular involvement by the abbots was reflected in the relaxation then abandonment of rules which required them to share living and sleeping accommodation with their brethren. By the later twelfth century this was marked by the appearance of a new expression of lordly architecture in the provision of a separate residence for the head of the community. In some cases, to preserve the fiction of the abbot sleeping in the same building as his monks, his chambers were attached to the dormitory, for example at Kinloss as an extension southwards from the common latrine block,[30] or at Crossraguel as a range extending eastwards from and communicating with the south end of the dormitory.[31] Increasingly, however, separate residences where they could entertain their visitors as befitted their status were provided.

Amongst surviving abbots' residences, that at Arbroath is the earliest surviving example of provision of accommodation wholly separate from the monks' dormitory. The earliest structure, datable to *c.* 1200, forms the eastern half of the enlarged late fifteenth-century Abbot's House.[32] It was a projection westwards from the junction of the south and west claustral ranges, the former containing the kitchen and refectory, the latter possibly guest accommodation. It comprised originally a rib-vaulted undercroft beneath a first-floor hall lit by tall lancet windows. This was substantially expanded in the late fifteenth century, when a new bedchamber with latrine and private gallery opening from it was added to the west of the thirteenth-century hall; a first-floor gallery in which was placed the main entrance reached by an external stair added on the north side; and accommodation for the abbot's servants provided in a second storey.

It is significant that the Abbot's House was not added to the cloister but was integral to the layout as conceived in the late twelfth century, in itself a mark of contemporary recognition of the changing role of the abbot of a major community. Its location, too, underscores the formal public role of the abbot as head of a seigneurially privileged landholding corporation. Its proximity to the gatehouse allowed control of traffic entering the precinct and, perhaps more important, meant that communication with the outside world, receipt of visitors and oversight of the business affairs of the abbey – which included supervision of the burgh which the abbot had been empowered to set up as part of the original

LORDSHIP AND
ARCHITECTURE
IN MEDIEVAL
AND
RENAISSANCE
SCOTLAND

❧

royal endowment of *c.* 1178 [33] – could be directed from a location where secular contamination of the community was minimised. Here, too, probably met the abbot's court, in which he exercised his seigneurial jurisdiction over the abbey's estates, until a separate courtroom was provided in the later thirteenth century in the gatehouse range for meetings of the regality court.

A supervisory role has also been suggested as an element governing location of the Abbot's House at Dunfermline.[34] Here, the lodging, of apparently mid-fifteenth-century date originally, but substantially altered and extended in the sixteenth century, lies north of the abbey church against the northern sector of the precinct wall overlooking the Maygate and Abbot Street.[35] The fifteenth-century building was of two storeys with a large first-floor chamber whose splendid traceried window overlooked the street, and permitted the abbot to 'keep an eye on his commercial interests in the town below, while still being in the sacred precinct'. [36] Here, the fiction of the abbot residing in the same complex as his monks was being stretched to the absolute limit.

Whereas at Arbroath the abbot's hall was integral to the claustral complex, at some older communities new provision was required for the abbot's lodgings. At Jedburgh, a structure which probably contained the abbot's house stood at the south-west angle of the cloister.[37] As at Arbroath, this adjoined the kitchen and refectory in the south range, and was originally of at least two levels with domestic accommodation on the first floor over service rooms in the undercroft. The upper levels of the building have long vanished, but the divisions of the undercroft suggest that the mid-thirteenth-century abbot's lodging comprised a hall with a private chamber and garderobe at its southern end. This was expanded in a post-Wars of Independence rebuilding, but the basic arrangement of first-floor accommodation over cellarage or service space was maintained.[38]

The elaboration of the abbots' houses at Arbroath and Jedburgh transformed modest but, in the case of the former, architecturally pretentious chambers into imposing semi-detached residences in keeping with the status of their occupants. At Melrose, a different approach was adopted. There, Abbot Matthew (1246–61) is recorded as responsible for the '... building of the abbot's great chamber, which is upon the bank of the river ...'.[39] This is the structure whose foundations lie north-east of the cloister, between the dormitory and the mill lade.[40] Abbot Matthew's work was a freestanding structure and comprised either a vaulted, aisled undercroft with hall and chamber on the upper floor, or a ground-floor aisled hall rising the full height of the building, probably with a private chamber added later at gallery level at its west end. On the inner face of the east gable wall are remains of a stone bench, which probably extended

along the side walls of the hall. Still in the thirteenth century, the building
was extended, probably to provide an enlarged chamber for the abbot.[41]
The whole measured a little over 10m wide by 25m long internally: this
was no modest suite but a lordly structure which rivalled the halls of the
great secular aristocrats. It was certainly in keeping with the economic and
seigneurial power of a thirteenth-century abbot of Melrose and a stark
monument to the abandonment of the austere principles of the Cistercian
order, whose poverty and piety had been regarded as physical reflections
of greater spirituality. It is a telling comment on the profound changes in
the monastic ethos that while the obits of twelfth-century abbots com-
mented on their piety and qualities as pastors to their flocks, that
of Matthew details his economic achievements, his commercial building
projects, and his physical betterment of the lot of his monks.[42]

Abbot Matthew's hall fell victim to the devastation wrought on Melrose
in 1385. Towards the middle of the fifteenth century, possibly under Abbot
Andrew Hunter (1444–71), it was replaced by the so-called Commendator's
House. When first built, this was a 'palatium', a form developed from the
freestanding hall tradition, and comprised a two-storey rectangular stone
block with timber penthouses on three sides, the first-floor chambers being
entered from a gallery or veranda on the east wall. There were at least two
rooms on either level, but the internal arrangements were remodelled in
1590 when it was fitted up as a residence for James Douglas, Commendator
of Melrose.[43]

In contrast to these detached residences, at Kinloss, Melrose's second
daughter house, the abbot's chambers extended southward from the dormitory range, linked to it by the latrines whose vaulted drain and garderobe
chutes survive. There is little evidence for the form of the medieval
accommodation at Kinloss, however, for Abbot Robert Reid (1526–41)
undertook its reconstruction in the 1530s. The fragments of Reid's building
show its core to have been a roughly rectangular tower of two principal
storeys and an attic over a series of barrel-vaulted cellars, one of which
served as a kitchen. The surviving jamb of a large rectangular window at
first-floor level indicates the position of the principal chamber.[44]

At Crossraguel, the link with the dormitory block was likewise maintained when a separate abbot's house was built in the fourteenth century.[45]
This formed the south side of a courtyard in the angle south-east of the
abbey church and the east claustral range. It comprised a first-floor hall
and chamber, entered via an external stair on the north side, over a range
of cellars. From the first, although there was a doorway from the abbot's
chamber to the common latrine, the main access to the abbot's house was
independent of the cloister. Visitors moved from the south court of the
abbey into a smaller courtyard to the south of the abbot's house, then,

LORDSHIP AND
ARCHITECTURE
IN MEDIEVAL
AND
RENAISSANCE
SCOTLAND

❧

via a passage beneath the west end of the block, into the abbot's court. Alterations in the fifteenth century saw provision of separate latrines within a projecting turret on the south side of the range, serving both the abbot's chamber and the hall, and the construction of a kitchen block at right angles to the house. The final substantial addition to this complex was a massive tower house abutting the south-east angle of the fourteenth-century range, probably representing a development contemporary with the gatehouse at the west side of the monastic court.

The tower house at Crossraguel, built either as part of Abbot Colin's general later fifteenth-century refurbishment or, more probably, in the 1530s by the aristocratic Abbot William Kennedy,[46] was part of a last flowering of domestic architectural patronage by monastic prelates in the early sixteenth century. Roughly contemporary with it was the work of Robert Reid at Kinloss, and also at Beauly Priory, of which he was commendator.[47] They did not mark the end of abbatial building operations, but the profound changes in the nature of the upper ranks of the monastic hierarchy in the early sixteenth century produced a rapid falling away in this field.

The reign of James V marked a new departure in prelatical building, a product largely of the increasing trend towards provision of commendators in place of resident abbots. This was nothing new in the Scottish Church, but had developed in the fifteenth century as a device to allow clerics to administer and enjoy the revenues of a benefice incompatible with their status; for example a bishop could be commendator of an abbey although he was not in monk's orders or even a member of a particular order. Increased royal control of nomination to benefices after 1487, however, led the Crown to extend the practice to laymen, in effect converting monasteries into landed possessions in the king's gift: lay commendators could draw revenue without fulfilling any spiritual function. Early commendators lived with the community of which they were head, simply taking over the existing abbot's lodgings – as at Melrose – or, as the communities dwindled away after the Reformation, converting portions of the cloister into houses – as at Balmerino.[48] The building activity of lay commendators, however, is a subject in itself and lies beyond the scope of this essay.

THE MONASTIC AND CATHEDRAL PRECINCT

Nowhere is the expression of secular lordship more apparent in a monastic context than in the precinct walls and gatehouses constructed from the later thirteenth century onwards.[49] The seigneurial symbolism of these enclosures has long been recognised. Robert Billings in 1845, for example, remarked of the gatehouse range and Regality Tower at Arbroath that '. . . it served to remind the world with out, that the coercive power of the abbot and his chapter was scarcely inferior to their secular dignity and their temporal magnificence'.[50] In spite of such recognition, however, the scanty ruins of most Scottish precinct walls and gatehouses have ensured that they remain a neglected study.

Monastic enclosures were constructed from an early date to guarantee the exclusivity and security from worldly affairs which the brethren craved, as well as for defence against physical dangers. In Scotland, no monastery occupied a truly deserted location, rendering boundaries necessary for the preservation of exclusivity, for example at Melrose, where the inhabitants of the land upon which it was established were called to witness its foundation.[51] Furthermore, the economic magnet of the monasteries acted as a stimulus for the development of settlements at the abbey gates – as at Whithorn – while the seigneurial perquisites of controlling a burgh encouraged several – such as Holyrood – to secure royal permission to develop their own chartered communities. Few traces of twelfth- or thirteenth-century circuits remain, but the featureless wall of granite boulders at Sweetheart offers some impression of the nature of these enclosures, while early engravings of Crossraguel show the extent and monumental nature of the outer court and precinct wall, of which no remnant survives.[52]

In terms of expression of lordship, the most significant feature which defined the limit of the jurisdiction of the head of the monastic community was the gatehouse. Indeed, as research in England has shown, while the remainder of the circuit could often be of relatively slight construction, or to have consisted of walls which might deter casual intrusion but not a determined attacker, the gatehouse structures were elaborated and loaded with the symbolism of seigneurial might.[53] Thus, for example, at St Albans, Bury St Edmunds, Kirkham or Thornton, the gatehouses are massive embattled structures, provided with crenellations and portcullis, and with visual indicators of lordship in the form of heraldic panels displayed prominently. In Scotland, such evidence is, with notable exceptions, more fragmentary. At Whithorn, for example, a truncated gatehouse displaying the royal arms as used by James IV, and with those of Bishop George Vaus (1482–1508) carved on the capitals of the jambs which support the archway, is incorporated into the modern street frontage.[54] Here is the physical demarcation between the precinct and the prior's burgh, which had been established as a free burgh by Edward Bruce before 1318, and which was incorporated into the regality jurisdiction granted to the prior in 1451 by James II.[55] This imposing frontage dominated the marketplace of the burgh and constituted a visible symbol of the prior's seigneurial rights over the burgesses. A similar gatehouse tower, of which only the

LORDSHIP AND
ARCHITECTURE
IN MEDIEVAL
AND
RENAISSANCE
SCOTLAND

❧

springers of the external arch and lower portions of masonry super-structure remain, marked the entrance to the chanonry at Brechin, here also positioned to dominate the marketplace of the bishop's burgh.[56]

A link between the receiving of grants of extensive seigneurial rights – what became regality jurisdiction – and the physical expression of the lordship implicit in such rights, can be traced from the later thirteenth century. In architectural terms, this trend was marked by the erection of monumental gatehouses, structures loaded with the symbolism of secular lordship. The earliest clear manifestation of this is at Arbroath, where rights which evolved into regality jurisdiction by the later thirteenth century were amongst the somewhat vaguely couched privileges granted by its founder, William the Lion, and at Dunfermline, where Robert I recognised the pre-existence of regality status which likewise evolved out of generous interpretation of earlier imprecise grants.[57] At Arbroath, together with the neighbouring presence of the abbot's burgh, self-awareness of the unique seigneurial status of the community triggered construction of the most impressive monastic gatehouse in Scotland. It was built before 1303, when the English chronicle *Flores Historiarum* described both Arbroath and Dunfermline as strongly fortified.[58] As it stands, the gatehouse is largely late thirteenth century, with nothing particularly ecclesiastical in its architecture. A gatehouse on this scale, however, was not part of the original scheme at Arbroath, as is evident from its relationship to the west front of the church; it covers the decorated lower façade of the south-western tower. Indeed, the range between the pend and the west front of the church is not bonded with the the tower, which suggests that there had been no earlier gatehouse on this alignment.[59] The existence of the burgh from the later twelfth century, however, makes an earlier enclosure highly probable, and positions further to the south – as is the case at St Andrews or Dunfermline, where the gatehouses adjoin the junctions of the south and west claustral ranges – or further to the north as part of a circuit which wholly enclosed the main complex of buildings, as occurred at Jedburgh and Whithorn, are possibilities.

The decision to build a new gatehouse at Arbroath represented a major undertaking and constituted a programme designed to reflect the enhanced status of the community which had arisen from its own interpretation of the rights bestowed upon it. It provided structures both symbolic of that status and with a practical function under it. The gatehouse is divided into three segments: an east range, a pend, and a west range. The east range probably contained guest accommodation, while the west range, which terminates in a machicolated tower, was the location of the regality courthouse. Significantly, the precinct wall of the monastery ran south from the south-west angle of the pend, with the result that the court house, although entered from within the pend, lay outwith the precinct, presumably an arrangement designed to reconcile the contradiction of an ecclesiastical community armed with a secular jurisdiction which extended to capital pleas.

The development at Arbroath is paralleled by the construction of an imposing entrance at Dunfermline in the earlier fourteenth century. There, the gatehouse formed part of a rebuilding occasioned by the sack of the abbey in 1304 [60] and which was well advanced by 1329 when Robert I gave a cash grant towards the rebuilding of the refectory which it adjoins,[61] but the description of the abbey in *Flores Historiarum* indicates that a fortified circuit existed in the late thirteenth century, presumably to separate the secular jurisdiction of the abbot's burgh from the ecclesiastical liberty of the monastic site. That this was already a regality jurisdiction was confirmed by Robert I in 1321,[62] and this exalted secular lordship was again reflected in the distinctly non-ecclesiastical character of the gatehouse tower

Prelatical Builders: A Preliminary Study, c.1124–c.1500

Figure 1.6 Glasgow, Bishop's Palace: from Swan's Views of Glasgow *(1828). RCAHMS, A 75902P*

Engraved by Joseph Swan, with Permission, from an Original Drawing in the Possession of Alex.r Mc.Grigor Esq.r of Kernock.

ARCHIEPISCOPAL PALACE & CATHEDRAL.

LORDSHIP AND
ARCHITECTURE
IN MEDIEVAL
AND
RENAISSANCE
SCOTLAND

ʾʿ

at the south-west angle of the cloister.[63] That regality jurisdiction was the catalyst which triggered building of these strongly secular symbols is underscored by the fact that the two monasteries identified by *Flores Historiarum* as fortified were the two where such jurisdiction seems first to have evolved in the ecclesiastical sphere.

At St Andrews, changing jurisdictional status also lay behind provision of a monumental entrance to the monastic precinct. Here, the building of the Pends represented the first major demarcation between the burgh – founded by the bishop of St Andrews before 1144 and continuing under the superiority of the bishops and archbishops down to 1620 – part of the barony of the bishop, the barony of the Culdees of St Mary on the Rock, and that of the prior centred on the cathedral-priory. These three blocks had by 1309 come under the extended seigneurial jurisdiction of the regality of the bishop of St Andrews. The construction of the Pends, therefore, appears to be linked to explicit definition of the respective spheres of authority set out on parchment in 1309.[64] Evidence for a change in masonry style within the 1.6km circuit of precinct wall, with the upper portion and the towers representing a sixteenth-century addition, indicates that the Pends was just the most elaborate feature of a mid-fourteenth-century enclosure of the priory complex.[65] The delay between the formal clarification of the jurisdictional position and the building of the gatehouse and enclosure can be explained by the disturbed political situation in Scotland in the early fourteenth century.

A grant of regality certainly prompted the projection of elevated secular lordship through architectural expression at the small Augustinian priory at Pittenweem, where a sophisticated circuit of walls and gatehouses was constructed in the middle of the fifteenth century. Of this, only stretches of featureless curtain and a fifteenth-century gate at the east of the enclosure remain.[66] The main gate lay in the north of the enclosure, but this stretch, which terminated in a tower at the north-east angle, was demolished in the nineteenth century.[67] From here, however, comes an armorial panel bearing the arms of Bishop Kennedy of St Andrews (1440–65), who held the priory *in commendam*, while a second panel bearing Kennedy's arms was recovered from the west claustral range.[68] In 1452, Kennedy secured a regrant of regality jurisdiction for the lands of the church of St Andrews, extended to include his priory at Pittenweem,[69] and the construction of the walls and gatehouses there must surely have commenced shortly thereafter.

Provision of symbolic architecture to project the secular power of the monastic community was, however, not always an immediate development. At Paisley, the Stewarts' own foundation, Robert III in 1396 continued Stewart patronage of the monastery through erection of its lands in regality.[70] This special favour perhaps arose from the king's geographically circumscribed powers – the Stewartry lands in the west were one of his few centres of influence – but reflected also the ambitions of its abbot: in 1395 Abbot John had secured papal permission to use the mitre, ring and other pontificals, the spiritual equivalent of the grant of regality.[71] John's ambitions, however, did not extend to the architectural embellishment of his abbey, and at his death in 1412 there had been little progress in the reconstruction begun after its burning in 1307. Troubled and disputed provisions to the abbacy in the early fifteenth century, compounded by the inactivity of the largely absentee Thomas Morow, brought a decline in monastic morale. When Thomas Tarvas was provided in 1446, he found, according to the Auchinleck chronicler, '... the place all out of gud rewle and destitut of leving and all the kirkis in lordis handis And the kirk unbiggit ...'.[72] Even allowing for hyperbole, it is clear that Tarvas was faced both with a physically dilapidated and financially despoiled community. It is against this background that the confirmation of the regality by James II in 1452 should be viewed.[73]

While Tarvas's predecessors were incapable of enforcing their regalian rights in the absence of a strong royal patron, in the changing political climate of the 1450s the abbot was determined to broadcast his privileged status. His priority may have been completion of the abbey church, the Auchinleck Chronicle informing us that '... The body of the kirk fra the bricht stair up and put on the ruf he biggit and thekit It with sclait and riggitt it with stane and biggit ane gret porcioun of the steple ...', but changes to reflect elevated lordship were made to the fabric of the monastic enclosure with the building of '... ane staitlie zethous [gatehouse] ...'.[74]

Tarvas's 'staitlie zethous' provided his monastery with a physical projection of the seigneurial rights conferred upon it by the Crown. It was an authority, however, which received reinforcement later in the fifteenth century when Abbot George Shaw added to Tarvas's arrangements. The reason for this was the grant to Shaw in 1488 of the right to erect the town which had grown up on the west bank of the Cart opposite the abbey into a burgh of barony under the abbot's supervision.[75] The lordship of the abbey over the burgh, then, was marked symbolically in the heightening of the gatehouse, while the demarcation of the sphere of Shaw's secular and spiritual jurisdictions was given concrete expression in the building of a monumental circuit to enclose the monastic precinct.[76] This wall, nearly one mile in circumference, was more than a simple boundary, being richly embellished with statuary, heraldic devices and inscription-bearing plaques.

Similar circumstances obtained at Crossraguel. Here, the abbey lands had been erected into a free barony by Robert I in 1324,[77] and in 1404

Figure 1.7
Crossraguel Abbey,
Ayrshire: aerial view.
RCAHMS, AY/4089

Robert III extended this to a grant in regality, including jurisdiction over the four pleas normally reserved to the Crown.[78] The seigneurial jurisdiction enjoyed by the abbots of Crossraguel exceeded that of the principal local magnate, Gilbert Kennedy of Dunure, and placed them at the peak of the local hierarchy of power. In the fifteenth century, redevelopment of the abbot's house reflected the enhanced status of the abbot of Crossraguel and the need to accommodate the extended household which his position brought. A more forceful statement of the secular authority which rested within the monastery was made in the sixteenth century when Abbot William Kennedy (1520–47), brother of the 2nd earl of Cassilis, added the massive three-storeyed gatehouse which still dominates the site.[79] Provided with gunloops and flanked by stretches of parapeted curtain wall, this was no sham fortification, but an uncompromising statement of the worldly power of the abbot.

Perhaps nowhere is the visible symbolism of secular lordship enjoyed by

ARBROATH ABBEY. Pl.2.

Published Aug.ᵗ 26.1790 by J. Hooper.

a head of a monastic community made more forcefully than at St Andrews. Here, Prior John Hepburn (c. 1483–1522) heightened the fourteenth-century precinct wall and provided it with mural towers, and rebuilt the gates known as the Teinds Yett and the Mill Port or Sea Yett, all of which bear his arms as prior of St Andrews.[80] Hepburn's work, despite the provision of elaborate hooded niches which originally contained religious effigies, is decidedly martial in its appearance, the towers being furnished with gun loops to provide flanking fire along the face of the curtain wall, while a parapeted wall walk ran round the whole circuit. For all its military air, however, this was still a structure designed rather to keep out casual intruders and to proclaim the secular authority of the head of the most powerful monastery in the land, than to resist a determined siege, for its very scale would have required a small army to man it. For all its apparent practicality, Hepburn's wall is the lineal descendent of the twelfth-century bishops' castles, wrapping an ecclesiastical centre in the trappings of conventional secular lordship, updated to accommodate the new architectural symbols of social cachet of the sixteenth century.

For all its apparent incongruities to modern eyes, the appearance of

Figure 1.8 Arbroath Abbey, Angus: gatehouse range, from Grose's Antiquities (1790). RCAHMS, AND/7/24

21

LORDSHIP AND
ARCHITECTURE
IN MEDIEVAL
AND
RENAISSANCE
SCOTLAND

❧

fortification in an ecclesiastical context in Scotland in the Middle Ages was simply the manifestation over time of the intensely aristocratic character of the medieval Church in its upper strata. The loading of a not exactly unwilling Church with the trappings of secular lordship in the form of landed estates and attendant jurisdictions merely reinforced that character. In the medieval mind there was no incompatibility in the exercise of secular jurisdictions by a spiritual authority, and modern discomfort with that phenomenon is largely a product of post-Reformation rejection of such jurisdiction by the Church. In an age when the Church was increasingly serving as an office of government, far from striving to keep their temporal and secular roles separate, late medieval prelates revelled in their dual status: 'Princes of the Church' is more than just a poetic description of the status of these men. Just as new arrivals on the aristocratic plane in England sought to advertise their status through provision of crenellation on their residences – and sought formal royal authority so to do in the form of a licence to crenellate – so too did ecclesiastical lords seek to advertise their seigneurial authority.[81] Crenellation, however, was more than just 'a cachet of gentility',[82] it was a symbol of the legal lordship which accompanied nobility. There was no more potent, or acceptable, symbol of lordship through which medieval prelates could proclaim their worldly might.

NOTES

1. For the purposes of this essay, the 'higher clergy' is defined for the secular beneficed clerics as the holders of the most senior offices – bishops and archbishops – and for the regular clerics as priors and abbots. The parameters of the chronological range of the study are set by the introduction of monastic foundations of the reformed continental orders and the reorganisation of the diocesan structure in the early twelfth century, and by the beginning of the pre-Reformation phase where the appointment of lay commendators to monasteries gained in prevalence.

2. *The Earliest Document Relating to Glasgow: the Inquest of David*, ed. and trans. J. T. T. Brown (Glasgow, 1901).

3. R. D. Oram, 'Alexander Bur, Bishop of Moray (1362–1397)', in *Church, Chronicle and Learning in Medieval and Renaissance Scotland*, ed. B. E. Crawford (East Linton, 1999), 195–214; A. Grant, 'The Wolf of Badenoch', in *Moray: Province and People*, ed. W. D. H. Sellar, (Edinburgh, 1993), 143–62 at 145–9.

4. K. J. Stringer, *Earl David of Huntingdon: a Study in Anglo-Scottish History* (Edinburgh, 1985), 71–2.

5. P. Yeoman, *Medieval Scotland* (London, 1995), 88.

6. *Wigtownshire Charters*, ed. R. C. Reid (Scottish History Society, 1960), 2 and note 1, 3; D. J. Craig, 'Pre-Norman Sculpture in Galloway: Some Territorial Implications', in *Galloway: Land and Lordship*, eds. R. D. Oram and G. P. Stell (Edinburgh, 1991), 45–62.

7. See, for example, E. J. Talbot, 'Early Scottish castles of earth and timber: Recent fieldwork and excavation', *Scottish Archaeological Forum*, vi (1974), 48–57; J. M. Steane, *The Archaeology of Medieval England and Wales* (London, 1984), 38.

8. G. D. B. Jones, 'Investigation of a cropmark site near Muir of Ord, Ross and Cromarty' [Tarradale], *Manchester Archaeological Bulletin* (1994), 13–19 at 13 and Appendix A;. E. J. Talbot, 'Castlehill, Caithness: a Viking fortification?', *PSAS*, 108 (1976–7), 378–9: E. J. Talbot, 'The defences of earth and timber castles', in *Scottish Weapons and Fortifications 1100–1800*, ed. D. H. Caldwell, (Edinburgh, 1981), 1–9 at 3.

9. C. J. Tabraham, *Scottish Castles and Fortifications* (Edinburgh, 1986), 32.

10. T. E. McNeill, *Anglo-Norman Ulster* (Edinburgh, 1980), 65–8, 85–7; R. D. Oram, 'A family business? Colonisation and settlement in twelfth- and thirteenth-century Galloway', *SHR*, lxxii (1993), 127–8.

11. Yeoman, *Medieval Scotland*, 94.

12. *Chron. Wyntoun* (Laing), ii, lines 2149–64.

13. S. Cruden, *St Andrews Castle* (Edinburgh, 1958), 5–6, 7; S. Cruden, *The Scottish Castle* (Edinburgh, 3rd edition, 1981), 21–2..

14. E. g. P. Fergusson, 'Porta patens esto: notes on the early Cistercian gatehouses in the north of England', in *Medieval Architecture in its Intellecutual Context: Studies in Honour of Peter Kidson*, ed. E. Fernie and P. Crossley (London, 1990), 47–59; for a discussion of the role of the gate-keeper, see G. G. Simpson, 'Claves Castri: the Role of the Gatekeeper in Scottish Medieval Castles', *Chateau Gaillard*, xv (1990), 319 24.

15. J. Lewis and D. Pringle, *Spynie Palace and the Bishops of Moray* (Society of Antiquaries of Scotland, Edinburgh, 2002); D. Pringle, *Spynie Palace* (Edinburgh, 1995); Yeoman, *Medieval Scotland*, 100–1.

16. G. W. S. Barrow, *Robert Bruce and the Community of the Realm of Scotland* (Edinburgh, 3rd edition, 1988), 151, 155, 163.

17. Pringle, *Spynie Palace*; Yeoman, *Medieval Scotland*, 101.

LORDSHIP AND
ARCHITECTURE
IN MEDIEVAL
AND
RENAISSANCE
SCOTLAND

☙

18. W. D. Simpson, *Kildrummy and Glenbuchat Castles* (Edinburgh, 4th edition, 1978), 9–10.

19. Cruden, *St Andrews Castle*, 3–4, 6; RCAHMS, *Fife*, no. 465.

20. C. J. Tabraham, 'The Scottish medieval towerhouse as lordly residence in the light of recent excavation', *PSAS*, 119 (1988), 267–76; G. Stell and M. Baillie, 'The Great Hall and Roof of Darnaway Castle, Moray', in *Moray: Province and People*, ed. Sellar, 163–86.

21. Myln, *Vitae*, 16.

22. M. E. B. Simpson, *Dunkeld Cathedral, Perthshire* (Edinburgh, 2nd edition, 1950), 7.

23. Yeoman, *Medieval Scotland*, 94; A. L. Murray, 'Preserving the Bishop's Castle, Glasgow, 1688–1741', *PSAS*, 125 (1995), 1143–61.

24. *RMS*, ii, nos. 13, 14, 20 etc.

25. Pringle, *Spynie Palace*; Yeoman, *Medieval Scotland*, 101–2.

26. J. Gifford, *The Buildings of Scotland: Highland and Islands* (Harmondsworth, 1992), 568–9.

27. *Chronicles of the Frasers: the Wardlaw Manuscript*, ed. W. Mackay (Edinburgh, Scottish History Society, 1905), 115–16.

28. N. Tranter, *The Fortified House in Scotland, iv, Aberdeenshire, Angus and Kincardineshire* (Edinburgh, 1977), 139–41.

29. RCAHMS, *Argyll*, vii, no. 115.

30. H. F. Kerr, 'Kinloss Abbey, Moray', *Transactions of the Scottish Ecclesiological Society*, xii pt i (1936–7), 61–4 at 63–4; R. D. Oram, *Moray and Badenoch: a Historical Guide* (Edinburgh, 1996), 97.

31. C. A. R. Radford, *The Cluniac Abbey of Crossraguel* (Edinburgh, 1970), 18–19.

32. R. L. Mackie and S. Cruden, *Arbroath Abbey* (Edinburgh, 1954), 37; R. Fawcett, *Scottish Abbeys and Priories* (London, 1994), 110.

33. *RRS*, ii, no. 197.

34. Yeoman, *Medieval Scotland*, 21.

35. RCAHMS, *Fife*, no. 199.

36. Yeoman, *Medieval Scotland*, 21.

37. J. Lewis and G. Ewart, *Jedburgh Abbey: the Archaeology and Architecture of a Border Abbey* (Edinburgh, 1995), 61.

38. Ibid., 142.

39. *Chron. Melrose*, 189–90.

40. R. Fawcett and R. Oram, *Melrose Abbey* (Stroud, 2004), 197–9; J. S. Richardson and M. Wood, *Melrose Abbey, Roxburghshire* (Edinburgh, 2nd edition, 1949), 21.

41. RCAHMS, *Roxburghshire*, ii, 287; Fawcett and Oram, *Melrose Abbey*, 198.

42. *Chron. Melrose*, 190.

43. RCAHMS, *Roxburghshire*, ii, 287; Fawcett and Oram, *Melrose Abbey*, 199–202.

44. MacGibbon and Ross, *Ecclesiastical Architecture*, i 421; Kerr, 'Kinloss Abbey', 64.

45. Radford, *Crossraguel*, 18–19.

46. Ibid, 19–20; Fawcett, *Abbeys and Priories*, 111.

47. R. Fawcett, *Beauly Priory and Fortrose Cathedral* (Edinburgh, 1987), 14–15.

48. MacGibbon and Ross, *Ecclesiastical Architecture*, ii, 509–12; Fawcett, *Abbeys and Priories*, 121.

49. For an excellent discussion of this phenomenon in an Anglo-French setting, see: C. Coulson, 'Hierarchism in Conventual Crenellation: An Essay on the Sociology and Metaphysics of Medieval Fortification', *Medieval Archaeology*, 26 (1982), 69–100.

50. R. W. Billings, *The Baronial and Ecclesiastical Antiquities of Scotland*, ed. A. W. Wiston-Glynne (Edinburgh, 1908), i, 1–2.

51. *Melrose Liber*, i, no. 1.

52. J. S. Richardson, *Sweetheart Abbey* (Edinburgh, 2nd edition, 1951), 10; *Charters of*

the Abbey of Crossraguel, i, (Ayrshire and Galloway Archaeological Association, 1886), e.g. plate 1 – Crossraguel Abbey in 1762, after John Clerk of Eldin.

53. Coulson, 'Hierarchism in Conventual Crenellation', 72–5; Fergusson, 'Porta patens esto'.

54. C. A. R. Radford and G. Donaldson, *Whithorn and Kirkmadrine* (Edinburgh, 1953), 28.

55. *RMS*, i, App. I, no. 20; *RMS*, ii, no. 453.

56. D. G. Adams, *Celtic and Medieval Religious Houses in Angus* (Brechin, 1984), plan p. 24.

57. *RRS*, v, 39–41; *Arbroath Liber*, nos. 231, 278; *RMS*, i, no. 863.

58. *Flores Historiarum*, ed. H. R. Luard, iii (Rolls Series, 1890), 311.

59. Mackie and Cruden, *Arbroath Abbey*, 39–41.

60. *Flores Historiarum*, iii, 311–12; RCAHMS, *Fife*, 114–15.

61. *ER*, i, 215.

62. *RMS*, i, App. I, no. 24; *RRS*, v, no. 188.

63. RCAHMS, *Fife*, 114–16 and fig. 242.

64. *St Andrews Liber*, xxxii; *RRS*, v, 39.

65. RCAHMS, *Fife*, no. 460; S. Cruden, *St Andrews Cathedral* (Edinburgh, 1950), 18; Fawcett, *Abbeys and Priories*, 116.

66. RCAHMS, *Fife*, no. 444.

67. A. T. Simpson and S. Stevenson, *Historic Pittenweem* (Scottish Burgh Survey, Glasgow, 1981), 11, 21.

68. RCAHMS, *Fife*, 223.

69. *RMS*, ii, no. 1444.

70. *RMS*, i, App. II, no. 1728.

71. Cowan and Easson, *Religious Houses*, 65.

72. *Chron. Auchinleck*, f. 113v.

73. *RMS*, ii, no. 523.

74. *Chron. Auchinleck*, f. 119r.

75. *RMS*, ii, no. 1768.

76. A. T. Simpson and S. Stevenson, *Historic Paisley* (Glasgow, Scottish Burgh Survey, 1982), 36–7; MacGibbon and Ross, *Ecclesiastical Architecture*, 9.

77. *Crossraguel Charters*, i, no. 10.

78. Ibid, no. 22.

79. Radford, *Crossraguel*, 20–1; MacGibbon and Ross, *Castellated and Domestic Architecture*, iii, 385–6.

80. RCAHMS, *Fife*, no. 460.

81. Coulson, 'Hierarchism in Conventual Crenellation', passim.

82. Ibid., 71.

Chapter 2

✵

ADAPTING TRADITION?
THE EARLDOM OF
STRATHEARN, 1114–1296

Fiona J. Watson

Figure 2.1
Earldom of Strathearn
properties mentioned
in the text.

The castle, especially the stone castle, is, without doubt, one of the most evocative images of the Middle Ages. Its development within the British context is also intimately associated with the 'feudalisation' or 'Normanisation' of the kingdom of England, and subsequently of Scotland. While historians continue to debate the definitions of these labels, and the appropriateness of using them at all, it is still the case that something strikingly new arrived in England after its conquest by William of Normandy: the knight, his fief, and its heart, the castle.[1]

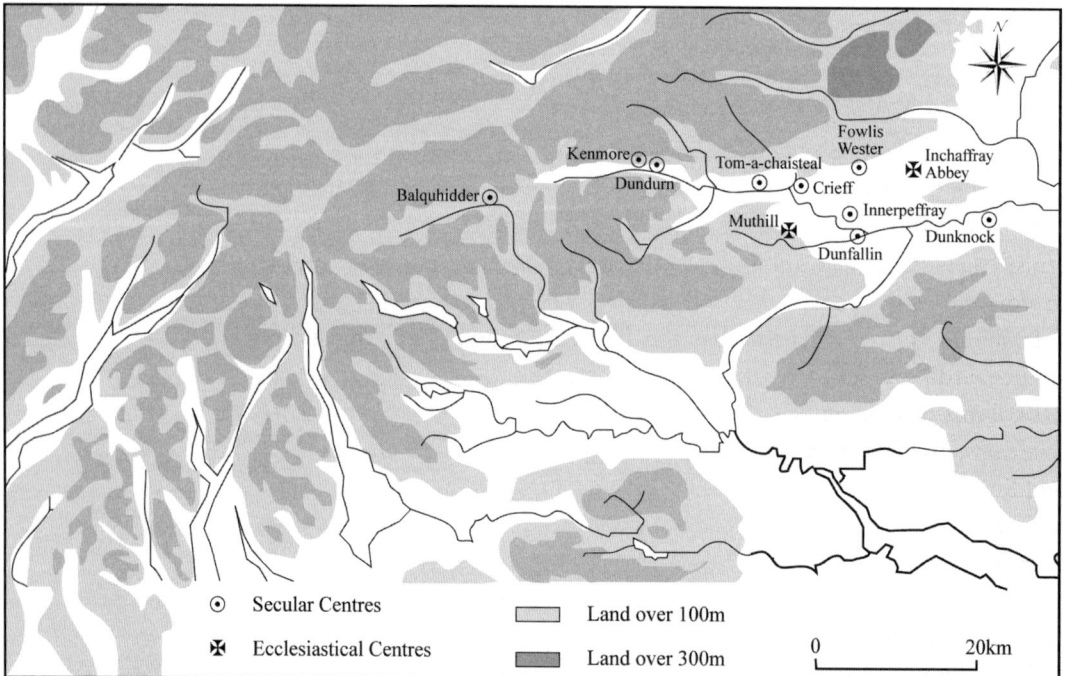

Secular Centres   Land over 100m

Ecclesiastical Centres   Land over 300m   0   20km

That these features gradually made their way into Scotland cannot be denied, though Scottish historians would strenuously reject the proposition that this was part of a 'civilising' process. Indeed, the extent to which Scottish society was transformed by the introduction of Anglo-Norman customs and institutions, particularly in relation to feudalism, is now hotly debated, even if this has, as yet, rarely made it into print.[2] Although, for example, knights' fees, with their implications for military service, were certainly a novelty in the twelfth century, it seems just as likely that much of the impression of general innovation owes more to the new habit of writing things down, often under different names, than any systematic and wholesale alteration to the structure of society.

A cursory glance at the map indicates clearly that the distribution of castles in Scotland before the outbreak of war with England in 1296 poses certain problems, given their predominance in the south and east, with a rich scattering in the far west.[3] To put it more usefully, a reading of the map argues clearly that castles were not a prominent feature in the heart of the kingdom, the original Scotia identified as that area between the Forth, the Spey and Drumalban; equally, it is no coincidence that the majority of Scotland's earls, whose origins stretched back perhaps beyond the formation of the kingdom, held land in Scotia.[4] It is stating the obvious, therefore, to conclude that Scotland's ancient earldoms, even in the thirteenth century, were not places in which to find the up-to-date apparatus of a 'Norman', or 'feudal', lord.

But how can this be: the role of the castle as an expression of status and prestige is surely an uncontroversial subject? Certainly there is undeniable evidence that the arrival of Anglo-Normans in Scotland, particularly after 1124, provided a new set of intimates for the king, but it is not the case that the 'native' earls were deprived of their status and influence within the kingdom as a result.[5] We cannot therefore conclude that these earls lacked the *ability*, in terms of status and landed resources, to 'modernise' their residences; the only alternative is that they had no *inclination* to do so.

It should be remembered that the Norman conquest of England was an extraordinary series of events which should not be categorised as a natural process; certainly, it has been argued that, contrary to earlier assertions, the Normans did not import a technique of large-scale castle-building but found it prudent to adopt such a policy on their lands on both sides of the Channel at around the same time.[6] They were thus adapting to changing conditions – as we would expect – rather than unconsciously applying a cultural norm. Scotland was not, as a political entity, conquered dramatically by an alien group, with all the accompanying social and political upheaval; rather, the kingdom evolved less sensationally

LORDSHIP AND
ARCHITECTURE
IN MEDIEVAL
AND
RENAISSANCE
SCOTLAND

ॐ

through the piecemeal conquest of surrounding territory by its kings and their supporters, and the assimilation of a number of ethnic groups, including the useful Anglo-Normans, into the wider whole. We should not expect, therefore, that the history of lordship in the northern kingdom would develop along the same lines as in post-Conquest England.

The 'native' elites already presided over a system of lordship, with all its many attributes, which was essentially well suited to the purposes for which it had developed; on the other hand, given that the kings of Scots had recognised the usefulness of the system developed by the Normans, it is equally likely that elements of it would be attractive to other members of the Scottish elites. In order to understand more fully why the traditional picture of a medieval castle as the heart of lordship does not generally seem to have been deemed appropriate for the earls of Scotia, I will now look in depth at the history of one of them: Strathearn.

The medieval earldom of Strathearn has its origins in the very creation of Scotland itself: one glance at the richness of prehistoric symbols shown on the Ordnance Survey map serves to illustrate the long history of settlement in the area. By the ninth century, the separate kingdoms of the Picts and the 'Scots' (Irish) of Argyll had joined together, creating a new 'Scottish' kingdom of Alba. It was reputedly divided into seven provinces (whose leaders, the mormaers, supposedly later became the first Scottish earls); Fortriu was the name given to the one which later divided into the earldoms of Strathearn and Menteith. The great fort of Dundurn, situated a few miles east of St Fillans at the east end of Loch Earn, was originally its most important seat and was allegedly still used as a stronghold as late as the twelfth century (although archaeologists today doubt that it was in use any later than the tenth).[7]

Strathearn sat right in the middle of the kingdom of Alba, or (in Latin) Scotia, bounded by mountains to the north, the earldom of Menteith and the Ochil Hills to the south, the lands of Argyll to the west, and the earldoms of Fife and Angus to the east. 'Of all the ancient earldoms, Strathearn was strategically the most important in the eyes of kings who desired to consolidate the government of Scotland beyond the Tay …'.[8] Equally, the very clear evidence visible even today of a Roman presence in the broad plains of the Earn valley serves as a reminder of the area's ability to resist conquest and assimilation.

The first member of the Strathearn family to be named as earl was Malise, who attested the foundation charter of the priory of Scone in 1114 or 1115.[9] However, there is no evidence for the activities of Earl Malise other than his few appearances as a witness to royal charters. Fortunately, this situation changes in the latter half of the century. Malise's son, Earl Ferteth, is most famous, in terms of 'national' history, for leading a revolt of 'Celtic' magnates in 1160 against King Malcolm IV, who had outraged these traditionalists by accompanying King Henry II of England on campaign to the Continent. As the representatives of families which perhaps occupied positions of power even before the Scottish kingdom was formed, Earl Ferteth and his cohorts were allegedly most alarmed by the implications of inferior kingship which such military service appeared to acknowledge.[10] As remarked above, even though the king's intimates were men from Anglo-Norman families, such as de Soules, Olifard and de Morville, who had mostly been given lands in south-east Scotland, Malcolm seems to have paid attention to the concerns of his more traditional advisers.

Because Earl Ferteth appears to have reacted to the activities of his king and, by implication, the influence of 'Anglo-Normanism' in such a manner, it seems reasonable to investigate more closely the mechanisms of power operated by such an apparently conservative magnate and his successors.[11] It is hoped, therefore, to present a more accurate picture of the form of lordship practised by members of this 'Celtic' nobility and their reaction to the changes taking place around them. Their relationship with the Crown is certainly of importance: as earls they were among the top rank of the nobility and all took part, to a greater or lesser extent, in national politics. Equally, however, as 'rulers' of an ancient province, they did not overtly owe their position to the Crown, however much the trend was towards establishing kingship as the ultimate political expression of power in Scotland and kings as the fount of all landownership.

Lordship was long-established in Strathearn and its exercise almost certainly relied less on the relationship of its earls with individual kings and more on networks with the many families who lived on, or adjacent to, their extensive estates. In a comparatively uncentralised power structure, these networks constructed between noble families are at least as worthy of study as those connecting the localities to the centre. On the other hand, it should be remembered that the exercise of lordship takes place in a physical environment, rather than a theoretical one, and the form of the structures employed by the earls in their relationships with those over whom they wielded power is vital to our understanding of how lordship actually worked.

One of the most frustrating elements of charter evidence pertaining to the earls of Strathearn is the almost complete absence of references to the place where the charter was given. It is thus almost impossible to say with any absolute degree of assurance where the earldom's main seats of government and administration were located. Nevertheless, on the few occasions when the place of the charter grant is given, what is striking is the apparently unfortified nature of the sites: the island at Kenmore near

LORDSHIP AND
ARCHITECTURE
IN MEDIEVAL
AND
RENAISSANCE
SCOTLAND

❧

St Fillans, Fowlis, Crieff, Dunfallin, Innerpeffray, Muthill and, finally, Inchaffray, the monastery founded by the third earl, Gilbert. As Neville puts it, '… until the last decade of the thirteenth and the first years of the fourteenth centuries, when the earl of Strathearn first clashed with royal authority and his lands were ravaged, the people of the earldom lived a comparatively undisturbed, peaceful existence. There was little need to erect strongholds capable of withstanding prolonged and violent assault'.[12] This would imply a province at ease with itself.

Tantalisingly, impressive masonry remains suggest that a significant stone castle was located at Tom-a-chaisteal, a promising hillock some three miles east of Crieff and within the ancient thanage of Strowan. Certainly local legend, and the impressive view which it commands over the Earn valley up to Comrie, opens up the distinct possibility that this was an important Strathearn castle, but it cannot be proved. Equally, all grants of land, both within and without the family, concern estates located on the broad plain of the Earn east of Crieff, and also across onto the south side of the Ochils; it might therefore be presumed that the comital demesne lands (which should be kept as intact as possible to provide for the earls' own households) were largely, though not exclusively, located in the other, western, part of the earldom.

Though the evidence is essentially negative, based primarily on the documentary silence regarding this western portion, together with its topography, it might be tentatively suggested that the heart of the earldom, in the sense of the greatest concentration of demesne, was located in the narrow funnel of land between Crieff and Loch Earn. Neville would not agree – she places the heart 'in a comparatively small area of land dominated by the waters of the River Earn and the burns of Pow and Cowgask'.[13] There is certainly no doubt that the balance of surviving evidence places the earls' administrative activity almost entirely in the eastern part of the earldom; however, the very paucity of this evidence should make us cautious in using it without alternative corroboration, and it could be argued (as Neville does in another context) that the very existence of written evidence might, in itself, indicate unusual activity. As has been most incisively noted elsewhere, 'It was feudalism …' or, in this case, certain selected aspects of it, '… that was driven by parchment, not the traditional lordships'.[14]

Despite the fact that the majority of records surviving from this period relate to the foundation and subsequent endowment of the Augustinian abbey of Inchaffray, only one charter was recorded as being granted by the earl at the abbey and that was not until 1287.[15] We may presume, surely, that the foundation charter of 1200 was granted at Inchaffray and it has been suggested that if, as seems likely, other grants were made there, the scribes would not bother to record the fact because it was such a normal occurrence.[16] A most striking association of the abbey with the earls' administration is to be found in the claim made by Maitland Thomson (although he does not provide a source) 'that the 'Sair Law', used by the earls of Strathearn for executions, lies on the slope to the north of the abbey, and is clearly visible therefrom'.[17] Given that another likely key administrative centre and potential castle-site, Fowlis, is located only a few miles north of this alleged gallowhill, Dr Thomson may well be correct, but it would be imprudent to say any more without corroborating evidence.

There is certainly no obvious structure remaining today at Fowlis out of which the earl might have operated; nevertheless, 'less than one mile east of the village of Fowlis Wester, on a farm known as Castleton, there is visible a grassy mound upon which Ordnance Surveyors have identified the remains of a castle'.[18] Equally, Dunfallin, which is no longer marked on modern maps but was situated approximately at Mills of Earn (NN 9216), was indeed the location of the earls' mill, and, so far as it can be judged, not much else; as the site of 'the full court of Malise, Earl of Strathearn' held on Tuesday 29 September 1284, this indicates most clearly that the administration of this great earldom was essentially a matter of practicalities, rather than prestige. Given that large amounts of grain belonging to his tenants would doubtless require to be milled so soon after the harvest, Earl Malise might well have decided to hold his court at the same time as he was overseeing the smooth running of this lucrative element of a landowner's rights.[19]

Innerpeffray, upstream from Dunfallin, is the site of a castle which, though constructed in the seventeenth century, was almost certainly established on an earlier fortification.[20] It is likely to be significant that the charter granted there, which allocated an annual fee of 10 merks to Inchaffray Abbey from the earl's holding at Pitcairn, near Dunning, was dated 25 March 1283, in other words, New Year's Day.[21] Doubtless the earl required to mark the dawning of a new year in a substantial residence, where he could celebrate in style with family and friends. Nevertheless, we should not conclude, given the evidence of the maps, drawn from the (admittedly limited) archaeological evidence, that Innerpeffray was a stone castle.

Muthill was another site named in a charter but not apparently equipped with any obvious fortification; it also seems to have formed part of the estate of Sir Malise, brother of Earl Gilbert, and was probably used later in the thirteenth century to endow other younger sons, since Malise apparently had no heirs. Most interestingly, Muthill was the site of a school which may have had its origins in the period of Celtic Christianity then being so earnestly pushed aside to make way for orthodox Roman practices.[22]

Crieff must surely also lay claim to operating as a key administrative

LORDSHIP AND
ARCHITECTURE
IN MEDIEVAL
AND
RENAISSANCE
SCOTLAND

⁂

centre in Strathearn. Three charters are recorded as being granted there, compared with the two given at Kenmore. In addition, Brice, parson of Crieff, was one of the most regular witnesses to comital charters between 1199 and his death around 1223; his son Malise, who succeeded him as parson, witnessed two of Earl Robert's charters. The post then went to sir Nicholas, who was a son of Sir Malise, Parson of Gask, and grandson of Earl Gilbert of Strathearn. Nicholas also acted as chamberlain, the chief financial officer, for his cousin, Earl Malise, in the 1250s. The traditional Celtic practice of keeping things in the family, even among those clergymen potentially bound by the tighter rules of celibacy advocated by Rome, was clearly still espoused even in the later thirteenth century.[23] Tradition also has it that the earls of Strathearn held courts on an artificial mound surrounded by a wall of earth and stone situated to the south of the town, commonly known since 1475 as the 'Stayt' of Crieff.[24]

Finally, there is the whole vexed question of 'leyle de Kenmer' (island of Kenmore) which again has faded from modern cartographic evidence, although there is reference to the 'eilean' (island) – 'a small flat promontory situated where the River Earn meets the loch, opposite present-day St Fillans'. If, as Neville suggests, this dwelling occupied a crannog, we are faced with the possibility of a very ancient site indeed; equally, its continued use, right up into the fourteenth century, is surely a striking example of the apparent unwillingness of these earls to transform any aspect of their life and work merely because other members of the Scottish political community were doing something different.[25] Certainly, the fact that the earls maintained a house at the most westerly end of their territory should also serve to remind us that, while the changing orientation of Scottish national politics gave greater prominence to the south and the east, traditional relationships with the west and the north were still very important. This is also attested to by the presence as witnesses of James, parson of Balquhidder, on no fewer than six occasions in the 1260s and 1270s, and Duncan of Balquhidder in 1284.[26] Although Balquhidder is a considerable distance from the administrative centre of Strathearn, the journey becomes less problematic if a boat is taken across Loch Earn. Finally, as with Innerpeffray, the earl celebrated New Year's Day at Kenmore, indicating that this was an important – and, presumably, spacious – comital residence.[27]

The evidence, sketchy though it is, for the places from which the earls of Strathearn administered their estates, provides an impression, even in the later thirteenth century, of well-established practice which still functioned effectively. The earls appear to have been prepared to be active the length and breadth of their domains; they were fortunate, perhaps, in that this was a compact earldom which was generally bounded, rather than

Figure 2.2
Dunknock, Perthshire:
aerial view.
RCAHMS, A 29474

divided, by more difficult natural features. Equally if, as members of the native nobility, the earls of Strathearn felt at all threatened by the impact of the Anglo-Norman newcomers on the political map of Scotland, they certainly did not attempt to compensate by building ostentatious up-to-date power centres. This may, of course, have been because of a lack of sufficient hard cash.[28] However, as mentioned above, the overriding impression created by their activities in the thirteenth century particularly suggests that they did not do so because they were entirely confident of their power and authority where it mattered: on their own lands.

LORDSHIP AND
ARCHITECTURE
IN MEDIEVAL
AND
RENAISSANCE
SCOTLAND

ॐ

This still begs the question of what sort of residences the earls lived and worked in. The lack of excavation makes this difficult to answer. However, Stephen Driscoll has provided considerable illumination on the question of the site and form of the caput of the thanage of Dunning, one of four thanages within the earldom, which may well have a bearing on the kind of structures prevailing elsewhere in Strathearn:

> Just south of Dunning is a slight hill, known as Dunknock, upon which once stood a multi–vallate fortification, not unlike the small hillforts of the Early Historic Period. No earthworks remain; the site survives only as a cropmark and has not been excavated. However, taking into account both its situation adjacent to the post-medieval manor of Pitcairn and its proximity to the parish church of St Serf, this enclosure is the most likely site of the caput of the thanage. It is significant that the interior is relatively spacious and level.[29]

Presumably the earl would have occupied a more ostentatious construction than one of his thanes; however, the basic principle may well have been the same. It should also be stated that highly sophisticated and impressive structures can be made from wood; one of the reasons for the eventual predilection for using stone in elite construction in Scotland was perhaps due less to a belief in its superiority over timber, but more because climate change rendered it more suitable.

However, such a prosaic interpretation of architectural change, or the lack of it, has not been the usual view taken by historians. These 'native' earls have often been characterised as 'traditional', even 'conservative', heralding the conclusion that stone castles were not built because of a suspicion of innovation and, by implication, a lack of understanding of the merits of the 'Norman' system. Certainly, Neville goes so far as to suggest that:

> ... as late as the middle of the thirteenth century, Strathearn had not been greatly influenced by the significant political, and especially cultural, changes which had occurred in Scotland in the one hundred years after the accession of King David I.

So, Strathearn was allegedly a backwater out of touch with the 'progressive' developments taking place in areas closer to the 'centre' of Scottish government.

> Under a thin veneer of conformity to the newer feudal customs and practices prevalent in larger parts of the realm, they managed to preserve in their earldom much that was Celtic and native.

This allegedly changed from the latter half of the thirteenth century, under a succession of Malises who emerged from the shadow of their Celtic past into a political landscape that was neither native, nor Anglo-Norman, but Scottish.[30] However, this interpretation runs into some difficulty given that, once this apparent transformation has taken place, there is still no evidence for any upgrading of the physical manifestions of lordship, surely one of the most obvious indicators of 'modernisation'. Equally, as will be shown below, the evidence also suggests that one of the other key elements of a 'modern' administration – knight's fiefs – actually seems to go out of fashion in thirteenth-century Strathearn.

The evidence in support of the change to a more 'modern' outlook under the later earls of Strathearn lies partly in the fact that Earl Malise (II) played a prominent role in the turbulent politics of the minority of Alexander III (1249–60), partly because of clear changes in the organisation of the comital household and retinue, but most particularly because the earls could not fail to become involved in the wars with England after 1296.[31] It is not the intention of this essay to discuss this last period, which could easily form the subject of an article in itself; however, and as further justification of a cut-off point in the 1290s, it is my contention that the wars with England changed the face of Scottish politics and affected every noble family of whatever political complexion.[32] This was almost certainly caused less by the actions of Edward I than those of Robert Bruce, who succeeded in radically redefining Scottish politics by virtue of the murder of the most important political figure in Scotland, John Comyn of Badenoch, and the subsequent seizure of the throne.[33]

The accusation that the earls of Strathearn paid mere lip-service to 'feudal' innovation, while seeking to preserve their ancient customs in the teeth of a royally sanctioned trend, is an important theme which has considerable bearing on the exercise of lordship and the role of the castle. Certainly there is evidence to suggest that King William the Lion made a deliberate attempt to encourage the introduction and spread of knight service to Strathearn through his grants to Earl Gilbert and his family.[34] Subsequent reference to the earl's knights, which has been interpreted as a '... form of expression ... used of those who discharged the military service due from their lord's land',[35] implies that the Crown achieved a degree of short-term success in this respect.

However, the longer-term failure of the earldom to use its landed resources for the production of knights, in preference to the practice of feu-farming in particular, should by no means be automatically ascribed to machinations by the earls. By the second quarter of the thirteenth century feu-farming appears to be sufficiently widespread (though by no means uniform) to suggest that there had been a general change in attitude towards the exploitation of Scotland's resources. Perhaps this was a result

LORDSHIP AND
ARCHITECTURE
IN MEDIEVAL
AND
RENAISSANCE
SCOTLAND

❧

of the Crown's waning interest in acquiring the northern counties of England (the traditional stamping-ground of Scottish military activity in previous centuries), provoking a corresponding decrease in the need to exploit the military capability of the kingdom. The expansion of royal power to the north and west (technically controlled by Norway) was accomplished largely through the endeavours of individual magnates such as Farquhar MacTaggart, later Earl of Ross, and William Comyn, who became Earl of Buchan. It seems to have become increasingly clear that there was much to be gained by renting out lands for a high rent but with security of tenure attached.[36]

The Scottish kings, like so many of their nobility, were by no means concerned to change for change's sake; they were certainly not intent on slavishly emulating practices from south of the Border, however willing they were to borrow certain features. As mentioned above, it would be rather old-fashioned, at best, to suggest that the Scottish national government was a pale imitation of English government; there is perhaps equally little justification for suggesting that the 'native' Scottish earldoms were always in the re-arguard of change. Such a presumption makes sense only if we expect that any innovation emerging in Scotland automatically had its origins in similar developments in England.

The question of knight service may turn out, in Scottish history, to be something of a red herring. In terms of the lands controlled by the earls of Strathearn, only three knights' fees can be identified: Madderty, granted to Earl Gilbert by King William in the late 1180s; Kincardine near Auchterarder, granted to Malise by the same earl, his brother, around 1173; and Meikleour and Lethendy, granted by King William again to Earl Gilbert c. 1195–9. There were almost certainly more, granted by the earls to their own immediate tenants, if the use of the term 'my knight', noted above, which can be found in approximately the same period, is anything to go by.[37]

From 1200 onwards, lands were held by the elites in Strathearn by feu-ferme, by blench-ferme (a token payment, such as a pair of spurs at Christmas), or in frankalmoign (free alms: a grant of land wherein the grantor has waived all rights to the exaction of any secular due). The barony of Kincardine, a knight's fee in the 1170s, was granted to Sir David Graham a century later for a blench-ferme rent of one silver penny.[38] Land grants made under blench ferme indicate a desire to show favour (they were often made to members of the earl's own family); they also imply an arrangement constructed not out of the imposition of an exaction which is an end in itself (such as rent or knight service) but one which is designed to create bonds of loyalty based on a much more complex, and less military-orientated, relationship.

Knights are certainly a prominent feature in the administrative and social life of the earldom throughout the period: excluding the earls themselves, there are references to at least twenty who maintained a reasonably close association with Strathearn, either as members of the comital family or household, or by virtue of a major landholding. Referring back to the point made earlier about renaming, it seems likely that the earls of Strathearn (before they were even called such) were leaders of a local cavalry elite both in pre-Norman times (of the type illustrated so impressively on the beautiful carved stones such as the one at nearby Dupplin), and after the brief period of the overt and systematic attempt by the Crown to create knights' fiefs.

However, the bonds of loyalty between the earls and their greatest tenants seem to have owed less by the end of the thirteenth century to military obligations than to long-standing traditions of a common involvement in the administration of the earldom. This is illustrated most clearly by the fact that, when Scotland was plunged into civil war, and then war with England, after the death of Alexander III, Earl Malise issued at least three – and doubtless more – discharges of extraordinary military service to tenants.[39] As these discharges make clear, even Sir William Murray, an important member of the earl's inner circle, only owed traditional Scottish service for his lands, rather than a quota of knights. This, together with the clear evidence for the continued and increasing exploitation of the area's economic resources such as, for example, the clearing of woods for arable land, balancing the need to maintain pastures in the face of an increasing demand for land for housing, the careful preservation of the ultimate authority of the earl's court, the attempts to prevent the escape of serfs,[40] reflects a lack of concern over the exploitation of military resources which is evident throughout most of Scotland.[41] In this respect, as in so many others, national and regional trends did, in fact, mirror each other. This should come as no surprise: in a comparatively uncentralised kingdom, royal and comital administrations were effectively based on the same governmental principles and were affected by the same issues, even if the details look different.

No earl ruled alone. Like the king, he relied on constructing and maintaining effective networks of power and patronage with the leading men within his orbit. If the conservative picture of the earldom before the thirteenth century painted by Neville holds true, then we would expect to see a markedly greater reliance placed thereafter on the kind of men, originally Anglo-Normans, who had earlier been preferred as administrators by the kings of Scots because of their abilities, rather than because their families were traditionally associated with the office. And surely these men, at least, would wish to live in castles?

LORDSHIP AND
ARCHITECTURE
IN MEDIEVAL
AND
RENAISSANCE
SCOTLAND

⁂

The comital household was clearly an important element in the exercise of power, since many of the administrative functions pertaining to the earldom were performed by members of it. At the beginning of the period for which documentary evidence remains, such men maintain a remarkably Celtic look to both their names and their offices; by the end of the thirteenth century, many of the Celtic offices have disappeared and the families forming the nexus of the comital administration are clearly not of native origin. Neville deals thoroughly with this subject in her thesis [42] and it is not intended to repeat her work here. Instead I would like to offer some more general conclusions, which may differ from her interpretation.

Once again, the extent of change can be exaggerated. The comital officers of the earlier period are indeed much more prominent in witness lists than they are after the accession of Earl Malise (II) (1245), and there is certainly a change in the offices themselves, with the disappearance of a host of Gaelic titles, and the introduction of both a marshal and a chamberlain in the 1240s. It has been suggested that 'the earl's attention to his revenues ... became more rigorous with the appointment of a chamberlain who had clerical experience, the seneschalcy (stewardship) apparently fading in importance, at least as a financial office'.[43] This last point is debateable. Certainly it is clear that the stewardship of Strathearn remained within one family (progressing eventually through marriage to the Murrays of Tullibardine) in typical Celtic fashion. It is also clear that the traditional habit of involving other male members of the steward's family in the execution of his responsibilities [44] continued throughout the thirteenth century, and that this included the oversight of the collection of all comital dues. As a single indication of these points, it was recorded that, on 2 February 1256:

> Robert, brother of the Steward of Strathearn, while they (the abbots of Lindores) and their men enjoyed peaceable possession of the right of taking timber from the wood of Glenlitherne (Glenlichorn) in Strathearn, for maintaining and repairing their buildings on their land of Fedal, which is in Kather Mothel, and likewise for the purposes of agriculture, the said Robert in violation of justice deprived the aforesaid abbot and convent of the aforesaid peaceable possession ...

This Robert was presumably a brother of Sir Malise, Steward of Strathearn, and grandson of Anecol, Thane of Dunning.[45]

The question of 'Anglo-Norman' infiltration into the earldom is extremely pertinent to any analysis of the elements of change and continuity occurring there. Despite the reliance on ancient families to serve as officers within the comital household, it is quite clear that many of the key families

Figure 2.3
Muthill Old Parish
Church, Perthshire:
view from south-east,
c. 1870–80.
RCAHMS, PT/4874

of the earldom were of foreign extraction right from the beginning of the documented period. Tristram of Gorthy, who possessed a holding from which he took his name to the west of Fowlis and north-west of Inchaffray Abbey, would appear to have had Breton origins. [46] Nevertheless, his son Henry, and perhaps his brother, both served the earls of Strathearn as *rennaire* or food-divider, clearly an office of Celtic origin. Equally two families who were named from the early period as the earl's knights – Kinbuck and Dolpatrick – were also originally incomers. It could be inferred that their introduction to Strathearn at the same time as the drive to create knights' fiefs provides evidence of attempted interference in the power structure of the earldom by the Crown. Whether or not such a conspiracy theory is correct, the continual presence of these men and their successors in the affairs of the earldom, together with their early assumption of the name of their lands as a surname, indicates that they soon became assimilated: these are men of Strathearn, whatever their origins, even in the twelfth century.

Other families joined the first ranks of the earls' social and administrative networks as the thirteenth century progressed. Interestingly, out of the top twenty lay witnesses throughout the period, five families can be identified as being related to the earls by marriage: Kinbuck, Ruthven, Graham,

LORDSHIP AND
ARCHITECTURE
IN MEDIEVAL
AND
RENAISSANCE
SCOTLAND

❧

Comyn of Buchan, and Murray.[47] Marriage by no means guaranteed permanent entry into the earls' closest circles; however, the witness lists do indicate that such a sign of comital favour tended to be an acknowledgement of an already rising star, rather than an attempt to create brand new links.

The two men who ranked top of the Strathearn hierarchy by the later thirteenth century must surely be Sir Patrick Graham and Sir William Murray, who appear to have acted as tutors or guardians during the minority of Earl Malise III.[48] Although the lack of any older male members of the comital family presumably resulted in the guardianship going to outsiders, both families can be seen to have played a part in Strathearn politics as early as the era of Earl Robert, rather than Earl Malise (II) who is usually credited with bringing in very different policies and personnel.[49] There is little need to look for some sinister force at work bringing such men to the forefront of Strathearn politics. Just as the Anglo-Normans had originally gained lands and political power in Scotland through model service to the Crown, so surely did their descendants take root throughout Scotland by means of similar loyalty and service to the major native dynasties. As the example of Henry, son of Tristram, the *rennaire*, so graphically illustrates, the process of cultural and political assimilation was by no means one-way.

We look in vain, however, to find any evidence for castle-building of the 'Norman' type by these incomers, even when they arrived through a grant of a knight's fee, as appears to have been the case with Kinbuck and Dolpatrick at least. Equally there is no evidence in the thirteenth century for Sir David Graham seeking to grace his lands of Kincardine with a significant stone structure, even though the remains of a later castle certainly exist today. In the end, we are forced to the conclusion that Strathearn was dotted with manor-houses, hall-houses and even, as at the possible fort at Dunning, structures with a more ancient history.[50]

We should not be surprised that this is so: architecture, as with the other mechanisms of lordship, tends to develop out of the requirements of the time and place, though fashion and tradition can play their part. The structures of Strathearn, even in 1300, serve as examples of an indigenous architectural tradition, which, if the climate had not changed and the kingdom not been turned upside down by warfare, might well have remained the norm in Scotia for much longer. Ultimately, however, their example should serve to make us aware of an alternative form of late medieval lordship and architecture to what might be termed the 'Ivanhoe' tradition. It will never displace this popular image of the Middle Ages but we must certainly be aware of it if we are to understand fully how power and lordship functioned in late medieval Scotland.

NOTES

1. See, for example, R. Eales, 'Royal Power and Castles in Norman England', in *The Ideals and Practice of Medieval Knighthood*, iii, eds. C. Harper-Bill and R. Harvey, (Woodbridge, 1988), 49–78; S. Reynolds, *Fiefs and Vassals*, (Oxford, 1994).

2. S. Reynolds, in her book, *Fiefs and Vassals* (Oxford, 1994), has even gone so far as to challenge the predominance of 'feudalism' throughout Europe, never mind Scotland.

3. *Atlas of Scottish History to 1707*, eds. P. G. B. McNeill and H. L. MacQueen (Edinburgh, 1996), 430, 432.

4. See D. Broun, 'Defining Scotland and the Scots', in *Image and Identity: The Making and Remaking of Scotland*, eds. D. Broun, R. Finlay and M. Lynch (Edinburgh, 1998).

5. See, for example, A. A. M. Duncan, *Scotland: The Making of the Kingdom*, (Edinburgh, 1992), 133–142.

6. R. Eales, 'Royal Power and Castles', 54.

7. *Scots Peerage*, viii, 239; S. Driscoll, 'Formalising the mechanisms of state power: early Scottish lordship, ninth to thirteenth centuries' in *Scottish Power-Centres from the Early Middle Ages to the Twentieth Century*, eds. S. Foster, A. Macinnes and R. MacInnes (Glasgow, 1998).

8. *Inchaffray Chrs.*, lviii. This quote is really referring to fourteenth-century Scotland, an important fact to note since, of course, early Scottish government was quite at home north of the Tay and only moved its focus south of the Forth in the later Middle Ages.

9. *Scone Liber*, no. 1.

10. See, for example, *Chron. Wyntoun* (Laing), ii, 422–3.

11. The earls of Strathearn have already been the subject of a most innovative PhD thesis by Cynthia Neville (The Earls of Strathearn, unpublished PhD thesis, 2 vols., University of Aberdeen, 1983). However, it has sadly never been published and the present author has taken advantage of this, and most particularly the appendix of Strathearn charters included in the thesis, to write this article. It thus owes a great debt to Dr Neville.

12. Neville, Strathearn, i, 32–3.

13. Ibid., i, 33.

14. Driscoll, 'Formalising the mechanisms of state power'.

15. *Inchaffray Chrs.*, no. 117.

16. Neville, Strathearn, i., 25.

17. *Inchaffray Chrs.*, 272, note to no. 25.

18. See *Lindores Chartulary*, 250, note to no. 43.

19. Neville, Strathearn, i, 16.

20. Ibid., i, 20.

21. *Moray Registrum*, 466–7.

22. See Neville, Strathearn, i, 22.

23. *Inchaffray Chrs.*, no. 115.

24. *Lindores Chartulary*, liii-liv.

25. Neville, Strathearn, i, 20.

26. *Inchaffray Chrs.*, nos. 95, 96, 100, 102, 105, 106; *Moray Registrum*, 465–6.

27. *Inchaffray Chrs.*, no. 87.

28. Neville, Strathearn, i, 238–40.

29. Driscoll, 'Formalising the mechanisms of state power', op. cit.

30. Ibid., xxxiii.

31. Neville, Strathearn, i, xxxiii.

LORDSHIP AND
ARCHITECTURE
IN MEDIEVAL
AND
RENAISSANCE
SCOTLAND

⁊

32. The exception to this were the native magnates of the Hebrides who, having been brought forcibly into the Scottish polity only in 1266, tended to play a very different political game from their peers on the mainland.

33. See, for example, F. Watson, 'The Enigmatic Lion: Scotland and the Wars of Independence', in *Image and Identity: The Making and Remaking of Scotland*, eds. D. Broun, R. Finlay and M. Lynch (Edinburgh, 1998).

34. For example, *RRS*, ii, no. 136; *HMC*, Seventh Report, part II, 704, no. 2.

35. *Melrose Liber*, p. xvi, note.

36. See F. Watson, 'Expressions of power in a medieval kingdom: thirteenth-century stone castles', in *Scottish Power-Centres from the Early Middle Ages to the Twentieth Century*, eds. S. Foster, A. Macinnes and R. MacInnes (Glasgow, 1998). It is, of course, impossible to tell whether the crown was the initiator or the imitator of such a policy until a fuller study of Scottish landholding is forthcoming.

37. Kinbuck would be such an example.

38. Neville, Strathearn, ii, nos. 59, 59a.

39. *Inchaffray Chrs.*, no. 117; *Moray Registrum*, 470; Fraser, *Grant*, iii, no. 12. Earl Malise was acknowledging that the military service required in these traumatic times was unprecedented and that its performance was at the goodwill of the tenant, rather than as an obligation owed to him as lord. However, these grants might also provide evidence of the fact that any form of military service was highly unusual in the more settled times of the later thirteenth century.

40. The first two activities indicate the pressure placed on the land through population growth (*Inchaffray Chrs.*, nos. 43 and 44; *Lindores Chartulary*, no. 28; Neville, Strathearn, ii, no. 60).

41. Watson, 'Expressions of power'.

42. Neville, Strathearn, i, chapter 4.

43. Duncan, *Making of the Kingdom*, 432. As noted above, the chamberlain was Earl Malise's cousin, Nicholas, parson of Crieff.

44. In the decades spanning the turn of the thirteenth century, the family of Strathearn stewards comprised a father, son and grandson operating in this way (See *Inchaffray Chrs.*, nos. 4, 5, 9, 11, 12, 14, 15, 19, 25, 28, 33).

45. *Lindores Chartulary*, no. 111. See Dr Neville's very useful family tree of the stewards of Strathearn in Strathearn, i, 177. The abbey of Lindores presumably justified their position by virtue of a grant made to them by Sir Fergus, brother of Earl Gilbert, before 1244, of the lands of Fedal '. . . with the common easement and liberty of taking material from my wood, where it shall be best and most suitable for them, for building and keeping up necessary and reasonable buildings in the aforesaid lands, and for those things which pertain to agriculture' (*Lindores Chartulary*, no. 24).

46. Neville, Strathearn, i, 271. The influence of Earl Gilbert's first wife, Matilda d'Aubigny – clearly a lady of considerable power, who witnessed nine of her husband's charters – must also be acknowledged as the potential source of any innovation around this time.

47. Ysenda, Earl Gilbert's second wife, was sister of Sir Richard of Kinbuck; Cecilia, Earl Gilbert's daughter, married Walter Ruthven; Annabella, daughter of Earl Robert married, as her second husband, Sir Patrick Graham of Kincardine; Maria, daughter of Earl Malise (II), married Sir Nicholas Graham of Dalkeith and Abercorn; and Earl Malise (III) married a daughter of Alexander Comyn, earl of Buchan. Sir William Murray, who acquired the lands of Tullibardine, was a great-nephew of Countess Ysenda (*Scots Peerage*, viii, 239–50; i, 451). This is not meant to imply that all the above would have regarded themselves predominantly, or even partially, as Strathearn men: Alexander Comyn clearly

would not, although his cousin, Comyn of Badenoch, had lands at Gask, just east of the earldom (*Inchaffray Chrs.*, nos. 108–9); Sir Patrick Graham also owned considerable estates in the Lennox (*Scots Peerage*, vi, 208–9).

48. *Inchaffray Chrs.*, no. 113; Neville, Strathearn, ii, no. 65.

49. As noted above, Earl Robert's daughter, Annabella, married Sir Patrick Graham, and her brother, Earl Malise, confirmed his earlier grant to Patrick's father, Sir David, of the barony of Kincardine. The unknown Gilbert de Murray witnessed four of Earl Robert's charters; Sir Malcolm Murray, who, according to the editor of the Inchaffray Cartulary, might well have been the son of this Gilbert (*Inchaffray Chrs.*, 279), and was certainly father of Sir William, witnessed three.

50. A grant from King Edward I in 1304 refers to a house at West Gask which 'must have been one of the strongholds on the Trinity Gask estate, perhaps Gascon Hall – then in the possession of the Earl of Strathearn or William Murray of Tullibardine' (E. M. Graham, *The Oliphants of Gask*, (London, 1910), 19; *CDS*, iv, p. 475). This is presumably yet another example of the kind of structure preferred in this area.

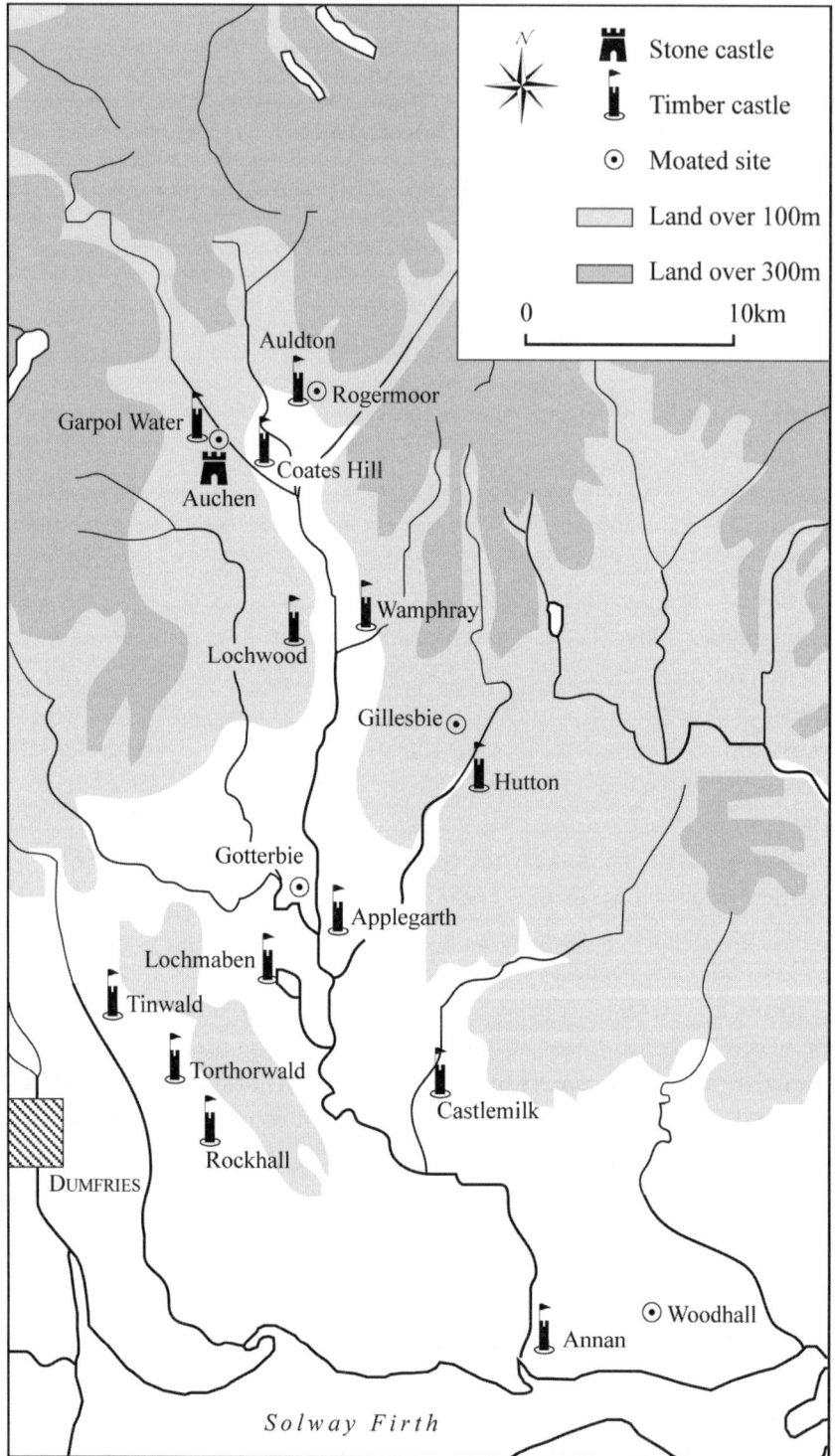

Legend:
- Stone castle
- Timber castle
- Moated site
- Land over 100m
- Land over 300m

0   10km

Auldton
Rogermoor
Garpol Water
Coates Hill
Auchen
Wamphray
Lochwood
Gillesbie
Hutton
Gotterbie
Applegarth
Lochmaben
Tinwald
Torthorwald
Castlemilk
Rockhall
DUMFRIES
Woodhall
Annan

Solway Firth

Figure 3.1
Bruce lordship of
Annandale.

Chapter 3

ॐ

THE BRUS LORDSHIP OF ANNANDALE, 1124–1296

Peter Corser

From 1124 until the outbreak of the Wars of Independence in 1296 the Anglo-Norman family of Brus, in a succession of Roberts relieved only by a single William, enjoyed unbroken suzerainty of the Lordship of Annandale. This chapter, which follows from an archaeological survey of Eastern Dumfriesshire by the Royal Commission on the Ancient and Historical Monuments of Scotland,[1] looks at the timber castles built by the incoming Anglo-Norman lords and considers the problem of other estate centres. It is not a study of standing buildings in the conventional sense, as the sites of the timber castles are marked only by their earthwork substructures and their defensive ditches and banks. Impressive though these may sometimes be, we are left to use sources like the Bayeux Tapestry, the stave churches of Norway, the timberwork in a handful of English bell-towers, and skuomorphs of timberwork preserved in stone buildings of the period to conjure our mind's-eye images of the high-quality timber buildings that might have stood upon some of these sites.

The enfeoffment of Robert de Brus, Lord of Cleveland, as Lord of Annandale in 1124 was the first recorded royal act of David I. It has been persuasively argued[2] that it was part of a wider military and political initiative pursued in concert by David and Henry I of England to establish, on Henry's part, firm control over the northern counties of England, and, on David's part, to make secure the southern counties of Scotland. Essential to the success of this strategy was the containment of any threat from Galloway where Fergus, Lord of Galloway, regarded himself as independent of the King of Scots. To this end Robert de Brus was established in Annandale, whilst Robert Avenel and Ranulf de Soules were established in Eskdale and Liddesdale respectively to control the routes into Teviotdale and the North Tyne. To the south lay the lordship of Carlisle held by Ranulf le Meschin until 1120 or soon after.

It is in this context that the timber castles of Annandale should be

Lochmaben, *NY 0820 8220*

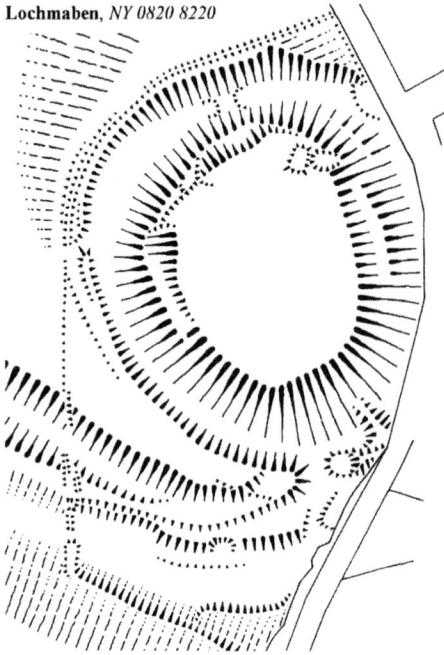

Auldton, *NT 0938 0583*

Applegarth, *NY 1043 8419*

Torthorwald, *NY 0328 7825*

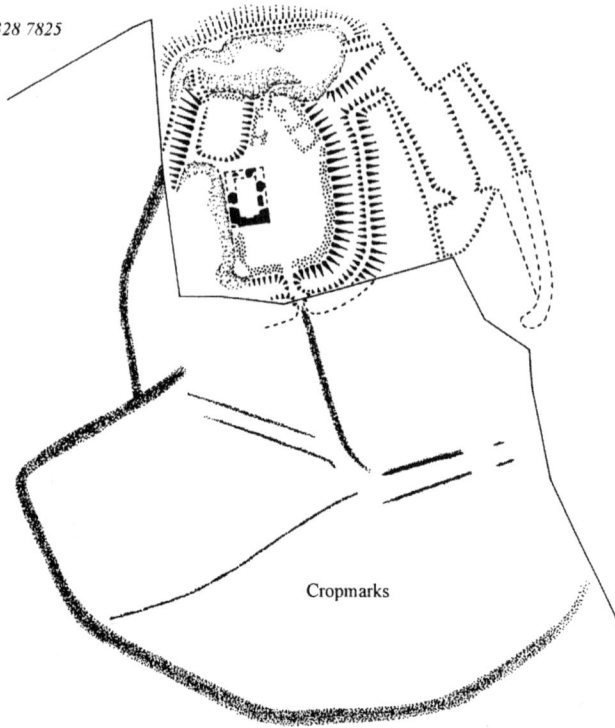

Figure 3.2
Timber castles:
comparative plans
(sheet 1) RCAHMS

Cropmarks

N

| 50 | 100 | 150 | 200m |

Timber Castles of the Brus Lordship

Lochwood, *NY 0846 9686*

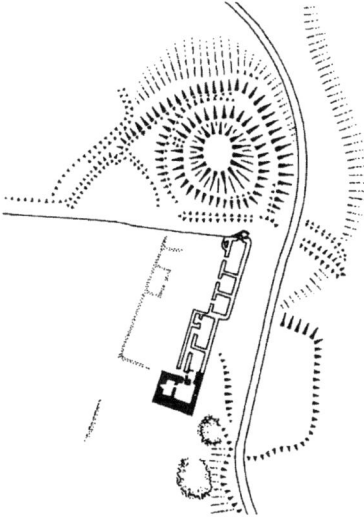

Hutton, *NY 1635 8936*

Figure 3.3
Timber castles:
comparative plans
(sheet 2) RCAHMS

Wamphray, *NY 1282 9648*

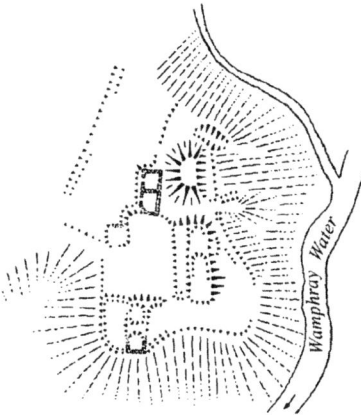

Wamphray Water

Rockhall, *NY 0546 7665*

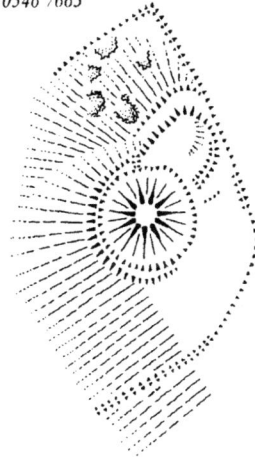

Coates Hill, *NT 0721 0412*

Garpol Water, *NT 0505 0402*

47

LORDSHIP AND
ARCHITECTURE
IN MEDIEVAL
AND
RENAISSANCE
SCOTLAND

❧

viewed, bearing in mind Cruden's caution against strategic interpretations of castle siting. 'The co-existence of castles conveniently grouped according to strategic theory,' he said, 'is frequently explained in terms such as "a chain of castles", "commanding a pass" or "controlling a frontier". Of no very precise meaning, these phrases overemphasise the military function … they tend to confuse modern and medieval geography as well as military technique and underestimate the domestic functions which considerably influenced design and situation'.[3] Mackenzie[4] was equally definite in asserting that 'the selection of a site for a baronial castle … was settled mainly by the occurrence of what was taken to be a suitable position in some quarter of the barony and had no reference to any other principle'. However, when looking overall at the locations of the early Annandale castles, and accepting that they may not have presented a serious obstacle to even a modestly sized field army, it is impossible not to be impressed by the presence of strategic considerations, even if only in terms of their ability to monitor movement and deter small raiding parties. This does not, of course, preclude their other functions as lordly residences, perhaps expressing the status of their owners, seats of local government and the centres of estates that were the basis of the emerging parish structure. This last point is well illustrated by the proximity of churches or chapels to all but two of the Annandale timber castles, Coates Hill and Garpol Water. Unfortunately the other functions of timber castles are much more difficult to demonstrate simply on the basis of their surviving earthwork remains.

Brus constructed his first castle close to the Solway coast, on the east bank of the Annan Water at what has become the modern town of Annan, thereby securing the short estuarine link with English Cumbria. The charter of 1124[5] reads as if the castle was in existence at that date, and it may be that Brus was already in Annandale. He certainly seems to have been in Scotland between 1114 and 1121 when, like David for most of this time, he does not appear as a witness to any of the surviving charters of Henry I.[6] Some time later the castle of Lochmaben was built at the heart of the lordship, on a site which secured the routeways north through Annandale, and also, because Lochar Moss effectively barred the route westwards to Dumfries, the alternative route into Clydesdale through Nithsdale.

There is no direct evidence to date the construction of Lochmaben and the abandonment of Annan. Lochmaben, however, was the scene of William I's confirmation of Annandale to Robert de Brus II, probably in 1172,[7] and that the castles co-existed, at least for a time, is implicit in a statement by Benedict of Peterborough in 1173 that William held both 'the castle of Annan and the castle of Lochmaben, which were the castles

of Robert de Brus'.[8] This is also the last reference to the castle of Annan, which, if the fragmentary state of the motte is anything to go by, may have fallen victim to the destructive power of a swollen river. Whether this was a result of the curse of St Malachy upon Brus and Annan, invoked when Robert de Brus II hanged a thief whose life he had promised Malachy that he would spare, is a question outside the scope of conventional scholarship, though Malachy's unhappy visit probably took place several decades earlier, in the 1140s.[9]

The castles of Rockhall, Tinwald, and Torthorwald are on what might be termed the forward defensive edge of the lordship, looking from the heights of the eastern lip of Nithsdale directly into Galloway, which lay beyond the extensive mosses of the lower Nith. Hutton and Coates Hill

Figure 3.4
Lochmaben,
Dumfriesshire:
vertical aerial view.
RCAHMS,
543/RAF/436/F21/0221

49

LORDSHIP AND
ARCHITECTURE
IN MEDIEVAL
AND
RENAISSANCE
SCOTLAND

❧

occupy similarly elevated positions with wide views. Coates Hill stands upon the spur that carries the Roman road into Clydesdale and looks across Threewater Foot, where the Evan, Annan and Moffat Waters come together and the important routes to and from Tweeddale and Yarrow enter the main body of the valley. The Brus demesne castle at Auldton, on the edge of present-day Moffat, did not enjoy the same lofty location, but was still well-placed to observe the Tweed and Yarrow routeways. Hutton stands only a little over 1km to the east of the Roman road up Dryfesdale, which proceeded via Craik Cross to the valleys of the south-east and the heart of David's kingdom. Even Wamphray, at first sight lying in something of a backwater, might have been placed to police a minor route up the Wamphray Water and over the watershed into the Ettrick valley.

It may be straining the argument too far to suggest that Applegarth and Lochwood were placed to control the north-south route through Annandale – both lie within 2km of the Roman road – but Garpol Water is ultimately the only timber castle in Annandale for whose siting no strategic arguments whatsoever can be advanced. A major consideration in its location may have been the hunting in the hills of northern Annandale, a function probably also to be ascribed to Auldton.

There are dramatic differences in scale between the major and minor castles of the lordship, with Annan, Lochmaben and Torthorwald emerging as castles of the first rank. Annan has suffered badly from both river erosion and from the activities of gardeners in the bailey (and was not resurveyed for this study), but the motte, crowned by its timber superstructure, must have towered impressively over the river. The motte at Lochmaben does not achieve the same elevation, but impresses by its sheer bulk. It stands 7m in height, its summit measures 60m in diameter, and its ditch is up to 15m in breadth. It was also accompanied by a large bailey which occupied the area between the motte and the loch to the west, although the defences of this bailey only survive on the south. The parish church stood immediately to the north of the bailey, where the burgh of Lochmaben subsequently developed, though given the size of the bailey it would not be surprising to learn that it had accommodated an early urban centre. A similar set of circumstances is in evidence at Torthorwald, where a substantial motte, formerly measuring about 60m by 50m, but mutilated by later quarrying, is accompanied by a large bailey. The bailey defences of Torthorwald have been ploughed down almost to the point of invisibility, but the line of the ditch, dug in a series of straight sections, has been recorded as cropmarks on air photographs. As at Lochmaben, an urban centre developed immediately to the north of the castle, though the parish church stood to the east.

The remaining timber castles are much smaller and a conventional motte is the principal feature of all but Garpol Water. Furthermore, with the exception of Coates Hill, there is at least circumstantial evidence to suggest that each was accompanied by a bailey. Indeed, the Brus demesne castle at Auldton is a textbook motte-and-bailey, though Garpol Water is a much more idiosyncratic affair, having been fashioned entirely from a natural hillock. The elongated summit of the hillock has been levelled to form the motte and a terrace on its north side serves as a bailey; both motte and bailey are enclosed within a stony bank and, except on the east, there is a broad ditch and external bank around the base of the hillock. At Tinwald, cropmarks have revealed an oval bailey defended only by a palisade, a fact which may be of significance to the many small mottes elsewhere not apparently accompanied by baileys. The motte itself has

*Figure 3.6
Garpol Water,
motte-and-bailey,
Dumfriesshire: aerial
view.
RCAHMS, B 16719*

been reduced by later agriculture to a somewhat formless mound, but the ditch around its base appears clearly as cropmarks on the same photographs.

Whilst an impressive tower house was built upon the motte at Tor-thorwald in the fourteenth century, and the baileys at Lochwood and Wamphray were occupied by late medieval stone buildings, including a tower house at Lochwood, there is no clear evidence for the rebuilding of any of the Annandale timber castles in stone before 1296. The only stone castle of this period was built at Auchen by the Kirkpatricks, on an entirely new site 1.4km east-south-east of their motte-and-bailey at Garpol Water. It is an underrated and misinterpreted site and, as an example of a castle crudely and perhaps hastily revamped as an artillery fortification, a remarkable survival, though the artillery works lie well outside the period of the Brus lordship.

Figure 3.7
Tinwald,
motte-and-bailey and
parish church,
Dumfriesshire: aerial
view.
RCAHMS, B 24078

Its original form was that of a quadrangular enclosure measuring 40m by 36m within a curtain wall 2.8m to 3m thick, which still stands to a height of 5m. The entrance was set towards the west end of the north curtain, where it was flanked by a circular angle-tower which was solid at least to first-floor height. A forework was subsequently added to afford further protection to the entrance and the whole was surrounded by a broad, water-filled ditch. The only evidence of the internal arrangements is a garderobe in the east curtain. The simple enclosure and the dogleg forework both point to an early date – the mid-thirteenth century would not be out of the question – and the enclosure can be paralleled at Kinclaven and Kincardine, both securely placed in the first half of the thirteenth century.[10]

The likely builders of most of the Annandale timber castles can be

LORDSHIP AND
ARCHITECTURE
IN MEDIEVAL
AND
RENAISSANCE
SCOTLAND

ఇక

*Figure 3.8
Auchen Castle,
Dumfriesshire: aerial
view.
RCAHMS*

identified. The Brus family are directly responsible for Annan, Lochmaben and Moffat, the Johnstones probably constructed Lochwood, whilst a castle they later held, Wamphray, was probably the work of the Corries. Garpol Water was held by the Kirkpatricks, and Tinwald may have belonged to the family of de Mundeville, one John de Mundeville of Tinwald appearing on record in about 1220.[11] Torthorwald was presumably held by the family of that name and David de Torthorwald, knight, is witness to a charter of Robert de Brus between 1245 and 1295.[12] In another charter Robert de Brus grants to David de Torthorwald that no escheat be taken within the barony of Annandale and the tenement of Torthorwald.[13] Hutton was probably the castle of Gilbert, Lord of Hutton, and his wife Juliana, passing to their son, Adam, before 1193 when he granted the chapel of Hutton to Jedburgh Abbey on condition that it should become parochial.[14]

However, a brief examination of the witness lists of the handful of Brus charters surviving for the late twelfth and thirteenth centuries reveals numerous family names which do not appear above. Amongst others are to be found Herries, Crosby, Bois, Humez, Hoddom, Maleverer, Heneville and Dinwoodie. Of course not all witnesses were necessarily resident in Annandale, though most probably were, and some possessed sizeable holdings for which no medieval estate centre has been identified. For example, at the end of the twelfth century Walter del Bois held Carruthers, then an independent parish. Around the same time William de Brus granted to William de Heineville lands around Sark[15] which may have formed an estate based on Logan and accompanied by a chapel said to have stood at Chapelknowe, 700m east of Logan Mains. Another estate which can be identified around 1200 is Kinmount, which Adam de Carlyle received from William de Brus in exchange for Lockerbie.[16]

There were also men and families perhaps of lesser means. Robert de Tremor is a shadowy figure, but his name still appears on modern maps as Turnmuir (Turnmuir Burn, Turnmuir Mill NY 1189 8119). In 1604 Turnmuir, or Turmor, was part of a compact estate on the east bank of the Annan, at the crossing point from Lochmaben into Dryfesdale, which included the aptly named Robert's Hill, Mantarig and Tuikisholm.[17] A similarly shadowy figure is Richard de Penresax (modern Pennersaughs), whose family held land in the former parish of Pennersaughs until the early fourteenth century when Robert I granted to Stephen Kirkpatrick the lands of Pennersaughs previously held by John Penesax.[18] It is not beyond the bounds of possibility that the Anglo-Norman placename Rickerby, preserved in the name Rickerby House, which stands only 500m north-west of Pennersaughs, may recall the original toun of Richard de Penresax or one his forebears. Rickerby belongs to a series of placenames which bear the names of settlers who must have followed Robert de Brus into Annandale and includes Sibbaldbie, Lockerbie, Pearsby, Warmanbie, 'Roberdsbi', 'Willambi', Gillesbie, Gimmenbie and Wyseby. Many of these men may have been of Flemish origin, brought by Brus from his Cleveland lordship, into which there was significant Flemish immigration in the first half of the twelfth century.[19]

What is revealed by the documents is that there were significantly more estates in Annandale in the twelfth and thirteenth centuries than there are surviving estate centres represented by timber castles. This discrepancy is heightened if the assumption is made that the parish structure emerging in this period reflects the estate structure and that each timber castle represents the caput of a single barony likely to be coterminous with a medieval parish. Over thirty parishes are known in medieval Annandale as against twelve timber castles.

LORDSHIP AND
ARCHITECTURE
IN MEDIEVAL
AND
RENAISSANCE
SCOTLAND

೨ౣ

It is possible that other timber castles formerly existed, but have been destroyed. It has, for example, been suggested that the late medieval tower of Castlemilk stood upon a motte. Unfortunately the drawing published in the Dumfriesshire *Inventory*[20] is misleading and it is clear on the original 'Platte of Castlemilk' that the sixteenth-century surveyor was merely seeking to depict the steep river cliffs which bound the site. The general conclusion remains, however, and a significant number of twelfth- and thirteenth-century estate centres in Annandale are still to be identified.

Of course we do not know what form these estate centres may have taken, nor do we know the lowest level of landholding at which castle-building would have been permitted. Barrow[21] suggests that it may be possible to draw a clear line between whole, half, or, in the thirteenth century, quarter knight's fees, and all the lesser fractions, with those above the line exercising baronial jurisdiction, though whether a similar division might apply to castle-building is yet another unknown. Furthermore, documentary references to subinfeudation in Annandale are limited to a handful of examples. The only full knight's service recorded applies to Dryfesdale, where Hugh, son of Ingebald, was restored to the lands his father had held on the terms upon which his father had held them, that is for the service of two vills and the service of one knight in the king's army.[22] Kinmount was held for one quarter of a knight's service,[23] whilst the lands of Torbeck, Willamby and the toun of Blackwood, all in the fee of Pennersaughs, together with two carrucates of the lands of Pennersaughs itself, returned one-eighth of a knight's service.[24] The unidentified estate of Cnoculeran returned one-twentieth of a knight's service.[25]

The five recognised moated sites in Annandale fill some of the gaps. The moated site at Rogermoor, only 600m north of the ruinous tower of Frenchland, is noted on the first edition Ordnance Survey 6-inch map[26] as a chapel of the Templars, but this claim is not substantiated and it is more likely to have belonged to the family of French who held lands in the vill of Moffat in the thirteenth century. Possibly about 1250, Roger, son of William French, exchanged with Robert de Brus two oxgangs of land near Warmanbie for two oxgangs in Moffat which Roger's father had formerly held.[27] The site is of considerable interest in its own right, for whilst only two arms of the ditch are still visible, it enclosed two substantial building ranges which survive as grass-grown stone wall-footings on opposite sides of a yard. Water was led into the ditch by a burn and there is some evidence for the damming of its north-west arm at its south-west end, where a small rectangular platform may be the site of a mill.

It is ironic that nothing is known of the history of Gotterbie Moor, the finest moated site in Annandale, whilst that at Woodhall, which is no longer visible, can be placed in a convincing historical context. Wood-hall, alternatively known as 'The Stank', was described in 1792 as 'an acre of ground surrounded by a fosse of considerable depth ... now drained and mostly filled up'.[28] It lay on the perimeter of a park created by Robert Crosby in the wood of Stapleton before 1230,[29] and, as its name suggests, was presumably the hall of that park. The park occupied approximately the northern third of the parish of Dornock and the moat on its south side would have served both the park and a putative estate comprising the remainder of the parish. Unfortunately there is no evidence that the Crosby family held any other land there.

It should be pointed out that there are considerable problems in distinguishing between moated sites and rectilinear prehistoric settlements in southern Scotland, and excavation might reclaim some medieval estate centres from the latter category. Others may lurk amongst the miscellaneous earthworks and enclosures, recorded both as upstanding remains and crop-marks, and excavation of an unusual cropmark enclosure at Dinwoodie Green in Annandale revealed it to be of medieval date.[30] The enclosure, now largely destroyed by road construction, was oval on plan, measured 55m by 34m within a ditch up to 3.7m wide and up to 1.4m deep, and was adjoined on the west by an annexe measuring 35m by 12m within a ditch 2.5m wide and 0.9m deep. Medieval pottery was recovered from the fill of the ditch and from cobbling within the enclosure itself, whilst several squared sandstone blocks were found both in the fill of the ditch and in a pit in the interior; a number of Bronze Age urns were also found, but their presence was thought to be no more than coincidence.

An estate of Dinwoodie probably existed around 1200, when Adam of Dinwoodie was witness to a Brus charter.[31] John, lord of Dinwoodie, is on record in 1362,[32] and in the late Middle Ages a tower house, now vanished, stood at Dinwoodie Mains, some 2km north of Dinwoodie Green. Admittedly the Mains is where a continuing estate centre would be expected, but a late medieval relocation cannot be ruled out and, whatever the status of the site at Dinwoodie Green, it appears to have functioned in the Middle Ages on the estate of Dinwoodie.

The Church as a landholding institution figures relatively little in the history of Annandale in this period, and the lands held by the bishops of Glasgow prior to 1124 had passed to the Brus lords by the middle of the twelfth century. The bishops nevertheless retained rights to the churches of Hoddom, Castlemilk, Dryfesdale and 'Aschebi', and following a dispute these rights were confirmed in 1187–89, when the churches of Moffat and Kirkpatrick-Juxta were also ceded to Glasgow.[33] But there was no Brus religious foundation to match that of Hugh de Morville at Dryburgh, or, more modestly, that of Turgis de Rosdale, who established the small

LORDSHIP AND
ARCHITECTURE
IN MEDIEVAL
AND
RENAISSANCE
SCOTLAND

❧

Augustinian house of Canonbie within sight of Liddel Strength, his great timber castle on the English side of the Border. Robert de Brus I had, of course, endowed the Augustinian priory of Guisborough in his Cleveland lordship, and Brus support of that house was continued from Annandale, where, in 1170, the churches of Annan, Lochmaben, Cummertrees, Kirkpatrick-Fleming, Redkirk and Gretna were all granted to Guisborough. This resulted in a dispute with the bishop of Glasgow which was temporarily settled in 1223, when the priory resigned patronage in return for an increased share of the teinds.[34]

Virtually nothing of the medieval churches of Annandale remains standing to illustrate the nature and extent of patronage in the lordship. The church which must have benefited most from Brus patronage, Lochmaben, was, prior to its demolition in 1818, 'an ancient Gothic fabric with a large choir'.[35] Hoddom too, demolished in 1812, may have been a building of some pretensions, though probably due to the efforts of the Carlyle family in the late Middle Ages. There are, however, pointers to significant Romanesque work at Dornock, where four small capitals, currently propping up a medieval coped grave cover in the churchyard, are reminiscent of those seen in eleventh- or twelfth-century belfries, and at Gretna, where, according to an early eighteenth-century description, there were 'heads hewen out of stone round the head of the walls of the church & queir supposed to be the heads of the Apostles and saints'.[36]

These hints, for they are little more, turn our thoughts back to the nature of the vanished buildings of Anglo-Norman Annandale. In this respect the timber castles are a vitally important archaeological resource, but it is equally important to identify other sites illustrative of the spectrum of lordship and lordly building in this period, the halls of Robert de Tremor and his like.

NOTES

1. RCAHMS, *Eastern Dumfriesshire.*
2. W. E. Kapelle, *The Norman Conquest of the North: the region and its transformation, 1100–1135* (London, 1979).
3. S. Cruden, *The Scottish Castle* (Edinburgh, 3rd edition, 1981), 100.
4. W. M. Mackenzie, *The Medieval Castle in Scotland* (Edinburgh, 1927), 79.
5. Lawrie, *ESC,* 48–9.
6. Kapelle, op. cit., 207.
7. *RRS,* ii, no. 80.
8. Anderson, *Scottish Annals,* 247.
9. A. A. M. Duncan, 'The Bruces of Annandale, 1100–1304', *TDGNHAS,* 3rd series, lxix (1994), 89–102 at 92.
10. J. G. Dunbar and A. A. M. Duncan, 'Tarbert Castle: a contribution to the history of Argyll', *SHR,* l (1970), 1–17 at 8–13.
11. R. C. Reid, 'De Amundeville', *TDGNHAS,* 3rd series, xxxiv (1955–6), 74–83 at 78.

12. *CDS*, i, no. 706; A. Macquarrie, 'Notes on Some Charters of the Bruces of Annandale, 1215–1295' *TDGNHAS*, 3rd series, lviii (1983), 72–9 at 75–6, 78.
13. *CDS*, ii, no. 1683; Macquarrie, op. cit., 74, 78.
14. W. Rogerson, *Hutton Under the Muir. Notes on the Past of an Annandale Parish* (Dumfries, 1908), 3; Cowan, *Parishes*, 84.
15. G. W. S Barrow, *The Anglo-Norman Era in Scottish History* (Oxford, 1980), 154; *CDS*, i, no. 605.
16. Fraser, *Annandale*, no. 2.
17. *Retours*,Dumfriesshire, no. 26.
18. *RMS*, i, App. II, 296, 510.
19. Barrow, *Anglo-Norman Era*, 47–8.
20. RCAHMS, *Dumfriesshire*, lxii.
21. Barrow, *Anglo-Norman Era*, 135.
22. *CDS*, i, no. 635.
23. Fraser, *Annandale*, no. 2.
24. Ibid., no. 3.
25. Ibid., no. 7.
26. 1861edition, sheet xvi.
27. *CDS*, i, no. 705; Macquarrie, *op. cit.*, 73, 78
28. *OSA.*, ii, 24.
29. Fraser, *Annandale*, no. 8; Duncan, 'Bruces of Annandale', 96.
30. K. S. Hodgson and W. F. Cormack, 'Excavations at Dinwoodie Green, Annandale' *TDGNHAS*, 3rd series, li (1975), 18–28.
31. *CDS*, i, no. 606.
32. *RRS*, vi, no. 282.
33. Cowan, *Parishes*, 127, 148, citing *Glasgow Registrum*, nos. 72–3.
34. G. Neilson and G. Donaldson, 'Guisborough and the Annandale Churches', *TDGNHAS*, 3rd series, xxxii (1953–4), 142–54.
35. *NSA*, iv, Dumfries, 393.
36. Macfarlane, *Geographical Coll.*, i , 382.

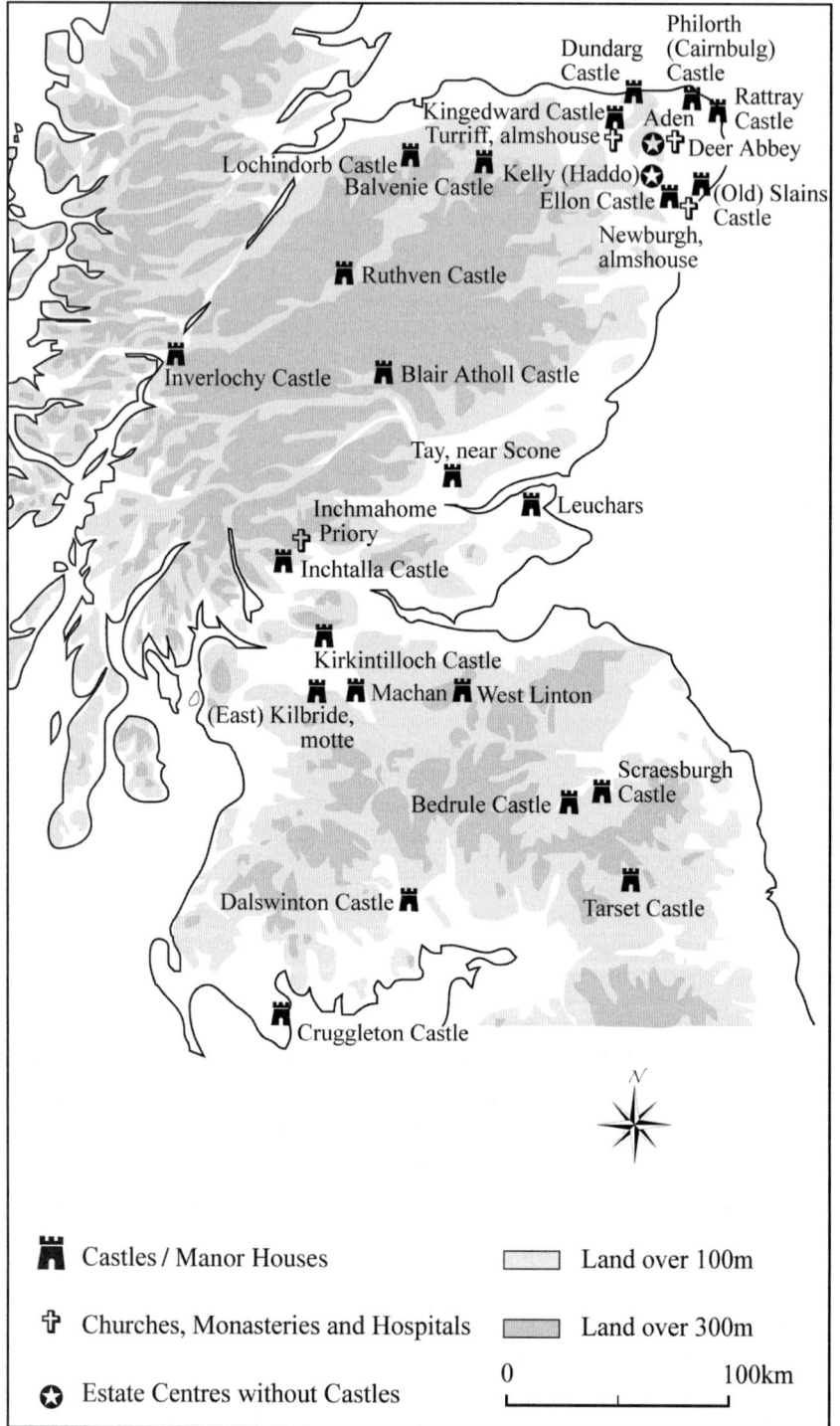

Philorth
(Cairnbulg)
Castle

Dundarg
Castle

Rattray
Castle

Kingedward Castle
Turriff, almshouse

Aden

Deer Abbey

Lochindorb Castle

Kelly (Haddo)

(Old) Slains
Castle

Balvenie Castle

Ellon Castle

Newburgh,
almshouse

Ruthven Castle

Inverlochy Castle

Blair Atholl Castle

Tay, near Scone

Inchmahome
Priory

Leuchars

Inchtalla Castle

Kirkintilloch Castle

Machan

West Linton

(East) Kilbride,
motte

Scraesburgh
Castle

Bedrule Castle

Dalswinton Castle

Tarset Castle

Cruggleton Castle

N

Castles / Manor Houses

Land over 100m

Churches, Monasteries and Hospitals

Land over 300m

Estate Centres without Castles

0   100km

Figure 4.1
Comyn properties
mentioned in the text.

Chapter 4

𝕒𝕓

THE COMYNS TO 1300

Alan Young

The thirteenth century could be regarded as the Comyn century of Scottish history[1] because of that family's territorial strength and domination of the political scene. In the 1250s, according to Walter Bower, the Comyns were 'multiplied beyond number in the ranks of magnates of the kingdom … at that time they were reckoned to be thirty two knights of this name'.[2] That may be an exaggeration by an anti-Comyn source keen to emphasise the dangers of overmighty subjects[3] to the Scottish monarchy. There were, however, three branches of the Comyn family – the Badenoch, Buchan and Kilbride lines – who acquired land and lordships in Scotland in the period *c.* 1150 to *c.* 1300. Thus the family were, in fact, as formidable a power in the land as Bower implied even if his figures were not strictly accurate.

The physical signs of the secular and ecclesiastical lordship which accompanied the Comyns' territorial and political power should be set in a number of contexts. Their architectural patronage should be seen in the context of their family fortunes, their landholding and management of estates, as well as their financial resources in both Scotland and England. It is also important to set the Comyns' architectural lordship in the context of the family's relationship with the Scottish Crown. They have, until recently, been depicted as overmighty subjects,[4] a threat to the stability of the Scottish monarchy. Yet the Comyns were, in practice, agents for the Scottish king, pillars of the Scottish monarchy for most of the thirteenth century.[5] The visible signs of their lordship should therefore be seen as symbols of their leadership of the aristocratic community and as complementary to their royal responsibilities. In contrast to the alliance between Comyns and the Scottish monarchy was the growing rivalry and antagonism after 1286 between the Comyns who held political power and the Bruces who did not – until 1306! The visible symbols of Comyn secular power should therefore be seen in the context of Bruce rivalry both before and after 1306. Finally, in 1296 the Comyns as leaders of the Scottish political community had to face warfare with England. Thus the military and

LORDSHIP AND
ARCHITECTURE
IN MEDIEVAL
AND
RENAISSANCE
SCOTLAND

ૐ

strategic importance of Comyn castles should be seen in the context of Anglo-Scottish warfare.

The Comyns quickly transferred from a clerical/ecclesiastical base in early twelfth-century England to an important secular landholding level in Scotland in the second half of the twelfth century. The link between England and Scotland was provided by William Cumin,[6] protégé of Geoffrey Rufus in the English chancery of Henry I. William was chancellor of Scotland by c. 1136 and soon became established, together with several nephews, at the Scottish court. He played a full part in David's ambitions to secure control over northern England during the civil war in Stephen's reign. David I, in turn, supported Cumin's ambition to succeed his former tutor, Geoffrey Rufus, as bishop of Durham when Rufus died in 1141. In return for renouncing his claims in 1144 William ensured that one of his remaining nephews, Richard – two of his nephews, William and Osbert, had died during the struggle – received the castle and honour of North-allerton (North Yorkshire), to be held of the bishop of Durham.[7] This is the first castle linked to the Comyn family and it was Richard (d. 1179) who founded the family's secular fortunes in northern England and southern Scotland.

Between 1144 and 1152 King David and Earl Henry granted Richard Cumin the important Tynedale lands of Walwick, Thornton, Staincroft and Henshaw (south-west Northumberland west of Hexham) on his marriage to Hextilda, daughter of Uhtred of Tynedale and Bethoc, only daughter of Donald III Ban, brother of Malcolm III and son of Duncan II, king of Scots.[8] Scottish royal support and a good marriage – factors in the rise of the Comyns throughout the twelfth and thirteenth centuries – enabled Richard to develop sizeable estates in southern Scotland as well as Tynedale. Earl Henry granted him the lands of West Linton, Peebles-shire, and together with other grants he was by 1152 a substantial landowner in north-west Peeblesshire.[9] Richard Cumin's marriage to Hextilda also brought possession of the lordship of Bedrule in Roxburghshire, probably between 1150 and 1170.[10] William the Lion's bestowal of the office of justiciar of Lothian on Richard Cumin between c. 1173 and 1178 can be seen as a consequence of his increasing importance as a landowner in southern Scotland.[11] It also further increased the status of the family and linked the Comyns more firmly to the Scottish monarchy.

Richard's eldest surviving son, William, the future earl of Buchan (c. 1212), had already extended the family's landholding considerably by 1200. By then he had gained the lordships of Kirkintilloch and Len-zie[12] and by 1190 the lands of Machan.[13] The Comyn family gained another lordship in central Scotland when David, a younger son of William, married Isabel de Valognes, lady of East Kilbride, before 1215.[14] The

family's increasing status in royal administration was shown when William
Comyn became sheriff of Forfar (c. 1190–1214) and Justiciar of Scotia (from
c. 1205). These are the first signs that the king was planning to use the
Comyns to represent his interests in the north.[15] It is significant that three
successive Comyn earls of Buchan – William, Alexander and John – held
the office of Justiciar of Scotia for sixty-six out of one hundred years
between c. 1205 and 1304. It has been recognised that the office of justiciar
was 'the most significant bridge between the king's court and the localities'[16]
and that of the three justiciarships in Scotland, that of Scotia had most
senior status. Comyn power in the north was further enhanced shortly
after 1205 when William became the first 'Norman' earl in Scotland on
marriage to Marjorie, the heiress of Buchan, c. 1212.[17] It is possible to see
this marriage as reward for William Comyn's military efforts against the
MacWilliam rebels in Ross and Moray in 1211–12 – William was, for a
time, warden of Moray in this emergency. It is also clear that the earldom
gave him the landowning status to match his political and administrative
role as chief agent for the crown in the north. Alexander II again appointed
William to the wardenship of Moray when this area rose in revolt in
1229–30. The king, however, sought a longer-term solution to this problem
by creating a hereditary lordship of Badenoch (the lordship of Lochaber
went with it) for the Comyns. Walter Comyn, William's second eldest
son, held the lordship of Badenoch from c. 1229.[18]

Together with Buchan, the acquisition of Badenoch and Lochaber meant
that by 1230, and with firm royal support, Comyn landowning power
stretched right across northern Scotland from the extreme east to Loch
Linnhe on the west coast. By 1230 also, the three main branches of the
family – the Badenoch, Buchan and Kilbride lines – had been established.
Emphasis on the scale of Buchan and Badenoch power in the north should
not detract from the combined landed interests of all three branches
elsewhere – especially in southern and central Scotland. Walter Comyn as
lord of Badenoch and Lochaber also acquired the earldom of Menteith
c. 1234 on marriage to Isabella heiress of Menteith,[19] although the earldom
did not remain in Comyn hands after Walter's death in 1258. The Badenoch
branch of the family, by the end of the thirteenth century, held land in
Atholl,[20] Perthshire (Findogask and Ochtertyre),[21] the lordships of Kirkintilloch and Lenzie as well as land at Machan in Clydesdale, land in
Nithsdale (Dalswinton was certainly in Comyn possession by 1250) and
the lordships of Bedrule and Scraesburgh in Roxburghshire.

The Comyn earls of Buchan, apart from most of Buchan, had consid-
erable landed interests elsewhere. These included land in Strathisla,[22] in
Strathbogie,[23] in Mar (near the Durward barony of Onele),[24] and in the
Mearns.[25] Further south they had a manor house on the Tay, near Scone.[26]

LORDSHIP AND
ARCHITECTURE
IN MEDIEVAL
AND
RENAISSANCE
SCOTLAND

They also held substantial properties in Fife, the lordship of Fithkil (now Leslie) and land at Kennoway.[27] Alexander Comyn, earl of Buchan, gained further considerable estates in Scotland after 1264 through his wife Elizabeth, one of the three daughters and co-heiresses of Roger de Quincy, 2nd earl of Winchester. When Roger died in 1264, Alexander acquired estates in Fife, Galloway, Dumfriesshire and Lothian.[28] In addition, he also secured the office of constable as a result of the de Quincy inheritance, which brought additional lands in Perth, Clackmannan, Inverness and Cowie, near Stonehaven.[29] This combination of Buchan lands and de Quincy inheritance made the Comyn earls of Buchan great territorial magnates. Their position in the north was further consolidated when Earl Alexander exchanged part of the de Quincy inheritance in East Lothian for Mortlach (Balvenie) in highland Banffshire between 1264 and 1282.[30] The castle and barony of Balvenie, located only twenty miles from Badenoch's eastern boundary, was an invaluable bridge between the Comyn-held earldom of Buchan and lordship of Badenoch. It is clear that the de Quincy inheritance did not divert the Comyn earls of Buchan southwards: both earls Alexander and John surrendered part of the de Quincy inheritance to consolidate their north-eastern stronghold. Earl John surrendered some of the properties which he had acquired through descent from Elizabeth de Quincy in the lordship of Galloway in return for King John Balliol's grant of Formartine and (probably) Belhelvie.[31]

*Figure 4.2
Lochindorb Castle,
Moray: general view.
R. D. Oram*

Figure 4.3
Inverlochy Castle,
Inverness-shire: view
by Bouquet, 1849.
RCAHMS

The Kilbride branch of the family, although junior to the Badenoch and Buchan lines and less extensive landowners, also held land elsewhere in Scotland than their lordship of East Kilbride, in north-west Peeblesshire and around Falkirk.[32] All three branches of the family held land in England, and this should not be forgotten when the resources behind the family's architectural patronage are investigated. The Badenoch branch held valuable land in Tynedale in Northumberland from the mid-twelfth century, and in Lincolnshire.[33] The Kilbride line, after 1215, held land in Northumberland, Norfolk, Suffolk, Essex and Hertford,[34] while the de Quincy inheritance brought the Comyns of Buchan substantial estates in England after 1264[35] – in northern England (in Cumberland, Yorkshire, Lincolnshire and Derbyshire); in the central Midlands (especially in Leicestershire, Warwickshire, Northamptonshire and Huntingdonshire); in the south-east (in Cambridgeshire, Bedfordshire, Buckinghamshire, Hertfordshire and Essex); and in the south-west (stretching through Oxfordshire, Berkshire, Gloucestershire and Wiltshire as far as Dorset on the south coast).

The most visible symbols of Comyn secular lordship throughout their vast landholding are in the north of Scotland, principally the castles of Lochindorb in Moray, Inverlochy in Lochaber and Balvenie in Banffshire. In terms of ecclesiastical lordship, the Comyns are represented by the impressive remains of the Augustinian priory of Inchmahome in Menteith

*Figure 4.4
Balvenie Castle,
Moray: aerial view.
Historic Scotland,
A4272-1*

and the Cistercian abbey of Deer in Buchan. These remains should first of all be set in the wider context of all known Comyn architectural patronage. Is there any evidence, for instance, of buildings on the first lands acquired by the family in southern and central Scotland – in Roxburghshire, Peeblesshire, Nithsdale, Dunbartonshire and the Clyde valley? The Comyns held Bedrule in Roxburghshire from *c.*1160. There appears to have been a motte at Bedrule[36] formed from a natural spur. The site (NT 595182), known locally as Castle Knowe, stands above an old ford on the west bank of the Rule Water. The motte was superseded by a castle of enceinte. Although the enclosure is not complete, the discernible features suggest a courtyard arrangement approximately 61 feet from north-west to south-east and 40 feet wide. There was a gatehouse on the north-west projecting from the curtain wall and facing towards the Rule Water, a circular tower on the south and two intermediate circular towers on the west and south-west and it can be assumed that there were two further towers on the north-west side. The layout suggests a late thirteenth-century date for this castle's later development: Edward I visited the castle in 1298.[37]

Of the other twelfth-century Comyn holdings in southern Scotland,

West Linton and Machan, there are inferences rather than physical evidence of Comyn architectural lordship. There was a church at West Linton dating from the twelfth century and there is reference to a steward of Linton (perhaps West Linton?) in 1166. The oldest secular building at West Linton seems to be a small sixteenth-century manor house [38] but it is possible that the Comyns had a manor house there in the twelfth century. Similarly, there was probably a Comyn residence, perhaps a manor house, at Machan from the late twelfth century. A steward of Machan is referred to in a Comyn charter *c.* 1212 x 1233.[39] A charter of Alexander III was issued there in 1264, as was a charter of William Comyn of Kirkintilloch in 1290.[40] It was natural that Kirkintilloch, caput of the lordship of Lenzie, the first known military fief to be granted to the Comyns by William the Lion before 1200, should have an early castle associated with it. There is documentary evidence that a castle existed in the early thirteenth century, when a 'Mr P. of the castle' is witness to a charter of 1212 x 1226.[41] In 1211 William Comyn received from King William the important right to have a burgh at Kirkintilloch and a market every Thursday, [42] and it is probable that a castle already existed at this time. The Comyns seem, in fact, to have taken over a Roman earthwork as the site of their castle.[43] This was located strategically at the junction of the Luggie and the Kelvin. The earliest castle at this site seems to have been a typical late twelfth-century motte, rectangular in shape, measuring 30 metres by 17 metres and with a broad, deep ditch on its south and east sides. Details of how Kirkintilloch developed as a castle during the thirteenth century are lacking, though in the eighteenth century it apparently had a 'double rampart of hewn stone, strongly cemented with lime'.[44] References to it in the 1290s and 1300s indicate its strategic significance in the Anglo-Scottish war. In 1304 there is a reference to a garrison comprising one esquire, eleven other men at arms, six officiarii, twenty crossbowmen and thirty-eight archers.[45]

Another early castle site of the Comyns belonged to the lords of East Kilbride. When David, younger son of William Comyn, Earl of Buchan, became lord of East Kilbride through marriage to Isabella, lady of East Kilbride, *c.* 1215, he inherited a castle in existence *c.* 1175 x 1190.[46] There are, however, three possible motte sites at East Kilbride – Mains, East Kilbride parish (NS 627428), Castle Hill, East Kilbride parish (NS 589563) and Castle Hill, East Kilbride parish (NS 612557). When Ure visited the present Mains Castle in the late eighteenth century, he mentioned the ruins of an older castle 70 yards [64 metres] north of that late fifteenth- or early sixteenth-century tower,[47] surrounded by a fosse much larger than that around the tower. This could have been the castle of the Comyns of East Kilbride. The castle at East Kilbride was regarded as the main residence of the family in 1290 and is referred to in the 1290s.

LORDSHIP AND
ARCHITECTURE
IN MEDIEVAL
AND
RENAISSANCE
SCOTLAND

꘎

Other Comyn castles in the south of Scotland were Dalswinton in Nithsdale and Scraesburgh in Roxburghshire, both belonging to the Badenoch branch of the family. Land at Dalswinton was in the possession of the Comyns by 1250 and possibly soon after 1185.[48] Dalswinton commanded Nithsdale and appears, like Kirkintilloch, to have been built on a Roman site: it occupied part of the site of a large Agricolan fort. Nothing remains of this castle, but an eighteenth-century account reported that a part of the walls were standing in 1792:

> They were 12, and in places, 14 feet [3.7 and 4.3 metres] thick, and bits of burnt wood were still clinging to them. The old cowshed was a great curiosity and was entire with its heavy stone wall, its outer door of wrought iron bars fastened with iron rivets. The Nith formerly came close to the castle and there was a pool called 'Comyn's pool' which belonged to the old water course and connected itself with the backwater in the Willow Isle by way of the Lady's Meadow.[49]

This brief record of an apparently substantial fortification together with its

*Figure 4.5
Inchmahome Priory,
Perthshire: aerial view.
RCAHMS, PT/4683*

role as the key southern base of the Comyns of Badenoch in the Anglo-Scottish wars – in 1301 Dalswinton seems to have been used as a recruitment base – indicates the significance of Dalswinton Castle.

It is known that the Comyns held Scraesburgh, alias Hunthill (Roxburghshire), by 1296 [50] at the latest, though they held Bedrule also in Roxburghshire from as early as 1160 (and may have held Scraesburgh by *c.*1200). There is evidence of an earthwork at Scraesburgh, which like many other earthworks in Roxburghshire was a low-lying structure and 'evidently designed for habitation and presumably contained wooden buildings'. [51] The site had a commanding view to the east and south-east across the Pleasants Burn and the valley of the Oxnam Water though it was easily approached from all directions and therefore was not a good defensive site. In this situation the defences themselves had to provide the chief strength. The oval earthwork measuring 65 metres from east to west by 55 metres from north to south consisted of a single massive rampart with an external ditch.

The evidence for early Comyn architectural lordship in southern Scotland is fragmentary, with little visible evidence, yet there is enough to infer that they did have a significant presence there through castles and manor houses by the early thirteenth century. Further, it is possible to suggest that Kirkintilloch, Dalswinton, East Kilbride and Bedrule were significant symbols of Comyn power in the south at the end of the thirteenth century. Historians must be conscious of Bruce's need to destroy or dismantle symbols of Comyn power in the south as in the north, where the 'Herschip' of Buchan after 1308 is generally acknowledged as destroying much thirteenth-century visible evidence.

The elevation of the Comyns from prominent landowners in the south to the earldom of Buchan *c.*1212 was a major step in the increasing political status of the family. It was natural that this move, apparently supported by the crown in an attempt to strengthen royal authority in northern Scotland, should be marked by visible signs of Comyn lordship. The 'herschip' of Buchan by Robert Bruce has destroyed much visible evidence of thirteenth-century building in Buchan, and there is also sparse survival of thirteenth-century documents. The scant remains of Deer Abbey, a Cistercian house on the banks of the river Ugie, founded by William Comyn earl of Buchan *c.*1219, are a useful starting point as visible symbols of Comyn architectural patronage. [52] Deer, originally a Celtic monastery, was refounded as a Cistercian house for a colony of monks from Kinloss in Moray and became the religious centre of the Comyn earldom. Earl William was buried there when he died in 1233. Deer's main estates were in the old parishes of Deer and Peterugie running in a swathe through central Buchan. [53] Deer was always a small house with a simple cruciform

LORDSHIP AND
ARCHITECTURE
IN MEDIEVAL
AND
RENAISSANCE
SCOTLAND

❦

plan for the church. The nave was 29.9 metres long and 12.2 metres wide, the total length of the church being 47.8 metres.[54] The Cistercians, as an austere order, did not require elaborate architecture, but it is apparent that Deer was in 1267 more than usually spartan. In that year Adam of Smailholm, abbot of Deer, a monk of Melrose, 'voluntarily resigned his office; since he preferred the sweet converse of the Melrose monks, whom he had fully proved, to having rule over the *hovel* of the monks of Deer'.[55] This may imply that permanent accommodation for the monks was not yet completed by that date, though it is probable that the church itself was complete. The abbey suffered in the 'herschip' of Buchan but the site was also well plundered two hundred years ago.

It is probable that the Comyns' ecclesiastical patronage in Buchan in 1219 was complemented by visible signs of secular lordships at the same time, though the sparseness of documentary, architectural and archaeological evidence makes this difficult to confirm. Documentary evidence only confirms the presence of two castles in thirteenth-century Buchan – Slains, by 1261, and Kinneddar (Kingedward) by 1272.[56] The few remains

*Figure 4.6
Blair Atholl Castle,
Perthshire: aerial view.
RCAHMS, PT/12025*

*Figure 4.7
Deer Abbey,
Aberdeenshire: aerial
view.
Aberdeenshire Council,
AAS/82/1-2/S2/23*

from thirteenth-century castle sites in Buchan, a tribute to the thoroughness of Bruce's 'herschip' in 1308, and later rebuilding, also makes precise dating difficult. The use of fourteenth-century documentary evidence to supplement the thirteenth-century material can, however, help to determine the main centres within the earldom [57] and the probable sites for Comyn architectural patronage. The caput of Buchan in the pre-Comyn and in the early-modern era was Ellon where there is a mound, possibly a motte, subsequently known as 'Earlshill', but there is no evidence of thirteenth-century buildings [58] and there was much rebuilding later in the Middle Ages. A more significant centre for the Comyn earls was Kelly (now Haddo). At least two of Earl Alexander's charters were issued there, in 1261 and 1272,[59] the latter being witnessed by King Alexander III himself as well as the leading barons of the land. That Kelly was where the king and his court were entertained indicates its significance but there is no evidence that there was a castle, and it appears more probable that there was a medieval manor house there.

As a coastal earldom, it is not surprising that Buchan was defended by an impressive grouping of well-sited castles along its coastline. On the north coast there was Dundarg (New Aberdour), standing within the ramparts of an Iron Age promontory fort. It was impressively sited on a rock of red sandstone looking northwards over the Moray Firth.[60] The inner ditch of the promontory fort was widened to form the castle moat. It seems probable that there was a castle here in the thirteenth century though archaeological evidence alone is inconclusive. East of Dundarg, in

71

LORDSHIP AND
ARCHITECTURE
IN MEDIEVAL
AND
RENAISSANCE
SCOTLAND

❧

the corner of Buchan, is Cairnbulg (originally known as Philorth). Standing on a fairly prominent mound which was probably a motte, later cut down to form a platform for the stone building, Cairnbulg's impressive tower house rises over a mid-thirteenth-century basement.[61] Further down the coast at Rattray there is another probable motte site,[62] which commanded the chief port of thirteenth-century Buchan. Recent excavation of two-thirds of the castle mound has revealed the foundations of the main thirteenth-century phase, with perimeter wall including two mural buildings and harbour side entrance and a multi-storeyed building free-standing on the mound centre.

Further south is Slains, standing on a rocky peninsula, where documentary evidence has shown there was a castle in 1261. There is, however, little archaeological or architectural evidence to show the structure of that thirteenth-century castle.[63] At Slains there is a stone tower of the fourteenth century; the outer ward, on the slopes of the mainland, enclosed a wall and was defended by earthen ramparts 'which may be older than the stone castle'.

A known inland castle of Buchan was at Kingedward[64] whose constable was referred to in 1272. This was an important Comyn stronghold with a prominent site on a bold precipitous rock protected by the Kingedward Burn on the south and on the north-west angle by a deep ditch which severed the neck of the peninsula. Like other Comyn castle sites in Buchan, Kingedward suffered in Bruce's 'herschip' and was subsequently rebuilt. It is therefore difficult to detect its thirteenth-century form. It appears to have been a motte and the ground plan indicates a castle belonging exclusively to the thirteenth century. Its enclosing walls had no angle towers.

There are few visible remains of the thirteenth-century Comyn castles of Buchan, though as a group they provide an impressively sited and strategic network of military strength. However, if we study Buchan after the fall of the Comyns, an administrative pattern emerges with the castles acting as the head of the baronies which were formed.[65] Kingedward, Rattray, Slains, Dundarg and Cairnbulg all acted as administrative centres. Of the new baronies, only Kelly and Aden (formed out of the Comyns' hunting reserve) did not have castles. Kelly and Ellon, with Ellon probably kept in Crown hands after 1314 as the legal caput of the suppressed earldom, acted as domestic and legal centres of Buchan. Around the fringes of the earldom there were five local subdivisions – Kingedward, Dundarg, Cairnbulg, Rattray and Slains – each based on a major castle and run presumably by constables and/or bailies. The components of most of the baronies lie fairly close to the castles. Slains consisted of a compact block of land roughly equivalent to the adjoining parishes of Slains and Cruden;

the components of Rattray lay within a four-mile radius of the castle; most of Kelly's components are within a six-mile radius; and those of Dundarg are within a five-mile radius. The unforfeited Ross share of the earldom became the baronies of Kingedward and Aberdour. The majority of the components of these lie close to the castles though more are scattered across the north of the earldom.

The sparseness of documentary and architectural/archaeological evidence for Comyn castles in Buchan makes it difficult to date the Comyns' architectural patronage. Evidence of the family's ecclesiastical patronage gives some clues. The foundation of Deer occurred in 1219, but Earl Alexander also founded two almshouses in Buchan, in 1261 and 1272. One was founded in the south-east of the earldom at Newburgh, probably the earldom's main burgh, in 1261.[66] This was for one chaplain and six poor people living in the burgh. It was supported by half-an-acre of land near the burgh gate, four chalders, fourteen bolls of oatmeal a year from the earl's mill at Forvie, and eighteen shillings a year for clothing paid by the burgh's provost from the burgh ferme. The second almshouse, rather larger, was founded at Turriff to the west of the earldom in 1272.[67] The foundation grant was to maintain a master, six chaplains and thirteen poor chosen by the earl from the poor 'husbandmen' of Buchan. It is probable that visible signs of secular lordship on motte sites in Buchan complemented the foundation of Deer. It is also probable that more architectural patronage on secular sites accompanied the foundation of two almshouses. The more settled political conditions after the minority of Alexander III ended, *c.* 1258, also suggest that more building activity would take place then.

It should be remembered that the Comyns of Buchan possessed land outside the earldom. It is known that they had manor houses in Leuchars, Fife, and on the Tay, near Scone. The de Quincy inheritance greatly added to the landholding of the Buchan Comyns and gave them important new lands in Galloway. After 1264 Earl Alexander inherited the castle of Cruggleton, originally a stronghold of the lords of Galloway.[68] Cruggleton was well situated on a clifftop but had been provided with a motte in the twelfth century. Excavation has revealed that this was replaced in the middle of the thirteenth century by a substantial stone castle of enclosure with a keep located on the summit of the motte. Responsibility for the construction of the first stone castle may lie with either Roger de Quincy or Alexander Comyn, while a phase of further strengthening occurred under the Comyns towards the close of the thirteenth century. In 1292 Edward I gave John earl of Buchan permission to export lead from the Isle of Man to cover eight towers at Cruggleton.[69]

The de Quincy inheritance did not distract the Comyns from their main base in the north. This is shown when Earl Alexander exchanged part of

LORDSHIP AND
ARCHITECTURE
IN MEDIEVAL
AND
RENAISSANCE
SCOTLAND

❧

the inherited property, Tranent in East Lothian, for the Banffshire lands and castle of Balvenie. Geoffrey Barrow has appropriately described Balvenie as a 'Comyn stepping stone'[70] between the earldom of Buchan and the Comyn lordship of Badenoch. Balvenie came into Comyn hands between 1264 and c.1282 and was obviously an important possession as it featured prominently in the movements of Edward I in the north of Scotland during his third full-scale invasion of Scotland in 1303 and Robert Bruce's movements against the Comyn power base in the north in 1307 and 1308. Perched on a promontory high above the River Fiddich, it commanded the mouths of Glen Rinnes and Glen Fiddich, the passes to Huntly, Keith and Cullen and the route to Elgin.[71] It is not certain how much building was actually undertaken by the Comyns of Buchan after the acquisition of Balvenie, though the acquisition by itself could be seen as part of a Comyn castle-strengthening programme. The earliest plan of the castle, a large quadrangular court (48.2 by 39.9 metres) enclosed by high walls (over 7.6 metres in places and 2.1 metres thick) with towers (now gone) at the west and north corners with another tower probably at the east where there is now a large sixteenth-century round tower, has been dated to the close of the thirteenth century,[72] which suggests most of the work was done after the Comyns acquired the site. One of the most noteworthy features of Balvenie Castle is the wide (averaging 12.2 metres) flat-bottomed ditch, 3.7 metres deep in places, which enclosed the castle on three sides. This great outer ditch, together with the wall walk which crowned the thirteenth-century enceinte, formed the chief defence of the castle.

The lordship of Badenoch with Lochaber was created for the Comyns as a military and political response to the revolt centred on Ross of 1229–30. Gillescop MacWilliam's rebellion had destroyed some wooden fortifications in the vicinity of Inverness and killed Thomas de Thirlstane, lord of Abertarff at the south end of Loch Ness. Alexander II wanted the Comyns of Badenoch to control the vitally important passes from both the north and west Highlands into the basin of the Tay.[73] The key Comyn castles of Badenoch and Lochaber – Ruthven and Inverlochy, supplemented by Lochindorb in the hill country between Badenoch and the Moray coast and Blair in Atholl – are strategically sited.[74] Ruthven commanded the northern end of two passes over the Mounth, Drumochter and Minigaig; Blair Atholl controlled the southern end of Drumochter and the southern end of the Glen Tilt route from Deeside; Lochindorb, although not in Badenoch but integrally related to it, was strategically situated on a loch between Forres and Grantown and fully occupied its island site one acre in extent; Inverlochy, the principal castle of Lochaber, commanded the entrance to the Great Glen, securing its southern sea outlet, and the scarcely less important overland route to the Spey by way of Glen Spean.

The clear military and political purposes behind the lordship of Badenoch suggest that castle-building took place, under Walter Comyn, shortly after its creation *c.*1229. Walter has been accused by Matthew Paris[75] of aggressively building castles in Lothian and Galloway, thereby precipitating a confrontation between the English and Scots in 1244. Rather more trustworthy evidence from the English Close Rolls refers to a Comyn castle at Tarset in Tynedale, which Walter had armed and supplied before 1244.[76] Walter had become earl of Menteith in 1234 and, like his father William after acquiring the earldom of Buchan in 1212, marked his elevation by founding a monastery. Earl Walter founded the Augustinian priory of Inchmahome in 1238[77] on the largest of the three islands in the Lake of Menteith. Inchmahome is the finest visible symbol of Comyn ecclesiastical lordship, and as Earl Walter was regarded as the leading baron in Scotland in 1237,[78] it is also a fitting monument to Comyn architectural patronage generally. There is evidence, however, that the foundation was not necessarily made for purely spiritual reasons.[79] It was probably founded in more matter-of-fact circumstances as part of a complex settlement of a dispute between Earl Walter and the bishop of Dunblane over rights in a number of local churches.

Walter did not hand down the earldom, after his death in 1258, to his nephew John, who only inherited the lordship of Badenoch, and after 1258 the Stewarts, through Walter Stewart, became the main patrons of Inchmahome. It is therefore difficult to assess the degree of Comyn architectural patronage at the priory. Richard Fawcett has noted that there were signs of modification to the original design, pointing to interruptions in the operation similar to those at Dunblane.[80] It is also, apparently, unlikely that the construction of the nave was under way before the mid-thirteenth century. It can only be surmised whether the nave was started before Earl Walter's death in 1258. Certainly there was plenty of political unrest in the 1240s and 1250s[81] – conflict between the Comyns and the Bissets in 1242, confrontation between English and Scottish armies in 1244 and the minority of Alexander III from 1249 to 1258 – to distract Earl Walter's resources. Economy does seem to have become an issue during the building of Inchmahome.[82] The west front of the church is impressive, with a central doorway below a three-light window. The church, however, was relatively small and entirely unvaulted though there were some architectural flourishes and the stone was of good quality.

There is no physical evidence of Earl Walter's main residence in Menteith but it would seem that there may have been a hall on an island adjacent to Inchmahome, Inchtalla. The remains there are late medieval, but it seems probable that there was a castle on the island in the mid-thirteenth century.[83]

Given the building activity in which Walter was engaged in the 1230s and 1240s, it seems probable that a programme was also started in Badenoch at this time. Ruthven, regarded as the caput of Badenoch, was a possible early motte site although now unfortunately covered by the eighteenth-century Ruthven Barracks.[84] The barracks stand on a prominent hill artificially scarped, rising from the flat floor of the Spey valley. There is documentary evidence for the existence of a castle at Ruthven in 1289.[85] Geoffrey Barrow has argued convincingly that Ruthven was built before 1269.[86] It is known that John Comyn I of Badenoch had built a castle at Blair in Atholl at that time.[87] This, now like Ruthven covered by later building, controlled the southern end of the Drumochter and Minigaig passes. As Barrow has pointed out, 'a fortress to guard the southern outlets makes little sense unless it can be matched by one to keep the northern outlets also'. It is probable, therefore, that Ruthven was established by 1269 at the latest and probably in the time of Walter Comyn (d.1258). Blair Atholl in 1269 can be seen as part of a developing Comyn castle-building strategy.

There are rather more substantial remains of Lochindorb, the importance of which to the Comyns is attested by John Comyn II's death there *c.*1302.[88] Documentary evidence suggests that the castle was in existence by 1279 at the latest, while architectural evidence points to buildings of the second half of the thirteenth century.[89] Lochindorb consists of a large quadrilateral curtained enclosure, its walls 2.1 metres thick and 6.1 metres high, with each angle strengthened by round towers of relatively slight projection. Only one of the towers survives in a reasonable condition, though all were still standing in 1793. In the north-east and south-west towers can be seen long fish-tailed slits heavily plunged downwards (which suggest a date in the second half of the thirteenth century) and some small square windows (again a thirteenth-century feature).[90] The castle is entered from the east where there is a landing place but it is noteworthy that no special arrangements have been made to strengthen the gate defences. Another interesting point to note is the outer work, a forewall on the south, usually said to be an addition of Edward I who stayed there for about a month in 1303.

Inverlochy, the chief castle of the Comyns in Lochaber, has been dated on architectural grounds to *c.*1270–80.[91] Documentary evidence shows that it was a key military centre by 1297. In Scotland it is a rare example of the quadrangular castle (27.4 by 30.5 metres) with high curtain walls, fortified with round corner towers (a type not uncommon in England and Wales: *cf.* Kidwelly 1275, Flint 1277 and Harlech 1283). Inverlochy is perhaps not an advanced version of this type as its corner towers do not control the curtain walls. Nevertheless the towers project boldly from each corner

*Figure 4.8
Tarset Castle,
Northumberland:
aerial view.
CUCAP, BAI -99*

LORDSHIP AND
ARCHITECTURE
IN MEDIEVAL
AND
RENAISSANCE
SCOTLAND

and one tower, the donjon (Comyn's Tower), is larger than the others. This was apparently planned as a keep with residential accommodation. The towers were floored and equipped with long narrow loops with fish-tailed slits. Like Lochindorb but unlike Harlech, Inverlochy has no gatehouse. It has two entrances, plain pointed-arch openings through the centre of two opposite sides. The entrance is simply a doorway in which hung a heavy two-leaved door secured by a drawbar and protected by a portcullis. Beyond the curtain wall, which with the towers stands to a height of 9.1 metres, is a wide ditch and outer bank. The ditch is clearly definable round three sides; the fourth confronts the River Lochy which fed the ditch. There is thus defence in depth.

A combination of documentary and architectural evidence points to a concentrated programme of strategic castle-building and -strengthening by the Comyns of Badenoch from c.1260 to c.1280. Evidence points to John Comyn I, head of the Badenoch branch of the family from 1258 to c.1278, as the man chiefly responsible, almost literally building on the foundations left by Walter Comyn in the 1230s and 1240s. He was behind the building of Blair Atholl in c.1269 and in 1267 had been given permission by Henry III of England to fortify Tarset in Tynedale.[92] The foundations of Tarset exist and have been described[93] by Philip Dixon as outlining a long rectangular building with angle turrets with a narrow chemise, the whole lying within a ditched enclosure.

By inclination John Comyn I was much involved in military affairs, as the chronicles for the years 1242 to 1269 testify. Fordun and Bower emphasise his military prowess, Bower referring to him as 'a keen fighter and a most outstanding participator in all knightly encounters'.[94] He fought for Henry III against his baronial opponents in England in 1264 and 1265[95] and was also involved in a Scottish military expedition to Man in 1275.[96] The years 1260 to 1280 were a particularly active period for castle-building and -strengthening by the Comyns of Badenoch – the branch was responsible for work at Lochindorb, Inverlochy, Blair Atholl and presumably Ruthven in the north and Tarset in Tynedale. It should not be forgotten that the Comyns of Badenoch were also responsible for Dalswinton in Nithsdale and Kirkintilloch in Dunbartonshire, both substantial castles by the end of the thirteenth century, as well as Bedrule and Scraesburgh in Roxburghshire.

Evidence from the Buchan branch suggests that the period after 1260 saw a parallel burst of building activity. The foundation of two almshouses in Buchan in 1261 and 1272 was matched by a castle-strengthening programme at the destroyed Buchan castle sites of Slains, Kingedward, Cairnbulg, Dundarg and Rattray. Documentary and architectural evidence from the Buchan-held castle of Balvenie, itself acquired in the period *c.*1264 x 1282, also suggests concerted castle-building activity after 1260. The Comyns of Buchan were also responsible, after 1264, for the upkeep of Cruggleton in Galloway, where archaeological evidence indicates building phases in the 1260s and 1280s.

Both political and financial circumstances helped to indicate the optimum time for castle-building as far as the nobility were concerned. It was unlikely that much building took place during times of political crisis such as the minority of Alexander III. The extensive architectural patronage of the Comyns, especially in castle-building, required large financial resources. All three branches of the family were extensive landowners in Scotland as well as England. Rather more information about the financial value of this landholding is available for the Comyns in Buchan. The de Quincy inheritance undoubtedly increased their financial wealth in Scotland and England: the value of Comyn's de Quincy lands in Scotland can be estimated at *c.* £150 per year;[97] as for the English lands from the inheritance, the important Leicester lands of Whitwick were worth £100 a year, and another important Leicester manor, Shepshed, was worth £34 a year.[98] Yet this was much less than the income from Buchan. In 1293 Earl John was asked for a relief of 1,471 merks to succeed to his overall Buchan inheritance in Scotland.[99] In 1311 the widow of Alexander Comyn of Buchan asked the English king, in consideration for the loss of her lands, for £500 yearly for her support.[100] Rather less financial information is available for the landholding of the Comyns of Badenoch in northern and southern Scotland, though a similar value can perhaps be assumed. In England the Tynedale lands of this branch were worth 500 merks a year[101] and John I gained further rewards for service to Henry III in 1264 and 1265 – he had a yearly fee of £50 and was also granted land to the value of £300 in England.[102] The Comyns had considerable financial resources, if not quite on a par with the 'rich and powerful' Balliols.[103]

By the end of the thirteenth century, the Comyns had control of a network of major castles, and therefore main lines of communication, across Scotland. Their power in northern Scotland was virtually viceregal, from Inverlochy in the west to Slains in the east – their castles controlled the western passes through the Mounth as well as the east-west passage across northern Scotland via the Spey and Spean valleys. With Inverlochy, the Comyns controlled the southern end of the Great Glen, the other main east-west route. They had acquired Buchan *c.*1212 and then the lordships of Badenoch and Lochaber with the support of the Crown in order to extend royal authority in northern Scotland. The Comyns' role as the pillars of Scottish monarchy was further emphasised in the period after 1260. The military, political and administrative strength of their network of castles was strengthened significantly through their appointment as sheriffs and keepers.[104] This not only

LORDSHIP AND
ARCHITECTURE
IN MEDIEVAL
AND
RENAISSANCE
SCOTLAND

⁊

helped to defend Scotland from the Norwegian military threat but caused a further definition of royal authority in the north and west. Thus the strength of the Comyns of Buchan in the north and south-west was complemented by the employment of Alexander Comyn, also Justiciar of Scotia, as sheriff of Dingwall and Wigtown and bailie of Inverie (Knoydart) in the period 1263 to 1266. There was a castle at Inverie and Alexander was responsible for outlay on its drawbridge, and 104 shillings on food for eight soldiers for six months. William Comyn of Kilbride was also given extra responsibility in the west as sheriff of Ayr *c.*1265–66. John Comyn earl of Buchan was sheriff of Wigtown and Banff between 1288 and 1292. In these difficult years after Alexander III's death, John Comyn was given added responsibility in Kirkcudbright in 1288–92 and was also sheriff of Aberdeen in 1291. His brother, Alexander, was also sheriff of Dingwall in 1292–93, and as an officer of Edward I held the castles of Tarradale and Urquhart and the sheriffdom of Aberdeen in 1303–5.[105] Comyn territorial power and the strategic position of their castles were recognised by Edward I when he became overlord of Scotland during the 'Great Cause' of 1291–92. The Comyns of Badenoch with their strength at Dalswinton in Nithsdale and Kirkintilloch in Dunbartonshire were justiciars of Galloway in 1258 and 1275. Their strength in southern and northern Scotland was acknowledged by Edward I in the responsibility that John Comyn II held for the castles of Jedburgh and Roxburgh, Dull and Clunie in Stormont, and Kilbride and Brideburgh (Dumfriesshire) between 1291 and 1293.[106]

Without control over the north, no authority could be secure in Scotland.[107] The Comyn strength in Buchan, Badenoch and Lochaber was enhanced by their alliance with the MacDougalls of Argyll who added the castle of Dunstaffnage to the Comyn strength in the north.[108] Comyn castles, especially in the north, played key roles in Edward I's attempt to establish control over Scotland after 1296 as well as Robert Bruce's attempt to establish his authority after 1306. Of particular importance were Lochindorb and Balvenie, both visited by Edward I in 1303. In 1303, after having 'scoured the highlands and lowlands both on the far side and on the near side of the mountains, he arrived in person at Lochindorb. He stayed there for some time and accepted the submission of the northern areas'.[109]

In 1307 and 1308 Robert Bruce marched on Inverlochy and Balvenie as well as Tarradale and Urquhart which were in the hands of Alexander Comyn of Buchan. He then undertook the 'herschip' of Buchan and its castles. For much of the thirteenth century, Comyn castles had complemented, and, in fact, symbolised the royal authority of Alexander III, the Guardians and John Balliol. If Edward I and Robert Bruce hoped to exercise effective power in Scotland after 1296, these symbols of Comyn architectural lordship had to be controlled.

1. G. G. Simpson, 'Kingship in miniature: A seal of minority of Alexander III 1249–1257', in *Medieval Scotland: Crown, Lordship and Community*, eds. A. Grant and K. J. Stringer (Edinburgh, 1993), 131. See now A. Young, *Robert the Bruce's Rivals: the Comyns, 1212–1314* (East Linton, 1997).

2. *Chron. Bower* (Watt), v, 323.

3. A. Young, 'Noble families and political factions in the reign of Alexander III', in *Scotland in the Reign of Alexander III*, ed. N. H. Reid (Edinburgh, 1990), 1–2.

4. 'The Challenge of the House of Comyn' in D. E. R. Watt, 'The Minority of Alexander III of Scotland', *TRHS*, 5th series, xxxi (1971), 1–23.

5. Young, 'Noble families', 13–16; M. Lynch, *Scotland: a New History* (London, 1991), 89–92.

6. A. Young, *William Cumin: Border Politics and the Bishopric of Durham, 1141–1144* (Borthwick Paper No. 54, University of York, 1978), 1–29; A. Young, 'The Bishopric of Durham in Stephen's Reign', in *Anglo-Norman Durham 1093–1193*, eds. D. Rollason, M. Harvey and M. Prestwich (Woodbridge, 1994), 353–69.

7. Symeon of Durham, *Symeonis Monachi Opera Omnia*, ed. T. Arnold (Rolls Series, 1882–5), ii, 316.

8. *Calendar of Charter Rolls*, ii, 40–1.

9. *Kelso Liber*, i, no 274; *Holyrood Liber*, 210–11; *Morton Registrum*, ii, 4.

10. *Glasgow Registrum*, i, 195; *OPS*, i, 358.

11. *Newbattle Registrum*, 289; *Melrose Liber*, i, 12–13.

12. NAS, GD 101/1; *RRS*, ii, 406–7.

13. *RMS*, i, no. 72, App. I, no. 109, App. II, no. 604; *Kelso Liber*, nos 9 and 13; *RRS*, ii, 364, 440.

14. *CDS*, i, no. 632.

15. A. Young, 'The earls and earldom of Buchan in the thirteenth century', in *Medieval Scotland*, eds. Grant and Stringer, 177.

16. A. A. M. Duncan, *Scotland: the Making of the Kingdom* (Edinburgh, 1975), 595.

17. Young, 'Earls and earldom of Buchan', 174.

18. Ibid., 177–8; *Moray Registrum*, no 76.

19. *Scots Peerage*, vi, 127.

20. *Coupar Angus Charters*, i, 134–5.

21. *RMS*, i, App. II, no. 448.

22. *Aberdeen-Banff Ill.*, ii, 427.

23. NAS, RH 1/2/32.

24. NAS, RH 1/2/31.

25. *Arbroath Liber*, i, no 132.

26. *Scone Liber*, no. 146.

27. *St Andrews Liber*, 253–4, *Inchcolm Chrs.*, nos 25–7.

28. *ER*, i, 22–3; Stevenson, *Documents*, i, 329–30; *RMS*, i, App. II, nos. 308, 319, 361, 497; NAS, RH 6/59/6, GD 175/24.

29. Young, 'Earls and earldom of Buchan', 195.

30. Ibid., 193; NAS, RH 6/59.

31. *CDS*, ii, no 1541.

32. *Morton Registrum*, ii, 3–4; *Newbattle Registrum*, 135 6.

33. *Calendar of Charter Rolls*, ii, 40–41.

34. *Book of Fees*, i, 919, ii, 911, 1118; *CDS*, i, nos. 1523, 1558.

35. Young, 'Earls and earldom of Buchan', 195.

36. RCAHMS, *Roxburghshire*, i, no. 28; J. R. Baldwin, *Exploring Scotland's Heritage: Lothian and the Borders* (Edinburgh, 1989), 92.

37. RCAHMS *Roxburghshire*, i, 62, citing Gough, *Itinerary of Edward I*, ii, 169.

LORDSHIP AND
ARCHITECTURE
IN MEDIEVAL
AND
RENAISSANCE
SCOTLAND

❧

38. RCAHMS, *Peeblesshire*, ii, 273; Baldwin, *Lothian and the Borders*, 92–3.
39. *Morton Registrum*, ii, 5; for Comyn possession of Machan in the late twelfth century, see *Kelso Liber*, 17, no. 13, and 10, no. 9.
40. *Glasgow Registrum*, i, no. 547; *Kelso Liber*, i, no. 186 (G. G. Simpson, *Handlist of the Acts of Alexander III, the Guardians and John*, (Edinburgh, 1960), no. 50).
41. *Cambuskenneth Registrum*, xxx–xxxi.
42. *RRS*, ii, no. 501.
43. RCAHMS, *Lanarkshire*, 21 no. 59; *Kirkintilloch by Select Contributors*, ed. J. Horne, ed. (no date), 26, 30, 33.
44. RCAHMS, Lanarkshire, 21, citing J. Horsley (1732).
45. *CDS*, v, 185.
46. *RRS*, ii, 285 n.; *Glasgow Registrum*, no 55; G. P. Stell, 'Provisional List of Mottes in Scotland', Appendix 1 of G. G. Simpson and B. Webster, 'Charter evidence and the distribution of mottes in Scotland', in *Essays on the Nobility of Medieval Scotland*, ed. K. J. Stringer (Edinburgh, 1985), 19.
47. MacGibbon and Ross, *Castellated and Domestic Architecture*, i, 233.
48. *Melrose Liber*, 280–1; *Kelso Liber*, i, 11.
49. J. Ferguson, 'On the House of Comyn', *Transactions of the Buchan Field Club*, xi (1914), 76.
50. *CDS*, ii, nos. 766, 823, 1816.
51. RCAHMS, *Roxburghshire*, i, no. 466.
52. MacGibbon and Ross, *Ecclesiastical Architecture*, iii, 274–8; Cowan and Easson, *Religious Houses*, 74.
53. Young, 'Earls and earldom of Buchan', 185–6, 201.
54. MacGibbon and Ross, *Ecclesiastical Architecture*, iii, 274–5.
55. *Chron. Melrose*, 197–8.
56. *Aberdeen Registrum*, ii, 276–7; ibid., i, 30–4.
57. Young, 'Earls and earldom of Buchan', 188 and n. 1.
58. Ibid., 185, 187.
59. *Aberdeen Registrum*, ii, 276–7; i, 30–4.
60. Young, 'Earls and earldom of Buchan', 188 and n. 1.
61. W. D. Simpson, 'Cairnbulg Castle, Aberdeenshire', *PSAS*, xlviii (1948–9), 32–44.
62. H. K. Murray and J. C. Murray, 'Old Rattray, burgh and castle', *DES* (1986), 10.
63. W. D. Simpson, 'Slains Castle' *Transactions of the Buchan Field Club*, xvi (1940), 39–40.
64. MacGibbon and Ross, *Castellated and Domestic Architecture*, iii, 112–13; J. Godsman, *King Edward, the Story of a Parish* (1952), 26–7.
65. Young, 'Earls and earldom of Buchan', 188–90.
66. *Aberdeen Registrum*, ii, 276–7.
67. Ibid., i, 30–4.
68. G. Ewart and others, *Cruggleton Castle, Report of Excavations 1978–1981* (Dumfries, 1985); A. E. Truckell and J. Williams, 'Medieval pottery in Dumfriesshire and Galloway', *TDGNHAS*, 3rd series, xliv (1966–7), 133.
69. Stevenson, *Documents*, i, 329.
70. G. W. S. Barrow, 'The Highlands in the lifetime of Robert the Bruce', in *The Kingdom of the Scots* (London, 1973), 378.
71. I. A. G. Shepherd, *Exploring Scotland's Heritage: Grampian* (Edinburgh, 1986), no. 29.
72. J. S. Richardson and M. E. B. Simpson, *The Castle of Balvenie, Banffshire* (Edinburgh, 1961).
73. G. W. S. Barrow, 'Badenoch and Strathspey, 1130–1312, i, Secular and Political', *Northern Scotland*, viii (1988), 6.
74. Ibid., 7.
75. Matthew Paris, *Chronica Majora*, ed. H. Luard (Rolls Series, 1872–83), iv, 379–80.

76. *Calendar of Close Rolls, 1242–7*, 222.

77. *Inchaffray Liber*, xxix–xxxii.

78. E. L. G. Stones, *Anglo-Scottish Relations 1174–1328* (Oxford, 1965), 35–7.

79. R. Fawcett and D. Breeze, *Inchmahome Priory* (Edinburgh, 1986), 15–16.

80. R. Fawcett, 'Ecclesiastical architecture in the second half of the thirteenth century', in *Scotland in the Reign of Alexander III*, ed. Reid, 161.

81. Watt, 'Minority of Alexander III'.

82. Fawcett, 'Ecclesiastical architecture', 161.

83. Fawcett and Breeze, *Inchmahome Priory*, 15–16.

84. Barrow, 'Badenoch and Strathspey', 9; Barrow, 'Highlands in the lifetime of Robert Bruce', 377–8.

85. *Coupar Angus Charters*, i, 134–5.

86. Barrow, 'Badenoch and Strathspey', 9.

87. *Chron. Bower* (Watt), v, 373.

88. *Chron. Wyntoun* (Laing), ii, 311–2.

89. Barrow, 'Badenoch and Strathspey', 8; S. Cruden, *The Scottish Castle* (Edinburgh, 3rd edition, 1981), 61–2; MacGibbon and Ross, *Castellated and Domestic Architecture*, i, 70–2.

90. Cruden, *Scottish Castle*, 61.

91. Ibid., 57–64; MacGibbon and Ross, *Castellated and Domestic Architecture*, i, 73–8; J. Lewis, 'Inverlochy Castle', *DES* (1989), 28–9.

92. *Calendar of Patent Rolls, 1266–72*, 178.

93. P. Dixon, 'From hall to tower: the change in seignurial houses on the Anglo-Scottish border after 1250', in *Thirteenth Century England*, eds. P. R. Coss and S. D. Lloyd, iv (1991), 89, 103.

94. *Chron. Bower* (Watt), v, 181.

95. *CDS*, i, no. 2678.

96. *Annals of Furness* in *Chronicles of the Reigns of Stephen, Henry II and Richard I*, ed. R. Howlett (Rolls Series, 1884–90), ii, 570–1.

97. Young, 'Earls and earldom of Buchan', 197.

98. *CDS*, ii, no. 421; *CDS*, i, no. 2366.

99. Stevenson, *Documents*, i, 393. The thanages of Formartine and Belhelvie granted by King John Balliol were worth over 250 merks a year (*Aberdeen Registrum*, i, 55).

100. *CDS*, iii, no. 233.

101. *CDS*, iii, no. 512. Tarset itself was said to be worth 200 merks in 1296.

102. *Calendar of Patent Rolls, 1258–66*, 198, 551; *Calendar of Liberate Rolls*, v, 198.

103. G. Stell, 'The Balliol family and the Great Cause of 1291–2', in *Essays on the Nobility of Medieval Scotland*, ed. Stringer, 157. Edward I demanded a relief of £3,290 for John Balliol's succession to his mother's Scottish lands.

104. *ER*, i, especially 1–51.

105. Ibid., i, 49; *CDS*, ii, no. 1633.

106. Stevenson, *Documents*, i, 247–8, 275, 312; *Rotuli Scotiae*, i, 12b, 17a. 'Brideburgh' appears to be Barburgh where there is a motte and bailey castle (NX 892901), referred to as Dinning Motte in RCAHMS, *Dumfriesshire*, no. 65. I am most grateful to Mr. A. M. T. Maxwell-Irving for this information.

107. A. Grant, *Independence and Nationhood: Scotland 1306–1469* (London, 1984), 11–12, 206–7.

108. Barrow, 'Highlands in the lifetime of Robert Bruce', 377–8; Cruden, *Scottish Castle*, 58–62, notes similarities between Dunstaffnage and the Comyn castles of Lochindorb and Inverlochy.

109. *Chron. Bower* (Watt), vi, 297.

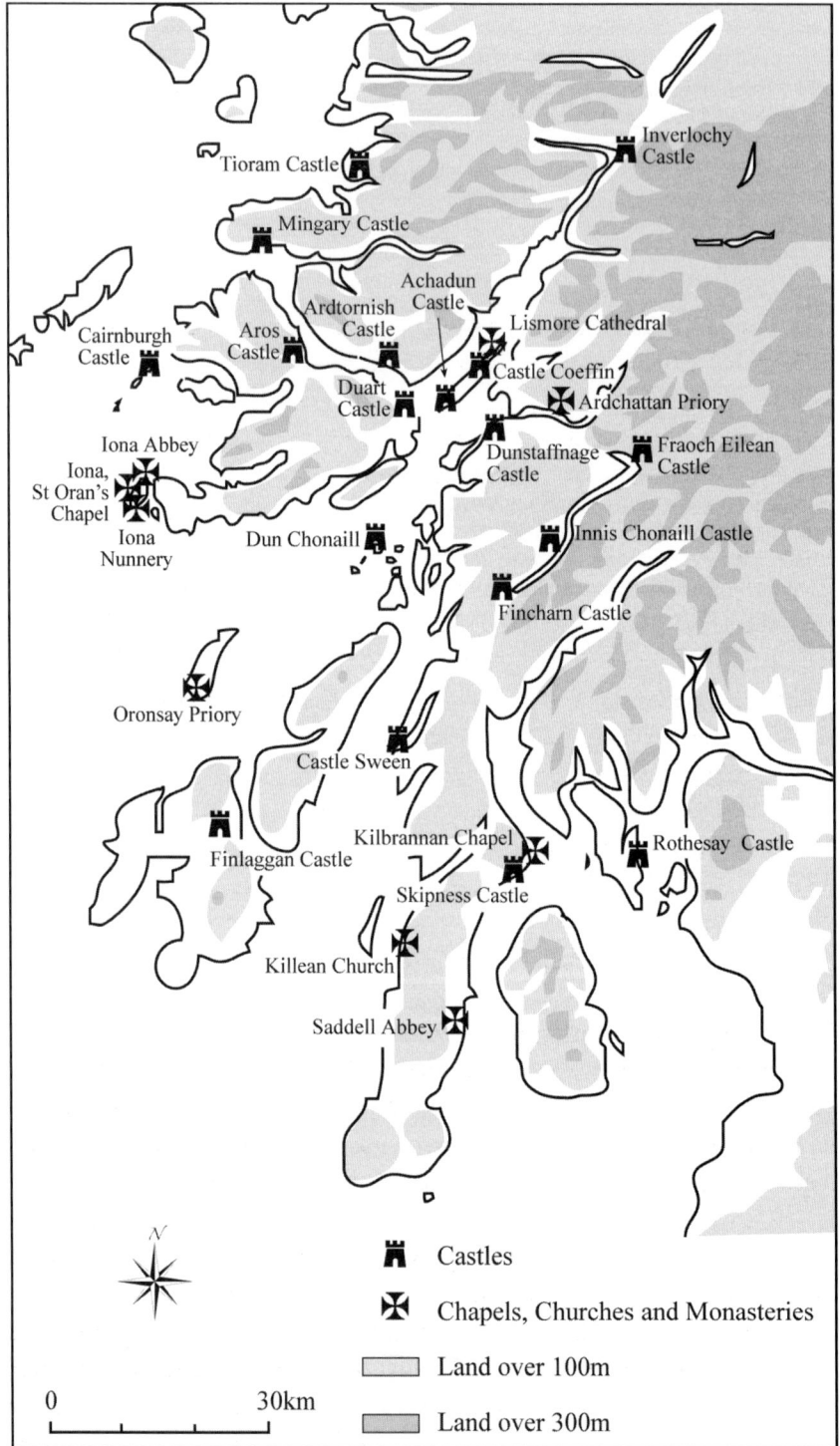

Tioram Castle

Inverlochy
Castle

Mingary Castle

Achadun
Castle

Cairnburgh
Castle

Ardtornish
Castle

Aros
Castle

Lismore Cathedral

Castle Coeffin

Duart
Castle

Ardchattan Priory

Iona Abbey

Dunstaffnage
Castle

Fraoch Eilean
Castle

Iona,
St Oran's
Chapel

Innis Chonaill Castle

Dun Chonaill

Iona
Nunnery

Fincharn Castle

Oronsay Priory

Castle Sween

Kilbrannan Chapel

Rothesay Castle

Finlaggan Castle

Skipness Castle

Killean Church

Saddell Abbey

N

Castles

Chapels, Churches and Monasteries

Land over 100m

0   30km

Land over 300m

Figure 5.1
Heirs of Somerled

84

Chapter 5

ૐ

THE HEIRS OF SOMERLED

Ian Fisher

The western seaboard of Argyll, bordering the Firth of Lorn and the Sound
of Mull, preserves one of the most remarkable concentrations of thirteenth-
century castles in Britain. To the south, a group of related kindreds
including the MacSweens of Knapdale held strongholds such as Castle
Sween, Skipness and Fincharn,[1] and Innis Chonaill on Loch Awe was the
first known residence of the Campbells.[2] The most important families,
however, both as castle-builders and patrons of churches, were heirs of
Somerled (d. 1164), the *regulus* or provincial king (Irish *rí*) of Argyll and
the Isles.[3] The MacDougalls, descended from his son Dugald, held the
mainland lordship of Lorn together with Mull and adjacent islands. The
widespread territory of another son, Reginald, was divided between his
sons Donald, who received Islay and Kintyre, and Ruari who held the
northern lordship of Garmoran together with the Small Isles and most of
the Outer Hebrides. A notable feature of all three lordships was their
combination of mainland territories in the kingdom of Scotland with
Hebridean islands which until 1266 were held from the Norwegian Crown.
The possession of island castles was an important issue in the dispute
between Ewen MacDougall 'of Argyll' and King Alexander II which led
in 1249 to a royal invasion of Argyll. Half a century later, Inverlochy,
Dunstaffnage and Castle Sween were to appear in historical or literary
documents of the Wars of Independence. Although this period of conflict
greatly diminished the power of the MacDougalls, their chief was still
styled 'lord of Argyll' in an agreement made in 1354 with his cousin and
namesake John (MacDonald) of Islay, 'Lord of the Isles'.[4]

The earliest surviving buildings of mortared stone in the West Highlands
are churches of the twelfth century. Somerled was engaged, in the year of
his death, in abortive negotiations to bring a celebrated reforming abbot
from Derry to the Columban monastery on Iona. At about the same
period the small chapel of St Oran in the burial-ground of Iona was
embellished with a doorway in Romanesque style.[5] It came to be used as
a mortuary chapel and burial-place for the MacDonald lords of the Isles,

LORDSHIP AND
ARCHITECTURE
IN MEDIEVAL
AND
RENAISSANCE
SCOTLAND

ॐ

and this dynastic function may have been intended by their ancestor Somerled himself. The second half of the century saw the introduction of reformed monastic orders with the foundation of the Cistercian house of Saddell in Kintyre, probably by Reginald who also endowed the Cluniacs of Paisley. Its physical remains and historical documentation are alike fragmentary, but moulded stones in Irish Romanesque style are consistent with a fourteenth-century record of its status as a daughter of Mellifont, Co. Louth.[6]

Reginald is credited in Clan Donald tradition with the introduction of Benedictines to Iona, which was achieved soon after 1200 despite opposition from the clergy of Ulster. The pattern of landholding revealed by the papal confirmation of 1203 also suggests the active support of Dugald (if still alive) and his son Duncan, both recorded as benefactors of the Benedictines of Durham in 1175. The tentative suggestion that this belated foundation of black monks may have been related to John de Courcy's establishment of the order at Downpatrick (Co. Down) is strengthened by recent excavations which indicate that the first church of the cathedral priory there was of simple cruciform plan, like that postulated at Iona.[7] The family link between Reginald and de Courcy, through the kings of Mann, was only one element in the elaborate web of friendly and hostile relationships around the Irish Sea and the North Channel at this period, and an Irish affiliation is also likely for the Augustinian nunnery on Iona.[8] This foundation is again ascribed by seventeenth-century Clan Donald historians to Reginald, and the tombstone of his sister, inscribed

Figure 5.2
The heirs of Somerled:
genealogical tree.

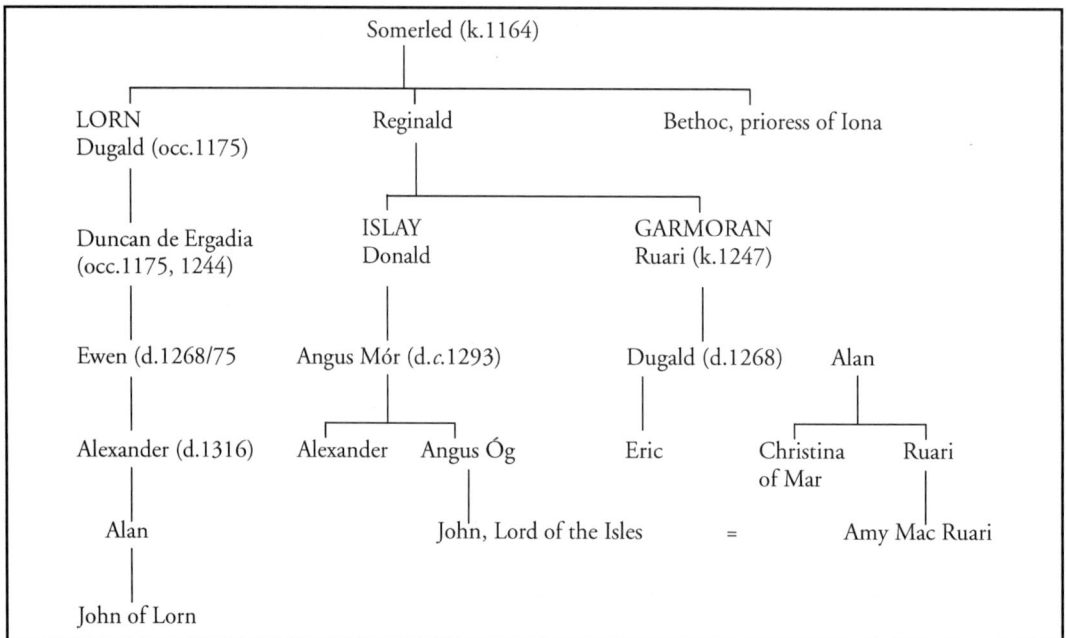

Behag nijn Sorle vic Il vrid priorissa ('Bethoc daughter of Somerled son of Gille-Brigte, prioress') was recorded at the end of that century. The nunnery church was a Transitional building with Irish features, and the original compact claustral lay-out was probably completed during the thirteenth century. The church of the Benedictine abbey was extended, probably before its completion, by an elegant choir with undercroft, and construction of the monastic buildings continued until the completion of the refectory at about the end of the thirteenth century.[9] An ambitious project of the same period, a massive south transept perhaps intended to house relics of St Columba, was carried no higher than the lowest courses of its walls, whether because secular patronage was disrupted by warfare or for some domestic reason within the monastic community.

Whatever the degree of their involvement at Iona, the MacDougalls became monastic founders in their own right about 1230 when Duncan established a Valliscaulian priory at Ardchattan on Loch Etive, direct from the principal house in Burgundy.[10] One of three Scottish foundations by an otherwise purely French order (the others being at Beauly and Pluscarden), this was perhaps inspired by Alexander II at a time when Duncan's allegiance had come under scrutiny following the Norwegian expedition of 1230. Little survives of the original buildings of this small community, but the church was enlarged in the early sixteenth century and remained the burial-place of leading members of the family. The MacDougalls also gave generous endowments to the see of Argyll, and the cathedral on the island of Lismore, whose choir appears to date from the late thirteenth or early fourteenth century, probably owed much to their patronage.[11] Another notable symbol of family piety was the mid-thirteenth-century chapel near Dunstaffnage Castle,[12] more elaborate than any parish church in the region and equalled in scale only by the extended church at Killean (Kintyre) and the somewhat later Kilbrannan Chapel near Skipness Castle.[13]

The achievement of these linked kindreds as monastic founders bears comparison with that of any baronial family in mainland Scotland,[14] and was added to by John MacDonald, first Lord of the Isles, with a rare fourteenth-century foundation for Augustinian canons on Oronsay.[15] Many of the surviving parish churches and chapels of late twelfth- and early thirteenth-century date are also on the families' lands, in Kintyre, Islay, Lorn and Mull.[16] As well as witnessing to a developing parochial system they required skills in construction, perhaps originally imported from Ireland, which in the coming century were to be turned to secular ends.

The Iron Age in the West Highlands, with its profusion of fortified residences which are classified by archaeologists as forts and duns, is

followed by a long period when little is known of secular building. Even the few mottes or allied earthworks, mainly in Cowal, need be no earlier than the masonry castles.[17] The first of these was probably the Stewart stronghold of Rothesay, whose circular shell-keep may have been inspired by comparable plans in twelfth-century castles of the Welsh marches. At Castle Sween, at about the beginning of the thirteenth century, the enclosing wall was adapted to a rectangular courtyard format which in Anglo-Norman England had been favoured for episcopal palaces rather than secular residences.[18] This plan was to be used in MacDougall territory at Achadun and Duart,[19] and by the Campbells at Innis Chonaill.[20] At Dunstaffnage, Mingary and Tioram the curtain-walls followed the outlines of roughly triangular rock-summits in a local adaptation of the small polygonal enclosures found in Ulster.[21] A common European type was the first-floor hall range or 'hall house', found in England both in castle enclosures and free-standing in manor houses. This type had a long life in the West Highlands, but there is architectural and historical evidence of thirteenth-century date for the hall houses at the core of Skipness Castle[22] and in the MacNachtan island castle of Fraoch Eilean in Loch Awe.[23] More primitive styles of fortification were also employed, in a region where crannogs and small island-dwellings remained in use until the seventeenth century. The island fortresses of Cairnburgh in the Treshnish Isles[24] and Dùn Chonaill in the Garvellachs[25] were defended by strong tides and formidable cliffs, augmented by cross-walls

Figure 5.3
Castle Sween, Argyll:
view from south-west.
RCAHMS, AG/13225

on the approaches to the summit plateaus and drystone walling in other gullies. In contrast to these towering sea-rocks, the principal residence of the Clan Donald was to be a low-lying island in Loch Finlaggan, Islay.[26]

The heart of the MacDougall lordship lay at the junction of the Firth of Lorn and Loch Etive, where Dunstaffnage Castle rises on its rock overlooking a sheltered anchorage.[27] The demonstration in recent excavations that the angle-towers were early additions increases the similarity of the original enclosure to those at Mingary and Tioram. The series of tall archers' embrasures in the landward curtain, however, is a sophisticated feature, and the castle with its nearby chapel may belong to the period between the political crises of 1249 and 1263. A few miles to the south-west, the crag on which the early historic fortress of Dunollie once stood [28] dominates the north entrance of Oban Bay. It may have been occupied in the thirteenth century, although the existing tower house is of late medieval type and the nearby house, still home to the chief of the clan, is of the eighteenth century.[29] The other known MacDougall castles on the mainland, Ardmaddy [30] and Gylen,[31] appear to have been of fifteenth- and sixteenth-century origin, but at least for a period at the beginning of the fourteenth century the family also controlled three castles on Loch Awe (*infra*). The island of Lismore with its cathedral, although legally part of the lordship of Lorn, may have been one of the causes of friction between Ewen MacDougall and Alexander II. Its north-west coast was

guarded by the 'castle or manor' on the bishop's township of Achadun and, much closer to the cathedral, by the hall house of Coeffin, both on rocky crags overlooking the main channel of Loch Linnhe.[32]

The pattern of MacDougall landholding in the Norwegian territories can be reconstructed from documents of the fourteenth century, supported by scanty and imprecise earlier references. The author of *Haakon Haakonsson's Saga* describes Alexander II's demand of 1249 that Ewen of Argyll should surrender 'Biarnaborg ... and three other castles, which he held of King Haakon'.[33] The named island was surely the larger of the two Cairnburgh islands, in the Treshnish group between Mull and Tiree, and another may have been its lower-lying neighbour, which is probably to be identified with the 'Iselborg' ('low fort') of fourteenth-century sources. Their counterpart in the channel south-east of Mull was Dùn Chonaill, the 'great castle of Dunquhonle' of Fordun's late fourteenth-century description.[34] The fourth of the contentious strongholds may have been Duart, if the rectangular courtyard-castle already existed at this time, or else the predecessor of Fordun's 'very strong tower' at Loch an Eilean, Tiree.[35] Another Mull castle, which was to become a major seat of Clan Donald, was the massive hall house and enclosure at Aros, guarding the shortest land-crossing from the Sound of Mull to the west coast.[36] A surviving Y-traceried window,

however, resembles others at Kilbrannan Chapel and Iona Abbey refectory, indicating a date no earlier than the late thirteenth century.

Sources for the early ownership of mainland northern Argyll are entirely lacking, yet the great peninsulas of Morvern and Ardnamurchan have important early castles.[37] The hall house at Ardtornish is a fragmentary equivalent of that at Aros on the opposite shore of the Sound of Mull, and likewise had a long history as an important residence of the Lords of the Isles.[38] Mingary Castle, finely situated on the south coast of Ardnamurchan at the head of the Sound of Mull, preserves much of its thirteenth-century enclosure, with details of the original wall-head fossilised in a later heightening.[39] Here, as at Dunstaffnage, features of the original hall range are preserved despite post-medieval rebuilding, including attached mural chambers and garderobes. The possibility that Mingary was a MacRuari castle is increased by its similarity to that on the tidal or 'dry' island in Loch Moidart, Eilean Tioram, which in the Latin form *insula sicca* is named in a charter of the 1320s granted by the MacRuari heiress, Christina of Mar.[40] The polygonal enclosure is dominated by late-medieval courtyard buildings and an imposing turreted tower of the late sixteenth century, all dating from its use by the Clan Ranald, the senior cadets of the Lords of the Isles. As at Mingary, however, sections of the original crenellated wall-head are preserved by later heightening.

Castle Tioram is unusual in its secluded position, sheltered by the rocks and shallows of Loch Moidart, but the strongholds of the MacDougalls, on their islands or rocky promontories, make a dramatic assertion of authority in a maritime lordship, on the boundary between two conflicting kingdoms. Symbolism may even have outweighed strategic value in some

*Figure 5.6
Cairnburgh Mor
Castle, Argyll: view
from north-east.
RCAHMS, AG/5195*

LORDSHIP AND
ARCHITECTURE
IN MEDIEVAL
AND
RENAISSANCE
SCOTLAND

⅋

cases, for the anchorage at Duart was dangerously exposed and tradition states that the late medieval MacLean lords kept their galleys some miles away in Loch Spelve. The castle's position at the junction of three great seaways was a dominating one, however, even before the addition of the great MacLean tower house in the late fourteenth century. Similarly, the defensive strength of the island fortresses of Cairnburgh and Dùn Chonaill was not matched by true ability to control the surrounding waters, for they lacked any anchorage and landing was dependent on winds and tidal currents. However, Cairnburgh was so valued as a place of refuge during the MacLean period that a Hanoverian garrison was maintained there to prevent such use as late as the 1740s.

The construction during the thirteenth century of numerous stone castles, as well as religious houses at Iona and Ardchattan, reflects the semi-regal ambitions of the MacDougalls and MacRuaris, both of whom were recognised by the Norwegian Crown as viceroys in the Hebrides. It also testifies to economic resources capable of maintaining a considerable force of skilled stonemasons, who raised walls with confidence at the edge of sheer cliffs and imported freestone from the rare local quarries in Mull and Morvern. The islands of Mull, Coll and Tiree were to play an important part in the post-medieval cattle-droving trade, and cattle products are likely to have been among the goods traded as far as Bristol and Ireland by Alexander MacDougall in his own ships in the late thirteenth century.[41] The western seaboard of Lorn also included some of the best arable land in Argyll, and land might be attached to castles for

*Figure 5.7
Mingary Castle,
Argyll: aerial view.
RCAHMS, AG/9051*

their maintenance. A glimpse of this system is seen in the grant of the constabulary lands of Dunstaffnage to Arthur Campbell about 1321.[42]

The increase of Scottish power in Argyll was marked by the acquisition by the Stewarts of MacSween territory in Knapdale, shortly before Haakon's expedition of 1263.[43] This may have been among the reasons for Ewen MacDougall's reversal of his earlier support for the Norwegian king, despite Haakon's earnest entreaties. The family enjoyed both their mainland and island properties under Scottish overlordship until the end of the century, despite the antagonism of the Campbells of Loch Awe, whose chief they killed in battle in 1294. Their high position among the Scottish baronage was marked by the marriage of Alexander MacDougall to a daughter of John Comyn of Badenoch. A report of 1297 to the English court showed the inhabitants of the Comyn lordship of Lochaber supporting Alexander's son, Duncan, and his brother-in-law, Lachlan MacRuari, against the pretensions of Alexander MacDonald of Islay, who in retaliation burnt two great galleys at Inverlochy when a hail of arrows from the castle prevented him from removing them.[44]

The MacDougalls had an uncertain relationship with the English Crown until the murder of Alexander's nephew, the Red Comyn, by Bruce in 1306. Their implacable enmity to the new king, coupled with the strategic position of their lordship, inevitably made them the main target of Bruce's campaigns in Argyll. John of Lorn, son of Alexander MacDougall, reported to Edward II in 1308 or 1309 that against Bruce's approach with a great force he was guarding three castles and a loch twenty-four miles long with its fleet of galleys.[45] Both the loch and the castles, like those of 1249, have been the subject of various identifications, but Bower's reference to the same length and the same number of castles in his description of Loch Awe removes any doubt.[46] The castles were presumably the MacNachtan hall house of Fraoch Eilean, that of Fincharn in the lordship of Glassary, and Innis Chonaill which may have been in MacDougall possession since the death of Cailean Mór Campbell. The decisive encounter took place at the north end of the loch, in the Pass of Brander, and thereafter, as Barbour narrates:[47]

> The king that stout wes stark and bauld,
> Till Dunstaffynch rycht sturdely
> A sege set and besily
> Assaylit the castell it to get,
> And in schort tym he has thaim set
> In swilk thrang that tharin war than,
> That magre tharis he it wan,
> And ane gud wardane tharin set.

LORDSHIP AND
ARCHITECTURE
IN MEDIEVAL
AND
RENAISSANCE
SCOTLAND

⅌

John of Lorn, after holding out for some time in the castle of Loch Awe (Innis Chonaill), escaped to the English court and was to serve Edward II as admiral of the western seas, while his father also died in English service. There is little evidence as to the landholdings of John's son and grandson, Alan and John, who re-established the MacDougall lordship in Lorn, nor of the history of Dunstaffnage after the grant to Arthur Campbell. Their island properties, however, were irretrievably lost, and the grant by David II to John MacDonald of Islay in 1343, with the quitclaim by John MacDougall in 1354, probably recognised a Clan Donald superiority which went back to the first decade of the century. John, 'Lord of the Isles', also acquired the lands of Garmoran through his marriage to Amy MacRuari, and for four centuries Castle Tioram was to be the seat of the lordship of their son, Reginald, and his Clanranald descendants. Meanwhile the offspring of John's son-in-law, the first MacLean of Duart, were the ultimate heirs to the island castle-building achievement of the thirteenth-century MacDougalls.

NOTES

1. W. D. H Sellar, 'Family origins in Cowal and Knapdale', *Scottish Studies*, 15 (1971), 21–37; N. Murray '"A Clan on the run?" The Mhic Suibhne Migration to Ireland *c.* 1240–1400' (forthcoming).
2. See Boardman, 'Pillars of the Community', *infra*.
3. A. A. M. Duncan and A. L. Brown, 'Argyll and the Isles in the Earlier Middle Ages', *PSAS*, 90 (1957), 192–220; W. D. H. Sellar, 'The origins and ancestry of Somerled', *SHR*, 45 (1966), 123–42; R. A. McDonald, *The Kingdom of the Isles. Scotland's Western Seaboard, c. 1100-c. 1336* (East Linton, 1997).
4. *Highland Papers*, i, 76–8.
5. RCAHMS, *Argyll*, iv, no. 12.
6. RCAHMS, *Argyll*, i, no. 296.
7. RCAHMS, *Argyll*, iv, no. 4; information on Downpatrick from the excavator, Mr. N. Brannon.
8. RCAHMS, *Argyll*, iv, no. 5.
9. Ibid., no. 4.
10. RCAHMS, *Argyll*, ii, no. 217.
11. Ibid., no. 267.
12. Ibid., no. 243.
13. RCAHMS, *Argyll*, i, nos. 287, 277.
14. R. A. McDonald, 'Scoto-Norse kings and the reformed religious orders: patterns of monastic patronage in twelfth-century Galloway and Argyll', *Albion*, xxvii (1995).
15. RCAHMS, *Argyll*, v, no. 386.
16. J. G. Dunbar, 'The Medieval Architecture of the Scottish Highlands' in *The Middle Ages in the Highlands*, ed. L. Maclean (Inverness, 1981), 38–70.
17. RCAHMS, *Argyll*, vii, nos. 108, 109, 113, 120, 125.
18. Ibid., no. 119.
19. RCAHMS, *Argyll*, ii, no. 276; RCAHMS, *Argyll*, iii, no. 339.
20. RCAHMS, *Argyll*, ii, no. 292.

21. RCAHMS, *Argyll*, ii, no. 287; RCAHMS, *Argyll*, iii, no. 345; C. J. Tabraham, *Scotland's Castles* (London, 1997), 33, 35; T. E. McNeill, *Anglo-Norman Ulster: the History and Archaeology of an Irish Barony, 1177–1400* (Edinburgh, 1982).
22. RCAHMS, *Argyll*, i, no. 314.
23. RCAHMS, *Argyll*, ii, no. 290.
24. RCAHMS, *Argyll*, iii, no. 335.
25. RCAHMS, *Argyll*, v, no. 402.
26. See Caldwell and Ruckley, 'Domestic Architecture', *infra*.
27. RCAHMS, *Argyll*, ii, no. 287; J. Lewis, 'Dunstaffnage Castle, Argyll and Bute: excavations in the north tower and east range', *PSAS*, 126 (1996), 559–603.
28. L. Alcock and E. A. Alcock, 'Reconnaissance excavations on early historic fortifications: Dunollie', *PSAS*, 117 (1987), 119–47.
29. RCAHMS, *Argyll*, ii, no. 286.
30. Ibid., no. 310.
31. Ibid., no. 291.
32. Ibid., nos. 276, 282; Duncan and Brown, 'Argyll and the Isles', 208–10.
33. Duncan and Brown, op. cit.; Anderson, *Early Sources*, ii, 555–6.
34. RCAHMS, *Argyll*, iii, no. 335; RCAHMS, *Argyll*, v, no. 402; *Chron. Fordun*, i, 43.
35. RCAHMS, *Argyll*, iii, nos. 339, 344; *Chron. Fordun*, i, 43.
36. RCAHMS, *Argyll*, iii, no. 333.
37. The editors of *Acts of the Lords of the Isles* speculate (p. xx) that Ardnamurchan and Morvern formed part of the early lordship of Clan Donald, while Moidart, Arisaig, Morar and Knoydart comprised the MacRuaridhs' mainland lordship of Garmoran.
38. RCAHMS, *Argyll*, iii, no. 332.
39. *Ibid.*, no. 345.
40. McDonald, *Kingdom of the Isles*, 189 n. 120.
41. *CDS*, ii, no. 63.
42. *RMS*, i, App. ii, nos. 353, 368. Duncan (*RRS*, v, 242) explains this as a subordinate part of the sheriffdom.
43. Murray, 'Clan on the run'.
44. Stevenson, *Documents*, 190–1.
45. *CDS* , iii, no. 80.
46. *Chron. Bower* (Watt), i, 191.
47. Barbour, *Bruce*, 367.

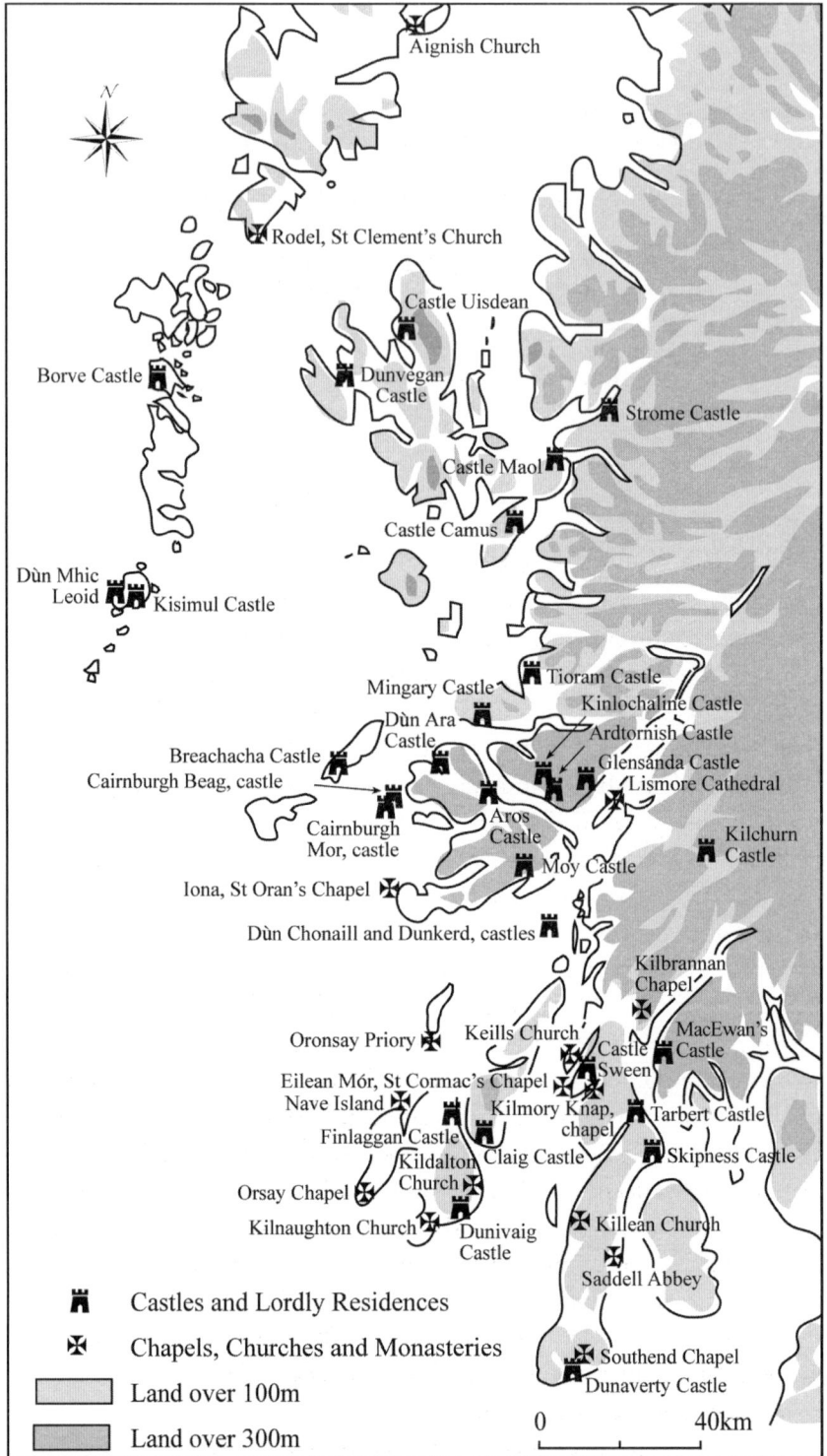

Aignish Church

Rodel, St Clement's Church

Castle Uisdean

Borve Castle

Dunvegan Castle

Strome Castle

Castle Maol

Castle Camus

Dùn Mhic Leoid

Kisimul Castle

Mingary Castle

Tioram Castle

Kinlochaline Castle

Dùn Ara Castle

Ardtornish Castle

Breachacha Castle

Glensanda Castle

Cairnburgh Beag, castle

Lismore Cathedral

Cairnburgh Mor, castle

Aros Castle

Kilchurn Castle

Iona, St Oran's Chapel

Moy Castle

Dùn Chonaill and Dunkerd, castles

Kilbrannan Chapel

Oronsay Priory

Keills Church

MacEwan's Castle

Eilean Mór, St Cormac's Chapel

Castle Sween

Nave Island

Kilmory Knap, chapel

Tarbert Castle

Finlaggan Castle

Claig Castle

Kildalton Church

Skipness Castle

Orsay Chapel

Kilnaughton Church

Dunivaig Castle

Killean Church

Saddell Abbey

Southend Chapel

Dunaverty Castle

Castles and Lordly Residences

Chapels, Churches and Monasteries

Land over 100m

Land over 300m

0   40km

Figure 6.1
Lordship of the Isles.

96

Chapter 6

๛

DOMESTIC ARCHITECTURE
IN THE LORDSHIP
OF THE ISLES

David H. Caldwell and *Nigel A. Ruckley*

INTRODUCTION

The architecture of the Western Isles and adjacent Highlands in the later medieval period is one of the elements which make the Lordship of the Isles seem so distinctive in our eyes. Many cultural traits like the Gaelic language, dress and the clan system were by no means confined to the area of the Lordship,[1] but the cultural package of the Lordship as a whole under the power and patronage of the MacDonalds was very different from that of Lowland Scotland. It was conservatively Celtic in a way which probably suited the Lords, well aware of their heritage as princes or kings. It resisted the establishment of Lowland institutions like burghs, and repelled any significant settlement by new families without a Gaelic background.

Any study of the architecture of the Lordship owes an enormous debt to the Inventories of Monuments, and scholarship, of the Royal Commission on the Ancient and Historical Monuments of Scotland (RCAHMS). There is also an important survey of medieval Highland architecture by John Dunbar.[2] Even so, it is still impossible to identify with any degree of precision which buildings belong to the period of the Lordship, approximately the fourteenth and fifteenth centuries. We therefore give some consideration to the problem of dating, taking into account the buildings inherited by the Lords, those deemed to have been erected in the fourteenth and fifteenth centuries, and other structures of less certain date but which seem to have some relevance to our theme. We also give some prominence to the results of our own work at Finlaggan on Islay rather than concentrating on already well described monuments.

A narrow study of patronage of architects and architecture by the Lords

LORDSHIP AND
ARCHITECTURE
IN MEDIEVAL
AND
RENAISSANCE
SCOTLAND

themselves would not take us far. We have only the names of two sculptors, Donald O'Brolchan, who was working at Iona in the mid-fifteenth century, and Mael-Sechlainn O'Cuinn, responsible for some of the cloister arcade and a fine commemorative cross at Oronsay Priory about 1500, and a grave slab with a warrior effigy at Iona.[3] It is not clear if either had any wider responsibility for the design and construction of buildings.

The West Highland sculpture they and others produced is very definitely a local phenomenon but in the twelfth and early thirteenth centuries it is possible to trace the influence of Irish work in local church architecture, for example at Saddell Abbey in Kintyre and on Iona at the abbey, the nunnery and St Oran's Chapel.[4]

Here we will look at the wider picture of what sort of houses the Lords and their people chose to live in. Given the lack of contemporary documentary evidence for the Lordship, archaeological excavation may offer the key to further understanding of the architecture of the Western Isles and Highlands. We also believe that much more can be learned from a geological approach, sourcing quarries for building stone and slates, and examining building techniques and patterns. The geologically based work we present here is still in its early stages and must, as yet, be regarded as an indication of its potential rather than a definitive conclusion.

There is a distinct lack of what might be termed monumental architecture. Churches tend to be small and plain. This, however, must be balanced against a remarkable flourishing of sculpture in the form of commemorative crosses and grave slabs. Although outwith the scope of this essay, patronage by the Lords and their chief men of the sculptors who produced this monumental art, and other craftsmen and artists, more than made up for the apparent lack of quality architecture.

It appears at first sight a fruitless task to search out a strategic pattern of fortifications in the Lordship belonging to the period of MacDonald domination. Some of the castles they inherited may relate to the mid-thirteenth-century tension between the kings of Scots and Norway, like Tarbert and the strongholds on the Treshnish Islands, and Dun Chonaill in the Garvellachs. Almost all castles are on the coast where they could have some role in watching or guarding the sea lanes which were so crucial in a world where galleys were the main means of transport, especially of men of war.

In most of these cases ease of access to good land was probably more significant; but this does not hold good for castles in the Treshnish Islands to the east of Mull, in the Garvellachs in the Firth of Lorn and on Am Fraoch Eilean in the Sound of Islay. A modern assessment might well be that they had limited potential as landing places, but all had space to draw up boats in time of need, or could call on galleys based nearby, either to challenge enemy forces or give advance warning of trouble.[5] Claig Castle on Am Fraoch Eilean is likely to have been a castle built by the Lords but the others date back to Norse times, and, remarkably, are double strongholds – in the Treshnish Islands Cairn na Burgh More and Cairn na Burgh Beg on two adjacent rocks, and in the Garvellachs Dun Chonaill and Dunkerd, both on the one small island.[6]

It might have been expected that Inverlochy, an impressive towered castle of the thirteenth century built by the Comyns, would have been of importance to the Lords of the Isles in protecting the route up the Great Glen to Inverness and the centre of their Earldom of Ross at Dingwall. While there is documentary evidence that it was given to the Earl of Huntly in 1506 with powers to have it rebuilt and garrisoned, recent archaeological excavations have failed to identify MacDonald occupation.[7]

MASONRY STYLES AND DATING EVIDENCE

There is practically no early documentary evidence for dating Lordship buildings. The presence or absence of a castle or residence in a list of island houses drawn up by the historian Fordun in the late fourteenth century, and the 1549 account of the Isles by Dean Monro, provide some clue.[8] Such evidence does not, of course, date individual elements of the places concerned, and is it going too far to assume that Claig Castle in the Sound of Islay was built after Fordun and in ruins before Monro on the basis that it appears in neither list? At least this would not seem improbable. A seventeenth-century MacDonald history not improbably ascribes the construction or restoration of chapels at Finlaggan, Orsay and Eilean Mór in the MacCormac Isles to John I, Lord of the Isles (1336–87).[9]

Archaeological excavations, particularly at Finlaggan and Breachacha Castle on Coll, have failed to come up with finely tuned independent dating evidence. Nor has a comparison of mouldings and architectural design features in Lordship buildings with those elsewhere significantly enhanced our understanding of their date. Many buildings are characterised by their lack of freestone dressings, and often, where such features exist, they can only be assigned to a period of a hundred years or more.

An alternative approach to this problem is to study the different types of wall construction to determine whether there might be changes with time. There are several difficulties with this type of research, not least recent restoration of several monuments which has either obscured or altered the original building pattern. We must also be aware that there is no uniformity to the geology of the study area, and so the buildings have a multitude of different rock types. The differing qualities of these rocks in terms of weight, hardness, ease with which they could be split, and so

LORDSHIP AND
ARCHITECTURE
IN MEDIEVAL
AND
RENAISSANCE
SCOTLAND

⁂

on, might be instrumental in determining the favoured method of using them. It is not surprising that where detailed examination has been made of particular edifices, the stone, with the possible exception of freestone dressings and quoins, and roof-slates, is all obviously of local origin.

The stone used in building may either have been quarried, gathered as field stones or off shores and river beds, or else re-used from earlier structures. Boulders and pebbles might be split to achieve a flat face, quarried blocks might be rough-dressed to approximate rectangles. Again it has to be borne in mind that the availability of these different sources of stone and the ease with which they could be worked might be of significance in deciding on building styles.

The main type of wall construction in the better buildings of the Lordship is random rubble. This was probably the cheapest method of mortared stone construction, depending largely on the mortar for its strength. Compared with ashlar constructed walls, it was extravagant in the use of mortar, but in the Western Islands this was no problem with local supplies of limestone and shell. Our preliminary analysis of medieval West Highland architecture suggests that there are four main traditions of work, as follows:

(1) Coursed work, mainly with long, low rectangular blocks. This type of masonry is seen in the main walling and west wing of Castle Sween in Knapdale and the main work of Skipness Castle in Kintyre. In all cases there is a certain admixture of boulders, normally split to present a flat face. Such work can confidently be dated to the twelfth century – perhaps the third quarter – in St Oran's Chapel, Iona, by the decoration of the doorway and later documentary sources.[10] Just outwith the Lordship, the castle of the bishops of Argyll at Achadun on Lismore can reasonably be dated to the late thirteenth century on the basis of documentary evidence and the presence of masons' marks here which also occur at the nearby cathedral.[11] All other examples of this coursed work might date to the twelfth and thirteenth centuries. Similar work notably occurs outwith the West Highlands in late twelfth-century work at Rushen Castle in the Isle of Man, and in Orkney in twelfth-century work at St Magnus Cathedral and the Bishop's Palace in Kirkwall, but here the fissile quality of the local flagstone insures that it is impractical to create masonry markedly different.

In some work of this style in the area of the Lordship there is lavish use of freestone for dressings and quoins. At Skipness Castle, Kilbrannan Chapel and Saddell Abbey this is red or white sandstone, thought to be from quarries in Kintyre or Arran. In the enclosure castle at Duart on Mull the dressings and quoins are from a sandstone probably quarried

on the opposite shore of Morvern at Inninmore Bay.[12] At Mingary and Castle Tioram the need for quantities of freestone for quoins was avoided by rounding the external corners of the curtain walls.

Where masonry of this type occurs in contexts where there is little other guidance as to dating, we may tentatively assign it to the twelfth or thirteenth century, for instance the earlier stonework in the curtain wall of Aros Castle in Mull and some of the walling of the castle on the Council Island at Finlaggan.

(2) Coursed work, with blocks and boulders and through courses of pinnings.

The best-quality work of this type occurs at the Iona Nunnery. Here the blocks are mainly rectangular, and a colourful effect is created by the contrast between the red granite and grey basalt and the Iona Series fine-grained metasediments, and also the yellow of the sandstone dressings, thought to have been quarried at Carsaig in Mull. More striking is the horizontal zoning achieved by through courses of pinnings between each main course of blocks. On architectural grounds it can be dated to the early thirteenth century, which conveniently suits the limited documentary evidence.[13]

The same effect of horizontality with courses of pinnings is achieved in the nave of Killean Parish Church in Kintyre, thought to date to the twelfth century.[14] Here the pinnings of red sandstone provide a good contrast with the rest of the stone. Similar quality stonework is found in Kintyre in Saddell Abbey, in Knapdale in the parish church of Keills and the chapel at Kilmory Knap, on Islay in the parish church of Kildalton

Figure 6.2
Skipness Castle, Argyll:
view from north-west.
RCAHMS, AG/502

LORDSHIP AND
ARCHITECTURE
IN MEDIEVAL
AND
RENAISSANCE
SCOTLAND

❧

and the chapel on Nave Island, and outwith the Lordship at Dunstaffnage Chapel in Lorn, all dateable to the late twelfth or early thirteenth century on the basis of architectural mouldings. These buildings use sandstone for dressings and quoins, but only sparingly at Keills, and not at all at the chapel on Nave Island. Other buildings with similar masonry may date to the same time, like the church at Kilnaughton on Islay and parts of Dunivaig Castle, including the stretch of wall with the sea-gate and substantial portions of the hall house. At Aignish Church in Lewis some stonework of this type is built over type 1 masonry.

(3) *Coursed boulders and blocks with panels of pinnings.* Masonry of this type may be a variant of type 2. Here blocks and split boulders are laid with gaps, filled up with copious quantities of pinnings, often forming panels little smaller than the main blocks themselves. The work varies greatly in quality or regularity, and unlike the best of type 2 masonry,

*Figure 6.3
Dunstaffnage Chapel,
Argyll: exterior of
south wall, 1972.
RCAHMS, AG/4536*

was probably not done for its decorative effect. Nevertheless, where the pinnings are made of fissile rock, for example slates and phyllites, and the panels are regularly placed, the work has an attractive appearance, not unlike galleting. Sometimes through courses of pinnings are evident, as in the refectory at Iona Nunnery, where there may have been a conscious attempt to mimic the earlier type 1 masonry. RCAHMS suggest a late fifteenth-century date for the refectory.[15]

Type 3 masonry is ubiquitous in the northern area of the Lordship, from the Mull group of islands to Lewis and Skye, and elsewhere in the West Highlands. The main work at Iona Abbey from the early thirteenth to the fifteenth century is of this type. It is also to be found in several castles of the period, including the hall houses at Aros and Ardtornish on either side of the Sound of Mull, Kisimul on Barra, Breachacha on Coll and work in the bottom part of the tower house of Moy on Mull.

(4) Compact blocks and boulders. The stone used in this work often tends to be of no great size and more rounded or square in shape than the typical long blocks of type 1 masonry. In the best work care has been taken to get as tight a fit as possible between different stones without resorting to pinnings or excessive use of mortar. Regular courses are more apparent in some work than others. In some places, remains of early or original harling can be traced, for instance at Orsay Chapel and Moy Castle.

A good example of type 4 work is to be found in the round tower containing latrines, on the west wing of Castle Sween, work dated by RCAHMS to *c.* 1300.[16] It is also to be seen on the south, or seaward side of Dunivaig Castle on Islay where it underpins masonry of type 2 in the hall house, implying a date in the thirteenth century or earlier. It is also the type of stonework to be seen in the fragmentary curtain and towers of King Robert I's castle at Tarbert.

On the other hand, much masonry of this type is clearly of later date, for instance in the chapels at Finlaggan and on the island of Orsay, said to have been built by John I, Lord of the Isles (see above), and late fourteenth- and fifteenth-century work at Oronsay Priory. The work at Castle Sween and Dunivaig appears particularly neat compared with much of the rest but we hesitate to press this as a chronological marker. Some structures with this type of masonry show absolutely no use of freestone for dressings or quoins. Such is the case at the chapel on Orsay.

DRESSINGS AND QUOINS

The diverse geology of the area of the Lordship provides only limited quantities of freestone suitable for carving dressings and quoins. Permian

LORDSHIP AND
ARCHITECTURE
IN MEDIEVAL
AND
RENAISSANCE
SCOTLAND

ત્ર

sandstones can be found in North Kintyre, and also across the water in Arran. Upper Old Red sediments occur in the southern portion of Kintyre, while Lower Old Red sediments are known in an area stretching from the Antrim coast at Cushendall to the south-east tip of Kintyre, between Carskey Bay and the southern approaches to Campbeltown Loch. The arc continues south to Sanda Island and then eastward to Arran. Sandstones of Permo-Triassic age form isolated outcrops on Mull, Ardnamurchan, Rum and Skye.

There is no evidence for the quarrying of these rocks in the medieval period other than their presence in the monuments and, so far, no concerted attempt has been made to match carved stones with quarries. Published identifications are generally tentative and dependent on examination using the naked eye or an eyeglass rather than thin sections or chemical analyses. There is thus much vagueness.

Two points, however, are clear. First, sandstone was transported over relatively long distances by sea for some building projects. Second, there is a clear divide in the distribution of the sandstone dressings in the buildings of the Lordship. In Kintyre and the Islay group of islands they are all ascribed an origin in Arran, Kintyre or Ulster, while in the Mull group of islands, Ardnamurchan and Morvern, the sources all appear to be quarries at Carsaig in the Ross of Mull, and Inninmore, Ardtornish and nearby Lochaline in Morvern.

In Kintyre it is not surprising to find buildings like Killean parish church, the chapel at Southend and Dunaverty Castle making use of local outcrops of sandstone. It is understandable that Saddell Abbey, the chapel at Kilbrannan and the adjacent Skipness Castle should all make use of sandstones thought to be from Arran, only a few miles across the water. It is less easy to believe that quarries on Arran were the source of the sandstones utilised at Oronsay Priory, Claig Castle by Jura, and Finlaggan, Kildalton Parish Church and Dunivaig Castle in Islay. Their shipment would have involved a long circuitous route round the Mull of Kintyre. Surely it would have been easier to bring it from Ireland or MacDonald lands in Kintyre?

Sandstones from Lochaline, Ardtornish and Inninmore have a reasonably limited distribution at buildings along the Sound of Mull and on Lochs Linnhe and Etive. The furthest afield they have been identified is outside the Lordship at Ardchattan Priory in Lorn. Sandstone from some twenty buildings around Mull, Coll, Tiree, Ardnamurchan, Morvern, Lismore, the Garvellachs and Lorn has been ascribed to the quarries at Carsaig. This sandstone has also been identified at Rodil Church on Harris. It tends to be fine-grained, greenish-yellow in colour, and does not wear well. Carsaig belonged to Iona Abbey and was only a short distance away

Figure 6.4
Ardtornish Castle,
Argyll: from south.
RCAHMS, AG/7212

by sea. It is not surprising to find it there in all the major medieval building projects.

Whatever its source, sandstone was used only sparingly, if at all, in many monuments, and there is evidence of its re-use, for example in the great hall at Finlaggan (see below) and in MacMillan's Tower, a late fifteenth-century addition at Castle Sween in Knapdale. It is possible that there was no new sandstone used in the Islay group of islands after the mid-fourteenth century, whereas it is clear that Carsaig stone, on the basis of work at Iona, was being won throughout the fifteenth century, and into the sixteenth century for Rodil Church.

Where sandstone was not used for dressings and quoins, the plentiful range of metamorphic and igneous rocks of the region was used, rough-dressed for the purpose. One group of these rocks is of particular interest, the metabasites and chloritic schists (previously called epidiorites and green schists) of Dalriadan origin, extending in a large band embracing Loch Awe and Loch Sween, south-westwards to take in parts of Jura, Islay and Gigha.[17] Rocks of this type were used for the quoins in MacMillan's Tower, of type 4 masonry, at Castle Sween, and in the remodelling of the hall house (in the fifteenth or sixteenth century?) at Dunivaig. They were also used for sills and lintels elsewhere, well away from their source, for example the door sill (fourteenth century?) of the great hall at Finlaggan, and the cloister arcade of *c.*1500 at Oronsay Priory.

Impressive expertise was acquired by local sculptors in carving this material – which surely did not all come from the one identified quarry at Doide on Loch Sween[18] - into graveslabs and commemorative crosses from the fourteenth to the sixteenth century. Did this industry develop from skills learned in using the rock in buildings, or did the builders learn from the sculptors?

LORDSHIP AND
ARCHITECTURE
IN MEDIEVAL
AND
RENAISSANCE
SCOTLAND

❧

ROOF SLATES

The ruin of every medieval structure in the region along with the lack of archaeological excavation may mean that the extent to which buildings were roofed with slate has been underestimated. With the information currently available we can only identify medieval slate roofs at Iona and Finlaggan.

Some of the slates at Finlaggan are local phyllites, others are from the Easdale slate belt, which extends south-westwards from the coast of Lorn through the 'slate islands' down the length of Jura. A third type, a slightly metamorphosed siltstone, or very fine-grained sandstone, has not yet been sourced, and certainly does not appear to be from Islay. It was the main roofing material for the great hall, perhaps from the fourteenth century. The Easdale type slate was used at the same time, while the evidence from the excavations suggests that the local phyllites may have been used for roofing at an even earlier date. Iona Abbey, and the nunnery, were covered with slabs derived from the Moine schists of the Ross of Mull.[19]

CONCLUSION

Our limited architectural and geological studies to date suggest there were two main schools of architecture under the Lords of the Isles, operating in different geographical regions. From Mull northwards building work of the fourteenth and fifteenth centuries is characterised by type 3 random rubble and the use of sandstone from Carsaig and quarries on the Sound of Mull for dressings and quoins. Type 4 masonry seems much more limited, occurring in the upper parts of the tower house at Moy on Mull and, also in the fifteenth century, at Glensanda Castle overlooking Loch Linnhe.

In Islay, Kintyre and Knapdale, building work of the period is predominantly in type 4 masonry. No type 3 masonry has been identified here. There is limited use of sandstone, except in Kintyre where there were local quarries, and such sandstone as there is may largely be re-used material from earlier structures. The exception is Oronsay Priory with considerable quantities of sandstone from an unidentified source in Arran, Kintyre or Ulster. Local builders showed themselves adept in rough-dressing metamorphic and igneous rocks for quoins, lintels, sills and jambs.

MEDIEVAL RESIDENCES

The buildings we have to deal with include castles and the residences of the upper strata of society. In the case of the secular structures it has been the most impressive elements, the hall houses, tower houses and enclosure castles which have hitherto attracted almost all the attention. It is worth bearing in mind that such terminology is essentially modern and may not have served well to distinguish the different dwelling types. In most cases, except at the very bottom of the social scale, residences were not single buildings but a complex of structures.

We propose here that secular residences normally consisted of an enclosure or plot of ground containing one or more buildings. 'Castle' is the preferred term, backed up by contemporary documentation, for the places more obviously provided with walls and defences to keep out hostile human forces. The dividing line between such castles and the rest, variously described in the past as fortified dwellings, crannogs (artificial islands), houses, and so on, must always remain inexact. Perhaps, as we attempt below, it would be more useful to analyse medieval house-types and their grouping within these residences rather than just note them for their most striking architectural features. But first some comments on enclosures.

ENCLOSURES

A house enclosure or plot might be defined by a battlemented stone wall or a turf dyke, by the limits of an island or summit of a rock. In the most striking Lordship castles like Castle Sween, Skipness, Mingary and Castle Tioram the enclosure takes the form of a thick, high wall, taking in a relatively small area. In all of these cases the wall acts as a support for buildings ranged around its interior.

In other castles the enclosing stone wall is less substantial but encompasses a relatively greater area with free-standing buildings. Hall houses and tower houses always appear to be positioned on the edge of such an enclosure rather than inside. This is, for example, the case with the hall house at Aros where there is reason to think, on the basis of differences in stonework, that the hall-house is a later addition. It is also the arrangement at Breachacha on Coll and Kisimul on Barra where it is believed that the enclosures are contemporary with the towers.

At Eilean Mor, Finlaggan, the enclosure around the whole island took the form of a timber palisade with a wooden walkway behind it. Erected sometime in the late thirteenth or fourteenth century, it had gone out of use before the end of the fourteenth century.[20] This work has only been discovered through excavation and it is possible that others remain to be detected at other Lordship residences.

LORDSHIP AND
ARCHITECTURE
IN MEDIEVAL
AND
RENAISSANCE
SCOTLAND

꒰꒱

The following is an attempt to identify the main types of buildings that make up medieval residences, placing particular emphasis on those deemed to be for living in.

(1) Simple dwelling houses and halls. These buildings are simple in plan form and relatively small. There appear to be considerable differences in the materials and methods of construction.

Firstly there are those which are rectangular with rounded corners, suggesting that they had hipped roofs. Often they have two opposed doorways towards one end of their long sides. None has walls surviving to a height of more than a metre, or any evidence of windows, but it is probable that the walls were load-bearing, supporting roof timbers from the wall heads or cruck slots in the wall thickness. RCAHMS in its descriptions has often assumed that the walls are of drystone construction but excavation experience gained at Finlaggan suggests that some could have had clay or mortar bonding. They vary in length from 6 to 10m and have a width of from 3.5 to 5.5m.

Three buildings of the type have been excavated at Finlaggan, two manifestly of later date than the forfeiture of the Lords of the Isles in 1494, but nevertheless included here for their apparent relevance to earlier structures. On Eilean na Comhairle (the Council Island), building (a) was 10.8 by 6.7m with rounded corners and walls from about 1.3 to 1.5m thick. The apparent cross-wall planned by RCAHMS [21] turned out to be a low bank of redeposited soil created by nineteenth-century landscaping of the island and removal of tumble. Only a little of the internal and external wall faces survived, showing the use of rough dressed blocks and split boulders, but not enough to categorise the masonry. The wall core consisted of smallish pieces of rubble. A gravelly soil within the building may have resulted from the disintegration of poor-quality lime mortar after the collapse of the walls, although none was observed *in situ*. The floor was of earth with a hearth positioned in the middle between the two entrances. Samples from this were taken for archaeomagnetic dating by GeoQuest Associates and gave date ranges of either AD 1230–1310 or AD 1420–1475. On stratigraphical grounds it is certain that the latter range is to be preferred.

The two other buildings at Finlaggan are on the main island, Eilean Mor. Building B was 7.6 by 5.5m overall with walls about a metre wide standing to a height of over half a metre. In plan it is rather like a barrel, with opposed entrances in its long sides and a hearth on the earth floor near one end of the interior. The walls are of coursed blocks and boulders of local stone with an average size of 380 × 470 × 230mm (type 4 masonry?). Limestone rubble formed the majority of the wall core and the stonework was bonded with poor-quality lime mortar. Much or all of it was evidently re-used, including some with plastered faces and pieces of carved freestone. The doorway through the west wall was a simple opening 0.58m wide, its jambs, and probably lintel, lying in the rubble inside it, all being of undressed local stone. The building partially overlies the dismantled remains of the great hall, thought to have been taken down in the 1490s, and may date to soon afterwards in the sixteenth century.

The third hall building of this type excavated at Finlaggan is building K, also on Eilean Mor. It was rectangular with rounded corners, with overall dimensions of 11.9 by 7m, and walls about 1.5m thick composed of a mixture of boulders and cut blocks of local stone types laid in courses. There was no evidence of any sort of mortar and the walls were apparently of drystone construction. They survive to a maximum height of three courses, about half a metre above the internal floor surface. Two entrances were identified, one in the long north wall 0.8m wide and another in the south wall, 1m wide, but not exactly opposite each other. Its floor was of earth and it is assumed that there would have been an open hearth in the unexcavated area in the western portion of the interior. The remains of a barrel padlock were found under the collapsed stonework in the north entrance and nearby were several nails, staples and at least one piece of a hinge strap, probably all from a wooden door. Dating evidence is limited but there is one base sherd of earthenware (SF 2047) with bright green glaze on its exterior and mottled brown and yellow glaze inside which can be assigned a sixteenth-century date.

Excavation of another medieval building of the type (building II) has been undertaken on an island in Loch Glashan near Lochgilphead in Knapdale.[22] Other structures of comparable size and shape can be traced as surface remains on other sites in the area of the Lordship, for example building C on an island in Loch Corr, Islay, and building D on the island settlement in Loch Ballygrant, Islay, which in the 1540s was in the possession of the MacLeans of Duart.[23] There is another on Dùn Ban, Ulva,[24] presumably a stronghold of the MacQuarries. Compare also the house on Eilean da Ghallagain at the head of West Loch Tarbert, some 12.8 by 6.8m over walls up to 1.5m thick. It has two doorways, one each in its long sides. John, Lord of the Isles, granted a charter to Paisley Abbey at this place in 1455.[25] All the buildings so far mentioned have two entrances but this may not necessarily be a defining characteristic. More excavation may prove otherwise.

Our second sub-type of halls and dwelling houses had turf, earth and/or wooden walls, and tend to be ovoid or barrel-shaped in plan. The walls

LORDSHIP AND
ARCHITECTURE
IN MEDIEVAL
AND
RENAISSANCE
SCOTLAND

❧

in these houses were presumably not load-bearing, the roofs being supported on couples. Again we turn to Finlaggan for excavated examples. The best preserved was building 12.2, supposed to be of fifteenth-century date, a relatively small house, about 8m long with a maximum width of 3.6m, represented by stone packing for a timber superstructure, set in the crest of low banks representing the remains of earlier houses. At the external corners were stone pads interpreted as the bases for roof couples. The entrance was in the middle of one side. The earlier houses (12.3, 12.4) underlying building 12.2 had central hearths set in earth floors, but there was no obvious floor to go with 12.2, leading us to the cautious suggestion that it had had a sprung timber floor.

This certainly seems to have been the case in a larger structure (V) at Finlaggan which left beam slots and corner pads for roof couples set on substantially surviving earth banks revetted in the interior by drystone walling to a height of 0.7m. The overall size of this house was about 11 by 8m and its entrance was in the middle of one of the end walls. Its destruction is dated by a type 6 groat of James III, minted about 1485.

Houses with sprung timber floors, not dissimilar to building V, can be found in Late Viking towns in Ireland – Waterford, Limerick and Dublin – and elsewhere in Europe.[26] The small size of building 12.2 and its position adjacent to the kitchens may suggest an alternative functional explanation as a foodstore. Houses like 12.2 and V at Finlaggan would be very difficult to identify elsewhere from surface remains alone, but a not dissimilar house (building A), apparently of medieval date, has been excavated at MacEwan's Castle in Cowal.[27]

Other supposed medieval dwelling houses or halls have a more distinctly rectangular layout with properly formed corners, perhaps indicating they had gabled roofs. These are our third sub-group. An example of the type, building P, was excavated on Eilean Mor at Finlaggan. It was 11.5 by 6.8m over walls about 0.7m in thickness with masonry of rubble laid in lime mortar (type 4?). It probably had one entrance in one of its long sides, and an earth floor. A vertical slot, 260mm wide, was encountered midway along the internal face of its south wall. This is to be interpreted as a slot for one of the crucks holding up the roof. Roof slates (imported metamorphosed siltstone) were recovered from deposits within the building and on the adjacent shore, indicating how the building was roofed. A sherd (SF 5030) of Scottish late-medieval pottery (fourteenth- or fifteenth-century) from a mortar wash in the top of the foundation trench of one of the walls is evidence that building P belongs to the period of the Lordship of the Isles.

Another rectangular hall building in the castle on an island in Loch Gorm, Islay, has drystone walls standing to a maximum height of 1.8m

Domestic
Architecture
in the Lordship
of the Isles

because they have been buried in an earthwork fortification of 1615. It is possible that the building is somewhat earlier. Internally it measures 7.5 by 4m with one doorway in one of its long sides and no evidence for a fireplace. There are cruck-slots in the two long walls.[28]

Finally, we should consider in this sub-group halls, as at the MacLean castle at Breachacha on Coll, and Kisimul, the castle of Macneil of Barra, which are built against the interior of curtain walls. Both were originally one storey high and of no great size.

Our fourth sub-type contains some very large and impressive halls, deserving the adjective 'great'. The only partially excavated example is building A on Eilean Mor at Finlaggan, a rectangular structure, 18.6 by 8.8m with walls about 1m thick, now standing at most to a height of 0.7m. Its walls were built of long, low blocks of local stones, well dressed to give smooth wall surfaces, set in courses with lime mortar and sparse use of small stones for pinnings. This is type 1 masonry, suggesting a date in the twelfth or thirteenth century. Its internal wall surfaces were coated in plaster.

It was almost totally dismantled or demolished, we believe in the 1490s.[29] Before that it had been substantially remodelled. Its slate roof, and possibly even its sprung timber floor, were features of the original design, but not the large fireplace spanning the west end wall and the screen wall, with string courses of slates, separating off a service area at the other. This screen wall is of type 2 construction and we might therefore assign it a date no later than the early fourteenth century. We might reasonably predict that the service area would have had its own door in the north wall, adjacent to the kitchens. It certainly had two doorways giving access to the hall. The main entrance into the hall was in the south long wall and it was framed with moulded sandstone jambs. These had obviously been reset, perhaps being re-used from an earlier door in another position. The mouldings, with a recessed shallow curve and a narrow hollow moulding, are difficult to date or parallel elsewhere. A sandstone corbel in the form of a human head, recovered from the adjacent but later building B, may originally have come from the hall. It is not unlike fourteenth-century work at the cathedral on Lismore.[30] Building B also produced a fragment of red sandstone carved with a band of nailhead decoration.

Large quantities of broken slates were found in and around the remains of the hall, showing that at the time of its demolition it was roofed mostly with imported metamorphosed siltstone slates along with a white sandstone roof-ridge. Some of the slates were from the Easdale slate belt and it was slate of this type that was used as pinnings in the hall screen wall. They may represent the original roofing of the building.

A rectangular recess, supposed to be the base of a latrine chute, was

LORDSHIP AND
ARCHITECTURE
IN MEDIEVAL
AND
RENAISSANCE
SCOTLAND

⁂

discovered in the south wall of the hall near the south-east corner. If this identification is correct, it implies there was an upper chamber over the service area.

This arrangement is to be found in the Bishop's House on Iona.[31] It measures about 14 by 7m over walls 0.6 to 0.8m thick, now all reduced to grass-covered foundations except for the partition wall, standing to a height of 3.7m. On the evidence of this the structure has walls of uncoursed boulders and blocks with pinnings and lime mortar. It is fortunate that there are two documentary sources to amplify the information ascertainable from ruins. They are a description of the building, then in ruins, by Sacheverell in 1688, and the illustration of Iona in Pennant's *Tour in Scotland*, showing it complete but for its roof.[32] The larger western chamber was the hall proper, open to the roof and containing a fireplace with a chimney in the west gable. The smaller eastern chamber, described as the buttery, was entered by a door in the cross-wall and there was an upper chamber here in the roof, possibly reached by a ladder and lit by a window in the east gable. RCAHMS suppose the Bishop's House dates to the 1630s.

It is an intriguing possibility that its design depends on a local tradition extending back into the medieval period to the great hall at Finlaggan. Even archaeological excavation may fail to identify if other halls are closely comparable since only their foundations remain. A possible candidate is the hall in Dùn Ara Castle, Mull, supposed to be a house of the MacKinnons.[33] The building has rounded corners and opposed entrances in its long walls, but the masonry is held together with lime mortar. The partition wall dividing off the service area is not bonded into the exterior walls and may be secondary. Its overall size is 15 by 8.5m.

Perhaps, too, the remains of a similar, but very large, hall may be incorporated in the ruins of Strome Castle in Wester Ross. The earliest reference to a stronghold here is in 1472 when Celestine of the Isles, Lord of Lochalsh, gave the office of constable of the castle to the Captain of Clan Cameron, but we may surmise that there was a castle here before the late fifteenth century. At present it appears to consist of the ruins of a very large hall, which in the past has been identified as a courtyard, on top of a steep-sided knoll, with a tower house, blown up in 1602, tacked on to one end. The tower house was evidently a work of the sixteenth century but the hall, some of the walling of which stands to a considerable height, is a multi-phase structure, some of which must date to the medieval period.

The interpretation offered here is that the original hall, with an overall width of about 13.5m, extended right to the end of the platform at the west end of the castle, albeit narrowing in breadth to accommodate itself

*Domestic
Architecture
in the Lordship
of the Isles*

on the top of the rock. The present west wall, evidently of later build than the north and south walls, has one large entrance and may originally have been a screen wall as in the hall at Finlaggan and the Bishop's House on Iona. The position of a latrine chute at the north-west corner of the site also bears comparison with the Finlaggan hall.

Whereas the north and south walls are characterised by the use of long, rectangular rough-dressed blocks (type 1 masonry), the cross-wall is of type 4 stonework. The doorway, with its arch-pointed opening with rough dressed voussoirs, is reminiscent of the doorway at the chapel on Orsay, said to be a work of John I, Lord of the Isles, in the fourteenth century.

The east end wall of the original hall may have lain just beyond the entrance door in the north wall, giving a possible overall length in the region of 28m. This would have excluded the well discovered in recent excavations and the north and south walls to the east of the entrance which look different in character. This hall, on the evidence of surviving joist holes, had a sprung timber floor, but with a width of 11m surely supported midway in some way.

The one other large hall is very fragmentary, only part of one, ivy-clad, wall standing to any height. It is at Castle Camus on Skye, originally a MacLeod residence which passed into MacDonald hands, possibly in 1463. It has walls of type 1 masonry, 1.5m thick, enclosing a rectangular space 7 by 18m with no evidence of partition walls. There is a latrine chute near one corner.[34]

(2) Hall Houses and First-Floor Halls. The distinction between these two types of buildings is not easy to define. Hall houses, probably wrongly, have been seen as stand-alone structures, strong houses, complete residences for high-status families, whereas first-floor halls have been seen as an element in a suite of buildings in major residences or strongholds. Our review will concentrate on the similarities rather than the supposed differences.

One of the largest and best-preserved hall houses in the Lordship is at Aros in Mull. Aros was a residence of the Lords of the Isles but there is no documentary evidence for when it was built, or by whom. RCAHMS suggest that it was erected in the thirteenth century for the MacDougalls but are unable to substantiate this by any analysis of its architectural features.[35] Its masonry is of type 3 and so does not provide any helpful clue. In so far as the hall house at Ardtornish is thought to have been constructed by the MacDonalds of Islay and is within easy reach of Aros, this might seem to lessen any requirement for the MacDonalds to have built the Aros one.[36]

Aros measures 25.3 by 12.5m externally, excluding a small jamb at its

LORDSHIP AND
ARCHITECTURE
IN MEDIEVAL
AND
RENAISSANCE
SCOTLAND

⁂

north end containing latrines. The ground floor was probably given over to two storage chambers while the first had the hall itself, rising, it may be assumed, to an open timber roof. There is now no trace of an entrance, but it is likely it was in the south wall, reached by steps from the courtyard. RCAHMS suppose that there was a solar (private withdrawing room) at the north end adjacent to the latrine-tower,[37] although there might as well have been a service area or buttery as reported for the Bishop's House on Iona. On the basis of surviving joist holes there was another chamber in a third storey in the north end of the building, and there is also evidence for a parapet walk. Of internal stairs there are no traces in the walls, and all the upper floors were of timber.

A second hall house of the Lords of the Isles is at Ardtornish on the coast of Morvern, within sight of Aros. The walling which survives is essentially of the ground storey only, indicating it was a building 17.2 by 8.8m in overall size, as Aros with a small jamb or buttress projecting at one end, interpreted as for latrines. The entrance was in the opposite end wall with a flight of steps in the wall thickness giving access to the hall above. There is no evidence of vaulting. A date in the second half of the thirteenth century is suggested by RCAHMS for its construction, at which time Morvern is thought to have been a MacDonald possession.[38] There is no recorded history for a castle at Ardtornish prior to 1380, the year in which John, 1st Lord of the Isles, is said to have died there.[39]

A fragmentary hall house, a residence of the MacDonalds of Islay, may be traced in the castle of Dunivaig on Islay. It is a composite structure ascribed by RCAHMS to the sixteenth century,[40] but on the basis of its type 4 stonework, superseded by type 2, dated by us to the thirteenth century. It is described by RCAHMS as a hall building rather than a hall house. It is a rectangular structure about 13.5 by 10m overall, set upon the summit of a precipitous rock by the sea's edge. There is evidence for only two storeys, both with timber-joisted floors. In its final form the ground floor may have contained a kitchen while the first floor had the hall itself, with a fireplace in its long south wall. Entrance to the building was gained from the west through one or other, or both, storeys.

The ruinous castle at Borve on the island of Benbecula has type 4 masonry and is said to have been erected for Amie MacRuari, the first wife of John, 1st Lord of the Isles, at some time in the latter part of the fourteenth century.[41] Although it had at least three storeys, it is interpreted here as a hall house rather than a tower house because of its overall dimensions and because it may be supposed to have had a large hall covering its second floor above two tiers of storage. In this respect it has been compared to Dundonald Castle.[42] It had an overall length of 18.9m and was over 11m wide. The structure was unvaulted, the joists for the

Figure 6.5
Aros Castle, Argyll:
view from south-east.
RCAHMS, AG/8133

upper two floors being supported on set-offs formed by the successive thinning of the walls. The entrance was at first-floor level in the middle of the long south wall. The stair up to it was enclosed in a secondary porch.

Skipness Castle, as remodelled in type 1 masonry in the late thirteenth century, had a first-floor hall, measuring about 15.2 by 6.1m internally. It was well lit, and had a latrine contained in the thickness of the wall at its west end. Otherwise details of its plan are now largely obscure.

A freestanding first-floor hall of type 4 stonework survives, re-roofed in recent times, at the priory on Oronsay, founded by John, 1st Lord of the Isles, in the second quarter of the fourteenth century. It has been identified as work of *c.* 1325–53 and is now known as the Prior's House.[43] First-floor halls were probably contained in other Lordship castles, built against the interior of their curtain walls. There is evidence for one in Mingary Castle on the south coast of Ardnamurchan.[44]

(3) Tower houses. Generally speaking, we would expect tower houses to have a more compact ground-plan than hall houses, a greater height-to-length ratio, and to give more prominence to accommodation in storeys above the hall. There is the curious situation with Glensanda Castle in Morvern that, although consisting only of a hall above an unvaulted cellar, it is counted a tower house rather than a hall house, presumably because it is reckoned to date to the fifteenth century, whereas hall houses are

LORDSHIP AND
ARCHITECTURE
IN MEDIEVAL
AND
RENAISSANCE
SCOTLAND

❧

often now dated to the thirteenth century or earlier.[45] Another at Castle Sween, with only a hall above ground-floor kitchens, is named MacMillan's Tower for one of its keepers, suggesting a date in the 1470s not inconsistent with its type 4 masonry.

Tower houses are very much a feature of the Scottish Lowland landscape but are relatively uncommon in the area of the Lordship of the Isles. Presumably it was a Lord of the Isles who erected Claig Castle in the Sound of Islay, and possibly MacMillan's Tower at Castle Sween. Others were built by the MacLeans, at Duart and Moy on Mull, Breachacha on Coll, and Kinlochaline and Glensanda in Morvern. The MacLeods had one at Dunvegan in Skye, the Macneils one at Kisimul in Barra. The tower house in Castle Tioram, possibly of fifteenth-century date, belonged to the MacDonalds of Clanranald, and Castle Maol on Skye to the MacKinnons.

As originally built, most of these tower houses were characterised by relatively simple plans, no vaulting, no turnpike stairs and no fireplaces. They had storage space on the ground floor, a hall at first-floor level, and one or more storeys above with private accommodation. The largest, built by the MacLeans at Duart on Mull, is L-plan, measuring 19.9 by 14m, the smallest Dùn Mhic Leoid (Castle Sinclair) in Barra, only about 5.5m square. They were strong houses rather than sophisticated fighting bases. They were, however, topped by battlements, and some, like Castle Uisdein and Dunvegan, both on Skye, were entered only at first-floor level.

The most complex in plan is Moy Castle on Mull, the residence of the MacLaines of Lochbuie. It is vaulted at ground- and first-floor level, has an original turnpike stair to give access to the upper floors, and has walls hollowed out with mural chambers. The vaulting of one contrived in the haunches of the lower vault rises above the floor level of the hall above, creating a raised step over almost a third of the floor area of the hall. This surely stems from the builders' inexperience with structures of such complexity or is the result of a change of plan after building had commenced. The latter explanation seems to be favoured by a difference in the tower's stonework from type 3 to type 4. Even Moy originally had no mural fireplaces; instead there were vents in the side walls for dispersing smoke from a central hearth or brazier in the hall.

The tower house in Castle Tioram, which badly needs more study, does have a vaulted ground floor, a turnpike stair as the main access from the first-floor hall to the storeys above, and a mural fireplace in the hall. The vaulting retains traces of wickerwork centring, an Irish type of construction, also found in the MacDougall tower house at Dunollie in Lorn. Irish builders may have been responsible for both, but we have to turn to the mainland castles of the Campbells, Kilchurn on Loch Awe, and the long-destroyed medieval castle at Inveraray on Loch Fyne, for likely work by Lowland Scottish builders before the end of the fifteenth century.

6. Other buildings. There is only space here for passing mention of other domestic structures. At Finlaggan the medieval kitchens were adjacent to the great hall, and contained small, free-standing ovens. Kitchens are also in evidence at Breachacha and Castle Sween. We have already mentioned building 12.2 at Finlaggan which may have been for storing food, and other stores and barns must have been a basic requirement of any residence of any permanence or size. At Castle Sween recent excavations have uncovered the remains of a smiddy.

TYPES OF RESIDENCE

It now remains to review the ways in which the different buildings were combined in Lordship residences, paying particular attention to the most prominent on each site.

In those castles with hall houses and tower houses there is no doubting that these structures are the most visible, and we may suppose that part of their function was to suggest the high status of their owners. In very few cases do they appear to have stood alone as self-sufficient houses. Moy Castle has no obvious traces of other buildings next to it, and it may be of significance that it is the most structurally complex of the Lordship towers with four main storeys and mural chambers.

The hall houses can only be interpreted as buildings which combined the classic medieval function of the hall with a certain amount of storage and physical security provided by high thick walls. The main task such a hall had to fulfil was the accommodation of a large household and guests, for food and entertainment, and for many, sleeping accommodation as well. The halls at other castles provided the same basic facility, and in the case of Eilean Mor, Finlaggan, we might speculate that there was no question of constructing anything but a ground-floor hall when there was a keep or castle on the neighbouring island.

The first-floor hall, hall house or tower house might have been the most prominent structure in the castles in which they occur, but they did not necessarily contain the residence of the chief man, not even in the remodelled great hall at Finlaggan and the hall house at Aros where there were probably private chambers or solars. At these places, as at many others – for instance Ardtornish, Glensanda and Dunivaig – it is possible to trace the foundations of other houses which may have been more modest halls for the private use of the owner and his family, or else a keeper.

117

LORDSHIP AND
ARCHITECTURE
IN MEDIEVAL
AND
RENAISSANCE
SCOTLAND

୬୯

Hall houses have only been identified at castles which were at least at some time residences of the Lords of the Isles – Ardtornish, Aros, Borve and Dunivaig. All would have looked impressive, perhaps relatively unencumbered by encompassing enclosure walls. As for the great halls at Strome and Camus, their early (unknown) history properly relates to the earldom of Ross.

The contrast between the relatively open Finlaggan, Aros and Ardtornish on the one hand, with their large halls for feasting, and on the other the castles of the Lords of the Isles' vassals, like Breachacha, Duart, Dunvegan and Kisimul, with their tower houses rising over courtyard walls, is striking, and may reflect an underlying reality in the Lordship. The vassals like the MacLeans, MacLeods and Macneils could not aspire to large feasting halls and instead erected towers. Vassals of lesser status or wealth made do with smaller ground-floor halls like the MacQuarries at Dùn Ban and the MacKinnons at Dùn Ara.

Of unique status and design was the lordly residence at Finlaggan, which, as has been argued elsewhere, might be considered a proto-urban centre. It was a meeting place for the Council of the Isles, the site of lordly inauguration ceremonies, and possibly a periodic gathering place for other activities which took place elsewhere in towns, particularly markets. Excavations have demonstrated a complex sequence of occupation on two islands in a freshwater loch extending back beyond the medieval period, and there are hints of other medieval structures around the neighbouring lochside.

The medieval occupation on the two islands may be simplified into two main phases as follows, the first dating approximately from the twelfth to the early fourteenth century, the second from the fourteenth century to the end of the fifteenth.

In phase I we are aware of a keep or castle on the smaller of the two islands, perhaps already connected to the larger one by a causeway. On the main island there was already a graveyard, perhaps now with a chapel, tenuous evidence of which was found in the form of fragments of white sandstone and roof slates made from the local phyllites. The original great hall also dates to this phase, some lesser buildings, and a timberwork defence around the whole island. The main means of access was probably by a causeway to the north tip of the island where there appears to have been an entrance tower. A fragment of a long cross penny (c. 1247–79) was recovered from it.

In phase II three lesser buildings replaced the castle on the Council Island: structure (a), described above (b) a small rectangular building, and (c) a small sub-oval house with opposed entrances. Our preferred interpretation is that (b) is the council chamber – hence the name for the island (a) is the hall of the keeper, and (c) his storehouse.

On Eilean Mor in phase II the timberwork defences were abandoned, leaving the island undefended except by the water. The main access was probably now by boat to a small jetty from which a system of paved roads gave access to all the other buildings. A chapel, possibly a larger replacement for a previous one, was built on the highest point of the island, and there was a commemorative cross nearby. The great hall was remodelled, and had kitchens adjacent to it. There were several other buildings, probably including dwellings, storehouses and workshops. The end of the island adjacent to the Council Island was partitioned off with a wall and had a another hall which may have been the private residence of the Lords.

Dean Monro wrote in 1549 that the Lords had Eilean Mor 'well biggit in palace-wark according to thair auld fassoun'.[46] Monro does not elaborate what this 'auld fassoun' was, but it is possible he meant the lack of curtain walls, the spread of separate buildings and the prominence of the hall. Perhaps at Finlaggan we are witnessing the architectural expression of real West Highland power. What need did the Lords have of stone and mortar defences when their authority rested on men, including the substantial bodyguard said to have been housed on the edge of the loch?[47]

Monro also describes the Council of the Isles meeting on the Council Island, even though the Lord was hunting, or playing other games. The discovery in the Finlaggan excavations of hunting arrowheads, fish hooks and gaming counters reminds us of this. The recovery of harp pegs, midden deposits containing sherds of wine jugs and butchered animal bones, along with the extensive kitchens, points to the real significance of the great hall in a society which measured the status of its chief men by their generosity in entertaining.

It is no accident that the Lords left the impressive castle of the Comyns at Inverlochy a ruin, that they gave the great island fortresses of their realm in the Treshnish Islands and the Garvellochs into the hands of vassals, and that the recorded events of their lives took place at Finlaggan, Aros and Ardtornish, with their great feasting halls, rather than their high-walled castles at Skipness and Castle Sween.

NOTES

1. Compare D. H. Caldwell and G. Ewart, 'Finlaggan and the Lordship of the Isles: an archaeological approach', *SHR*, lxxii (1993), 146–66.
2. J. G. Dunbar, 'The Medieval Architecture of the Scottish Highlands' in *The Middle Ages in the Highlands*, ed. L. Maclean (Inverness, 1981), 38–70.
3. K. A. Steer and J. W. M. Bannerman for RCAHMS, *Late Medieval Monumental Sculpture in the West Highlands* (Edinburgh, 1977), 106–9, 119–20; RCAHMS, *Argyll*, iv, 107, 235.
4. Dunbar, 'Medieval Architecture of the Highlands', 40–1.
5. There is a thoughtful account of the role of the castles in the Treshnish Islands

LORDSHIP AND
ARCHITECTURE
IN MEDIEVAL
AND
RENAISSANCE
SCOTLAND

and the Garvellachs in N. MacLean-Bristol, *Warriors And Priests. The History of the Clan MacLean 1300–1570* (East Linton, 1995), 23, 26–7.

6. This identification of Dunkerd, mentioned only in a document of 1390, is the one favoured in RCAHMS, *Argyll*, v, 268.

7. *RMS*, ii, no. 2950. We are grateful to John Lewis of Scotia Archaeology for information on recent excavations.

8. *Chron. Fordun*, ii, 39; *Monro's Western Isles of Scotland and Genealogies of the Clans 1549*, ed. R. W. Munro (Edinburgh 1961), 58.

9. W. F. Skene, *Celtic Scotland* (Edinburgh 1880), iii, 402–3.

10. RCAHMS, *Argyll*, iv, no. 12.

11. RCAHMS, *Argyll*, ii, no. 276.

12. RCAHMS, *Argyll*, iii, 193, no. 383.

13. RCAHMS, *Argyll*, iv, no. 5.

14. RCAHMS, *Argyll*, i, no. 287.

15. RCAHMS, *Argyll*, iv, 175.

16. RCAHMS, *Argyll*, vii, no. 119. This account does not actually spell out why the Commission date this tower to this time, but the reasons presumably include the nailhead-ornament on a doorway and the remains of a cross-shaped slit (see p. 256).

17. For a map see Steer and Bannerman, *West Highland Sculpture*, fig. 27.

18. RCAHMS, *Argyll*, vii, no. 236.

19. RCAHMS, *Argyll*, iv, 57.

20. The date for the timberwork's construction depends on the discovery of sherds of Saintonge polychrome pottery of the late thirteenth century in midden material under the rampart in trench 9. Its demise is signalled by sections flattened for the building of later structures including buildings H and P, and probably the chapel.

21. RCAHMS, *Argyll*, v, 276.

22. H Fairhurst, 'A Medieval Island-settlement in Loch Glashan, Argyll', *GAJ*, 1 (1969) 47–67; RCAHMS, *Argyll*, vii, no 146.

23. RCAHMS, *Argyll*, v, nos. 311, 309.

24. RCAHMS, *Argyll*, iii, no. 341.

25. RCAHMS, *Argyll*, vii, no. 141.

26. M. Hurley, 'Waterford in the Late Viking Age' in *The Illustrated Archaeology of Ireland*, ed. M Ryan (Dublin, 1991), 162.

27. D. N. Marshall, 'Excavations at Macewan's Castle, Argyll, in 1968–69', *GAJ*, 10 (1983), 131–42.

28. RCAHMS, *Argyll*, v, no. 406.

29. We cannot date the destruction of the hall itself from the excavations, but it is clear that building V was demolished at this time and there were other considerable changes. This is backed up by coin evidence.

30. RCAHMS, *Argyll*, ii, pls 33A, 34A-C.

31. RCAHMS, *Argyll*, iv, no. 14.

32. W. Sacheverell, *Account of the Isle of Man* (London, 1702), 135; T. Pennant, *A Tour in Scotland And Voyage to the Hebrides MDCCLXXII*, Part 1 (London, 1776), pl. XXI.

33. RCAHMS, *Argyll*, iii, no. 340.

34. Dunbar, 'Medieval Architecture of the Highlands', 49, identifies this work at Camus as a possible hall-house. His plan (fig. F2) differs significantly from that published by R. Miket and D. L. Roberts, *The Mediaeval Castles of Skye & Lochalsh* (Portree, 1990), 29.

35. RCAHMS, *Argyll*, iii, no. 333.

36. Aros does, however, bear such a superficial resemblance to Dundonald Castle in

*Domestic
Architecture
in the Lordship
of the Isles*

Ayrshire, and is almost identical in size, that there is surely cause to wonder if Dundonald is Aros's inspiration. Dundonald was erected in the late fourteenth century for King Robert II, the father-in-law of John I Lord of the Isles. Dundonald is normally described as a tower house but it seems more apt to the present writers to view it as a hall house with a particularly elevated and grand hall, as befitted the king. It was vaulted, unlike Aros, which like most other medieval buildings in the West Highlands relied on timber for floors and ceilings. See below for Borve Castle, also compared to Dundonald, by MacGibbon and Ross.

37. RCAHMS, *Argyll*, iii, 175.

38. RCAHMS, *Argyll*, iii, 173; *Acts of the Lords of the Isles*, xx.

39. Skene, *Celtic Scotland*, iii, 402–3.

40. RCAHMS, *Argyll*, v, no. 403.

41. *Collectanea de Rebus Albanicis* (Iona Club, 1847), 298.

42. MacGibbon and Ross, *Castellated and Domestic Architecture*, iii, 115–17.

43. RCAHMS, *Argyll*, v, no. 386.

44. RCAHMS, *Argyll*, iii, no. 345.

45. RCAHMS, *Argyll*, iii, no. 342; Dunbar, 'Medieval Architecture of the Highlands', 54.

46. *Monro's Western Isles*, 56–7.

47. M Martin, *A Description of the Western Islands of Scotland circa 1695* (Stirling, 1934), 273.

Innis
Chonaill
Castle

Inveraray Castle

Kilmun,
collegiate church

Castle Sween

Eilean Dearg,
castle

N

Castles

Collegiate Church

Land over 100m

Land over 300m

0   30km

Figure 7.1
Campbell properties
mentioned in the text.

Chapter 7

'PILLARS OF THE COMMUNITY': CAMPBELL LORDSHIP AND ARCHITECTURAL PATRONAGE IN THE FIFTEENTH CENTURY[1]

Stephen I. Boardman

Shortly before 19 January 1413, Duncan Campbell succeeded his father as lord of Lochawe and chief of Clan Campbell.[2] Duncan's long chieftainship (1412x1413–1453) was notable, amongst other things, for the initiation of an extensive building programme which saw long-established focal points of Campbell lordship refurbished and new centres for the exercise of secular and spiritual authority founded. Duncan's grandson and successor Colin, 1st Earl of Argyll (chief 1453–93), also invested heavily in the construction, repair or improvement of a number of castles and kirks in both long-held and recently acquired Campbell lordships. To some extent, the building projects of Duncan and Colin simply mark out the territorial and juris-dictional advances made by these fifteenth-century Campbell lords and their fourteenth-century predecessors. They also, however, reveal a great deal about the changing political and social status and ambitions of the chieftains of Clan Campbell in the years before and after 1400.

THE LORDSHIP OF ARGYLL

The origins of the rise of the chiefs of Clan Campbell to a position of regional dominance in late-medieval Argyll are usually sought in the period of dynastic and civil conflict now known as the Wars of Independence. In particular, the close personal and political relationship between Sir Neil Campbell of Lochawe (d. *c.* 1315) and King Robert I is seen to have laid the foundations for a wide-ranging expansion of the kindred's political

LORDSHIP AND
ARCHITECTURE
IN MEDIEVAL
AND
RENAISSANCE
SCOTLAND

❧

and territorial interests from their stronghold in the lordship of Lochawe. Neil and his kinsmen were certainly amongst the most loyal and prominent partisans of the Bruce cause and were handsomely rewarded for their support after Bruce's triumph over his Scottish enemies.[3] Sir Neil married the king's sister Mary and the couple received a grant of the earldom of Atholl which descended to their only son, John. In addition, Neil's brother Donald and his kinsman Sir Arthur Campbell received title to estates forfeited by the MacDougall lords of Argyll in Benderloch and Lorn.[4] Most of these grants, however, produced no lasting extension of Campbell territorial interests. John Campbell, Earl of Atholl, died childless at the battle of Halidon Hill in 1333, while Campbell ambitions in Lorn and Benderloch were restricted by the successful reintegration of the MacDougall lord, John *Gallda* of Lorn, into the aristocratic society of Argyll and the Hebrides during the 1350s.[5]

In areas to the south of Lochawe, however, a different picture emerged. From the early decades of the fourteenth century onward, Campbell power and influence swept south from mid-Argyll into Cowal and the sea lochs of the Firth of Clyde. The dramatic southward advance of Clan Campbell was based firmly on the family's naval capacity and the political patronage of the overlord of Cowal, Robert, Steward of Scotland (the future Robert II) and the Steward's kinsmen, the Menteith lords of Knapdale and Arran. The first significant intervention by the Lochawe Campbells into the politics of Cowal and the Firth of Clyde was in the Steward's service, after he had been ousted from his lordships of Bute, Cowal and Renfrew by agents of Edward Balliol, the English-backed pretender to the Scottish Crown, during 1333.[6] The Steward's counter-attack in 1334 was spearheaded by a Campbell galley force which forced the surrender of Dunoon Castle in Cowal.[7] It may well be that the Steward gave the keepership of the strategically vital fortress of Dunoon to Clan Campbell during 1334, although the evidence for Campbell occupation of the site thereafter is patchy.[8]

The assault on Dunoon heralded a dramatic expansion of the territorial interests of the Lochawe Campbells in the Firth of Clyde during the chieftainship of Gill-easbuig Campbell (*c.* 1342–1382 x 1387). Gill-easbuig's marriage to Isobel Lamont, a member of the most important local kindred in Cowal, confirmed the direction of Campbell policy and enterprise.[9] The spread of Campbell power in the region was aided by a series of resignations and sales of territorial rights in favour of Gill-easbuig during the 1350s, 1360s and 1370s. In particular, Gill-easbuig was the beneficiary of significant grants by Sir John Menteith, lord of Knapdale and Arran, and Mary, Countess of Menteith. In November 1353, for example, Sir John Menteith granted a substantial part of his lordship in Knapdale,

with the keeping of Castle Sween, to Gill-easbuig Campbell.[10] Probably at around the same time, Gill-easbuig received title to lands in Sir John's lordship of Arran, including Lochranza Castle.[11]

The granting of the keeperships of Sween and Lochranza, combined with the possible Campbell constableship of Dunoon, suggests that Gill-easbuig and his family had assumed the role of military agents for Stewart and Menteith lordship in Knapdale, Cowal and the islands of the Firth of Clyde. The strategic strongpoints handed over to Gill-easbuig both reflected and strengthened Campbell naval power, since all were associated with secure harbours from which galley forces could operate with relative impunity. The resignations made by Sir John Menteith seem to have been arranged by Robert the Steward in order to protect Robert's long-term interests in the Menteith estates and lordships. At the time of the grants Stewart/Menteith lordship in Knapdale, Arran and Kintyre was coming under increasing military pressure from John of Islay, Lord of the Isles. Moreover, Sir John Menteith was childless, and the Steward, Menteith's eventual successor as lord of Knapdale and Arran, may well have been keen to establish a politically reliable kindred in Knapdale and Arran before Sir John's death.[12] That Gill-easbuig was indeed active in and around the lordships of the Firth of Clyde which Sir John Menteith had held is suggested by his designation as Gill-easbuig 'of Arran' in a brief genealogy

Figure 7.3
Dunoon Castle,
Argyll: general view
from west.
RCAHMS, A 74270

of Campbell chiefs incorporated in a Gaelic poem of the early sixteenth century.[13]

Campbell aspirations in Arran and Knapdale, however, made little headway after Sir John's demise *c.*1360, and the most enduring territorial gains made by Gill-easbuig were in the Steward's lordship of Cowal. The most important acquisitions were made through a series of resignations by Mary, Countess of Menteith, in favour of the Campbell chief. Mary was the widow of Sir John Graham, Earl of Menteith, who was executed in 1347 following his capture by English forces at the battle of Neville's Cross.[14] Sometime between 1347 and 1361, Mary issued a number of charters by which she gave over all her lands in Cowal held directly from the Steward, including the lands of Kilmun with the patronage of the kirk of St Mun, to Gill-easbuig Campbell.[15] It seems probable that Countess Mary was forced or persuaded into these resignations by the Steward in order to prevent the rights to the Cowal estates passing to any future husband of Mary's daughter and heir, Margaret Graham. Margaret Graham was many times married, but the only spouse who seems to have objected to her effective disinheritance in Cowal was John Drummond, married to Margaret sometime before April 1360.[16] By May 1360 attempts were being made to bring to an end a serious feud between Drummond and a cadet branch of the Menteith family which was being backed by Gill-easbuig Campbell and his son.[17] Drummond's death before September 1361, and Margaret Graham's subsequent marriage to Robert, the third son of the Steward, failed to suppress the potential threat to the Campbell gains in Cowal. John Drummond's marriage to Margaret Graham seems to have produced children whose interests in the Menteith inheritance were upheld by their Drummond kinsmen. The Drummonds had powerful political backing, because by 1362 Sir John Drummond's sister, Margaret, had become the mistress and intended bride of King David II.[18] King David, who viewed the

Steward as his chief domestic political rival, was keen to undermine the position of Robert and his allies in the west and soon made clear his determination to protect Drummond ambitions in the Menteith inheritance.[19] Tensions between Robert and David reached a climax early in 1363 when the Steward and his sons became involved in a full-scale rebellion against the king.[20] The role of Gill-easbuig and his family in the events of 1363 is uncertain, although it seems probable that the Campbells supported the Steward's rebellion and came into the king's peace at the same time as Robert shortly before David's controversial marriage to Margaret Drummond in or around April 1363. The king may well have had to promise concessions in order to secure Gill-easbuig's submission, for in the following month David confirmed the countess of Menteith's resignation of the barony of Kilmun and other lands in favour of the Campbell chief, effectively removing any threat to Campbell interests posed by the family of the new queen.[21]

By the mid-1360s, then, Gill-easbuig had attained territorial and political dominance in mid-Argyll and Cowal. There remained, however, a serious rival to the Campbell chief for the social and political leadership of the provincial aristocracy of Argyll in the shape of John of Lorn. In 1354, on his re-entry into the political life of the Scottish kingdom, John *Gallda* evidently hoped to resurrect his family's pretensions to the title 'lord of Argyll'.[22] John *Gallda*'s claims to regional pre-eminence were based on, and legitimised by, his descent and lineage. John was the head of one of the three great kindreds descended from Somerled which had dominated the lordships of Argyll and the Isles from the twelfth century onward.[23] John's status and authority were undoubtedly bolstered by the standing of his ancestors as illustrious figures in the history and political mythology of Argyll and the Hebrides, but of more immediate significance was the support John received from David II. John's return to Scotland seems to have been engineered, or at least encouraged, by King David, who probably regarded the MacDougall lord as another potential ally in his struggle with Robert the Steward and Steward's confederates in the west, including Gill-easbuig Campbell.[24] In 1357–58 John *Gallda* received the king's assistance in attempts to reclaim the territories and castles which had been held by his great-grandfather, Alexander of Argyll.[25] By 1362 John had married David II's niece and was acknowledged as the king's nephew, while later in the reign he was employed as a royal bailie in the Appin of Dull.[26]

In February 1371, however, the death of David II and the accession of Robert the Steward to the throne (as Robert II) transformed the balance of power in Argyll. King Robert's hostility towards John *Gallda* was based not only on John's political association with David II, but also the position

LORDSHIP AND
ARCHITECTURE
IN MEDIEVAL
AND
RENAISSANCE
SCOTLAND

⅋

of the MacDougall lord, a nephew by marriage of the dead king, as a possible dynastic rival to the Stewart.[27] While Gill-easbuig Campbell attended Robert's coronation in March 1371, John *Gallda* was removed from his royal bailiary in Perthshire and swiftly sank into political obscurity. King Robert's enmity towards the MacDougalls of Lorn and his disapproval of David's restoration of John *Gallda* may well have influenced the hostile depiction of the family in John Barbour's *The Bruce*, written for the Stewart royal court *c.*1375–76.[28] In *The Bruce*, John *Gallda's* grandfather and namesake, John of Lorn, is consistently (and rightly) identified by Barbour as Robert I's most relentless and implacable domestic foe. On at least two occasions Barbour emphasises the fact that John of Lorn was never reconciled to the Bruce king.[29] Barbour's determination to associate John with action against Robert I may well have resulted in the mis-identification of Bruce's enemy at the battle of Dalry (1306) as a 'lord of Lorn' and the entirely mistaken account of Lorn's imprisonment and death at Dumbarton.[30] Barbour's treatment of the MacDougalls would hardly have been appropriate for David II's court, where John *Gallda* was apparently held in high favour.

In any event, John *Gallda* died *c.*1376–77 leaving two daughters who were married off to brothers from a cadet line of the Stewarts.[31] John *Gallda's* illegitimate son, Allan, continued to act as chief of the Mac-Dougalls in Lorn, but the kindred which had once dominated Argyll was effectively reduced to a position of restricted local power and influence inside Lorn under their new Stewart overlords.

By the late 1370s, then, Gill-easbuig Campbell was unquestionably the leading political and territorial magnate inside the ancient province of Argyll. It was natural that Gill-easbuig and his successors should seek to claim the title and status of lord of Argyll. It also seems that Robert II was quite prepared to support, or at any rate acknowledge, the creation of a Campbell overlordship of Argyll. In 1382, the king granted Gill-easbuig and his son Colin an *hereditary* royal lieutenancy with extensive powers and rights which seems to have covered most of Argyll between the lordships of Lorn and Knapdale.[32] The Campbell chiefs now explicitly occupied an intermediate position between the 'barons' of Argyll and the Scottish Crown, and by 1395 Gill-easbuig's son and successor, Colin, was openly using the title 'Dominus de Ergadia'.[33]

As the fourteenth-century lords of Lochawe moved from a position of local to provincial dominance, it was inevitable that they would require new collection, storage and consumption points for the renders of recently acquired lordships, as well as suitable locations for the exercise of justice. The rapid acquisition of territorial interests and rights of lordship in mid-Argyll and Cowal after 1330 naturally affected the pre-eminent position

*Figure 7.4
Kilmun Church,
Argyll: detail of effigy
of Margaret Stewart,
Lady Campbell.
RCAHMS, B 19013*

*Figure 7.5
Kilmun Church,
Argyll: detail of effigy
of Sir Duncan
Campbell.
RCAHMS, B 19008*

of Innis Chonnell (fig. 1), an isolated island-fortress in Lochawe, as the principal stronghold of the family and the place where the Campbell chief conducted the bulk of his business. By 1400, Innis Chonaill lay at the northern edge rather than at the centre of Campbell interests. Despite this, the fortress retained a prominent role as a residence and centre of administration, while the lordship of Lochawe maintained its place as the symbolic ancestral heartland of Campbell power.[34]

Nevertheless, to the south of Lochawe, 'new' Campbell fortresses began to appear in the territories the family had acquired on the sea-lochs of the Firth of Clyde. In many cases, the Campbells seem simply to have refurbished sites formerly associated with Menteith and Stewart lordship. One such was Carrick Castle on the shores of Loch Goil, apparently renovated towards the end of the fourteenth century. Carrick (Fig. 2) would have consolidated the Campbell hold on Over Cowal, and probably served as a local administrative centre for the lands obtained by Gill-easbuig

LORDSHIP AND
ARCHITECTURE
IN MEDIEVAL
AND
RENAISSANCE
SCOTLAND

⅔

and his successors in the area.[35] In addition, Carrick secured the eastern end of one of the overland routes between Loch Fyne and Loch Long across the north of Cowal, and for a while acted as the most convenient point of contact and transit between Campbell lordship in Argyll and the Lennox/Dumbarton region.[36] A similar example is the island-fortress of Eilean Dearg in Loch Riddon, which was in Campbell possession by the 1440s, when Walter Bower could describe it as the 'impregnable castle of the lord of Loch Awe'.[37]

Carrick and Eilean Dearg formed part of an expanding network of fortifications, held by hereditary constables drawn from the cadet branches of the Campbells of Lochawe, which controlled important lines of communication linking and protecting the increasingly widespread territorial interests of the chiefly lineage. Despite their strategic location and the heavy investment in their construction, however, Carrick and Eilean Dearg never became major centres of Campbell lordship.[38]

It was not until the chieftainship of Gill-easbuig Campbell's grandson, Duncan, that the dramatic shift in the geographical and political orientation of Campbell power which had taken place during the fourteenth century found a more significant expression in two major building projects, the collegiate kirk of Kilmun on the Holy Loch and the castle of Inveraray on Loch Fyne. The nature of the work at both sites reflected not only the status and needs of the fifteenth-century lords of Lochawe as provincial rather than local magnates, but also the way in which that newly-won status had been threatened during the reign of James I (1406–37).

THE KING'S MEN?

During the fourteenth century the expansion of Clan Campbell had been tied intimately to the policies and interests of Robert the Steward. It would be a mistake, however, to think of the relationship simply as one of command and unquestioning service. For most of his adult life the Steward presided over what was, in effect, a controlled retreat of Stewart and Menteith influence from the Firth of Clyde in which the Campbells replaced, rather than sustained, Stewart lordship. The Steward's ability and inclination to function as an active, local lord in the area was hampered by his role as guardian of the kingdom for prolonged spells in the 1330s, 1340s and 1350s, and by the dramatic expansion of his territorial ambitions eastward into areas such as Atholl, Menteith and Strathearn during the same period. The reduction of the Firth of Clyde to an area of peripheral interest for the main Stewart line was confirmed rather than reversed by Robert's accession to the throne in 1371.

The events of 1371 were important for Clan Campbell in another regard, because the territories and personal relationships which made up the Steward's regional lordship in the west were thereafter effectively absorbed into the royal establishment. The Clan Campbell's later reputation (indeed their consciously developed image) as agents of the Scottish monarchy and as defenders of the social and cultural values of the lowland court and aristocracy should not obscure the fact that the family became 'king's men' in the fourteenth century largely by dynastic accident. In consequence, the process cannot be seen as one in which the Campbells were forced to make a series of stark choices or compromises between the culture, language and political dynamics of Gaelic society in Argyll and the attitudes and mores appropriate to a royal servant (even if it is legitimate to assume that there was a mutual incompatibility here). The Campbells of Lochawe remained unequivocally part of the Gaelic world in terms of their culture and the framework of their political ambitions. Gill-easbuig and his son Colin (chief 1382x87–c.1412) displayed little or no interest in advancing their status within the hierarchy of the lowland aristocracy. Both men took brides from Argyll-based families and, despite their manifest power and influence, neither man rushed to become a knight.[39] Instead, Gill-easbuig and Colin aspired to the leadership of the provincial aristocracy of Argyll. In papal supplications of the fourteenth and fifteenth centuries, moreover, kinsmen of the Campbell chiefs implicitly and explicitly identified themselves as members of Highland, Gaelic-speaking society.[40]

By the time of Robert II's death in 1390 the Campbells of Lochawe had become part of a recast 'royal' Stewart regional lordship in the south-west, which centred on Robert II's son, Robert, Earl of Fife and Menteith (from 1398 Duke of Albany). The place of the Campbells in Albany's affinity was reinforced by the marriage, sometime in the 1390s, of Colin Campbell's son, Duncan, to the duke's daughter Marjory. Albany's authority as a regional magnate extended across much of Scotland north of the Forth, particularly the earldoms and lordships of the south-western Highlands (Argyll, Lennox and Menteith), but also embraced areas such as Fife and the burghs of Dumbarton and Stirling.[41] In addition, for long periods Albany acted as guardian or governor of the kingdom in place of his elderly father Robert II, his incapacitated brother Robert III, and his nephew James I, who was held as a captive in England between 1406 and 1424. During the Albany guardianships and governorships, then, as in the reign of Robert II, Campbell chiefs were brought close to the sources of royal power and patronage in the Scottish kingdom through their involvement with a magnate who had a substantial regional power-base inside Gaelic Scotland before he came to dominate the exercise of royal authority.

The return of James I to Scotland in 1424 brought the fifty-year-old

LORDSHIP AND
ARCHITECTURE
IN MEDIEVAL
AND
RENAISSANCE
SCOTLAND

⚜

Campbell association with the highest echelons of royal government to an abrupt close. Duncan Campbell of Lochawe was one of the noble hostages sent to England in 1424 to act as a surety for the payment of James I's ransom to the English Crown.[42] Duncan's enforced sojourn in England was probably a huge stroke of luck, for it meant that he was absent from the kingdom in 1425 when James I launched a concerted political offensive against the Albany Stewarts and their allies in Lennox and Argyll.[43] On 24–25 May 1425 Murdoch Stewart, Duke of Albany, his sons Walter and Alexander, and his father-in-law Duncan, Earl of Lennox, were condemned to death by a parliamentary assise in Stirling and immediately executed.[44] In the same parliament Murdoch's son, James (known as 'the fat'), Bishop Finlay of Argyll, and a number of Lennox men who had been in rebellion against James I were forfeited.[45] Shortly thereafter, James 'the fat' and Bishop Finlay were forced to flee into exile in Ireland.[46]

Thus, when Duncan Campbell returned to Scotland between 16 July 1426 and 31 March 1427, he found a much-altered political landscape awaiting him.[47] The king's assault on the Albany Stewarts had decimated Duncan's kinsmen and political allies. The magnates executed in 1425 included Duncan's brother-in-law (Murdoch of Albany) and his uncle by marriage (Duncan, Earl of Lennox), while the refugee James the fat was Duncan's nephew.[48] Given Campbell's multiple links to the Albany Stewarts and the Lennox family it was hardly a surprise that King James seems to have regarded him with a degree of mistrust, especially given the continuing threat posed by the outcast James Stewart and the disgraced Bishop Finlay of Argyll.[49] Although not subjected to a direct royal attack, Duncan soon found his status and position in Argyll undermined by the king and his new agents in the west. Circumstantial evidence indicates that the king rescinded the heritable royal lieutenancy held by the Campbells of Lochawe in mid-Argyll since 1382.[50] As early as March 1427 James gave an indication of his willingness and ability to interfere in the affairs of Argyll in general, and those of Duncan Campbell in particular, by taking one-third of the lands of Glassary into royal possession while a dispute over the estates between Duncan and Sir James Scrymgeour was decided before the king's council.[51] The contest over the Glassary lands dragged on for the next five years, during which time Duncan was summoned before royal councils and parliaments in Perth and elsewhere, a process which consistently emphasised the primacy of the king's jurisdiction within Argyll.[52] James also increased his influence within the province by obtaining the appointment of the dependable George Lauder as a replacement for the rebellious Bishop Finlay.[53] As bishop of Argyll, Lauder appointed a number of Scots-speaking kinsmen and clerical supporters to benefices within his diocese.[54] That Lauder's control of ecclesiastical patronage was intimately tied to James I's political agenda in the region and dependent on the king's support is suggested by the backlash against the bishop's appointees following James' death in 1437.[55]

The conduct of James I's campaigns against the Lord of the Isles and other clan chiefs during 1428–29 may also indicate that Clan Campbell was not high in the king's favour.[56] In a council at Inverness in August 1428 the king arrested a number of Highland aristocrats, including Alexander, Lord of the Isles. Although many were imprisoned, two men, Alexander Macruarie of Garmoran and John MacArthur, were singled out for unspecified crimes and beheaded.[57] The identity of MacArthur is uncertain, but he may well have been a member of the Campbell family based around Strachur on Loch Fyne.[58] In the same parliament another Campbell, bearing the unusual name James, 'was hanged after being charged and convicted of the killing of John of the Isles'.[59]

Although Duncan Campbell seems to have supported James I's abortive siege of Roxburgh Castle in the winter of 1436–37 (a military failure which played a major part in the king's assassination in the Blackfriars of Perth in February 1437), there was little indication that the Campbells' 'special relationship' with the royal court and the family's position as the natural agents of the Crown in the west had been restored by the time of the king's death.[60] This was not through a lack of effort on Duncan's part, as the Campbell lord sought, like many others, to find a place in the new Crown-centred political community which James I was fashioning. An aggressive and interventionist monarch had brought home to Duncan Campbell the effect royal indifference or hostility could have on the territorial and political ambitions of Clan Campbell in the west. It was a lesson Duncan and his successors were quick to learn from and respond to. One of the features of James I's kingship was his use of knighting ceremonies to focus loyalty on the king and the dynasty he represented. In 1430, at the baptism of his infant sons, the twins James and Alexander, James I had knighted the sons and heirs of a number of noblemen.[61] The chronicler Walter Bower was clearly aware of the personal ties and obligations which this ceremony was intended to promote when he noted that 'All of these [new knights] were of tender years and are now fellow-soldiers with our reigning king' (i.e. James II).[62] There is no proof that Duncan had any part in the baptismal knighting ritual, which was clearly intended to create or strengthen links between the Crown and individual members of the greater aristocracy. It may be significant, however, that it was in 1430 that Duncan first appears in contemporary record as a knight.[63] Sir Duncan's entry into the knightly class was a decision made relatively late in life, and it represented a significant break from past practice; Duncan

LORDSHIP AND
ARCHITECTURE
IN MEDIEVAL
AND
RENAISSANCE
SCOTLAND

ᘔᕁ

was the first lord of Lochawe demonstrably to be knighted since his great-grandfather Sir Colin Campbell.[64] The previous Campbell indifference to the achievement of knightly rank and status thus seems to have disappeared at the same time as the Crown began to make greater use of the granting of knighthood as a means of securing aristocratic loyalty and of defining the dependable servants of the Crown, the aristocratic circle from which the monarch was expected to draw his secular office-holders.[65] The connection between knighting and loyalty to the king and dynasty was more explicit in the elevation of Duncan's son, Colin of Glenorchy, to the status of a knight in the aftermath of the assassination of James I in 1437.[66] Colin was one of the men who rounded up the regicides in 1437 and it is possible, indeed likely, that he became a knight at the coronation of James II.[67]

Following James I's death, then, Duncan and his eldest surviving son, Colin of Glenorchy, sought to reassert their autonomy and predominance in Argyll at the expense of men associated with the dead king, while paradoxically also identifying themselves politically with the interests of the king's widow, Queen Joan, her young son James II, and the Stewart dynasty in general.[68] In accepting knightly rank, the Campbell lords were not aiming to transform the nature of lordship and society in the region they controlled, but rather to identify themselves as loyal servants of a royal dynasty which was making increased use of chivalric forms and ceremonies to define and enhance its own status. The Campbell entry into chivalric class would, in fact, restrict the opportunities and incentives for future royal-backed intervention in Argyll by presenting the Campbell lordship as one which naturally upheld the Crown's interests.

Having entered the ranks of the knightly class, the lords of Lochawe experienced a rapid promotion through the hierarchy of new and established titles which were, in theory at least, in the gift of the Scottish Crown. Sometime in the period 1440–45 (and perhaps as early as 1437), Sir Duncan was granted, or simply adopted, the title Lord Campbell.[69] Recent work by A. Grant has outlined the growth, early in the fifteenth century, of a 'new' aristocratic elite, the Lords of Parliament, which employed an innovative naming style to denote its members' social and political pre-eminence in the localities and their consequent right to an individual summons to attend meetings of the kingdom's parliament.[70] Whether the origins of the new title lay in social competition and emulation as Grant suggests, or in a more formal act of invention located in the royal court, the fact that Duncan Campbell was one of the first lords to make use of the style was surely significant. The title demonstrated Duncan's determination to be regarded as part of the 'new' aristocratic community increasingly centred on the Scottish Crown and its institutions.

The quest for recognition of status in this context continued in the chieftainship of Duncan's grandson and successor, Colin, who in 1457–58 became Earl of Argyll. Overall, the comital titles granted out by the Crown in late-medieval Scotland tended to be honorific, conveying social prestige rather than lands or rights of lordship over defined territories.[71] In the case of the Campbell earldom of Argyll, the title probably did no more than recognise and ratify Colin's position as the provincial overlord of Argyll, a rank claimed by Campbell lords for at least sixty years before the royal grant of comital status. In the 1460s, Earl Colin moved beyond a simple royal endorsement of his local standing to develop a career as a 'court' aristocrat and an active royal administrator, serving as Master of the King's Household from c. 1464 before eventually attaining the Chancellorship of the kingdom, the highest secular office in the land, in 1483.[72]

The 'new' secular and ecclesiastical centres founded by fifteenth-century Campbell lords at Inveraray and Kilmun were thus shaped by the dual role of Campbell chiefs as the recently-established overlords of an ancient and self-aware Gaelic provincial community, and as court aristocrats and the self-appointed 'representatives' of royal power in the west.

KIRK AND CASTLE

The physical location of Inveraray Castle and the collegiate kirk of Kilmun attests immediately to the fact that Campbell territorial expansion in the fourteenth century had been most effective and enduring in Cowal and the sea-lochs of the Firth of Clyde. The construction of Inveraray (Fig. 3) has traditionally been ascribed to the period after Sir Duncan's death in 1453, when his grandson, Earl Colin, was reputedly a minor and in the ward of Sir Colin Campbell of Glenorchy.[73] In fact, it seems far more likely that Sir Duncan planned and initiated the work at Inveraray, and that the new stronghold was substantially complete by the time of his death.[74]

As a centre for regional lordship Inveraray held many advantages. The site on Lochfyne gave the Campbells direct maritime links to their newly acquired estates, castles and dependents in the south and east of Cowal, and general access to the Firth of Clyde and the sea lanes of the North Channel toward Ireland.[75] This fact became increasingly important in the second half of the fifteenth century when the export trade in salted herrings from the fisheries of the sea-lochs of the Firth of Clyde experienced rapid growth.[76] The castle also dominated an area where many of the most important land routes through Argyll intersected, gathering at the top of Lochfyne before striking east into Cowal and the Lennox.[77] The success

LORDSHIP AND
ARCHITECTURE
IN MEDIEVAL
AND
RENAISSANCE
SCOTLAND

❧

of the herring industry and the castle's general strategic significance no doubt helps to explain the growth of a small trading settlement in the lee of the Campbell castle. In 1474, this embryonic commercial centre was granted the status of a burgh of barony.[78]

Another indication of the importance of Cowal within the expanded Campbell lordship was the emergence of Kilmun Kirk on the Holy Loch as the main religious and ecclesiastical centre for the family.[79] Kilmun may have been the burial place of Gill-easbuig 'of Arran'(died 1382x85) and his son Colin (died 1412x14), but this is by no means certain, and the first Campbell chief unquestionably to be laid to rest on the shores of the Holy Loch was Sir Duncan Campbell (died 1453), who endowed Kilmun as a collegiate kirk in 1441–42.[80] The previous Campbell mausoleum is unknown, but from the mid-fifteenth century the 'lords of Lochawe' were, in fact, buried within sight of the Renfrewshire coast.[81]

The foundation of the collegiate kirk also had a political aspect, namely the assertion of Campbell control over ecclesiastical patronage in Argyll in the face of the activities of George Lauder, Bishop of Argyll. In the wake of James I's death Duncan Campbell appears to have orchestrated a campaign against men appointed to benefices in Argyll by the bishop, and the creation of the collegiate kirk was a vital part of that process. Duncan's request in the autumn of 1441 for the elevation of Kilmun to the status of a collegiate kirk proposed the annexation of the revenues of the parish kirks of St Connan of Dysart (*Diseart*) (i.e. the parish kirk of Glenorchy at Dalmally) and the 'Three Holy Brethren' of Kinlochgoil to the new institution.[82] Among the supplications which apparently reached Rome at the same time as Duncan's petition were a number attacking the Lauder-appointed incumbents of the two parish kirks earmarked for annexation to Kilmun. Thus one 'Morice Patricii Hilarii' supplicated the pope for provision to the vicarage of 'Disert', held by James Lauder, 'alleged priest', on the basis that Lauder 'is utterly ignorant of the idiom accustomed to be spoken in that church, whereby he is unable ... to preach the word of God to the parishioners, hear confessions and administer the sacraments ...'[83] Similarly, 'Archibald Martini' supplicated for provision to the kirk of Kinlochgoil because 'George bishop of Argyll granted it by his own temerity without the consent of the true patron to one Peter of Dalkeith, alleged priest, ... who cannot speak intelligibly the idiom of the parishioners, and intruded him by the secular power, ... by the negligence of the said Peter and his ignorance of the tongue many of the parishioners have died without the sacraments of the church ...'.[84] Peter of Dalkeith was also involved in a parallel dispute with Duncan Campbell over the arch-deaconry of Argyll. Sir Duncan's kinsman Neil Campbell, the previous archdeacon, had died *c.* 1436–37, whereupon Dugald of Lochawe, rector of Lochawe, and perhaps an illegitimate son of Sir Duncan, had been provided to the vacant office by the papal nuncio, Anthony Altani, Bishop of Urbino. It seems likely that this was yet another piece of crisis patronage directed towards the Campbells in the immediate aftermath of James I's assassination.[85] Bishop Lauder had certainly not been in favour of the grant and responded by appointing Peter of Dalkeith in opposition to Dugald of Lochawe although, as the supplications made by both parties in 1441 reveal, Lauder's man was never able to gain control of the office.[86]

In the short term, then, the creation of the collegiate kirk at Kilmun seems to have been designed to restrict the ability of the bishop of Argyll to impose his own candidates in benefices traditionally controlled by the Campbell lords. There were, however, undoubtedly more 'positive' factors underlying the considerable patronage directed by Duncan Campbell towards the support of his new foundation.

The determination to associate Campbell lordship with the kirk and relics of St *Fionntáin* (the form St Mun is from the hypocrostic *Mo-Fhintu*) is said to have reflected a long-standing Campbell attachment to the saint's cult which predated the acquisition of the kirk on the Holy Loch.[87] More pertinently, Campbell domination of the kirk of St *Fionntáin* undoubtedly helped to promote the claims of the lords of Lochawe to exercise authority over the native kindreds of Cowal. *Fionntáin* had given his name to a number of religious sites across Argyll, but the veneration of the saint was most obvious in Cowal, where the saint's crosier was held by a family of hereditary custodians at Inverchapel, just to the north of Kilmun.[88]

Moreover, the Campbell foundation, the most westerly example of a collegiate kirk in late-medieval Scotland, was clearly inspired by the changing patterns of religious devotion and expression found amongst Scottish aristocrats during the late fourteenth and early fifteenth centuries.[89] The chief function of a collegiate church was to provide masses for the souls of the founder and his or her family.[90] They were also usually intended, as in Kilmun's case, to be the burial place for the founder's successors.[91] Over time, the monuments of the dead multiplied, commemorating and celebrating the history and virtues of the noble line laid to rest within the kirk, and exhorting emulation from the living representatives of that lineage when they came to worship in the presence of their ancestors. Unfortunately, only the tombs of Sir Duncan Campbell (the founder of the collegiate kirk) and his wife Margaret Stewart survive at Kilmun (figs. 4 and 5), but they provide an interesting commentary on the way in which Sir Duncan and his spouse (or one of his successors if Sir Duncan did not commission the tombs during his own lifetime) wished to be remembered by their posterity.

LORDSHIP AND
ARCHITECTURE
IN MEDIEVAL
AND
RENAISSANCE
SCOTLAND

❧

The most important point is that the Kilmun tombs commemorate Duncan and Margaret as members of a chivalric aristocratic elite. Sir Duncan's effigy depicts the lord of Lochawe as a knight in full plate armour, a representation which stands in stark contrast to contemporary aristocratic sepulchres of the West Highland and Hebridean tradition.[92] Moreover, the effigies may, originally, have been associated with a heraldic panel depicting the royal arms, perhaps emphasising Sir Duncan's role in service to the Crown as lieutenant of Argyll.[93] Sir Duncan's tomb and, more certainly, that of Lady Margaret, seem to have been the work of a mason who was also employed in Margaret's native Renfrewshire to fashion effigies for Sir Patrick Houston, and his wife, in the parish kirk of Houston.[94] The Kilmun tombs may well reflect a regional armorial style associated with the lords and knightly families of the 'Westland'; the Kilmun and Houston effigies are certainly distinct, for example, from contemporary monuments depicting East Lothian and Berwickshire knights.[95]

Duncan Campbell's construction of a collegiate kirk, his flaunting of associations with royal government, his acceptance of knighthood, and his use of the style 'Lord Campbell' might at first point towards a deliberate and crude emulation of 'alien' aristocratic fashions and a dramatic break from the society of the province of Argyll. It could, however, be argued that these developments reflected the new way in which all great regional lords and lesser aristocrats across the kingdom had to present and promote their power in the face of a more assertive and intrusive royal establishment. In the case of the Campbells the contrast with the way in which they had previously exercised and advertised their power may have been starker, but the process of accommodation with royal power was essentially the same. Moreover, in many ways the aim seems to have been the consolidation of local power and the restriction of the outside interference by secular and ecclesiastical powers in the Campbell lordship which had characterised James I's reign. It is of interest to note that the Campbell-inspired campaign against Bishop Lauder's appointees made use of the notion that the monoglot Scots-speaking clerics introduced by Lauder were inherently unable to provide appropriate spiritual services for their Gaelic parishioners. The deployment of this argument may well have been more tactical than ideological; certainly the first glimpse we have of the personnel staffing the collegiate kirk at Kilmun (from 1452) suggests that a fair proportion of Duncan's chaplains were of lowland origin.[96] Nevertheless, the implication remains that many inside Argyll may have viewed Duncan's foundation of a collegiate kirk not as the imposition of an alien and threatening ecclesiastical innovation, but as a means of protecting the rights of Gaelic clerics and laymen against the arbitrary interference of a bishop of Argyll who had no social, political or cultural attachment to his diocese. Similarly, the confirmation of the royal lieutenancy was not a means of 'opening up' Argyll to the Crown's agents, but of securing the Campbell hegemony in the province.

Sir Duncan's effigy, which implicitly identified the Campbell chief as an upholder of the chivalric codes which lay at the heart of the lowland conception of acceptable secular lordship, was one of the earliest indications of the family's determination to present their regional power in a reassuring way to the royal court. The foundation of Kilmun as a collegiate kirk and the commissioning of the founder's tomb were combined with other mid-fifteenth-century developments which tended to dissociate the Camp-bells of Argyll, in lowland eyes at least, from the non-chivalrous Gaelic-speaking aristocracy of the Hebrides and Western Highlands. This was an important, perhaps necessary, development for men such as Sir Duncan and Earl Colin as they sought to justify their local power or advance their careers at the royal court, because of the negative view of Gaelic lordship and society which seems to have permeated the royal administration in fifteenth-century Scotland.

The censorious descriptions of Highland society found in some lowland chronicles, and occasionally government legislation, were undoubtedly en-couraged and exacerbated by the very immediate and practical problems encountered by the Crown and its agents in attempts to impose royal authority on the region. The terminology and intellectual framework through which these criticisms were voiced, however, reflected a general western European view of the nature of the struggle between 'civilisation' and 'barbarity'. This model was, in itself, ultimately derived from classical definitions of barbarity which focused on the division between Christianised and pagan society.[97] John Gillingham's work has highlighted the importance of twelfth-century English chroniclers, such as William of Malmesbury, in redefining barbarism in terms not of religious difference, but 'in terms of secular and material culture'.[98] Gillingham argues that this recasting increasingly allowed 'English' observers to condemn Scots, Irish and Welsh society (although undoubtedly Christian) as barbaric because of their customs, political organisation and comparative economic under-development. Thus, talking of the Irish, William of Malmesbury could claim that, 'ignorant of agriculture, they live in rustic squalor, unlike the English and the French who live in towns, who are familiar with commerce and enjoy a more cultivated style of life'.[99] By the mid-fourteenth century, some of the chroniclers of lowland Scotland had adopted the same language and ideology in their descriptions of the Scottish Gael. John of Fordun's mid-fourteenth-century account of the differences be-tween the Gaelic-speaking highlander and the English-speaking lowlander,

LORDSHIP AND
ARCHITECTURE
IN MEDIEVAL
AND
RENAISSANCE
SCOTLAND

❧

for instance, although often seen as a shrewd if biased piece of contemporary social observation, was a product of this tradition.[100] Fordun's use of language, and his description of the contrasting qualities of lowlander and highlander, clearly placed these groups in opposition to each other within the long-established and well-defined debate between 'civilisation' and 'barbarity',[101] although the image of a kingdom divided socially and culturally between a Gaelic-speaking Highland zone and an English-speaking lowland one was not confined to the pages of Fordun.[102] Fordun's fifteenth-century continuator, Walter Bower, Abbot of Inchcolm, returned with even greater enthusiasm to the theme that the linguistic/cultural division between Highland and Lowland Scotland was also a moral barrier: the gap between civilisation and barbarity, between civic government and disorder. Bower was explicit in his condemnation of the Gael as an 'untameable' barbarian, incapable of constancy, and a natural rebel against 'the kings and law-makers of Scotland'.[103]

How far Bower's view of the Gael was shared by his fellow lowland Scots is uncertain. Nevertheless, the fact that an influential cleric with a record of service to James I's administration articulated such hostile sentiments is significant in itself. There would undoubtedly have been an incentive for fifteenth-century Campbell lords to distance perceptions of themselves and their lineage from the prevailing perceptions of the Gael as a whole.

One way to achieve this goal was through the manipulation of the family's genealogy. The earliest recorded Campbell genealogy was a product of Gaelic scholarship, dates from c. 1400, and traced the Campbell chiefs back to King Arthur, a claim to Brittonic descent which, Sellar suggests, might well have reflected the family's early links to Stirlingshire and the Lennox.[104] While the Campbells' supposed 'Arthurian' descent remained a constant feature in poems and genealogies produced in the fifteenth and sixteenth centuries, two additional elements found their way into discussion of the family's origins which seem to have been designed to appeal to quite separate audiences. Perhaps around the middle of the fifteenth century (i.e. during the chieftainship of either Sir Duncan or Earl Colin) the Campbells began to claim continental antecedents. It was certainly in the decade 1460–70 that a medial 'p' was introduced into the Campbell surname (the predominant spelling of which had previously been Cambell), and this change may have been designed to strengthen a 'new' origin legend for the family, outlining their descent from a Frenchman who bore the name 'De Campo Bello' and who came to Scotland late in the eleventh century.[105] By the time Hector Boece wrote his *Scotorum Historia*, early in the sixteenth century, the Campbells' French ancestry had apparently gained wide acceptance in Lowland Scotland.[106] Moreover, Boece's account of a continental origin seems to have had the 'official' approval of the Campbell family. Boece specifically names John Campbell of Lundie, as one of the sources for his work and also makes mention of the role played by the 3rd Earl of Argyll in supplying manuscript sources for his history.[107]

The French descent claimed by the Campbells gave the family an honourable and natural place in the cosmopolitan aristocratic culture of western Europe and distinguished the family, in terms of ethnic origin and, by implication, social, political and cultural behaviour, from the Gaelic lords of Ireland and the Hebrides, stigmatised by Bower as inherently lawless, irrational and incapable of political constancy.

The Campbell lords' adherence to the core beliefs of the aristocratic caste to which they now claimed to belong, and the way in which this marked them off from Gaelic lords in general, are central features of Blind Hary's verse epic, *The Wallace*. Hary's work was written between 1476 and 1478, while Colin, 1st Earl of Argyll, was Master of the King's Household.[108] This period also saw a sustained conflict between John MacDonald, Lord of the Isles, and James III, a fact which clearly influenced

Figure 7.6
Carrick Castle, Argyll: view from south-east.
RCAHMS, A 37253CN

LORDSHIP AND
ARCHITECTURE
IN MEDIEVAL
AND
RENAISSANCE
SCOTLAND

❧

Hary's depiction of the Gaelic lords of the west as natural political rebels.[109] Hary took great care, however, to dissociate the ancestors of Colin Campbell from the fractious Gaels of Ireland and the Hebrides. Included amongst the victims of one of the numerous English 'atrocities' which enliven Hary's narrative were:

> … kynd Cambellis that nevir had beyne fals
> Thir rabellit nocht contrar thar richtwis croon.[110]

The rest of Hary's tale makes it plain that these virtues were not confined to these hapless individuals, but were the general characteristics of Clan Campbell. The Campbells' chief adversary in Hary's account was one Macfadzan, clearly modelled on the Lord of the Isles, who was allied to the English Crown and who brought Irish and Hebridean forces into Argyll in order to confront the 'gud Cambell'.[111] For Hary, the struggle between MacFadzan on the one hand, and Wallace and Campbell on the other, was more than a political conflict. On one level it involved a clash between the Islesmen and Irish in MacFadzan's service, and the 'native true born Scots' who supported Wallace and Campbell. Significantly, in terms of Hary's conception of the structure of fifteenth-century Scotland, men that 'borne war off Argill' were clearly regarded as full members of the Scottish kingdom. Even those Argyll men who had sided with Mac-Fadzan were, in Hary's view, Scots by birth and blood, to be accorded rights denied to their Irish and Hebridean allies. The bloody carnage which followed MacFadzan's final catastrophic defeat saw the pitiless slaughter of the usurper's Irish levies but,

> Born Scottis men baid still in-to the feild
> Keist wappynnys tham fra and on thar kneis kneild.

Wallace responded to this sight with a speech both merciful and chilling:

> Off our awne blud we suld haiff gret pete
> Luk zhe sla nane off Scottis will zoldyn be
> Off outland men lat nane chaip with the liff.[112]

Hary's ethnic distinction between the 'true born Scots' of the Campbell earldom of Argyll and the 'Outland' men of the Hebrides and Ireland makes little sense given the unified culture and language of these areas, but it was surely an attempt to express in racial terms the differences between these regions in terms of their political relationship with, and loyalty to, the Scottish Crown and kingdom late in the fifteenth century.

On another level again, Hary visualised the confrontation between Wallace and Campbell's forces and MacFadzan's men as a dramatic fight between 'civilisation' and 'savagery'. The advance of the Irish and

Hebrideans involved the flouting of all the chivalric conventions of war in a bout of terrifying and indiscriminate destruction:

> Barnys nor wyff thai peple sparyt nocht
> Wastyt the land als fer as thai mycht ga
> Thai bestly folk couth nocht bot byrn and sla.[113]

*'Pillars of the Community':
Campbell
Lordship and
Architectural
Patronage in the
Fifteenth Century*

Hary's picture of MacFadzan certainly made an impression on the poet William Dunbar, for the Gaelic warlord and his 'Erschemen' made an overtly demonic 'guest appearance' in Dunbar's 'The Dance of the Sevin Deidly Synnis'.[114]

In contrast, Hary viewed the Campbells of Lochawe as full members of civilised society in dress, weaponry and attitude, and this was most vividly expressed in the fanciful speech he attributes to the 'knycht Cambell' (a significant appellation) before his final clash with MacFadzan. Campbell rallies his troops with the observation that:

> yon bestly folk [the Irish and Islesmen] wantis wapynnys
>   and weid
> Swne thai will fle, scharply and we persew.[115]

Hary's portrayal of the lord of Lochawe as the resolute defender of the Scottish kingdom and civilised society against Macfadzan and his 'beastly' hordes probably reflected contemporary Campbell propaganda outlining the family's historic and continuing role within the kingdom.[116] The notion that Argyll and its lords represented a bulwark against the disorderly Gaels of the Isles and Ireland also surfaced in the mythic history of the Scottish kingdom provided by the sixteenth-century verse translation of Boece's chronicle. Here, Argyll was said to have derived its Latin name from one 'Argadus', a great lord of the region who, after initial problems, won fame for his good governance of the realm and vigorous enforcement of justice as governor and lieutenant to Scottish kings. Eventually Argadus met his death at the hands of a raiding force of Hebrideans under the command of a brigand significantly 'Borne in the Ylis within the occident se' who sought revenge for the execution of his friends and allies during one of Argadus' judicial tours.[117] That sixteenth-century lowland chroniclers could associate the very origins of the title 'dominus de Ergadie' with a figure who kept the violence of rebellious Islesmen in check and upheld the laws of the Scottish kingdom in the west says much about the way in which the contemporary Campbell earls of Argyll explained and justified their lordship to a lowland audience.

In Argyll and the Hebrides, on the other hand, the poets and genealogists employed by Clan Campbell sought to advance the status of their patrons by linking the family to prestigious figures in the historical mythology

LORDSHIP AND
ARCHITECTURE
IN MEDIEVAL
AND
RENAISSANCE
SCOTLAND

☙

shared by the Gaels of Scotland and Ireland. By the first half of the sixteenth century the sparse Arthurian genealogy of *c.* 1400 had been greatly elaborated and extended to trace the Campbell line back to figures from the *Leabhar Gabhála Éireann*, the standard account for late-medieval Gaelic scholars of the historical mythology of the Gael. Thus, the Campbells were descended, in this scheme, from Britán Máel (the supposed eponymous ancestor of all Britons), son of Fergus Lethderg and grandson of Nemed.[118]

The most important point is that the Campbells' various origin legends, although appearing mutually exclusive, were in fact being developed and deployed simultaneously to vindicate and legitimise the expansion of Campbell lordship in different cultural and political environments.

A CIVIL LORD?

If the accounts of Blind Hary and Hector Boece tend to dwell on the military role of Campbell lords as a 'front-line' defence against 'the Isles' and as enforcers of royal 'justice', there were other and more subtle ways through which fifteenth-century Campbell lords came to claim a prominent place in the aristocratic society of lowland Scotland.

Even before Sir Duncan's apparently sudden adoption of 'Crown-centred' aristocratic titles and styles in the 1430s and 1440s, Campbell chiefs had social and political links which spread far beyond the confines of Argyll.[119] As members of the great regional affinities of Robert the Steward and the duke of Albany, Campbell lords had inevitably been brought into social contact with noble families from the Stewart lordships clustered around the Firth of Clyde and the lords and lairds of Lennox, Stirlingshire, Renfrew, Cunningham and Ayrshire. In the chieftainship of Duncan Campbell, however, the links to families across this region became more numerous and more intense as the focus of Campbell marriage strategies shifted from Argyll to the Firth of Clyde and beyond. Duncan's own marriage to Marjory Stewart, Duke Robert's daughter, initiated the trend. After Marjory's death Duncan looked to the Stewart aristocracy of the Firth of Clyde for his second bride, marrying Margaret, the daughter of John Stewart of Ardgowan, a natural son of Robert III who held property in Renfrewshire and Cowal.[120] One of Duncan's daughters married Andrew Cunningham of Glengarnock (Ayrshire), while there also seems to have been a match with the Somervilles of Carnwath (Lanarkshire).[121] More strikingly, Sir Duncan's ecclesiastical patronage also revealed and reinforced Campbell ties to the mendicant orders based in urban centres in west-central Scotland. In April 1387 the then lord of Lochawe, Colin Campbell, his wife and their children (presumably including Duncan) were granted admission to the benefits of the masses and prayers celebrated by the Carmelite order throughout Scotland. When the anniversary of Colin's death came to be celebrated in the friars' provincial chapter, it was to be observed as if he was one of the brethren of the order.[122] It seems likely that Colin's point of contact with the Carmelite order was through the house at Irvine. Duncan continued the connection with the Carmelites with a grant of an annual rent in favour of the Perth house (Tullilum) from his properties in the earldom of Menteith.[123] The chief beneficiaries of Duncan's largesse, however, were the Dominican friars of Stirling and, in particular, Glasgow.[124]

Sir Duncan's association with the Dominicans probably built on the order's long-term interest and influence in the diocese of Argyll. The Dominicans had a long tradition of providing bishops of Argyll, a practice which was brought to an abrupt close by the role of the Dominican bishop Finlay of Albany in the rebellion of the Albany Stewarts against James I in 1425–26.[125] A special Campbell interest in saints identified with the Carmelite and Dominican orders may explain the regular appearance of the Virgin Mary as a focus for devotion in grants made by Duncan Campbell, and the repeated use of the name Katherine for the daughters of fifteenth-century lords of Lochawe.[126]

One of the most significant aspects of Sir Duncan's links with the Dominicans and Carmelites is that they suggest a regular Campbell interest in the burghs of Glasgow, Stirling, Irvine and Perth.[127] A grant in favour of the Glasgow Dominicans by Sir Duncan's successor, Earl Colin, of an annual rent from the escheats of the bailiary of Cowal might imply that at least some of the surplus production of Campbell lordship (whether arising from rents, profits of justice, fines or tolls) was being marketed in the burgh during the Glasgow fair.[128]

The Campbell concern with the economic exploitation of the resources of their lordship through the forms of commercial organisation familiar to lowland Scots became manifest in the development of the new centres of Campbell power at Inveraray and Kilmun as burghs of barony late in the fifteenth century.

The granting of burghal status to Inveraray in 1474 has to be seen against the background of a dramatic rise in royal customs revenue levied on the export of salted herrings from the firth of Clyde dating from late in the 1470s. The role of Earl Colin's burgh in the rapid growth of the value of the herring fisheries is open to a variety of interpretations. Changes in climate or the natural migration of herring shoals could lead to the collapse of fishing industries in established areas and the transfer of processing and trade to new locations.[129] The Firth of Clyde may have benefited from a natural increase in easily accessible herring stocks in the

LORDSHIP AND
ARCHITECTURE
IN MEDIEVAL
AND
RENAISSANCE
SCOTLAND

ठॆ

second half of the fifteenth century which made exploitation on a larger scale economically attractive. Alternatively, the apparent surge in herring exports may have reflected only the increasing ability of the Crown to extract customs revenue from a long-established industry which had previously lain outwith the reach of the king's tax-collectors. The case of the unfortunate Bristol merchant William de Canville indicates that long-distance trade (without urban development) had been a feature of the economy of Lochfyne as early as the thirteenth century. On 27 October 1274 Canville landed unspecified merchandise at a site he describes as the 'port of Lochfyne' (*portu de Loghfyn in Scocia*) where a Scottish merchant 'Bryan de Dunbrecan' (a mistake for Dunbretan, i.e. Dumbarton?) seized Canville's ship and goods.[130] Although the commodities carried by Canville and the goods he was hoping to obtain at Lochfyne are unspecified, it seems likely that the Bristol merchant was dealing in salted herrings.

If there was already a strong (although technically 'illegal') export trade in salted herrings from various sites around Lochfyne, then the grant of burghal status to Inverary in 1474 may simply represent Earl Colin's attempt to establish a local monopoly backed by the Crown, which stood to benefit from any change which channelled the trade through a point where export taxes could be levied. In any event, the grant of burghal status to Inveraray in 1474 was clearly related to the surge in customs revenue and indicated the earl's conscious desire to promote, control and regulate the lucrative trade from the sea-lochs in partnership with the Crown.

The growth in the importance of the herring trade for royal finances and the leading role of Lochfyne (and presumably Inveraray) is apparent in the customs accounts from 1480 onwards. In 1480 the accounts of the custumar of Irvine, David Blair, abruptly began to record customs revenue levied on the export of salted herring custumed at Lochfyne.[131] In 1481 Blair was described as custumar of Irvine *and* Loch Fyne, and the value and volume of the custumed herring exports had doubled.[132] In the same year the custumar of Dumbarton also registered a dramatic leap in customs revenue from Lochfyne herring.[133] The escalating value of the herring customs prompted a redistribution and reorganisation of responsibility for the levying and collection of the sums due to the Crown. In 1483 the custumar of Dumbarton was renamed the custumar of Dumbarton and the 'Lowis'. The derivation of the 'Lowis' is uncertain, but there can be no doubt from later entries that the new area of fiscal assessment embraced Lochfyne and the other sea-lochs of the Firth of Clyde.[134] Throughout the 1480s the value of the herring customs from the region increased; in 1487 George Maxwell, the then custumar of Dumbarton, accounted for the duty on 397 lasts of herring from which the Crown was owed £286 4s.[135] Given that the royal customs duty represented only a small fraction of the total value of the herring traded, the profits of those men who dominated the industry in the Firth of Clyde were likely to be substantial. Accordingly, the protection of the economic rights and monopolies of the burghs and lords involved in the industry began to feature in parliamentary legislation from the 1470s onwards, latterly alongside measures to promote the efficiency and scope of the fisheries.[136]

At times, the Crown's cavalier treatment of the privileges of those directly involved in the exploitation of the western fisheries aroused resentment. The parliament of January 1488, for example, seemed to criticise James III's tendency to grant concessions to foreign merchants and others which allowed them to bypass established burghs.[137] The dissatisfaction with royal policy evident in the parliament of January 1488 may have contributed to the participation of Colin, Earl of Argyll, in a rebellion against James III later in the same year, which ended with the king's death at the battle of Sauchieburn (11 June 1488) and the elevation of his son and heir, James IV, to the throne.[138] Earl Colin was a prominent figure in the new regime, serving as James IV's chancellor, and it may well have been his influence which led to the inclusion of legislation regarding the western fisheries in the first parliament of James IV's reign in October 1488.[139] The terms of the parliamentary statute insisted that all foreign merchants should trade only at royal burghs such as Dumbarton, Ayr, Irvine, Wigtown, Kirkcudbright and Renfrew or other 'free' burghs. More pointedly, these merchants were not to buy unsalted and unbarrelled fish nor were they to trade at any location 'at the Lowis nor uthir Mane land' other than free burghs where the appropriate duties and customs could be levied. The legislation, if successfully enforced, would have confirmed the position of Inveraray as one of the few locations within the 'Lowis' where salted and barrelled herring could legitimately be sold to the Breton and French merchants who seem to have been the main carriers involved in the trade. Campbell domination of the western fisheries was confirmed in the month after James III's death when the new king's councillors (headed by Earl Colin) gave a three-year lease of the assise of the 'herrings of the western sea' to the earl's kinsman Colin Campbell 'Knightson'.[140] Moreover, in 1490 Earl Colin was allowed to establish another 'legitimate' commercial outlet in the 'Lowis' when he successfully petitioned James IV for Kilmun to be given the status of a burgh of barony, with a fair on 21 October, the feast day of St Mun.[141]

The Campbells' entrepreneurial activity in the Firth of Clyde may well have been significant for the expansion of the family's power in other areas of their lordship. R. Dodgshon's theoretical model of the way in which relationships of lordship and dependence could be established, consolidated and extended in the western Highlands and Islands through

LORDSHIP AND
ARCHITECTURE
IN MEDIEVAL
AND
RENAISSANCE
SCOTLAND

the ability to obtain and redistribute prestige items might suggest that luxury goods procured through trade in the 'Lowis' could have sustained and enhanced the status and influence of the Campbell lords elsewhere in Argyll and the Hebrides.[142] Economic power also affected Campbell relationships with lowland Scotland. Even before the upturn in herring exports and the foundation of Inveraray and Kilmun as officially sanctioned burghs, successive Campbell chiefs had been able to finance extensive building programmes and deals with lowland aristocrats in the marriage and land markets.[143] The attempt to promote the growth of economic centres within Argyll itself was thus informed by a long-standing awareness of, and familiarity with, the benefits of mercantile activity.

Commercial innovation was not a characteristic generally associated with aristocrats from Gaelic-speaking regions. Indeed, the economic conservatism and backwardness of Gaelic society in Scotland and Ireland had been a matter of derisory comment by jaundiced observers since the eleventh and twelfth centuries, and were seen to explain many aspects of the Gael's supposed 'savage intractability'.[144] Gerald of Wales, for example, expounded in his *Topographia Hibernica* that the Irish were 'a people who have not departed from the primitive pastoral life. Mankind generally progresses from the forests to the fields and thence to towns and the conditions of citizens; but this nation, despising agricultural labour, not coveting the riches of cities, and averse to civil laws, follows the same life as their forefathers in forests and open pastures, willing neither to abandon old habits or learn anything new'.[145] These stereotypical representations resurface in fourteenth- and fifteenth-century Scottish chronicles such as Fordun and Bower with their contrasting images of the industrious domesticated Scot and the indolent Gael.[146]

Earl Colin's foundation of the burghs of Kilmun and Inveraray was rooted in his immediate and practical desire for economic improvement and financial gain. It seems likely, however, that Argyll's vigorous promotion and exploitation of trade through forms of commercial organisation familiar to lowland society and linked to the Crown's taxation system became yet another element which was seen to mark off Clan Campbell, in lowland eyes, from the 'barbaric', rebellious and economically backward Gael of the Hebrides and the central Highlands (these three afflictions, of course, being interrelated). When the counsellors of James III and James IV regarded the Hebrides and the western Highlands, they no doubt saw a foreign and threatening land, unaffected by, and resistant to, the institutions and conventions which were regarded as essential for a 'civilised' existence elsewhere in the kingdom. In Argyll, however, the view lightened, for here the dark 'barbarian' tide broke on the redoubts of Campbell power. At Inveraray and Kilmun, according to the vision of social development with which most educated clerics were familiar, the Campbell lords had established and encouraged the pre-conditions for 'civilised' society: commercially minded, law-abiding and responsive to the legitimate demands of royal government.

The successful 'selling' of Campbell lordship to a lowland audience explains only a small part of the overall political achievement of the earls of Argyll during the fifteenth century. Clan Campbell faced west to the Hebrides and Ireland as well as east to the Firth of Clyde. It would be thoroughly misleading to suggest that the Campbells abandoned the traditions and imagery of Gaelic society and adopted, wholesale, the values and conventions of the lowland elites. It would be even more mistaken to propose that men like Sir Duncan and Earl Colin sought in some way to transform the social and cultural make-up of the province of Argyll through the introduction of new and 'alien' customs. Campbell earls continued to patronise the Gaelic learned orders: poets who propagated the image of their lord as a great and powerful leader of the Gael, and genealogists who sought to root the Campbells' origins, descent and current status in the historical mythology of the Gaelic world. [147] In a sense, the projection of these apparently conflicting images and justifications of Campbell power both east and west was part of a single unified propaganda effort which exploited symbols and definitions of power and status derived from a variety of sources in order to sustain and vindicate the personal lordship of the Campbell chiefs.

As far as lowland Scotland was concerned, the face of Campbell lordship remained reassuring. At Kilmun on the Holy Loch, the prayers of the provost and chaplains of the collegiate kirk and the 'citizens' of the tiny burgh celebrated the long and noble lineage of the lords who protected them: knights who claimed French descent and unshakeable loyalty to the Scottish Crown.

NOTES

1. The author would like to thank Dr Roger Mason, Dr Jane Dawson, Dr Martin MacGregor and Dr Norman Macdougall for their comments on earlier drafts of this paper.
2. *AT*, 19/1/1413.
3. G. W. S. Barrow, *Robert Bruce and the Community of the Realm of Scotland* (Edinburgh, 3rd edition, 1988), 289–90.
4. *RRS*, v, nos. 27, 46, 366, 374, 393; *RMS*, i, App. II, nos. 353, 368. Sir Arthur Campbell, in particular, accumulated claims to extensive estates in the north of Argyll. Sir Arthur's ambitions extended north from Lorn and Appin into Garmoran, for sometime in the 1320s Christina MacRuari heiress of Garmoran resigned her rights in these lands to Arthur's son (also Arthur). Faculty of Procurators (Glasgow).

LORDSHIP AND
ARCHITECTURE
IN MEDIEVAL
AND
RENAISSANCE
SCOTLAND

ॡ

5. *The Anonimalle Chronicle, 1307–1334*, eds. W. R. Childs and J. Taylor (Leeds, 1991), 165–7. For David II's role in the return of John *Gallda*, see S. Boardman, 'The Tale of Leper John and the Campbell Acquisition of Lorn', in *Alba: Celtic Scotland in the Medieval Era*, eds. E. J. Cowan and R. A. MacDonald (East Linton, 2000), 219–47 at 231–3. In January 1358 David II restored John of Lorn, his nephew by marriage, to all the lands which had belonged to Alexander of Lorn (John's great grandfather) in the lordship of Lorn and elsewhere in the kingdom. This grant invalidated the claims of various Campbell lords to estates within Lorn and Benderloch (*Acts of the Lords of the Isles*, 5–8; *Highland Papers*, ii, 142; *RRS*, vi, no. 165; K. A. Steer and J. W. M. Bannerman for RCAHMS, Late Medieval Moumental Sculpture in the West Highlands (Edinburgh, 1977), Appendix II, p. 204).

6. Balliol's forces had triumphed over those representing the young Bruce claimant, David II, at the Battle of Halidon Hill in 1332 (*Chron. Wyntoun* (Laing), ii, 407–8). As early as 1296 the then Campbell chief, Colin, was noted as possessing a significant galley force. In 1306, Colin's son, Neil, was capable of mounting large-scale naval operations in the Firth of Clyde. According to John Barbour it was Sir Neil who supplied the galleys which allowed the beleagured Robert I to escape the relentless pursuit of his enemies on the Scottish mainland (Barbour, *Bruce*, 130, 138–9).

7. Wyntoun's account implies that Robert had a close personal relationship with the Campbells of Lochawe before his discomfiture in 1334 (*Chron. Wyntoun* (Laing), ii, 414). Gill-easbuig Campbell, son of Sir Colin Campbell of Lochawe, received a grant of the lands of Kinlochstriven in the south of Cowal from Robert the Steward sometime in the period before 1371. The compiler of the Argyll Transcripts has placed the Steward's undated charter c. 1335, perhaps to suggest that Gill-easbuig played a leading role in the encounter at Dunoon. Wyntoun, however, clearly identifies the leader of the Lochawe Campbells in 1334 as Gill-easbuig's elder brother Dougal (*Chron. Wyntoun* (Laing), ii, 414; *AT*, i, ; *OPS*, ii, part 1, 59).

8. *Panmure Registrum*, 175–6; *Highland Papers*, ii, 143.

9. NAS, Register House Charters RH6/304; *Lamont Papers*, no. 26.

10. Fraser, *Menteith*, ii, 235–6.

11. *AT*.

12. Ibid. The insertion of the Steward's allies into Knapdale and Arran may well have been designed to ensure the hold of the Stewart family on these lordships in the increasingly likely event of Sir John Menteith's death without direct heirs. Knapdale, in particular, was vulnerable to John of Islay, Lord of the Isles, who was already embroiled in a dispute with the Steward over the neighbouring lordship of Kintyre (*Acts of the Lords of the Isles*, xxv–xxvii). The Steward's involvement is indicated by his appearance as a witness to the grant of Arran lands to Gill-easbuig at Stirling. (The Steward is described as guardian of the realm, which places the grant in the period 1346–1357). John, lord of Arran, was still alive in May 1360 (Fraser, *Menteith*, ii, 244).

13. *Scottish Verse from the Book of the Dean of Lismore* (Scottish Gaelic Texts Society, 1937), 162–3. Traditional sources suggest that Gill-easbuig's mother may have been Helen Menteith, daughter of the Sir John Menteith who died c. 1320. If this is true, Gill-easbuig's territorial designation may reflect the fact that he was raised by his mother's family on Arran. In the 1353 grant, Gill-easbuig is styled Sir John's 'fidelis consanguineus'. If Gill-easbuig's mother was Helen Menteith, then Sir John would indeed have been a first cousin.

14. *Chron. Bower* (Watt), vii, 261.

15. *AT*, ii, 1; *Analecta Scotica*, ed. J. Maidment (Edinburgh, 1834–7), 15–16; *RRS*, vi,

no. 293; ibid., Addenda, 528–9. Charter of confirmation by David II, 25 May 1363, of a charter of the lands of the barony of Kilmun and others by Mary, former countess of Menteith, to Gill-easbuig son of Colin, and, 11 October 1363, confirmation of Mary's charter of lands of Kilmun in Cowal (*HMC*, Fourth Report, 476, no. 47; *RRS*, vi, no. 304). These royal confirmations were issued during, and shortly after, the 1363 baronial rebellion against David II in which one of the chief issues was the status of the king's new queen, Margaret Drummond, whose brothers had been at feud with the Campbells over the Menteith inheritance (Fraser, *Menteith*, i, 239–46). It is unclear whether the countess's resignation included the barony of Over Cowal and the lands of Lochgoilhead, lying to the north of Kilmun, but these too had been acquired by Gill-easbuig before 1369. *RRS*, vi, no. 429, Perth 15 March 1369, David II confirmed to Gill-easbuig Campbell all grants and sales of land made to him in Craignish, Kilmelfort, Strachur and Cowal. Gill-easbuig's son and successor, Colin, was the lay patron of Lochgoilhead parish kirk by June 1392, while Over Cowal which was confirmed in possession of the Lochawe Campbells in 1407 (*CPL, 1378–94*, 175; *AT*, i, at date). Gill-easbuig also received title to the lands of Stronchuillin and Finnart in the barony of Kilmun in 1373, following on the resignation of Paul Glenn (*AT*, i, at date).

16. Theiner, *Mounumenta*, 315.
17. Fraser, *Menteith*, i, 239–46.
18. S. Boardman, *The Early Stewart Kings: Robert II and Robert III* (East Linton, 1996), 16–17.
19. Ibid.
20. Ibid., 17–18.
21. *RRS*, vi, no. 293; ibid., Addenda, 528–9. A royal confirmation of countess Mary's grant of the kirk of Kilmun followed on 11October 1363 (*RRS*, vi, no. 304). David II may well have been trying to woo Gill-easbuig from the Steward's affinity through these acts of patronage.
22. *Highland Papers*, i, 75.
23. J. W. M. Bannerman, 'The Lordship of the Isles: Historical Background', Appendix II in Steer and Bannerman, *Late Medieval Monumental Sculpture*, 201–5.
24. See Boardman, 'The Tale of Leper John', 231–3.
25. *RRS*, vi, no. 165.
26. *ER*, ii, 106, 352; *RMS*, i, no. 237; Boardman, 'The Tale of Leper John', 232.
27. Boardman, 'The Tale of Leper John', 232.
28. Barbour, *Bruce*, 112–121, 248–52, 258–62, 342–5, 360–66, 564–7.
29. Ibid., 342–5, 366. An implicit criticism of David II's attempt to re-instate MacDougall lordship in Argyll?
30. See Duncan's discussion of both these episodes (ibid., 112–14, 564–7).
31. Boardman, 'The Tale of Leper John', 232.
32. *RMS*, ii, no. 2128; *AT*, 10/5/1437. The exact boundaries of the lieutenancy are not given. Instead, the office is said to cover the area stretching from Carn Drome, near Tyndrum, to Lochgilphead (the northern and southern limits?) and from Loch Melfort to Loch Long (the western and eastern limits?). Loch Melfort marched with Lorn and Lochgilphead with Knapdale.
33. *St Andrews Liber*, 5, 'Duncano Cambell filio et herede Culini Cambell, domini de Ergadia'. It has been suggested that the title 'dominus', when used to describe the overlords of major Gaelic provinces such as Argyll or Galloway, denoted a figure whose title in the east would be Latin 'comes' and Scots earl (J. W. M. Bannerman, 'The Scots Language and the Kin-based Society' in *Gaelic and Scots in Harmony: Proceedings of the Second International Conference on the Languages of Scotland* (Glasgow, 1988), 7. In 1423–5 Colin's son and successor,

LORDSHIP AND
ARCHITECTURE
IN MEDIEVAL
AND
RENAISSANCE
SCOTLAND

✳

Duncan, appeared as 'Dominus de Argill' and as 'Cambel de Argyle', while in July 1432 Duncan's son and designated heir was styled 'Gillaspy Cambel of Ergile' (*Rotuli Scotiae*, ii, 242, 244–5, 254; *Highland Papers*, ii, 174).

34. In the early fifteenth century Sir Duncan Campbell invested in the reconstruction of Innis Chonaill and another focus of lordly power in Lochawe, the kirk of Inishail (RCAHMS, *Argyll*, ii, nos. 292, 247). Both sites continued to appear on the itineraries of Duncan and his successors. A Gaelic proverb, said to originate in a Campbell raid which captured the daughter and heiress of the thane of Cawdor in the late fifteenth century, revelled in Lochawe's inaccessibility as a feature which protected the clan from its enemies ('*S fhada glaodh o Loch Obha! 'S fhada cobhair o chlann dhaoine*, *The Book of the Thanes of Cawdor* (Spalding Club, 1859), 103–4.

35. Carrick may have provided the setting for the baronial court of Over Cowal. Attendance at the baronial court of Over Cowal was specified in a grant of 1398 by Colin Campbell of Lochawe of lands around the head of Loch Long to his kinsman, Arthur Campbell of Menstrie (*Highland Papers*, iv, 18–19).

36. In 1428, for example, a royal summons for Duncan Campbell, lord of Lochawe, to appear before the king's court at Perth was delivered by the sheriff of Dumbarton 'Apud le Carryk' (*Highland Papers*, ii, 158–9). The rectangular tower at Carrick displays some features also found at the great Stewart castle of Dundonald in Ayrshire, David's Tower in Edinburgh and Morton Castle (RCAHMS, *Argyll*, vii, no. 116). The parallels with Dundonald are especially significant given the Campbell/Stewart link in the political sphere.

37. *Chron. Bower* (Watt), i, 191. Eilean Dearg was almost certainly acquired from the Stewarts as part of the lordship of Ormidule.

38. When resident in Cowal, the lords of Lochawe preferred to conduct their business at Kilmun or Dunoon (e.g. *Panmure Registrum*, 175–6; *Highland Papers*, ii, 143).

39. Gill-easbuig, who was certainly not a knight as late as 1371, may have been knighted towards the very end of his life (*Highland Papers*, iv, 16; *Lennox Cartularium*, 6–8).

40. Invariably in cases where such a distinction helped the case of the supplicant. In 1366, for example, John and Mariota Campbell supplicated the pope to allow their marriage within the prohibited degrees of consanguinity on the basis that 'by reason of the diversity of dialects between the highlands (in which the said John and Mariota dwell) and the low lands of Scotland' there was little intermarriage between the regions, a situation which inevitably restricted the choice of suitable marriage partners (*CPL*, 56). In 1423 it was recorded that Neil 'Colini Cambel', the archdeacon of Argyll, had been provided to the rectory of the parish kirk of Glassary in opposition to James Scrymgeour who did not understand 'the language and idiom of the parishioners' (*CSSR, 1423–1428*, 10–11).

41. Boardman, *Early Stewart Kings*, 181–3.

42. M. Brown, *James I* (Edinburgh, 1994), 40–2.

43. Ibid., 60–7; *CDS*, iv, nos 941–2, 952–3, 960, 964, 973, 981, 983.

44. Brown, *James I*, 66; *Chron. Bower* (Watt), viii, 243–5.

45. Brown, *James I*, 66.

46. *Chron. Bower* (Watt), viii, 245.

47. *CDS*, iv, no. 983; *Highland Papers*, ii, 152–7.

48. *SP*, i, 150.

49. Although Finlay's parentage is uncertain, his style 'of Albany' suggests that he was a kinsman of the 1st or 2nd duke (D. E. R. Watt, *A Biographical Dictionary of Scottish Graduates to AD 1410* (Oxford, 1977), 4–5). Finlay's replacement as bishop of Argyll was appointed in 1427 on the basis of the previous incumbent's

death, but it is striking to note the safe-conduct obtained in June 1428 by one Finlay Murdochson of Scotland (at that time living in England) for a pilgrimage to St James's shrine at Compostella (*Rotuli Scotiae*, ii, 263). Could Finlay have been an illegitimate son of Duke Murdoch? In addition, Murdoch Stewart's son, Walter, is claimed to have had at least two sons, Andrew and Arthur, by 'a lady of the name of Campbell'. This women is described as 'a daughter of the knight of Lashow' (Lochawe) in a later pedigree (*ER*, iv, clxxix and clxvi; NLS, Advocates' Manuscripts, MS 33.2.36).

50. That James I had in some way annulled or infringed the 1382 lieutenancy is suggested by the fact that Duncan had a notarial copy of the original grant drawn up during the first general council after James I's death in 1437 (*AT*, 10/5/1437).

51. *Highland Papers*, ii, 152–7.

52. Ibid., 157–74; the king's return also seems to have coincided with the Scrymgeours gaining the ascendancy in a struggle for control of the patronage of the parish kirk of Glassary (*CSSR, 1433–1447*, 10–11, 80, 141, 195–6).

53. J. Dowden, *The Bishops of Scotland* (Glasgow, 1912), 385–6.

54. *CSSR, 1433–1447*, iv, nos. 787 (James Lauder to Glenorchy), 782, 808, 816, 818, 823, 879 (Peter of Dalkeith to the parish kirk of Lochgoilhead and the archdeaconry of Argyll)

55. Ibid.

56. Brown, *James I*, 97–100.

57. *Chron. Bower* (Watt), viii, 261.

58. Although the chiefs of this family typically bore the names Arthur and Ivar rather than John ('Strachur Writs' in *Highland Papers*, iv).

59. *Chron. Bower* (Watt), viii, 261. The victim is usually taken to be Sir John Mór, lord of Dunivaig and the Glens, although this identification was not made until the seventeenth century.

60. Brown, *James I*, 163–6.

61. *Chron. Bower* (Watt), viii, 263.

62. Ibid.

63. NAS, Muniments of the King James VI Hospital, GD79/3/4.

64. *APS*, ii, Appendix (Acts of James I), 28; *AT*, 10/5/1437.

65. See M. Keen, *Chivalry* (New Haven and London, 1984), 9–11, for a discussion of Ramon Lull's view of knights as natural and integral members of medieval government under the king.

66. Boardman, 'The Tale of Leper John', 223–4.

67. *RMS*, iii, no. 316.

68. Boardman, 'The Tale of Leper John', 224–5; *CPP*, iv, no. 791. Duncan's foundation of a collegiate kirk at Kilmun was said to be for the souls of James I, his widow Joan, and the then king, James II.

69. *APS*, ii, 55–6, 59; *AT*, 10/5/1437; A. Grant, 'The Development of the Scottish Peerage', *SHR*, lxvii (1978), 1–27, at 12–13.

70. Grant, 'Scottish Peerage'.

71. Grant, 'Scottish Peerage', 1–7. The chief point was that this status derived from a royal 'gift', which left little room for the concept of the earl as the accepted leader of a distinct 'provincial' community. The 'new' comital creations in Scotland from that of the earldom of Crawford (1398) onwards seem to have been sanctioned by full gatherings of the Scottish political community in parliament.

72. N. Macdougall, *James III: A Political Study* (Edinburgh, 1982), 54. In the years after 1460 Colin appeared as an auditor of exchequer (1462), a royal justiciar south of Forth, and (in 1464) as Master of the King's Household. Although

LORDSHIP AND
ARCHITECTURE
IN MEDIEVAL
AND
RENAISSANCE
SCOTLAND

⚜

Colin's ancestors had held a variety of important royal offices within their own region, the earl's appearance as a working member of the crown's central administration was a new departure for the chief of Clan Campbell.

73. *Taymouth Bk.*, 13; *Highland Papers*, ii, 96–7.

74. Inveraray was noted as a centre of Campbell lordship in the 1430s. Sir Duncan issued one of his last charters in February 1453 at Inveraray, while Colin's first recorded grant, in May 1454, was sealed at the same location (NAS, Society of Antiquaries Charters, GD 103/2/40; *Lamont Papers*, no. 35). Given that Colin's father seems to have died c. 1432, his 'minority' must have been of very short duration

75. . J. E. Dawson, 'The Origins of the "Road to the Isles": Trade Communications and Campbell Power in Early Modern Scotland', in *People and Power in Scotland; Essays in Honour of T. C. Smout*, eds. R. Mason and N. Macdougall (Edinburgh, 1992), 74–103, at 91–2.

76. See below, and note 129.

77. A. R. B. Haldane, *The Drove Roads of Scotland* (Edinburgh, 1952), 84–101.

78. *RMS*, ii, no. 1168.

79. After the mid-fourteenth century Campbell chiefs often issued charters and concluded agreements at Kilmun kirk. They also seem to have had a private residence very close to the kirk, 'manerium nostrum de Strathachi' (Strath Eachaig), of which no trace now remains (*Glasgow Friars Munimenta*, 163–4, 172–3, 192).

80. *CSSR, 1433–47*, no. 791; *RMS*, ii, no. 346.

81. Cases have been made for Inishail, Dalavich and Kilchrenan. Traditional tales present the first Campbell burial at Kilmun as the result of a storm which prevented the carriage of the body of a lord of Lochawe's son to the established burial ground at Inishail (N. D. Campbell, 'The Origin of the Holy Loch', *SHR*, x (1913), 29–34). A tomb in Kilchrenan kirk on Loch Awe was said to be that of Cailean Mór (d. c1296), but this identification is incorrect (*SP*, i, 320; RCAHMS, *Argyll*, ii, 149; *Taymouth Bk.*, 16). Archibald, 2nd earl of Argyll, was buried at Kilmun in 1513 following his death at Flodden.

82. *CSSR, 1433–1447*, no. 791. For the identification of Dysart, see W. J. Watson, *History of the Celtic Place-Names of Scotland* (Edinburgh, 1926), 256–7, 282; *OPS*, ii, part 1, 134.

83. *CSSR 1433–1447*, no. 787; I. Fraser, 'The Place-Names of Argyll – An Historical Perspective', *TGSI*, liv (1984–6), 3–37, at 9.

84. *CSSR, 1433–1447*, no. 823.

85. Cf. the papal nuncio's grant of a portable altar to Colin Campbell of Glenorchy in the same period. Dugald of Lochawe was one of the witnesses to the notarial instrument drawn up in May 1437 recording the grant of the lieutenancy of Argyll to Gill-easbuig Campbell in 1382 (*AT*, at date).

86. *CSSR 1433–1447*, nos. 782, 808, 816, 818.

87. N. D. Campbell, 'The Origin of the Holy Loch', 29–34. The evidence for this view is simply the appearance of sites dedicated to *Fionntáin* near centres associated with Campbell secular lordship. Without a clearer idea of the chronological relationship between these sites and the advent of Campbell lordship, however, it would be dangerous to assume that *Fionntáin* was a 'Campbell' saint before the acquisition of Kilmun (Cf. Watson, *Place-Names*, 307).

88. *RMS*, ii, no. 2385; *OPS*, ii, part 1, pp. 72–3. The Robert Dewar and John Dewar who appeared as witnesses to charters issued by Campbell chiefs in, respectively, 1442 and 1481, were probably members of the family charged with the keeping of *Fionntáin*'s crosier (*RMS*, ii, no. 346, NAS, GD1/426/1). The devotion of the

inhabitants of Cowal to *Fionntáin* was noted in a late fifteenth-century source (A. P. Forbes, *Kalendars of Scottish Saints*, (Edinburgh, 1872), 135, 414–16).

89. See D. E. Easson, 'The Collegiate Churches of Scotland', *RSCHS*, vi (1938), 193–215; idem. vii (1939), 30–47, at 36–7.

90. Easson, 'Collegiate Churches'.

91. D. E. R. Watt, 'Collegiate Churches', in *An Historical Atlas of Scotland, c. 400–1600* (St Andrews, 1975), pp. 78–80.

92. Steer and Bannerman, *Late Medieval Monumental Sculpture*, 28. The tomb provides an early confirmation of the adoption by the Campbells of a boar's head as their armorial crest (Cf. Laing, *Seals*, i, no. 154; D. E. Meek, 'The Gaelic Ballads of Medieval Scotland', *TGSI*, lv (1986–7), 47–72, at 52–6).

93. Steer and Bannerman, *Late Medieval Monumental Sculpture*, 28.

94. The same man may also have produced the tombs of Sir Robert Stewart of Lorn and his wife now at Culross Priory in Fife (M. C. Scott, Dress in Scotland, 1406–1460, unpublished Ph.D thesis, University of London, 1987, 132–4, 151, 154–7).

95. The phrase 'lords of the Westland' appears in a number of fifteenth-century chronicle and record sources. Although never precisely defined, the 'Westland' included Cunningham and Lanarkshire, and probably also embraced other areas around the Firth of Clyde, such as Ayrshire (excluding Carrick) and Renfrewshire (*TA*, i, 49, 92). The 'lords of the Westland' were seen to be politically and militarily active in areas such as Cowal, Knapdale, Kintyre, the islands of the Firth of Clyde and the Hebrides and were often associated with the Gaelic aristocrats of these areas while being distinguished from them in cultural terms. The Auchinleck Chronicle, for example, reporting on James II's campaign against the earls of Douglas in 1455, narrated that the king 'past to glasgw and gaderit the westland men with part of the ereschery' before raiding Douglasdale (C. A. McGladdery, *James II* (Edinburgh, 1990), 166). Scott suggests that the armour style depicted on the tombs at Houston, Kilmun and Culross is more 'old-fashioned' (that is, less influenced by contemporary trends in continental and English armour) than the types displayed on the monuments of the earls of Douglas and Lothian families such as the Borthwicks (Scott, Dress in Scotland).

96. *RMS*, iv, no. 791. The Provost in 1452 was Peter Wilson (conceivably the same as Peter of Dalkeith), with his chaplains Thomas Spens, Duncan Lindsay, Donald McAgrade, John Baxter, Duncan MacMillan, Alexander Dewar and Duncan 'Johannis Beg'. Sir Duncan's kinsman, Neil Campbell, archdeacon of Argyll, had used similar linguistic arguments in 1423–4 against James Scrymgeour in the dispute over the kirk of Glassary (*CSSR, 1423–1428*, 10–11).

97. See W. R. Jones, 'The Image of the Barbarian in Medieval Europe', *Comparative Studies in Society and History*, 13 (1971), 376–407, esp. 396 8; A. Pagden, *The Fall of Natural Man: The American Indian and the origins of comparative ethnology* (Cambridge, 1982), 15–26.

98. E. g. J. Gillingham, 'Foundations of a disunited kingdom', in *Uniting the Kingdom? The making of British History*, eds. A. Grant and K. Stringer (London, 1995), 48–64, at 59–60.

99. William of Malmesbury, *Gesta Regum*, ii, 485, quoted in Gillingham, 'Foundations', 59–60.

100. R. Nicholson, *Scotland: The Later Middle Ages* (Edinburgh, 1974), 205–6.

101. The chronicler's contrast between the 'docile', 'peaceful', 'law-abiding' lowlander and the 'fierce', 'untameable', 'hostile' and 'savage' highlander pointed to key characteristics which differentiated 'civilised man' from the 'barbarian' in classical and medieval texts (*Chron. Fordun*, i, 42). Even Fordun's apparently innocent

LORDSHIP AND
ARCHITECTURE
IN MEDIEVAL
AND
RENAISSANCE
SCOTLAND

𝕽

observational division of the Scots into mountain and coastal dwellers squared with the view of classical authors that rational civilised man lived in the cities and on the plains while the wild man or barbarian inhabited the woods and mountains. Similarly, the simplistic emphasis on the exclusive dependence of Gaelic society on pastoralism did not reflect the realities and complexities of agricultural production in upland zones, but did serve to identify the Gael with a lifestyle which was regarded as inherently primitive. For the scholars of medieval Europe, familiar with the Ciceronian notion of man's progression from 'a state of nature to a state of civilisation', the barbarian came to represent 'the retarded, disoriented, irrational infancy of mankind, before man had begun to achieve better things for himself through his submission to law and the exercise of reason', and it was a commonplace to contrast 'the sweet reasonableness and tractability of civilised man with the disorderliness and irrationality of the barbarian' (Jones, 'The Image of the Barbarian', 397).

102. 102 See, for example, note 40 above, for the Campbell supplication of 1366.
103. *Chron. Bower* (Watt), i, 48–9, viii, 8–9, 260–7, and especially vii, 359–61.
104. See W. D. H. Sellar., 'The Earliest Campbells – Norman, Briton or Gael?', *Scottish Studies*, xvii (1973), 109–22.
105. Cf. W. Gillies, 'Some aspects of Campbell History', *TGSI*, l (1976–8), 256–96, at 278–9, especially note 31, for an argument which suggests that the development of the Campbell form can be explained in linguistic terms and need not indicate the contemporaneous promotion of a Norman origin (Sellar, 'The Earliest Campbells'). The earliest indication of this process may, again, be provided by Sir Duncan Campbell's tomb at Kilmun. An eighteenth-century rendering of the now-illegible tomb inscription describes Duncan as 'Dominus le Campel, Miles de Lochaw' (G. Crawford, *The Peerage of Scotland* (Edinburgh, 1716), 17). The new spelling of the surname appeared in charters issued from the mid-fifteenth century onwards (e.g. *RMS*, ii, nos. 811 (1464), 989 (1469)).
106. H. Boece, *Scotorum Historia* (Paris, 1527), Bk. 12, f. 266v. I thank Nicola Royan for this reference. Cf. *The Chronicles of Scotland compiled by Hector Boece*, translated into Scots by John Bellenden 1531 (STS, 1938–41), ii, 169.
107. E. J. Cowan, 'The Angus Campbells and the Origin of the Campbell-Ogilvie Feud', *Scottish Studies*, xxv (1981), 25–38, at 28.
108. Macdougall, *James III*, 54.
109. Nicholson, *Later Middle Ages*, 480–2.
110. *Hary's Wallace*, i, 144. Colin Campbell had, in fact, played a leading role in the crown's military and political offensive against John of the Isles during 1476 (Macdougall, *James III*, 121–4).
111. John of the Isles had been charged with treasonable dealings with England and Edward IV in the parliament of November-December 1475 which had seen his forfeiture (Macdougall, *James III*, 121).
112. *Hary's Wallace*, i, 163–4.
113. *Hary's Wallace*, i, 157. That women and children should be protected by the self-restraint of chivalric warriors was one of the pious orthodoxies expounded in theoretical treatises on medieval warfare (*The Tree of Battles of Honoré Bonet*, trans. G. W. Coopland, (Liverpool, 1949), 185). I thank Dr Carol Edington for this reference (Cf. Keen, *Chivalry*, 227–37).
114. *The Poems of William Dunbar*, ed. W. M. Mackenzie (Edinburgh, 1932), 120–3.
115. *Hary's Wallace*, i, 162. The distinction implied here was economic as well as moral.
116. See M. Brown, ' "Rejoice to hear of Douglas": The House of Douglas and the Presentation of Magnate Power in Late Medieval Scotland', *SHR*, lxxvi (1997), 161–84, for the similar cultivation of an image of Douglas power and its place in

the Scottish kingdom; see also M. James, 'English politics and the concept of honour, 1485–1642', in *Society, Politics and Culture: Studies in early modern England* (Cambridge, 1986), 308–415, for the importance of lineage identities and loyalties in English politics.

117. W. Stewart, *The Buik of the Croniclis of Scotland*, ed. W. B. Turnbull (Rolls Series, 1858), i, 451–6, 476–9.

118. See Sellar, 'Earliest Campbells', and Gillies, 'Campbell History'.

119. In the 1370s and 1380s, for example, Gill-easbuig Campbell had attended the royal court on those occasions when Robert II returned to his ancestral lordships in the west (*Lennox Cartularium*, 1833), 6–8; Fraser, *Lennox*, ii, 39–51).

120. Sir John Stewart of Ardgowan had sold his lands in Cowal to Duncan's father, Colin, in 1404 (*AT*, 20/6/1404).

121. *Chron. Auchinleck*, 163. The traditional view that Duncan's eldest son, Gill-easbuig (d. c. 1432), married Elizabeth, a daughter of John, 2nd lord Somerville, is chronologically impossible (*Scots Peerage*, i, 332). If, however, Gill-easbuig had married an aunt or sister of the 2nd lord, the match would have been highly significant, since Thomas Somerville (John's grandfather) was a favoured servant of James I. Could this have been another attempt by Sir Duncan to overcome the king's initial hostility? That there was a link of some sort with the Somerville family is suggested by the fact that in 1459 John, lord Somerville, received a royal pardon for forging the seal of a lord Campbell (probably Sir Duncan) and attaching it to a financial discharge. In addition, the Somervilles of Plean were later to be found in the service of Earl Colin (*RMS*, ii, no. 690).

122. *AT*, 1/4/1387.

123. *AT*, 1432.

124. In 1429 and 1451 Duncan Campbell granted the Dominicans of Glasgow rents from various lands in Cowal (*Glasgow Friars Munimenta*, 163–4, 172–3 (nos. 21,30)). Duncan's grandson, Colin, also granted the Dominicans of Glasgow an annual rent from the escheats of the bailiary of Cowal (Ibid,, 192, no. 40; *Lamont Papers*, No. 15, a notarial transumpt made at Stirling in the House of the Friars Preachers, at the request of Duncan Campbell, lord of Lochawe, on 13 May 1433).

125. Watt, *Fasti*, 26–7.

126. The new dedication of the collegiate kirk of Kilmun in 1442, for example, was to the Virgin Mary and St. Mun. In the thirteenth century the dedication of Kilmun had been in favour of the traditional saint alone (*Paisley Registrum*, 132–4; *Glasgow Friars Munimenta*, 163–4 (no. 21)). Grants by Duncan in favour of Dunoon kirk and to support a ferry across Lochfyne were also made in honour of St. Mary. Mary was a figure of special veneration for the Carmelites and Dominicans, but Sir Duncan's generosity may simply have reflected a pan-European growth of interest in the cult of the Virgin Mary during the later Middle Ages (R. N. Swanson, *Religion and Devotion in Europe, c. 1215-c. 1515* (Cambridge, 1995), 144–5).

127. Earl Colin and his son, Archibald, 2nd earl of Argyll, would certainly later take an interest in a political struggle for control of Irvine between the Montgomeries and the Cunninghams.

128. *Glasgow Friars Munimenta*, 192, no. 40.

129. J. R. Coull, *The Sea Fisheries of Scotland: A Historical Geography* (Edinburgh, 1996), 54–78.

130. *Select Cases Concerning the Law Merchant AD 1270–1638*, ed. H. Hall (Selden Society, vol. 46, London, 1908–32), ii, 18–9; *CDS*, v, no. 62. Although Canville portrayed this act as an illegal seizure when he caught up with Bryan in Dublin

LORDSHIP AND
ARCHITECTURE
IN MEDIEVAL
AND
RENAISSANCE
SCOTLAND

❧

in 1283, it is possible that Bryan was working in defence of the rights of the burgesses of Dumbarton in preventing uncustumed trade through Lochfyne.

131. *ER*, ix, 65.56 lasts (1 last=12 barrels) worth £16 16s.

132. Ibid., 144–5.115 lasts worth £34 10s.

133. Ibid.,146.76 lasts 2 barrels worth £322 17s.

134. Ibid.,e.g. 210, 292, 339, 438, 542, xi, 371, xii, 371, 462, 592, xiii, 226. The custumar of the 'Lowis' received an unusually high fee for the 'great labours and expenses' involved in collecting the customs of the area, indicating that his duties involved visiting multiple sites around the 'Lochs' where herring was being processed and traded (Ibid., 543). Some of the accounts rendered after 1500 refer to the custumar's travels in the 'Isles' and Argyll.

135. Ibid.,542–3. This sum represented the high water mark in terms of royal revenues fom the western fisheries. During James IV's reign the annual sum collected was much more modest, only rarely exceeding £100.

136. *APS*, ii, 179, 183, 209, 235, 242.

137. Ibid.,ii, 183. The terms of the statute (Item 15) should probably be read in conjunction with the act passed in the parliament of October 1488 after James III's death.

138. N. Macdougall, *James IV* (Edinburgh, 1989), 27–44.

139. *APS*, ii, 209.

140. *ER*, x, 374, 499, 570, 638.

141. *RMS*, ii, no. 1993. It is uncertain whether Kilmun was intended to prosper as an outlet for the export of herring or as a location for trade in the general produce of Cowal and Argyll. The October fair would have allowed for the purchase of grain and perhaps also salt in preparation for the processing of a winter herring catch for sale in the major Lent markets of continental Europe (I am grateful to Dr Martin Rourke of the Department of Economic History, University of Edinburgh, for this suggestion). It is also of interest to note, that the Campbell habit of consuming as well as overseeing the trading of fish, a form of food traditionally considered rather 'ignoble' in Gaelic society, drew pejorative comments from the seventeenth-century Gaelic poet Iain Lom MacDonald of Keppoch (*Orain Iain Luim: Songs of John MacDonald, Bard of Keppoch*, ed. A. M. Mackenzie (Scottish Gaelic Text Society, 1964), 42–3). In his 'Oar-Song to MacLean of Duart', MacDonald describes the Campbells (*sliochd Dhiarmaid*) as the 'dirty rabble of the fishing' (*prasgan salach an iasgaich*). I am grateful to Dr Wilson McLeod, Department of Celtic, University of Edinburgh, for bringing this reference to my attention.

142. R. A. Dodgshon, 'West Highland chiefdoms, 1500–1745' in *Economy and Society in Scotland and Ireland 1500–1919*, eds. R. Mitchison and P. Roebuck (Edinburgh, 1988); Dodgshon, ' "Pretence of blude" and "place of thair duelling": the nature of Scottish clans, 1500–1745', in *Scottish Society 1500–1800*, eds. R. A. Houston and I. D. Whyte (Cambridge, 1989).

143. In the lifetime of Sir Duncan Campbell, for example, major work was completed or initiated at Kilmun, Inveraray, Innis Chonaill, Inishail and Eilean Dearg, while in the following chieftainship, Colin, earl of Argyll, rebuilt Castle Gloum in Dollar Glen (renaming it Castle Campbell) and added a new gatehouse to the fortress at Dunstaffnage. When Sir Duncan's daughter, Margaret, was married to Andrew Cunningham of Glengarnock, she was accompanied by a not inconsiderable dower of 800 merks (McGladdery, *James II*, 163). From the fourteenth century onwards the Campbells were also voracious procurers of feudal rights and legal titles inside Argyll, many of which were obtained by outright purchase, for example the estates in Cowal bought from the Stewarts of Ardgowan in 1404–6 for 200 merks (*AT*, i, at date). The most likely marketing

points for the surplus production of Campbell lordship in this period were burghs such as Dumbarton, Glasgow, Renfrew, Irvine and Ayr. See J. Dawson, 'The "Road to the Isles"', at 91–6, for a discussion of the trading links of Clan Campbell in the sixteenth century.

144. Gillingham, 'Disunited Kingdom', 58–64.

145. *Giraldi Cambrensis Opera*, ed. J. F. Dimock, Rolls Series (London, 1861–91), v, 151, quoted in Jones, 'Image of the Barbarian', 396.

146. E. g. *Chron. Bower* (Watt), vii, 359–60, where the kingdom is implicitly divided between 'Scotos silvestres catervanos' and 'eruditos domesticos'.

147. See Gillies, 'Campbell History'; W. Gillies 'The Invention of Tradition Highland-Style' in *The Renaissance in Scotland*, eds. A. A. MacDonald, M. Lynch and I. B. Cowan (Leiden, 1994), 144–56; W. Gillies, 'Heroes and Ancestors', in *The Heroic Process: Form, Function and Fantasy in Folk Epic*, eds. B. Almquist, S. Ó Catháin, P. Ó Héalaí (Dun Laoghaire, 1987), 57–73.

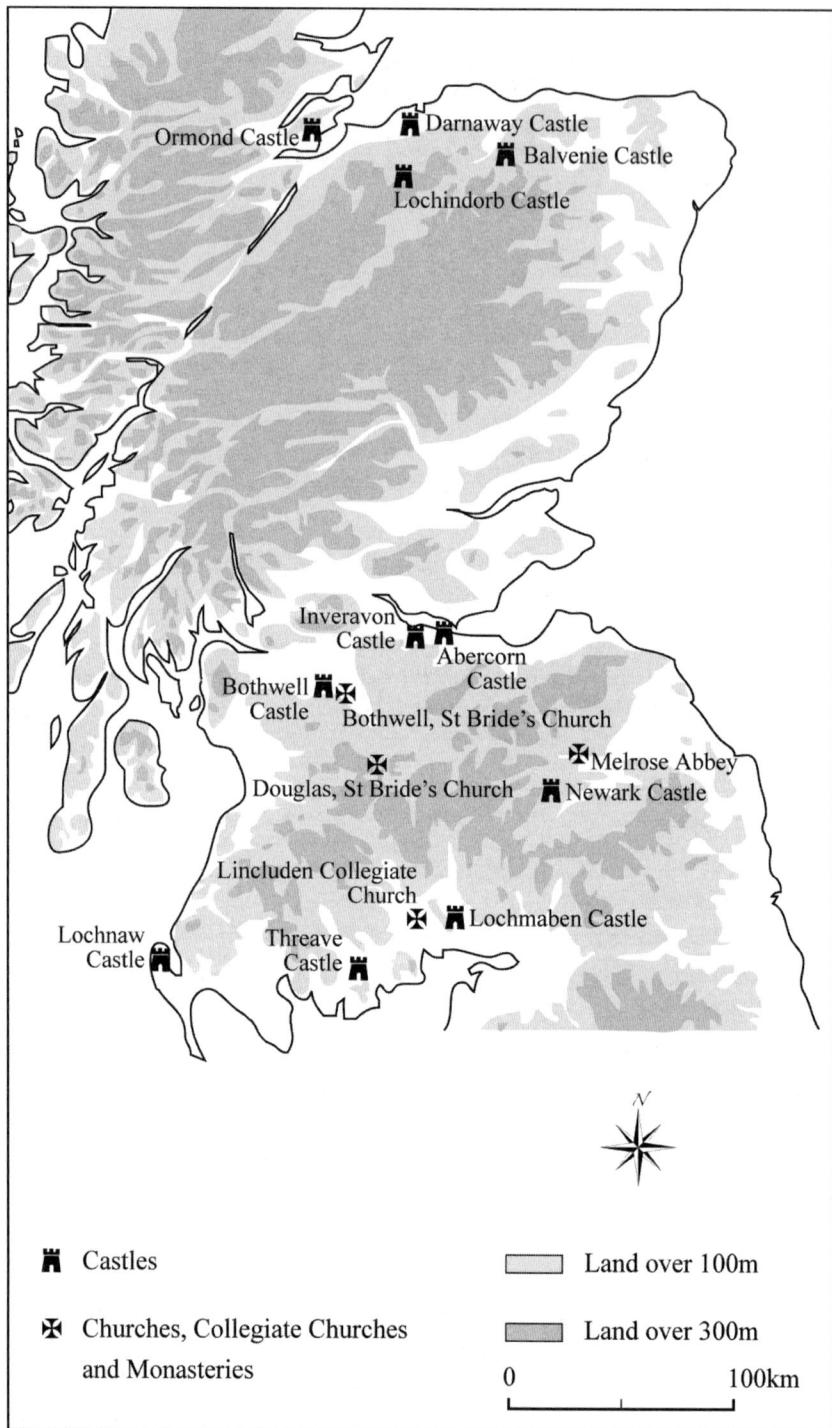

Castles

Churches, Collegiate Churches and Monasteries

Land over 100m

Land over 300m

0   100km

Ormond Castle
Darnaway Castle
Balvenie Castle
Lochindorb Castle
Inveravon Castle
Abercorn Castle
Bothwell Castle
Bothwell, St Bride's Church
Melrose Abbey
Douglas, St Bride's Church
Newark Castle
Lincluden Collegiate Church
Lochmaben Castle
Lochnaw Castle
Threave Castle

Figure 8.1
The Black Douglases.

Chapter 8

⚜

THE BLACK DOUGLASES,
1369–1455

Christine A. McGladdery

By the mid-fifteenth century the Black Douglases, who were among the few significant survivors of the mid-fourteenth century higher nobility, had become the most prominent magnate family in Scotland. The foundations for their rise to power were laid with the encouragement of David II, who wished to rebuild the administration and control of the marches after six decades of intermittent warfare.[1] The Douglases soon established a network of influence on the middle and western sectors of the Anglo-Scottish border. Their position was consolidated in 1369 when David II confirmed Archibald the Grim in the lands of Galloway between the Nith and the Cree, and when Archibald became 3rd Earl of Douglas in 1388, he inherited the entailed Douglas estates of Douglasdale, Lauderdale, Eskdale and the forest of Selkirk. This arose from the death of James, 2nd Earl of Douglas, at the battle of Otterburn in August 1388, leaving no legitimate heirs. A tailzie of 26 May 1342 had been drawn up to cope with such a crisis, and its terms allowed Sir Archibald, the illegitimate son of Robert I's lieutenant, Sir James Douglas, to inherit the earldom. Archibald's succession split the family into two main branches. From his labelling as the 'Black Douglas' and 'Archibald the Black' by the Pluscarden chronicler, Archibald's descendants became known as the Black Douglases.[2] The Douglases of Angus, descended from George, illegitimate son of William, 1st Earl of Douglas, and his mistress, Margaret, Countess of Angus, were, by contrast, labelled the 'Red Douglases'. The castle of Tantallon was the major stronghold of Red Douglas power, although in terms of landed influence, the Black Douglases far outweighed the Red.[3]

The origins of Archibald's rise lay in his marriage in 1362 to Joanna Moray. This brought possession of the lordship and castle of Bothwell in Lanarkshire as the centrepiece of a network of estates which stretched from Easter Ross to the Borders.[4] Walter Moray had acquired Bothwell from the Olifards in 1242, but work on the present castle began only around

LORDSHIP AND
ARCHITECTURE
IN MEDIEVAL
AND
RENAISSANCE
SCOTLAND

ᘏ

*Figure 8.2 (below)
Bothwell Castle,
Lanarkshire: aerial
view.
RCAHMS, LA/2898*

*Figure 8.3 (opposite)
Bothwell Castle,
Lanarkshire: south-east
tower ('Douglas
Tower').
Historic Scotland,
A.2562-2*

1280. It is a monumental expression of lordship and status, comprising a huge donjon at one end of a curtain-walled enclosure, itself entered through a gatehouse consisting of two projecting round towers closely flanking the entrance passage. Much of this ambitious scheme never advanced beyond foundation level, and the castle was eventually completed on a much-reduced scale. Destruction and rebuilding afflicted Bothwell throughout the Wars of Independence, with half of the cylindrical donjon being thrown down when the castle's owner, Andrew Moray, recaptured it from the English in 1337. It lay derelict after that slighting until about 1362, when rebuilding commenced under Archibald the Grim.[5]

The importance of Bothwell to the Douglases' expanding powerbase is implicit in the late fourteenth- and early fifteenth-century remodelling of the castle. A massive square tower, now reduced to its lowest courses, was constructed at the north-east angle of the courtyard as a replacement for the slighted donjon. This was a self-contained structure, a semi-detatched towerhouse which held the private chambers of the Douglas lords. Immediately adjacent to it was a massive hall block, comprising a formal chamber at first-floor level over a range of cellars. Attached to the southern end of this range was a chapel block, from which a further range of accommodation extended westwards along the south curtain wall.[6]

The wealth and sophistication of the Douglases is underscored in the

*Figure 8.2 (below)
Bothwell Castle,
Lanarkshire: aerial
view.
RCAHMS, LA/2898*

LORDSHIP AND
ARCHITECTURE
IN MEDIEVAL
AND
RENAISSANCE
SCOTLAND

ࣶ

remains at Bothwell. The size of its great hall indicates the scale of the household and following to be accommodated within the castle, while the embellishment of the wall-heads provides a memory of architectural exuberance. The corbels which carried the machicolation of the south-east tower are linked by small arches in a manner rare in medieval Scotland, indicating late fourteenth-century continental influence: the Black Douglases' exploits in France would have exposed them to such traditions.[7] It is also evidence of the family's desire to announce their status and position in such outward demonstrations of affluence.

Black Douglas status was further symbolised by the marriage secured in 1400 by Archibald for his daughter, Mary, to David, Duke of Rothesay, the eldest son of Robert III. Bower reports that the marriage took place in the collegiate kirk at Bothwell, which had been founded by Archibald in 1398.[8] Of this large church, only the chancel with its pointed barrel-vaulted roof and the adjoining sacristy survive of the medieval building – the site of the nave and crossing is occupied by the nineteenth-century parish church – but sufficient remains to indicate its former splendour.[9] When he died at Threave on 24 December 1400, Archibald was taken to Bothwell for burial in the collegiate church, breaking the Douglas tradition of burial at either Melrose Abbey or their older mausoleum in the parish church of St Bride at Douglas,[10] further emphasising the importance attached by Archibald to his upper Clydesdale holdings.

Archibald's power and influence increased steadily. In February 1372, Thomas Fleming, Earl of Wigtown, signed his earldom over to Archibald in exchange for a large sum of money.[11] The lordship of Galloway, divided since 1235, was re-united when this sale was ratified by royal charter in October 1372, although there is no evidence of a formal grant of the title, and the Black Douglases did not use it until at least 1406. Significantly, it was not a title used by them after James I's return in 1424, indicating that royal sanction for its use had never been given. The single occasion in the extant records when it was used after 1424 was in 1452, when the 8th earl of Douglas styled himself earl of Wigtown just prior to his murder by James II.[12]

To emphasise this impressive power base in Galloway, Archibald constructed Threave Castle on an island in the River Dee. There is a rich archaeological heritage of crannogs in the south-west of Scotland, and the positioning of Threave links it to this tradition of building on natural or man-made islands. The site itself may have been an early centre of lordship – the name, Threave, is derived from the p-Celtic noun *tref,* meaning a homestead, its simplex form stressing its importance – and Archibald had a massive tower house constructed there. The tower house became a very popular form of architecture for Scottish baronial families, being a simple

*Figure 8.4
Threave Castle,
Stewartry of
Kirkcudbright: aerial
view.
RCAHMS, KB/3036*

164

LORDSHIP AND
ARCHITECTURE
IN MEDIEVAL
AND
RENAISSANCE
SCOTLAND

𝔞𝔨

but effective construction well suited to the localised feuding which was the main form of aggression likely to be experienced by the inhabitants. Built around 1370, Threave is one of the earliest Scottish tower houses, and, like Craigmillar on the south-eastern outskirts of Edinburgh, built by another of David II's henchmen, Sir Simon Preston of Gorton, its model may have been the great tower begun by the king at Edinburgh castle. It rises to 26m through five storeys, entered at first-floor level and with access to the upper storeys provided by a single spiral stair in the thickness of the north-west angle. In its present form, drum towers closely flank three angles of the keep, linked by a curtain wall on the south and east sides, but excavation has shown this to be a mid-fifteenth-century arrangement radically different from its original late fourteenth-century layout. The stark impression created by the free-standing tower house at Threave belies the fact that, in its heyday, other buildings clustered around it forming a bustling castle complex. Excavation revealed the footings of two substantial structures extending east then south of the tower, interpreted as a hall range over built cellarage and an accommodation block with a chapel. Parallels with the planning of Archibald's work at Bothwell are immediately obvious.[13]

Before the excavations at Threave, despite the tower's massive scale, the accommodation provided appeared inadequate for the household of a man of Archibald's standing, and quite incapable of housing his retinue as earl after 1388. The discovery of the adjacent hall ranges has prompted a reassessment of the tower's role, however, and it, like its counterpart at Bothwell, can be seen as the spacious private apartments of the lord and his family. The tower contained, from the base, a cellar-cum-wellhouse, then a vaulted kitchen at first-floor level with the single entrance doorway accessible by a movable external timber stair. Above the kitchen was the hall, then the bedchambers and an upper hall. The eight-foot thick walls of the tower have slits for windows on the landward (east) side, but more generous embrasures with window-seats admitting light on the other sides which faced the river and marshland, and were thus deemed less vulnerable to attack. The tower's main defence was conducted from the wall-head, where timber platforms oversailed the wall face: the socket holes for the supporting beams are still clearly visible on the north, south and east sides. There is evidence of a stone box machicolation over the doorway and the overhanging hoarding would have been reached through window openings in the top storey of the tower. The Douglases, and the masons and craftsmen who built Threave, may have been influenced by the Norman and Angevin models seen during their times in France, a suggestion supported by similarities in the configuration of entry to stair and kitchen to service which does not compare with later Scottish tower house design.[14]

*Figure 8.5
Lincluden College,
Dumfries: chancel
showing monument to
Margaret, Countess of
Douglas, c.1880.
RCAHMS, B 18437*

The advent of new, powerful artillery in the fifteenth century prompted further defensive measures. It is suggested that the siege of Threave by James II in 1455, at which he employed his 'great bombard', was anticipated by the 9th earl in the hastily erected enclosure of drum towers and artillery wall. This new work entailed the demolition of the earlier hall and domestic blocks, the remains of which it partly overlies. This, however, would make it the earliest example of its kind in Britain and, while the Douglases' continental connections may have provided the background for such precocity, given some of the continuing uncertainties surrounding the archaeological and architectural evidence, it is equally possible that its construction post-dates the siege of 1455 as part of the royal consolidation of the castle, not necessarily on the part of James II himself, but by those acting on behalf of his successors some fifty or more years later.[15]

LORDSHIP AND
ARCHITECTURE
IN MEDIEVAL
AND
RENAISSANCE
SCOTLAND

❧

Although Threave is the most impressive example of Archibald the Grim's architectural patronage, he also established Lincluden Collegiate Church in 1389. This, sited on the west side of the Nith near Dumfries, was a college of secular priests which was endowed to celebrate masses for the souls of the founder and his family. It was a significant demonstration of wealth and status, and provided a more personal focus for the spiritual wellbeing of the Black Douglases themselves. The quality of the mason-work in the choir indicates the level of patronage commanded by the Douglases. Its designer may have been the Parisian master mason, John Morow, whose early fifteenth-century work at Melrose Abbey – a monastery with close links to the Douglas family – includes a panel inscribed with other Scottish commissions including work in 'Nyddysdayl' (Nithsdale).[16] Architectural details reflect the French influences to which the Black Douglases were open, particularly through the 4th earl's participation in French military action which earned him the title, Duke of Touraine. It is probable that the 4th Earl intended to be buried at Lincluden, but his final resting place following his death at Verneuil was the cathedral of his ducal capital, Tours. Instead, it is the tomb of his widow, Margaret, the eldest daughter of Robert III, which takes pride of place in the north side of the choir, emphasising her status with its magnificence.

The earldom of Douglas was inherited by the son of Archibald the Grim, also called Archibald. The new 4th Earl was captured by the English in September 1402 at Homildon Hill, then again in 1403 at Shrewsbury, having taken part in the Percys' rebellion against Henry IV. It was not until 1407 that he returned to a Scotland being ruled by an interim government on behalf of James I, who was just starting his eighteen-year imprisonment in England, and ripe for exploitation and acquisition by a magnate with strong territorial and kinship ties. Collusion with the Albany regime brought Douglas the earl of March's lordship of Annandale in exchange for the lordship of Dunbar, which had been held by the Douglases since the disgrace and expulsion of March and his family a decade earlier. Further increase in his personal wealth and influence followed. Complaints appeared in the exchequer accounts indicating that Douglas was subverting revenue from his work as royal justiciar by not rendering the money collected to the government exchequer but keeping it for his own purposes.[17] Use of Edinburgh customs revenue as private income during the early 1420s, and Douglas's independence in foreign policy from as early as 1400, demonstrated his true ambition. With substantial backing from lay and ecclesiastical landowners, his support for Albany was very much on his own terms with no obvious acknowledgement of the governor's political superiority.

Douglas was operating from a very powerful position. He held the earldom of Wigtown, the lordship of Galloway, Annandale, Eskdale and other Dumfriesshire lands, the lordship of Bothwell in Lanarkshire, Douglasdale, the lordship of Ettrick forest in the middle march and lands extracted from the earldom of March in the south-east. The Black Douglases held unrivalled power in the south of Scotland, controlling all three march wardenships following the disgrace of their rivals, the earls of March, in 1400. These wardenships carried with them special military and judicial powers and, by 1420, Douglas was using the title of 'Great Guardian of the marches of Scotland', an announcement, repeated in 1423, of his supreme power on the English border.[18] Douglas was also connected with the religious foundations of Coldingham, Dryburgh and Melrose, and, in Edinburgh, he held the keepership of the castle and was the 'principal protector' of Holyrood Abbey.[19] Indeed, Albany's son and successor as governor held so little sway in Edinburgh that he appeared there only three times, according to the extant records, between 1420 and 1424.[20] Flexibility and personal advantage lay behind Douglas's actions, although this was not necessarily indicative of outright lawlessness and anarchy. A vast connection of strongholds, disparate landholdings, offices and adherents brought its own problems of administration and control, and it is possible that the indenture drawn up between Douglas and Albany on 20 June 1409 was intended to control potentially violent conflicts of interest.[21] In the absence of strong and effective central government, local solutions had to be found and Douglas, with a shrewd eye to his own position, wanted to insure against the possibility of Albany one day becoming king with a written assurance of mutual aid, while keeping the alternative of James I's return always in view.[22]

Pressure on Douglas prior to the return of James I increased when the new earl of March succeeded in 1420 and William, Earl of Angus, attained his majority – both men bearing deep antipathy to the earl of Douglas. This may have encouraged his undoubted efforts to secure the king's release from captivity. The Albany Stewarts, during their time as regency governors, had been lamentably inefficient in labouring for James I's return, and the position from which Douglas was able to negotiate for the return of the king was enhanced by the fact that he was married to James's sister, Margaret. In addition to independent negotiations with the English, Douglas was also pursuing continental ambitions, and his dealings with the French king led, in 1423, to active military service in France.

Before leaving for France, Douglas arranged for the administration of his affairs during his absence, one of which was to create his eldest son, Archibald, Earl of Wigtown, with control of Black Douglas lands and offices. During preparations for his expedition to France, Earl Archibald

LORDSHIP AND
ARCHITECTURE
IN MEDIEVAL
AND
RENAISSANCE
SCOTLAND

❧

visited most of his chief residences, dispensing patronage and delegating the authority necessary for running his estates. In November 1423 Douglas was at Lochmaben, the chief stronghold of Annandale, before progressing to Bothwell by 10 December, where he spent some time sorting out his affairs in his Lanarkshire lands. He probably remained there for the Christmas season before returning to Edinburgh in early February.[23] During that period, Douglas issued charters concerning his lands in Galloway and Annandale, Berwickshire and Roxburghshire, preparing his vassals in them to accept temporary control by Archibald, Earl of Wigtown. The latter issued a charter on 10 January 1424, ratifying his father's confirmation of Michael Ramsay as keeper of Lochmaben Castle, and outlining the terms of his authority over Douglas possessions.[24] A notable exception was the earldom of Wigtown itself, and the lordship of Galloway. The control and administration of these estates was left, on the 4th Earl's authority, in the hands of his wife, Margaret Stewart, Countess of Douglas, and she continued to administer Galloway and Wigtown throughout James I's reign.[25] This may have been a simple matter of delegation, necessary when the Black Douglas landholdings were so geographically spread out, but another reason for Archibald, Earl of Wigtown's apparent exclusion from the administration of the earldom granted to him in 1419 may have been an attempt to forestall royal intervention. The 3rd Earl of Douglas had been granted the lordship of Galloway east of Cree by David II, but the acquisition of the earldom of Wigtown from the reluctant Fleming family at the beginning of Robert II's reign may have been sufficiently questionable to invite royal interest in the possible usurpation of Crown rights in the area, now exercised by the Douglases, such as the collection of the burgh customs of Kirkcudbright.[26]

An important adviser to Wigtown was his uncle, James Douglas of Balvenie, later known as James 'the Gross' because he was so fat. His landed power was based on the former Moray lordship of Balvenie in Banffshire and Ormond in Easter Ross, the lands and castle of Abercorn in West Lothian, and estates at Strathaven and Stonehouse in north-west Lanarkshire.[27] On 7 March 1427, he was granted royal charters confirming him in his West Lothian and Lanarkshire estates, centred on his castle of Abercorn. From this base, Balvenie was well positioned to exploit the customs of Linlithgow during the Albany governorship, relieving local merchants of over £750.[28] The role played by Balvenie between 1423 and 1425 was one of liaison between the Black Douglases and central government in the sensitive period around the return of the king. During the winter of 1423 Balvenie may have been negotiating a marriage with one of Albany's sisters, although this match was abandoned in favour of his subsequent marriage to Beatrix Sinclair, sister of William, Earl of Orkney.[29]

Distancing himself from the Albanys was shrewd enough politically, given
the return of James I, but the Sinclair marriage was more significant in
the sense that Balvenie would wish to establish himself at court not merely
as a representative of Black Douglas interests but with more independence
to look to his own position and exploit opportunities as they arose. The
marriage, too, secured him influential allies in Lothian, where he had
otherwise alienated many of the local political community. He anticipated
the position of favour which would have been held by the Sinclairs, as
Earl William's father, Henry Sinclair, had been tutor to James I and had
been captured with him and held captive in England for several years.
Also, Orkney already had ties with the Black Douglases, as the earl held
Nithsdale in right of his mother, Egidia Douglas, Balvenie's niece. In
addition, the barony of Herbertshire in Stirlingshire had been granted to
the Sinclairs by the 4th Earl of Douglas and the bailie appointed to
administer the barony was Alexander Livingston of Callendar, an active
member of the king's council destined to have considerable influence
during the minority of James II.[30]

Douglas influence on the king's council was sufficient to secure the
protection of their interests while the king was preoccupied with his
dealings with the Albany Stewarts, until the momentous news reached
Scotland that the Scottish army had been all but destroyed at Verneuil in
Perche, Earl Archibald and his younger son, James, being amongst the
dead.[31] At a stroke, the Black Douglas insurance policy was gone, and
irreparable damage inflicted on their apparatus of power in Scotland. James
I was ready to exploit the weakness of the new 5th Earl, as was evident
from as early as 12 October 1424 when Archibald and the king were at
Melrose for the installation of the new abbot. The 4th Earl of Douglas
had been described as 'special protector and defender' of Melrose, but
James I had clearly resumed that role for the crown.[32] The election of
John Fogo as abbot indicates the strands of interest involved: Fogo had
been the 4th Earl's confessor and went on to fulfil this role for James
I.[33] This was just one manifestation of a sustained onslaught on the Douglas
position, with James manoeuvring to ensure that the more personal offices
and local influences belonging to the 4th Earl of Douglas were not
automatically assumed by his son.[34]

Black Douglas influence in the south-east was eclipsed, based as it was
on the 4th Earl's personal control of the area from 1400 The affinity with
local families such as the Swintons and the Humes was weakened with
the deaths of John, Lord Swinton, and Alexander Hume of Dunglass at
Verneuil. In Lothian, the 4th Earl's keepership of Edinburgh Castle and
his special interest in Holyrood Abbey lapsed with his death: Edinburgh
Castle was placed in the 'janitorship' of loyal king's men, Robert Lauder

LORDSHIP AND
ARCHITECTURE
IN MEDIEVAL
AND
RENAISSANCE
SCOTLAND

❧

of the Bass and William Giffard.[35] With the resurgence of influence in the south-east of the earls of March and Angus, Douglas was obliged to accept the diminution of Black Douglas influence there, although he was less sanguine about the king's involvement in the affairs of Wigtown and Galloway, which had been left in the hands of Countess Margaret by her husband on his departure for France. James I maintained this state of affairs by confirming a charter to his sister concerning lands in Galloway, although official recognition of her status in regard to the lands she held was not actually confirmed until 1426.[36] Technically, the lands were still in Black Douglas hands as Margaret was the mother of the 5th Earl and no formal separation from the remaining family estates was suggested, but she was to hold the lands in life-rent only, thus leaving their ultimate fate upon her death open to question. Douglas certainly used the title 'lord of Galloway' during this time, but it may have been stressed to him that the title of earl of Wigtown was not to be used.[37] The loss of control over his hereditary heartland must have been a bitter blow, not least since rents collected from the area in 1456 amounted to £750, indicating that the income afforded to the Douglases from their Galloway lands would have been substantial.

The court met at St Andrews for Christmas 1425, following which Douglas accompanied the king to Edinburgh, appearing on a witness list to a charter issued there on 8 January 1426.[38] Between that appearance and the opening of parliament at Perth on 11 March, Douglas was busy with the administration of his lands in the west and middle marches, certainly spending time at his castle of Lochmaben in Annandale.[39] This was built around 1365 by an occupying English force, and was constructed on a courtyard plan on a promontory site with a clear intention of making it highly defensible, the strongest part of the edifice being the south front, which faced landward. The gatehouse was flanked by projecting wing walls which spanned the moat, providing a safe and protected anchorage for boats.[40] The castle fell into the hands of Archibald the Grim in 1384, four years before he inherited the Douglas earldom, and although there is no evidence of alterations carried out by the Douglases, they appear to have regarded it as an important stronghold from which to administer Annandale and conduct the judicial duties which went with their march wardenships.

In April and May 1426, James I pressed the issue of royal rights in Selkirk. The exchequer audit began in mid-April, but even before then, royal officials had been at work in Selkirk.[41] In early July, Douglas was at Newark Castle on the right bank of the Yarrow near Selkirk, the chief stronghold of his lordship of Selkirk and Ettrick forest, presumably to monitor the actions of Crown officials.[42] Douglas could not shrug off

Figure 8.6
Newark Castle,
Selkirkshire: general
view.
RCAHMS, SE/45

royal interference here, as the value, both strategic and financial, of the lordship of Selkirk and Ettrick was considerable. From Newark, the Black Douglases administered the middle march, collecting feudal revenue, conducting judicial business and dominating Selkirkshire. As its name suggests, it replaced an 'auld werk' and was constructed some time before 1423 by the 4th earl of Douglas. The castle now consists of an oblong tower which would once have been about five storeys high with walls ten feet thick. Only sections of the corbelled parapet remain. The existing entrance is at ground level in the north side and leads into a vaulted basement with the kitchen formed in a timber entresol floor. A straight stair in the north-west angle, changing into a turnpike as it ascends, rises to the great hall on the third stage of the tower. The original main entrance was at this level, reached by an external timber stair, as at Threave. In the north wall of the hall are three mural chambers, the largest of which may have been a guardroom. The upper floors, which have collapsed, were reached by a second turnpike stair in the south-east angle. A barmkin wall enclosed the tower, some substantial sections of which survive, as does a gatehouse.[43] The present image of a monolithic, free-standing tower within an otherwise empty enclosure, however, is, as at Threave, misleading. Substantial though the tower at Newark is, it could not meet the accommodation requirements of a magnate of the standing of Archibald, 4th Earl of Douglas. Reassessment of the site has revealed that the tower block again contained the private suite of the earl and formed the centrepiece of an extensive complex

LORDSHIP AND
ARCHITECTURE
IN MEDIEVAL
AND
RENAISSANCE
SCOTLAND

🦌

of hall, lodging and domestic ranges disposed along the east side of the barmkin.

In the 1450s the Crown rents for the lordship of Selkirk were calculated at £500, and even allowing for a slightly lower value in the 1420s, it represented a substantial sum for the Douglases which they would have been loath to see reduced. The basis of the king's interference was insistence on his feudal rights to specific pieces of land, perhaps in the burgh of Selkirk, overriding the rights of Douglas. This was a flexing of political muscle by James I, intended to deliver a message to Douglas about the changed nature of Scottish politics now that he was back in control, and the message was perfectly understood.[44]

A more subtle manifestation of royal encroachment was the absorption of men with traditional Black Douglas connections into direct royal service. Although it was normal practice for the king to draw his officials from the ranks of his major magnates' affinities, there was clear political manoeuvring involved in drawing off Douglas men and establishing a rival indebtedness. This further fuelled the political frustration which led Archibald to interfere in the affairs of the Kennedies in Carrick in 1429–31 and enter into private negotiations with the English warden of the west march. The outcome was a brief period of imprisonment in 1431 as a salutary lesson against independent action, following which he was restored to his office of warden of the west march only, wardenship of the middle march having been lost to the earl of March who had, in turn, given over the east march to the earl of Angus. Involvement in central government was all but over for Douglas for the rest of James I's reign and he remained in the south administering his local affairs from Bothwell and Newark.[45]

Black Douglas representation at court in the person of James Douglas of Balvenie was still very much alive. In 1430, at the ceremony to celebrate the birth of twin sons to James I and Queen Joan, Balvenie's son, William, was knighted. By 1435 Balvenie was sheriff of Lanarkshire, firmly involved in court service and steadily consolidating his local position. He kept close links with the rising Livingston family, while no doubt casting a wary eye on the favour being extended to the Crichtons within Lothian. William Crichton was a close councillor of the king and came to hold the offices of master of the king's household, sheriff of Edinburgh and keeper of Edinburgh Castle. His cousin, George, was elevated to similar influence in West Lothian, holding the office of sheriff and keeper of Blackness, an important fortress on the Firth of Forth within sight of Balvenie's own stronghold at Abercorn. Unfortunately, little more than grass-grown rubble remains of Abercorn Castle following its destruction by James II in 1455. It had commanding views up and down the Forth and across to Fife, coupled with proximity to Edinburgh, and Balvenie was well placed to involve himself in central politics while bolstering his self-esteem with the magnificence of his castle.[46] Provided James I felt that he could harness Balvenie's ambitious energy in royal service, he was happy to make use of his influence and experience, but the king's death in 1437 led to the unmasking of Balvenie's true ambition.

James I was assassinated at Blackfriars, Perth, on 20 February 1437, but the commission to act as lieutenant-general on behalf of the six-year-old James II was not granted to Archibald, 5th Earl of Douglas, until the summer, possibly arising from a general council held at Stirling in early June.[47] The delay in calling upon the senior representative of the Scottish nobility (and closest in line for the Crown after James II) to take this office probably stemmed from the unwillingness of the queen to bring back a man whom her husband had so clearly distrusted. It is possible that Balvenie used his influence to bring his nephew back to take office and, if this was the case, Archibald was quick to reward him as Balvenie had secured the title earl of Avondale by November 1437.[48]

To understand the renewed influence of the Black Douglases in this period, it has to be noted that they were one of the few surviving magnate families the heads of which were adults at the beginning of the minority of James II. The earls of Angus and Crawford were the others, with the earls of Sutherland and Menteith imprisoned in England as hostages for the ransom of James I. Magnate numbers were always subject to fluctuation due to forfeitures and failures of lines, but from the beginning of the fourteenth century the average was eight to ten; therefore only three adult earls demonstrated the severely depleted ranks of the higher nobility. To make matters worse, Angus died in October 1437, leaving a son of eleven, and Douglas died in 1439, leaving a fifteen-year-old heir. This, more than anything else, facilitated the rise of members of the lesser nobility such as the Crichtons and Livingstons, as they had held political office under James I and were well placed strategically as keepers of the royal castles of Edinburgh and Stirling respectively. Rivalries and disputes barely suppressed under the authoritarian rule of James I now surfaced, and Douglas, as lieutenant-general, was faced with the massive problem of imposing order on these rivals.[49] The lieutenant-general was at his castle of Newark on 4 May 1439 conducting business of his own, but the turmoil which faced his beleaguered government was compounded by an outbreak of plague which, according to the Auchinleck chronicler, began in Dumfries and was 'callit the plague but [without] mercy for thar tuk it nain that ever recoverit bot thai deit within xxiiii houris'.[50] Whether or not Douglas succumbed within twenty-four hours, he certainly died at Restalrig on 26 June 1439, leaving an heir neither old nor experienced enough to assume

LORDSHIP AND
ARCHITECTURE
IN MEDIEVAL
AND
RENAISSANCE
SCOTLAND

᠊᠁

the office of lieutenant-general. No obvious alternative was available, as the next adult male in line for the Crown was Malise Graham, Earl of Menteith, who had been sent to England in the second exchange of hostages in October 1427.[51]

Following the death of his nephew, Avondale became chief representative of Black Douglas interests, with only his nephew's two under-age sons standing between himself and the earldom of Douglas. The events of what came to be known as the 'Black Dinner' when, on 24 November 1440, the 6th Earl of Douglas and his younger brother David were invited to dine at Edinburgh Castle, strongly suggest the involvement of his great uncle. William, Lord Crichton, was chancellor and keeper of Edinburgh castle and, notwithstanding the political struggle in which he and Alexander Livingston had been engaged, he seems to have been working with Livingston in this dramatic action. The youths, in company with their close adherent Malcolm Fleming of Biggar and Cumbernauld, were given dinner, following which Earl William and his brother David were seized and executed on the grounds of treason. The sixteenth-century chroniclers, Buchanan and Pitscottie, make much of the haughty ambition of the 6th earl and his arbitrary actions which lay at the root of the breakdown of law and order,[52] but this is scarcely credible given that he can only have been sixteen years old at the time. Significantly, no specific charges survive, and the boys were not forfeited, allowing a large proportion of the wealth of lands and titles which formed the entailed Douglas estates to pass to Avondale. Sir Malcolm Fleming was executed on the following day, presumably to allow time to form the sentence of forfeiture passed against him.[53] It is virtually impossible to believe that Crichton and Livingston could have taken such extreme action independently, and Avondale, now 7th Earl of Douglas, exhibited no inclination for revenge and even took it upon himself to placate Fleming's enraged son and heir by ensuring that he was allowed to succeed to the lands forfeited by his father and giving one of his own daughters in marriage to Sir Robert Fleming, thus seeking to secure Fleming's indebtedness to him.[54]

The 7th Earl of Douglas lost no time in consolidating his new position as head of the Black Douglas family. The duchy of Touraine and other lands in France acquired by the 4th Earl were beyond recovery because of the absence of any living direct male descendant, although the ambition to recover the possessions persisted, compelling the French king to write a letter in 1448 in which he repudiated firmly all claims made by William, 8th Earl of Douglas.[55] The lordship of Annandale lapsed for the same reason, although the lordships of Galloway and Bothwell were regarded as recoverable as they had been inherited by the sister of the 6th Earl, Margaret Douglas, known to later chroniclers as the 'Fair Maid of

Galloway', to whom the 7th earl planned to marry his son, William. This marriage did not actually take place until after the death of the 7th Earl, but his ambition was clear.[56]

Earl James used his new-won political dominance to advance the interests of his sons. By somewhat dubious means, he secured the earldom of Moray for his third son, Archibald. In 1429–30 James Dunbar, Earl of Moray, died leaving two daughters, Janet and Elizabeth, as co-heiresses. Early in 1442 both sisters were married: the elder, Janet, to James Crichton, eldest son of chancellor Crichton, and the younger, Elizabeth, to Archibald Douglas. At the cost of alienating the Crichtons, James secured Archibald the title of earl of Moray and procured an entail excluding Janet Dunbar in order to give the action a semblance of legality.[57]

The extent of Douglas infiltration into all aspects of Scottish political life was not confined to the secular arm. The Church was, at this time, in schism and was thus vulnerable to political exploitation. John Cameron, Bishop of Glasgow, owed his meteoric rise in fortune to service in the Black Douglas household under Archibald, 5th Earl of Douglas, and his subsequent advancement in the service of James I. In his treatment by James, 7th Earl of Douglas, the divisions which existed in the Black Douglas affinity may be seen. The transfer of title and lands resulting from the 'Black Dinner' did not take place in an atmosphere of complete harmony and acquiescence. There was clearly considerable resentment and antipathy towards the 7th Earl and his immediate family from the families and retainers who had served the 5th Earl and his sons, and Cameron may have been sufficiently identified with the former Douglas line to make the 7th Earl suspicious of him, indicated in the very forthright terms in which Cameron was condemned in a petition sent to the Pope on 3 March 1441.[58] Douglas also endeavoured to gain a foothold in Church affairs by trying to have his second son, James, provided to the bishopric of Aberdeen, although in this he was unsuccessful. Douglas had thrown in his lot with the Council of Basle and the conciliar pope, Felix, but his gamble in seeking the council's support for Black Douglas ambitions did not pay off, as it was the rival pope, Eugenius, who emerged triumphant.

The aspirant bishop, James, was the younger twin brother of Archibald, Earl of Moray, his junior status marked by his father's choice for him of an ecclesiastical career. His failure to win advancement in the Church, however, provided him with the opportunity to prove his worth in secular affairs. This was reflected in an indenture of 26 August 1447, which declared James the elder twin.[59] While William, 8th Earl of Douglas, remained childless, the issue of succession to the earldom had to be settled, and as the next eldest brothers were twins, a decision had to be reached. It is possible that James had shown such prowess in arms and chivalric

LORDSHIP AND
ARCHITECTURE
IN MEDIEVAL
AND
RENAISSANCE
SCOTLAND

?

pursuits that he was considered more suitable for the role of Master of Douglas.

James, 7th Earl of Douglas, died in March 1443 and his son William succeeded as 8th Earl, rapidly assuming a very active role in central government. The Crichtons were edged out of positions of influence and came under attack as Douglas, in league with the Livingstons, set about consolidating his position in what was to be the culmination of a century of painstaking building of power through the acquisition of lands, titles, offices and strongholds. In parliament in June 1445, William's brothers were prominent participants, with Archibald appearing as earl of Moray, Hugh as earl of Ormond, and John as lord Balvenie. Margaret of Galloway held possessions in Aberdeenshire and Inverness-shire from the Moray inheritance absorbed by the Douglases at the time of Archibald the Grim's marriage to Joanna Moray and, following her marriage to William 8th earl of Douglas, the title of Ormond was created for Hugh out of the name of a former stronghold of the Morays in the Black Isle.[60] Only rubble foundations and low walls remain of Ormond Castle now, but the recent clearance of the formerly thickly wooded hill which it occupies has revealed its impressive site, commanding wide views of the Black Isle and Moray Firth. No evidence, documentary or otherwise, remains to indicate any expenditure by the Black Douglases or even how frequently Earl Hugh was present at his castle, but the strategic, elevated site argues for a stronghold affording status and control to its possessor.

The youngest brother, John, was infeft in Balvenie, his father's lordship in Banffshire, centred on Balvenie Castle, strategically situated in Glen Fiddich. Balvenie had been the property of the Comyn earls of Buchan, and was a thirteenth-century construction of fortress-like quality, comprising a quadrangular enceinte measuring 45.7 by 39.6 metres. The defensive nature of the castle is indicated by the 2.1 metre thick walls which rose to 7.6 metres. The enceinte is of massive coursed rubble, once crowned by a parapet, and there is a two-leaved iron yett (gate) within a pend, intended to withstand an onslaught from a battering ram.[61] Various alterations to the thirteenth-century structure are attributed to its period of Black Douglas possession. These included the removal of the thirteenth-century angle towers, and construction of a new hall and chamber block against the west curtain in the early fifteenth century. As at Ormond, however, there is no documentary evidence demonstrating Black Douglas presence at Balvenie.

Opposition to the seemingly unending rise of the Black Douglases certainly existed, but was neither sufficiently strong nor well organised to prevent the dominance of the Douglases and their allies at court for the remainder of James II's minority. It would be misleading to view these years as a time of unceasing conflict and aggression, for the Douglases and their circle provided a core of stability in government. The impressive list of allies built up by William, 8th Earl of Douglas, by 1445 included Sir James Hamilton of Cadzow. His immediate connection with the family was through marriage to Euphemia Graham, eldest daughter of Patrick Graham, earl of Strathearn, and widow of Archibald, 5th Earl of Douglas. With Douglas in a position of considerable influence, Hamilton may have considered his chances of advancement best served by overlooking any resentment felt by his wife towards the man who owed his position as earl of Douglas to the death of her sons. Euphemia's daughter Margaret was married to William, 8th Earl of Douglas, but the marriage did not take place until 1443, possibly indicating that the family of the former 6th Earl was reluctant to agree. Hamilton's advancement during the minority of James II certainly owed much to Douglas influence and patronage, and he was also connected to the Livingston faction through his mother Janet, the daughter of Sir Alexander Livingston of Callendar.[62]

Unchallenged at home, Black Douglas prestige on the continent also ran high. The 4th Earl had fought and died in France, securing Touraine from the French king in the process, and the chivalric reputation of James Douglas had clearly spread abroad.[63] In addition to this, William, 8th Earl of Douglas, travelled to the Papal jubilee in Rome in the winter of 1450–51, journeying by ship to Lille, where he was received by the duke of Burgundy, and thence to Paris where he held talks with Charles VII. He reached Rome by January 1451, travelling with a magnificent entourage and finding himself 'commended by the supreme pontiff above all other pilgrims'.[64] Doubtless this was heady stuff for Douglas, but events back in Scotland were running very much contrary to his interests.

Margaret, Duchess of Touraine, died at Threave some time during 1450,[65] prompting James II to seize the earldom of Wigtown which had been held by her in life-rent. The king had financial difficulties, as he had been unable to provide his new queen, Mary of Gueldres, with sufficient provision as agreed in their marriage settlement in 1449; therefore he feared that her uncle, the duke of Burgundy, would withhold further dowry payments. Such action was complicated by the fact that royal confirmation had been given in January 1450 to the resignation by Duchess Margaret of all the lands, lordship and regalities of Galloway 'above the water of Cree' to William, 8th Earl of Douglas.[66] It is certain that Douglas aspired also to the earldom of Wigtown by virtue of his wife's direct descent from the duchess, but, by launching this pre-emptive strike during the absence of the earl of Douglas, James II was giving notice that his minority was well and truly at an end, as was Black Douglas pre-eminence at court. Those left administering the 8th Earl's lands and possessions were in an

LORDSHIP AND
ARCHITECTURE
IN MEDIEVAL
AND
RENAISSANCE
SCOTLAND

❧

awkward position as they would not have wished to oppose the king by any use of force, while remaining conscious of their duty to safeguard Douglas's interests. It seems that the earl's deputies chose to ignore royal demands and summonses, hoping fervently for the earl's speedy return from Europe. Significantly, a justice ayre was held at Lochmaben in January 1451.[67] Although Lochmaben was a royal castle, it was part of Douglas's jurisdiction as warden of the west march and used frequently by him for business connected with his wardenship. The keepers were Douglas men, and the king's presence there indicates that he was assessing the area and gauging the strength of Douglas lordship.

When news of what had transpired reached Douglas, he returned to Scotland and established a wary truce with the king. In the June parliament of 1451 Douglas submitted formally to James II, overtly demonstrating his loyalty in the surrender of all his lands and titles. These were re-granted immediately, but the ceremony emphasised Douglas's indebtedness to the king for all he possessed. Significantly, the king continued to hold the earldom of Wigtown until October 1451 when it was re-granted to Douglas in the parliament held at Stirling. James II was under considerable pressure to resolve his differences with Douglas, as the men who formed Scotland's political community were very uneasy about the methods employed by the king in attacking the lands of such an important subject at a time when he was not there to plead his case.

From feeling himself to be the most powerful magnate in Scotland with considerable influence over the king, William, 8th Earl of Douglas, must suddenly have felt alarmingly vulnerable. Not surprisingly, he sought to bolster his position by seeking allies, and it was to this end that a bond was made between Douglas and the earls of Crawford and Ross. Both of these men had a history of troublemaking behaviour not calculated to endear them to the king, but as the bond has not survived, its contents are a matter for speculation.[68] It is likely that the bond contained nothing more sinister than the assurance of mutual assistance, but Douglas regained some influence as a result, and was in almost constant attendance at court witnessing royal charters, one of the most significant of which was issued at Edinburgh on 13 January 1452, on which Douglas used the title of earl of Wigtown.[69]

The reluctant re-granting of the earldom of Wigtown to Douglas in October 1451 had said nothing about the use of the title, sensitivity about which had persisted throughout the active reign of James I. An arrogant misreading of his true position may have contributed to the ultimate showdown between Douglas and James II, exacerbated by the discovery of the bond with Crawford and Ross which, given the tension between them, the king chose to interpret in a sinister light. The summons to attend the king at Stirling in February 1452 struck Douglas as sufficiently worrying to make him demand a safe-conduct. Douglas arrived in Stirling on 21 February, but it was on the following day that heated issue was taken over the bond, with the king demanding its dissolution. According to the Auchinleck chronicler, Douglas stated that:

> he mycht not nor wald nocht / Than the king said / fals tratour sen thow will nocht i sall / and stert sodanly till him with ane knyf and straik him in at the colere and down in the body.[70]

Other lords who were present assisted the king's direct physical attack on Douglas, to the extent that the murdered earl's body was said to have had twenty-six wounds. Two of the men named as being involved in the murder, William Cranston and Simon Glendinning, had demonstrable Douglas connections, therefore James II seems to have worked to exploit discontent with the Balvenie line amongst the formerly loyal vassals of the 5th Earl. The Galloway heartland of the original Black Douglas line may never have been committed with any enthusiasm to the family of James the Gross following his inheritance through the dubious means of the 'Black Dinner'. He and his sons spent most of their time in their Lothian and Lanarkshire strongholds of Abercorn and Douglas, together with Newark in Ettrick forest; therefore the more far-sighted of the south-western lairds may have realised that the removal of Black Douglas lordship would facilitate their rise to greater power and influence in their own areas. James II took advantage of this by travelling south immediately after the murder, appearing at Lochmaben, Jedburgh, Dumfries and the castle of Morton, where he issued charters mostly in favour of men with some Douglas connection.[71]

The Black Douglases were in a very difficult position in deciding how to respond, as outright opposition to the king was ultimately treasonable. The murder of the 8th Earl of Douglas by the king, while the former was under safe-conduct, would have been sufficiently shocking to necessitate some hard work by the king to explain his actions and reassure the political community. James II convened a parliament in Edinburgh on 12 June in which the three estates proceeded formally to exonerate him from blame for the murder. The 9th Earl of Douglas's defiant demonstration at Stirling in March and his withdrawal of allegiance[72] gave the king the excuse for a formal show of strength, and he summoned a general levy to appear at Pentland Muir which he led south in a series of raids during July. These raids were resented sufficiently to alienate some support from the king, and it was under pressure from the political community that he was compelled to conclude an agreement with the 9th Earl at Douglas Castle on 28 August. Douglas promised to forgive the king for the murder of

LORDSHIP AND
ARCHITECTURE
IN MEDIEVAL
AND
RENAISSANCE
SCOTLAND

๕

his brother, to renounce all treasonable leagues, to carry out his duties as march warden faithfully and to give the king such 'honour and worship' as he could render safely. Above all, Douglas undertook not to seek 'any entrie in the lands of the earldome of Wigtone' without the queen's consent, and not to obtain the lordship of Stewarton without the king's leave.[73]

Wigtown, it seemed, remained a bone of contention, although Douglas, aware of the uneasiness provoked by the king's actions which had awakened fears of a revival of the ruthlessness exhibited by James I, was ready to exploit his advantage by pressing the king to make good his assurances of good faith. Mounting pressure led the king to enter into a bond of manrent with Douglas at Lanark on 16 January 1453, in which he promised to restore the earldom of Wigtown to Douglas and to promote his marriage to the 8th Earl's widow, Margaret of Galloway.[74] However, Douglas entertained no illusions as to the true nature of his relationship with the king, and there may have been an element of buying time at the root of these negotiations.

The Douglas factions were busily fortifying their strongholds of Lochindorb, Darnaway, Inveravon, Douglas, Strathaven and Abercorn at this time, in apparent anticipation of a direct royal attack.[75] Darnaway and Lochindorb were held by Archibald Douglas as earl of Moray, the former, in the Findhorn valley, being the seat of the earldom. Thomas Randolph, Earl of Moray, nephew of Robert I, had developed it. Earl Archibald may have elaborated upon the castle which he inherited from his Randolph and Dunbar predecessors as earls of Moray, but it is impossible to ascertain the scale of any such work as the medieval building was all but obliterated in a massive rebuilding carried out between 1802 and 1812. The only significant survival from the original building is the roof structure of the great hall, which indicates something of the impressive proportions of the castle. This, an open timber oak roof of arch-braced collar-beam truss construction, with carved bosses at the hammer beams, was long believed to be of fifteenth-century date and to be the work of Archibald Douglas, but modern examination has shown it to be of later fourteenth century date, probably built for John Dunbar, Earl of Moray from 1372 to 1392.[76] Such a lordly setting as was provided by this magnificent chamber accorded well with the character of Archibald Douglas. He was very conscious of his status and eager to enhance his prestige with building work, and there is evidence that he was a patron of the arts, as Richard Holland's 'Buke of the Howlat', rich in political satire, was written under his patronage.

The other castle under the control of Archibald Douglas was Lochindorb, which stands on an island approximately an acre in area in a stretch of

Figure 8.7
Darnaway Castle,
Moray: roof over great
hall.
RCAHMS, B 19997

LORDSHIP AND
ARCHITECTURE
IN MEDIEVAL
AND
RENAISSANCE
SCOTLAND

��

water called Lochindorb, meaning 'lake of trouble' in Gaelic. The castle lies amidst moorland on the borders of Moray and Nairnshire, and consists of a quadrilateral enclosure forming a slightly irregular parallelogram with walls seven feet thick and twenty feet high. At one end is an outer curtain with a portcullis gate, enclosing the section of the island outwith the main enclosure. Round towers projected from each angle of the wall, although only one survives in a reasonable condition, demonstrating no great projection or internal stair, indicating that access would have been by ladder and trap-door. Entry to the castle is from the east, where there is a landing stage for boats. The castle was built in the thirteenth century by the Comyn lords of Badenoch[77] but became a royal castle on the fall of that family c.1308 before passing to Thomas Randolph in 1312 when he was created earl of Moray by Robert I. In the early 1330s the castle was held for the cause of Edward Balliol by David de Strathbogie, Earl of Atholl. Regained by the Bruce loyalists after 1335 and restored to Randolph possession until the extinction of that family in 1346, Lochindorb passed in 1372 into the hands of Alexander Stewart, Lord of Badenoch, the third son of Robert II, who won lasting infamy as the 'Wolf of Badenoch'. The castle may have passed to his bastard son, Alexander Stewart, Earl of Mar, on whose death without surviving heirs in 1435 it would have reverted to the Crown. Upon becoming earl of Moray, Archibald Douglas received possession of Lochindorb and further strengthened the defences of the castle. There is an interesting record of its eventual destruction in the form of a letter of warrant issued by James II to the thane of Cawdor. It seems that Cawdor had designs on a large iron gate, installed at Lochindorb by Archibald Douglas, and the letter gave Cawdor permission to remove the gate and take it back to his own castle, which would have been a small price to pay for Cawdor's co-operation in helping to destroy the northern Douglas stronghold at a cost to himself of £24.[78]

The final onslaught against the Black Douglases was launched by the king at the beginning of March 1455. The Auchinleck chronicler states that James II

> ... kest doune the castell of inverawyn (Inveravon) ... and passit to lanerik and to douglas and syne brynt all douglasdale and all awendale and all the lord hamilton's lands ...[79]

This cut the ground from under the feet of the Black Douglases, the siege of Abercorn marking a particularly crucial stage in their downfall, Abercorn being the principal stronghold of James the Gross's family. With the king undertaking personal supervision of the artillery bombardment of Abercorn, the 9th Earl of Douglas appears to have been unable to decide on a course of action to defend or rescue his castle. This vacillation was the last straw for his hitherto ardent supporter, James lord Hamilton, who, seeing no future for the Douglas cause, submitted to the king. This defection was crucial. Abercorn fell and was destroyed, following which the Douglases were summoned to appear before the king to answer charges of treason. Parliament convened at Edinburgh on 9 June 1455 to proceed with their formal forfeiture, although the 9th Earl, his mother Countess Beatrice, and Margaret of Galloway had fled to England.[80] The three remaining Douglas brothers, Archibald, Hugh and John, plundered and raided on the Borders until, on 1 May 1455, they were routed at Arkinholm by a party of southern lairds including Johnstones, Maxwells and Scotts. Archibald, Earl of Moray, was killed, Hugh, Earl of Ormond, was wounded, captured and subsequently executed, while John, Lord Balvenie, managed to escape to England.[81]

James II proceeded to lay siege to Threave, the last Douglas fortification to hold out against him. On this occasion Douglas did make an effort to save it by offering it to Henry VI, who made a payment of £100 to Douglas on 15 July 1455 'for succour, victualling, relief and rescue of the castle of Treve'. This last-ditch attempt was unsuccessful, and the king employed cannon newly arrived in his armoury from Burgundy to attack the castle which was surrendered when it became clear that no help would be forthcoming from the Black Douglases.[82]

The men who benefited most from the downfall of the Black Douglas family were previous Douglas tenants in the south, such as the Scotts, Johnstones, Maxwells and Kerrs. James, Lord Hamilton, who had remained on the Douglas side almost up to the end, was rewarded by the king, as was the Red Douglas, Earl of Angus. In May 1457 he was styled George, Earl of Angus, Lord Douglas and warden of the east and middle marches.[83] In rewarding loyalty and support offered during his crushing of the Black Douglases, James II was careful not to replace one concentration of power with another, particularly in the south-west where rewards sufficient to bolster their local positions of influence were enough to ensure the willingness of lairds such as the Johnstones and Scotts to take care to block any attempted Douglas resurgence.

NOTES

1. For a general discussion of the rise of the Black Douglases in the fourteenth century, see M. Brown, *The Black Douglases* (East Linton, 1998), Chapters 1–5.
2. *Chron. Pluscarden*, i, 339.
3. Brown, *Black Douglases*, 86–92.
4. *Scots Peerage*, iii, 612–13; Brown, *Black Douglases*, 53–60.
5. C. J. Tabraham, *Scotland's Castles* (London, 1997), 48–51, 64, 89–90.
6. *Ibid.*, 89–90; for an important discussion of the tower house/hall block

LORDSHIP AND
ARCHITECTURE
IN MEDIEVAL
AND
RENAISSANCE
SCOTLAND

❧

arrangement as a key element in later fourteenth-century lordly architecture in Scotland, see C. J. Tabraham, 'The Scottish medieval towerhouse as lordly residence in the light of recent excavations', *PSAS*, 118 (1988), 267–76.

7. S. Cruden, *The Scottish Castle*, 3rd edition (Edinburgh, 1981), 78–80.

8. *Chron. Bower*, 8, 31; *CPL*, Benedict XIII, 83.

9. McGibbon and Ross, *Ecclesiastical Architecture*, ii, 531–7.

10. *Ibid.*, 520–31.

11. *APS*, i, 560–1.

12. C. McGladdery, *James II* (Edinburgh, 1990), 65.

13. Tabraham, 'Scottish medieval towerhouse'; G. L. Good and C. J. Tabraham, 'Excavations at Threave Castle, Galloway, 1974–78', *Medieval Archaeology*, 25 (1981).

14. C. J. Tabraham, *Scottish Castles and Fortifications* (Edinburgh, 1986), 21–2, 48–53.

15. C. J. Tabraham and G. L. Good, 'The artillery fortification at Threave Castle, Galloway', in D. H. Caldwell (ed.), *Scottish Weapons and Fortifications, 1100–1800* (Edinburgh, 1981), 55–72; see also G. Stell, 'Late Medieval Defences in Scotland', in ibid., 21–54, at 47–8.

16. J. S. Richardson, *The Medieval Stone Carver in Scotland* (Edinburgh, 1967), 57–8.

17. *ER*, iv, 80.

18. *CSSR*, i, 142.

19. Fraser, *Douglas*, iii, 349.

20. *RMS*, ii, no. 48; Fraser, *Douglas*, iii, 60; Fraser, *Elphinstone*, ii, 226.

21. NAS, Register House Charters, 223; Fraser, *Douglas*, iii, 369–71.

22. J. Wormald, *Lords and Men in Scotland: Bonds of Manrent, 1442–1603* (Edinburgh, 1985), 39–41.

23. *RMS*, ii, nos. 143, 256, 12; *Melrose Liber*, ii, 507.

24. *RMS*, ii, no. 143.

25. Ibid., ii, no. 12.

26. *Scots Peerage*, viii, 523; *ER*, vi, cx.

27. *RMS*, ii, nos. 38–40, 43, 49; for detailed discussions of the career of James the Gross, see McGladdery, *James II*, Chapter 2 and Brown, *Black Douglases*, Chapters 11 and 12.

28. *RMS*, ii, nos. 43–9; *ER*, iv, 42, 113, 144, 193, 216, 244, 270, 296, 300–1, 365.

29. *APS*, i, 589; Fraser, *Elphinstone*, ii, 226–8; Brown, *Black Douglases*, 234–5.

30. Fraser, *Douglas*, iii, 81–2, 404, 422; *Scots Peerage*, vi, 570.

31. *Chron. Bower* (Watt), viii, Ch. 35. l. 14–57.

32. *RMS*, ii, no. 11; M. Brown, *James I* (Edinburgh, 1994), 52–3.

33. *CSSR*, i, 102, 106; *CPL*, vii, 214; *RMS*, ii, nos. 31, 142.

34. Brown, *Black Douglases*, 230–3.

35. *ER*, iv, 310, 481; *Glasgow Registrum*, ii, 344.

36. *RMS*, ii, nos. 12, 47; Brown, *James I*, 78–9.

37. Fraser, *Douglas*, iii, 383–5.

38. *RMS*, ii, no. 31.

39. Fraser, *Douglas*, iii, 386.

40. Tabraham, *Castles and Fortifications*, 45; Cruden, *Scottish Castle*, 53–4.

41. *ER*, iv, 400–27.

42. Fraser, *Buccleuch*, ii, 25.

43. Tabraham, 'Scottish medieval towerhouse', 270–1, 274.

44. Brown, *James I*, 77.

45. Fraser, *Douglas*, iii, 391–3, 395–8; *HMC*, ix, app. 6, no. 19; NAS, GD 119/164.

46. *Chron. Auchinleck*, f. 116v.

47. Fraser, *Melvilles*, 31.

48. Fraser, *Douglas*, ii, 301; Brown, *James I*, 199.

49. McGladdery, *James II*, 14–15.
50. *Chron. Auchinleck*, f. 109v.
51. Menteith was not destined to be released until 1453.
52. Buchanan, *History*, f. xv; Pitscottie, *Historie*, 40.
53. *Chron. Auchinleck*, f. 121r.
54. Fraser, *Douglas*, i, 446.
55. Ibid., iii, 305.
56. *CPL*, x, 130–1.
57. *Aberdeen-Banff Ill.*, 231–2.
58. *CSSR*, iv, 748; McGladdery, *James II*, 26–7.
59. *RMS*, ii, no. 301; Watt, *Fasti*, 3.
60. Pinkerton, *History*, i, 198.
61. Cruden, *Scottish Castle*, 51; Tabraham, *Castles and Fortifications*, 24.
62. McGladdery, *James II*, 34–5.
63. For a discussion of James, Master of Douglas, and his chivalric career, see *Chron. Auchinleck*, f. 113r; P. H. Brown, *Early Travellers in Scotland* (Edinburgh, 1891); McGladdery, *James II*, 41–3.
64. A. I. Dunlop, *The Life and Times of James Kennedy, Bishop of St Andrews* (Edinburgh, 1950), 124; J. Law, *De Cronicis Scotorum Brevia*, 1521. Edinburgh University Library DC7, 63, f. 128v.
65. Fraser, *Douglas*, i, 397–8.
66. *RMS*, ii, no. 309.
67. *ER*, v, 521.
68. McGladdery, *James II*, 61–4.
69. *RMS*, ii, no. 523.
70. *Chron. Auchinleck*, f. 114v; McGladdery, *James II*, 65–8.
71. McGladdery, *James II*, 69–70.
72. *Chron. Auchinleck*, f. 115r; Fraser, *Buccleuch*, ii, 49.
73. P. F. Tytler, *History of Scotland* (Edinburgh, 1828), ii, 386–7.
74. Fraser, *Douglas*, iii, 483–4; *CPR*, x, 130–1; McGladdery, *James II*, 82–3.
75. *APS*, ii, 76.
76. G. Stell and M. Baillie, 'The Great Hall and Roof of Darnaway Castle, Moray', in W. D. H. Sellar (ed.), *Moray: Province and People* (Edinburgh, 1993), 163–86.
77. Supra, Chapter 4, 'The Comyns'.
78. *Cawdor Book*, 21–2; ER, vi, 486; Cruden, *Scottish Castle*, 61–2.
79. *Chron. Auchinleck*, f. 116r.
80. *APS*, ii, 76.
81. *RMS*, ii, no. 772.
82. *CDS*, iv, no. 1272.
83. Fraser, *Douglas*, ii, 90, 437.

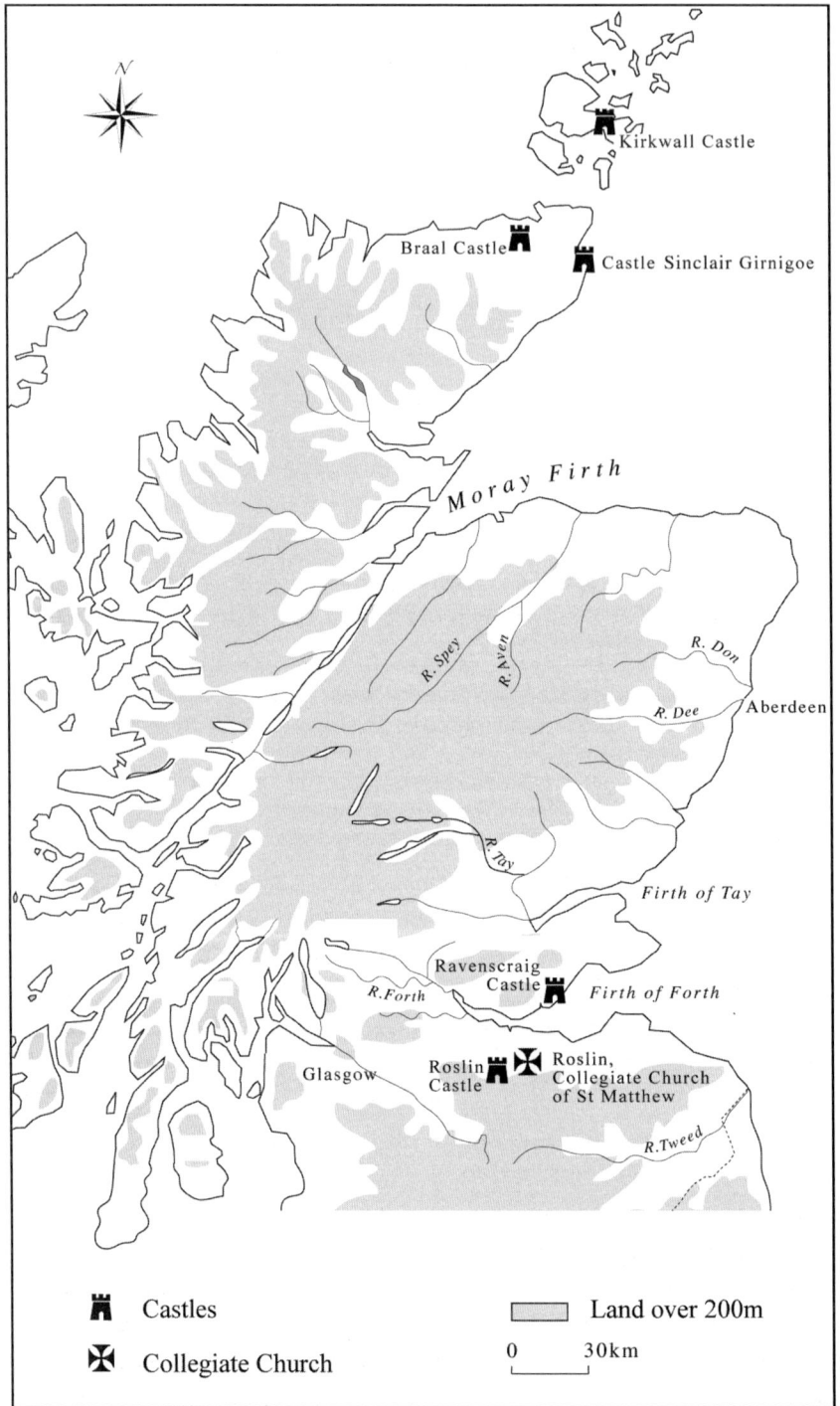

Kirkwall Castle

Braal Castle

Castle Sinclair Girnigoe

Moray Firth

R. Spey

R. Aven

R. Don

R. Dee

Aberdeen

R. Tay

Firth of Tay

Ravenscraig Castle

R.Forth

Firth of Forth

Glasgow

Roslin Castle

Roslin, Collegiate Church of St Matthew

R.Tweed

Castles

Land over 200m

Collegiate Church

0   30km

Figure 9.1
Sinclair properties
mentioned in the text

Chapter 9

✷

THE SINCLAIRS
IN THE LATE
MIDDLE AGES

Barbara E. Crawford

The first Sinclairs to be recorded in Scotland were based south of the Forth in Midlothian where the lands and barony of Roslin were granted to Sir William Sinclair on 14 September, 1280.[1] Cousland, Roslin and Pentland were named together as the baronies of the Sinclair family in 1325[2] but Roslin became the most important seat and Earl Henry called himself 'lord of Roslin' when granted his Orkney earldom title in the late fourteenth century. It was there that the family's main fortified residence was constructed on the dramatic ridge above the gorge of the River North Esk and where the flamboyant collegiate church of St Matthew was founded nearby by the last Orkney earl in 1446. Sir William was an active member of the nobility and a great favourite of Alexander III: he accompanied Alexander's queen, Yolanda de Dreux, to Scotland in 1285, and was justiciar of Galloway in 1287 when fealties were sworn to Edward I. He took a stand against Edward, however, on the king's invasion of Scotland in 1296 and defended the castle of Dunbar against him, for which he was sent to the Tower of London after surrendering. Father Richard Hay in his genealogy of the Sinclairs[3] wrote at length of the role of Sir William at the Battle of Roslin Moor in 1303, mentioning that an English prisoner advised him to rebuild his castle at Roslin in a stronger position on the rock: 'which counsell he embraced, and builded the Wall Tower with other buildings, and there he dwelt'.

Unfortunately, it is not always possible to be certain of Father Hay's information concerning his Sinclair heroes, although not unlikely that the origins of Roslin Castle do lie in this period of war and invasion in southern Scotland. The 'Wall Tower' is probably meant to refer to the rectangular defensive tower at the south-west side which is on the highest point of the castle enclosure. (Fig. 9.2) The family continued to distinguish

LORDSHIP AND
ARCHITECTURE
IN MEDIEVAL
AND
RENAISSANCE
SCOTLAND

✺

themselves in the Wars of Independence. Sir William's son, Sir Henry, supported Bruce and fought at Bannockburn; his second son was William, Bishop of Dunkeld, who also distinguished himself in the struggle against the English.

Sir Henry (d. 1335) was included as one of the barons of Scotland who supported the Declaration of Arbroath dated 4 April, 1320, but in the next year appears as royal bailiff in Caithness,[4] a rather surprising move north which anticipates the future role which the Sinclairs were to play in the Scandinavian parts of Scotland. It may have had something to do with his marriage to Alicia de Fenton, a northern heiress with lands in Ross, who survived him and suffered loss of her dower because of her position regarding Edward III. He was predeceased by his heir Sir William (d. 25 March, 1330) who was slain, and maybe also another son, John, in battle at Tebas de Ardales by the Moors of Granada while they were accompanying Sir James Douglas to Palestine with the heart of Bruce. This left a minor, another William (d. post-1358), who, after the death of his grandfather, must have come under the patronage of William, Earl of Ross, for he eventually (c.1350) married Isabella de Strathearn, eldest daughter of the second marriage and main heiress of Malise, Earl of Caithness and Orkney. In 1344 she had been designated as Malise's heir, who gave control of her marriage to her uncle, William, Earl of Ross.[5]

Figure 9.2
Roslin Castle and
Chapel, Midlothian:
general view, c.1880.
RCAHMS, C 22386

Drawn by R.W.Billings.

Engraved by G.B.Smith.

Figure 9.3 (left)
Roslin Chapel,
Midlothian: eastern
aisle by R W Billings.

Figure 9.4 (below)
Roslin Castle,
Midlothian: view
from north-west (from
MacGibbon and Ross,
Castellated and
Domestic Architecture,
volume 1 (1887), 368,
Fig. 318)

LORDSHIP AND
ARCHITECTURE
IN MEDIEVAL
AND
RENAISSANCE
SCOTLAND

⁊⁊

At about the same time a Thomas Sinclair, believed to be another son of Sir William,[6] was closely involved with John de Hay of Tulibothil,[7] sheriff of Inverness whose sister he married, as well as with members of the Ross family. By 1364 Thomas Sinclair was called 'baillie of the king of Norway' in Kirkwall, when he witnessed a charter of resignation of land to Hugh de Ross.[8] During this period in the 1350s and 1360s the Ross family dominated events in the whole north of Scotland, including Orkney, in the vacuum left by the death of Earl Malise *c*.1350 leaving no male heir. It was clearly through the patronage of the Ross family that the Sinclairs were catapulted into their premier position of power in the north of Scotland.[9]

This dramatic development of the fortunes of the Sinclair family must have entailed a process of adaptation to the completely different political and cultural circumstances which they encountered in Orkney and Caithness. They entered a Scandinavian world and, once William and Isabella's son Henry (d. *c*.1400) had had his claim to the earldom lands and rights of Orkney accepted by King Haakon VI Magnusson in 1379, he was the holder of the most ancient earldom in the kingdom of Norway. This brought new obligations and new honours, but also new and very different problems from any that the family had encountered before. Sadly, one can glean very little about the way in which the members of the Sinclair family adapted to their changed circumstances, but what evidence there is suggests that they took on the challenges of their position with energy and determination.

The process by which the lands of the earldoms of Orkney and Caithness were divided among the five daughters of Earl Malise is described in detail in the 'Genealogy of the Earls', a fifteenth-century history of the descent of the earls of Orkney and Caithness drawn up by Bishop Thomas Tulloch to support the claim of William, last Sinclair earl in the 1420s.[10] It is said there that Malise's 'lordschipis of lands and possessionis war dividit amongis thame' but that the son of the eldest daughter inherited the title to the earldom of Caithness 'be the law of Scotland and conswetude heritageble'. As far as Orkney was concerned, however, he only inherited 'ane soum part or quantite of the lands of Orchadie, as partinant or belangand, efter the law of Norwege, to the eldest sister be jure of heritage'. This did not include the title to the earldom, which could be granted to whichever member of the family made the best claim, and in fact the earldom was granted *without* the title to the eldest grandson, Alexander de Ard, for five years in 1375.[11] Presumably his government of the islands was unsatisfactory and in 1379 Henry Sinclair and his cousins, Alexander de Ard and Malise Sperra (as well as Henry's mother) attended King Haakon VI at Marstrand in south-east Norway, where Henry was awarded the title of earl of Orkney along with all rights and powers attached, as well probably as royal rights and powers. The document which Henry then issued acknowledging his grant as well as his numerous obligations (eighteen in number) laid on him by the Norwegian government still survives, one of which forbade him to build any fortifications in his earldom.[12] Hostages were left behind to ensure the fulfilment of obligations – one of them Henry's great rival Malise Sperra – who received permission in the following June to return to Scotland on condition that they themselves would make sure that the obligations were fulfilled. One letter survives, issued by Earl Henry at St Andrews in September 1379, in which he announces that he has promised King Haakon not to alienate or pledge any lands or islands in his earldom of Orkney.

The theoretical grant of the earldom was only a start, and clearly Henry had to establish himself in the islands where no earl had been in power since the death of Earl Malise nearly thirty years before. A power struggle with Malise Sperra developed, eloquent witness to which is provided by the 'Submission' of Malise in 1387 in which he pardoned all injuries and offences done to him by Earl Henry and his men and promised to restore and make satisfaction for any injuries committed by him or his men. My interpretation is that Malise had been given a grant of royal authority in Shetland, for the evidence shows that he was highly placed in the king's council in Norway and held a Norwegian knighthood.[13] Nothing in Earl Henry's installation document shows that Shetland was included in his grant of the earldom, but in 1386 Malise was behaving high-handedly in Shetland. The final clash between the two cousins occurred in Shetland in 1391, and the Icelandic Annals record that Malise was killed and seven men with him by the earl of Orkney, but one young man escaped in a six-oared boat and with seven others fled to Norway. This victory would appear to have given Henry Sinclair *de facto* control of Shetland, and in the same year he got his brother, David, to resign to him all rights and claims which he might have in Orkney and Shetland by reason of his mother, Isabella Sinclair, in return for a grant of land in Aberdeenshire.

All this evidence proves beyond doubt that the first Sinclair earl established his position in the Northern Isles with some degree of military force, and it is very likely that it was this earl who built the castle of Kirkwall in Orkney against the strict prohibition of his installation document.[14] However, he appears to have remained on reasonably amicable relations with his Norwegian sovereign: we know that Earl Henry was in Norway or Denmark in 1389 to acknowledge Erik of Pomerania's claim to the Norwegian throne[15] and we have evidence from a letter of Richard II of England to Queen Margaret of Norway (between February 1389 and April 1391) of cordial relations with her. This letter refers in particular to Earl Henry's complaints to Queen Margaret of 'the intolerable and extreme

LORDSHIP AND
ARCHITECTURE
IN MEDIEVAL
AND
RENAISSANCE
SCOTLAND

❧

hurt committed against him' by Richard's subjects.[16] The king comments that the same earl and his subjects together with the French and Scots have made war against him notoriously and he does not therefore feel inclined to give the safe-conduct to him which the queen has requested. However, by 1392 Richard had granted a safe-conduct to the earl and twenty-four companions to pass through his dominions – presumably to go to Denmark on some royal business. Where exactly the earl had been making war against King Richard is not clear, whether within his own territories or elsewhere, but his reference to attacks against him by English subjects is likely to be connected with fishing disputes in waters round the Northern Isles.

It is this situation of violence in northern waters which was probably responsible for the death of Earl Henry I, which is reported in the Genealogy as having taken place in Orkney when 'for the defence of the cuntrie (he) was sclane thair crowellie be his innimiis'.[17] This may be the occasion in 1400 when an English fleet landed in Orkney, as recorded by Walsingham. The Genealogy continues to give the highly interesting information that after his death his mother (Isabella, the main heiress of Earl Malise who married William Sinclair) came to Orkney and lived permanently there, surviving all her sisters and all her sisters' children, succeeding to them 'as anerlie ane and lawfull aire of the Eirledome of Orchadie, and of the lands of Cathanie, belangand till hire as till ane anerlie sister' excepting one portion only of the Caithness estates. This statement is made with the clear indication of some sort of reversal of inheritance which probably operated according to Norwegian legal custom in which women had recognised rights to family lands. In this case the operation of these rights put Isabella in the powerful position of gathering into her hands virtually all the lands which had been shared out among the five daughters of Earl Malise, and holding these until her grandson succeeded to her. This situation could help to explain why the next earl appears to have had very little to do with his northern earldom – his grandmother was in charge in Orkney and perhaps survived into the second decade of the fifteenth century, for the Genealogy, written in 1446, says: 'Of this thing thar bene faythfull witness as zit leweand on lyfe, quhilk saw the modir of Henrie the first, and spak with hir at lenth'.

Earl Henry I had at least ten children by his wife, Jean, daughter of Walter Haliburton of Dirleton. The heir to the earldom, his eldest son, Henry II, is said, as noted, to have succeeded to his grandmother as regards the northern lands and it is doubtful whether he ever visited his Norwegian overlord to receive a grant of the earldom title, although he used it from the date of his succession to his father. He was clearly fully occupied in central Scottish affairs, presumably based on his Roslin stronghold, and Father Hay says that he 'built the great dungeon of Roslin, and other walls thereabouts'.[18] Through his prestigious marriage to Egidia, granddaughter of King Robert II, he was very close to the royal court, as can be seen from his witnessing of important royal charters. At the beginning of his career he was taken captive at the battle of Humbleton (14 September 1402) and following his release was put in charge of Border defence, leading the Scottish forces at the siege of Berwick (1405). The next year he was again captured by the English while accompanying the king's son and heir on his way to France for greater safety, and was in and out of custody thereafter for some years.[19] His recorded movements were all southwards; in 1409 he travelled to England on the affairs of the captive James I; in 1412, along with the earl of Douglas and fifty horsemen, he had a safe-conduct to pass through England to France or Flanders; in 1416 he had a safe-conduct for twenty persons to come from and return to Scotland. From this very year there is some evidence that he as well as his brother, John, were more active in the administration of the Northern Isles, which makes one suspect that their grandmother, Isabella, died around this time; first of all a letter dated 11 December, 1416, of 'Henry erle of Orkynnay Lord ye Sincler and of Nyddesdale' made his brother-in-law David Menzies of Weem tutor testamentar of his son and heir, William, and other male or 'famale' children and governor of all his men, lands, rents, possessions and goods in Orkney until his heirs attained their majority.[20] Eighteen months later (21 September, 1418) John Sinclair received the very important grant of Shetland as a life fief with all royal rights, which made him the *foud* (Danish *foged* = royal official) and provides the first evidence that the Sinclair family had acquired control of Shetland.[21] Earl Henry among other magnates died of 'le qwhew' recorded by Bower in 1420.[22]

Although Earl Henry II's son and heir, William, appears to have been under age for a few years after his father's death, he was nonetheless proposed as a hostage for James I in 1421, and received safe-conducts in 1423 and 1424. He met James I at Berwick on his return to Scotland in April 1424, and was one of the assize which condemned the duke of Albany and his sons to death in 1425. By then he had put forward his claim to the earldom of Orkney, which had been controlled by the bishop, Thomas Tulloch, for a period since his father's death, followed by David Menzies. The remarkable 'Complaint of the people of Orkney' sent to the Queen of Norway in 1425 along with a letter asking that the young earl be appointed their governor shows clearly that there had been much disturbance in the islands between the followers of David Menzies and of Thomas Sinclair, a member of the family established in Orkney.[23]

LORDSHIP AND
ARCHITECTURE
IN MEDIEVAL
AND
RENAISSANCE
SCOTLAND

❧

William was not, however, formally invested as earl by King Erik until 1434. The conditions detailed in his installation document are similar to those of his grandfather's of 1379, with extra attempts to strengthen the number of sureties and referring specifically to 'illa turris' in the burgh of Kirkwall which had been constructed illegally and which had to be rendered up to the king on Earl William's death.[24]

By this date he had married Elizabeth Douglas, widowed twice previously, and for which a papal dispensation was granted in 1432 for them to remain in matrimony. Earl William was involved in protracted legal battles to assure her legal rights in her former husband's property, and in 1437, just after the murder of James I, as countess of Buchan and Orkney, she was given a grant of the fruits of the earldom of Garioch. Her brother at the time was lieutenant-general of the kingdom; this marriage had brought Earl William into close contact with the royal court, and in 1436 he had been chosen, as pantler and admiral of the fleet, to accompany the king's daughter on her journey to France for her wedding to the Dauphin (his father appears to have been admiral before him). His position of power intensified during the minority of James II when his relatives, the Douglases, were in control, nor did it diminish when the king came of age: he acted as steward at the young king's marriage to Mary of Gueldres in 1449, and in 1454 was appointed chancellor.[25] By that date his wife had died and he had broken with the Douglases and was active in the campaign against Threave Castle in 1455, also holding James, Lord Hamilton, in custody at Roslin.[26] In the same year he was granted the earldom of Caithness, thus succeeding in re-uniting the two ancient northern earldoms which had been separated since the death of Earl Malise c. 1350: it was made in compensation for his claim to the lordship of Nithsdale. His southern seat at Roslin was also being developed into a power centre commensurate with the standing of a magnate of Earl William's status. Amongst all the details of the magnificence of his retinues and standard of living, Father Hay says very specifically that 'he built the church walls of Rosline, haveing rounds with faire chambers and galleries theron. He builded also the foreworke that looks to the north-east: he builded the bridge under the castle and sundrie office houses'.[27] Commentators have interpreted the meaning of this in different ways: the Royal Commission's *Midlothian Inventory* assumed that 'church walls' is a mistake for 'castle walls',[28] whereas MacGibbon and Ross accepted that he did build a chapel in the castle and that the north-west wall with its eight great buttresses must have been part of it.[29] It can perhaps be accepted that this remarkable militarised structure which so puzzles architectural historians was indeed the work of this remarkable man. The collegiate church of St Matthew, lying above the castle rock, which he certainly founded in 1446, and of which only the eastern limb was ever completed, is a piece of architectural extravaganza which has never been satisfactorily explained in the light of contemporary architectural styles.[30] Roslin itself was erected into a burgh of barony in 1456.

From this position of power in the kingdom of Scotland Earl William's star rapidly waned. He ceased to be chancellor in the later months of 1456 and along with Bishop Kennedy moved to the sidelines as the young James II took a more aggressive line in both internal and external politics. In foreign matters the 'annual' of Norway loomed large and inevitably meant strained relations with the king of Denmark-Norway (who would have been Earl William's acknowledged overlord for his earldom of Orkney, but there is no evidence that he had ever been to do homage since 1434, although he had been summoned in 1446, when the present version of the 'Genealogy of the Earls' was written). Negotiations over the 'annual' took place in the late 1450s, and at a meeting of Danish and Scottish envoys in Paris in 1460 it became clear what James's intentions were regarding Orkney and Shetland. Undoubtedly, Earl William must have been aware of royal ambitions regarding his earldom and possibly attempted

Figure 9.5 Ravenscraig Castle, Fife: aerial view. RCAHMS, F/12858

LORDSHIP AND
ARCHITECTURE
IN MEDIEVAL
AND
RENAISSANCE
SCOTLAND

♒

to implement delaying tactics.[31] He also embarked on an expensive purchasing of odal lands in Orkney at this time, apparently with the intention of acquiring an estate which could not be encroached upon by the king.[32] The untimely death of James II in 1460 allowed the earl a breathing space to prepare himself better for the time when royal ambitions would once again focus on his rich northern possessions. During this period, he was once more called upon to guide the kingdom, and acted as one of the seven regents for the minority of James III, which provided him with an excuse for not being able to respond to King Christian's summons to him to attend the Danish court.

With the rise of the Boyds to power, aggressive policies were again directed towards the Northern Isles. The situation of tension over the 'annual' was used as a means to achieve these ambitions, in the marriage negotiations which were conducted at Copenhagen in the summer of 1468. The earl refused all attempts by King Christian to summon him, undoubtedly realising that his position as vassal of both kings made it exceedingly difficult for him to be involved in the negotiations. These resulted in the extraordinary acquiescence of King Christian in the demands of the Scottish envoys that Orkney be handed over as part of the dowry

Figure 9.6
Ravenscraig Castle,
Fife: from north-west.
Historic Scotland,
A.3136-4

of Princess Margaret.[33] Desperately short of cash and desperate for a good marriage, he agreed to pledge the islands as part-payment for the dowry; in the following year he agreed to pledge Shetland for most of the rest. There is little doubt that this transfer included all of the islands, and not just the royal estates as has been argued.[34] It remained for the ambitious councillors of James III to prevail upon the earl to give up all his rights in the earldom, which he did in 1470, thus assuring the Scottish Crown of permanent possessions in the islands, if the Danish monarchy ever succeeded in redeeming them. The impression that the earl came out very badly from the 'excambion' of 1470 is probably unjustified as he received in exchange for his 'right' in the earldom several remarkable privileges which he must have stipulated: a handsome pension of 400 marks and the very fine royal castle of Ravenscraig in Fife. This had only recently been constructed for the queen dowager and was perhaps the most up-to-date castle in Scotland, built for defence against gunpowder. It provided a caput for the estates which the family already had nearby.

From 1470 Earl William was known as 'earl of Caithness' until 1476 when he resigned this earldom in favour of the William who was the eldest son of his second marriage; thereafter he was only 'Lord Sinclair'. His latter years were occupied with family affairs, although he was named as an envoy to England once or twice. Family matters were problematical, although evidence suggests that his second marriage to Marjory Sutherland, daughter – possibly natural – of Alexander Sutherland of Dunbeath, was very successful.[35] At least there were fourteen children as a result. Alexander Sutherland's will, dated 1456, may indicate that Earl William's liaison with Marjory had not at that time been regularised, although it later was. Such a marriage, to a possibly illegitimate daughter of a member of the Sutherland family with no standing in the north, is very surprising. However, Alexander's will indicates that he had been a source of credit for the earl, perhaps to help with the land-purchasing policy in Orkney. The children of this marriage clearly took precedence over the son of the first marriage to Elizabeth Douglas, William 'the Waster', who was not considered suitable to be his father's main heir, although he did succeed in getting possession of the Fife estates after his father's death. Ravenscraig was thereafter the main seat of the Fife Sinclairs.

In 1476 the old earl had done his best to ensure that his main estates went to the elder sons of his second marriage, the earldom of Caithness to William, and Roslin and Ravenscraig to Oliver. Nonetheless, shortly after his death, in the early months of 1480, a great deal of in-fighting broke out between the half-brothers, to which several bonds and agreements bear witness. A verdict of idiocy was procured against the elder William in 1482, but his interests were well represented by his eldest son,

Figure 9.7 (opposite)
Castle Sinclair
Girnigoe, Caithness:
general view, c.1908.
RCAHMS, CA/192

Figure 9.8 (above)
Castle Sinclair
Girnigoe, Caithness:
aerial view,
RCAHMS, B
47452/CN

Henry, who eventually restored the fortunes of the family in the Northern Isles based on the 'conquest' estates acquired by his grandfather in Orkney which did not escheat to the Crown along with the earldom lands.[36] This was done in conjunction with his uncle, Sir David Sinclair of Sumburgh, an illegitimate son of the old earl who pursued a successful career in the service of both the kings of Scotland and of Norway, and who built up a personal estate in Shetland based on 'conquest' lands which he prevailed upon all his half-brothers and sisters to resign to him in 1498.[37] It is perhaps significant that the Sinclair fortified base in the Northern Isles was only ever Kirkwall Castle; there is no evidence that any other strongholds were built in the islands[38] until the advent of the Stewart earls and their followers (excepting earlier defensive structures like Cubbie Roo's Castle on Wyre). Even Sir David, who was captain of Bergenhus (the

LORDSHIP AND
ARCHITECTURE
IN MEDIEVAL
AND
RENAISSANCE
SCOTLAND

ૐ

fortified royal centre in Bergen), never built a castle at Sumburgh, his main Shetland residence. The situation was quite different in Caithness, where the younger Earl William probably had possession of Braal Castle, as the caput of the earldom (first referred to in March 1374/5), but is also said to have built Girnigoe Castle on the north coast in the late fifteenth century.[39] This castle, embellished in the early seventeenth century with the building on the landward side known as Castle Sinclair, was the main seat of the Sinclair earls. There are many more primitive defensive towers (like Old Wick and Ackergill), a likely result of the division of the earldom lands during the period in the mid-fourteenth century when there was no earl. In the saga period we also know that there had been fortifications at Lambaborg (Buchollie), at Scrabster, which the bishop held *c.* 1200, and at Thurso, where the earls had a castle at the same time. The contrast between Caithness and the Northern Isles in respect of castle-building is probably a result of greater control exercised by the earls over their Orkney earldom than their Scottish one.

NOTES

1. *Newbattle Registrum*, 290; *Scots Peerage*, vii, 564.
2. *CDS*, iii, no. 352.
3. Hay, *Sainteclaires*, 10–12.
4. *Diplom. Norv.*, v, no. 68.
5. *RMS*, i, App. I, no. 150.
6. *Scots Peerage*, vii, 567.
7. *Aberdeen-Banff Ill.*, ii, 384.
8. *Aberdeen Registrum*, i, 106.
9. B. E. Crawford, The Earls of Orkney-Caithness and their Relations with Norway and Scotland 1158–1470 (unpublished PhD thesis, University of St Andrews, 1971), 220–2.
10. *The Bannatyne Miscellany* (Bannatyne Club, 1827–55), iii, 65–85.
11. *Diplom. Norv.*, ii, nos. 437, 438.
12. Ibid., ii, no. 457, translated in *Orkney Recs.*, no. xi.
13. B. E. Crawford, 'The pledging of the islands in 1469: the historical background', in *Shetland and the Outside World 1469–1969*, ed. D. J Withrington (Aberdeen University Studies, no. 157, 1983), 39.
14. Hay, *Sainteclaires*, 17.
15. *Diplom. Norv.*, iii, No 484.
16. *The Diplomatic Correspondence of Richard II*, ed. E. Perroy (Camden Society, 3rd series, xlviii, 1933), no. 130.
17. *Bannatyne Miscellany*, iii, 81.
18. Hay, *Sainteclaires*, 20.
19. *Scots Peerage*, vii, 570–1.
20. Campbell of Monzie Papers, University of Guelph, Ontario.
21. *Diplom. Norv.*, ii, no. 467.
22. *Chron. Bower* (Watt), viii, 117.
23. *Diplom. Norv.*, ii, no. 691; ibid., vi, no. 423, trans in *Orkney Recs*, xviii, xix.

24. *Norges Gamle Love Anden Raekke 1388–1604*, ed. A. Taranger (Christiania, 1912–18), no. 74.

25. C. A. McGladdery, *James II* (Edinburgh, 1990), 85.

26. *Chron. Auchinleck*, 167, f. 116v.

27. Hay, *Sainteclaires*, 26.

28. RCAHMS, *Midlothian*, 109.

29. MacGibbon and Ross, *Castellated and Domestic Architecture*, i, 370–1.

30. B. E. Crawford, 'Earl William Sinclair and the Building of Roslin Collegiate Church', in *Medieval Art and Architecture in the Diocese of St. Andrews*, ed. J. Higgitt (British Archaeological Association, Tring, 1994), 100.

31. B. E. Crawford, 'William Sinclair, earl of Orkney and his Family: a Study in the Politics of Survival', in *Essays on the Nobility of Medieval Scotland*, ed. K. J. Stringer (Edinburgh, 1985), 237.

32. Ibid., 240–1.

33. B. E. Crawford, 'The Pawning of Orkney and Shetland: a reconsideration of the events of 1468–9', *SHR*, xlviii (1969), 39.

34. B. E. Crawford, 'The Earldom of Orkney and the Lordship of Shetland; a re-interpretation of their pledging to Scotland in 1468–9', *Saga-Book of the Viking Society*, xvii (1967–8), 167.

35. B. E. Crawford, *The History of Dunbeath in the medieval period* (Dunbeath, 1990), 12.

36. Crawford, 'Earl William Sinclair', 242.

37. B. E. Crawford, 'Sir David Sinclair of Sumburgh', in *Scandinavian Shetland. An Ongoing Tradition?*, ed. J. R. Baldwin (Edinburgh, 1978), 5.

38. Although it has been speculated that the Earl's Palace in Birsay may have originated as a Sinclair structure, the evidence is not conclusive.

39. The earliest reference to the castle of Braal or Brawl is in March 1375/6 (*RMS*, i, No 641). Girnigoe is said to have been built by Earl William between 1476 and 1486 (*Visits to Ancient Caithness*, 3rd edition 1982, 28), but the earliest reference I have found is 1496 (R. Saint-Clair, *The St. Clairs of the Isles* (Auckland, 1898), 187). A programme of excavation at Castle Sinclair Girnigoe is being undertaken by the University of York on behalf of the Clan Sinclair Trust. The findings to date point to its origin as an enclosure castle of late fourteenth- or early fifteenth-century date, subsequently remodelled in at least three major phases.

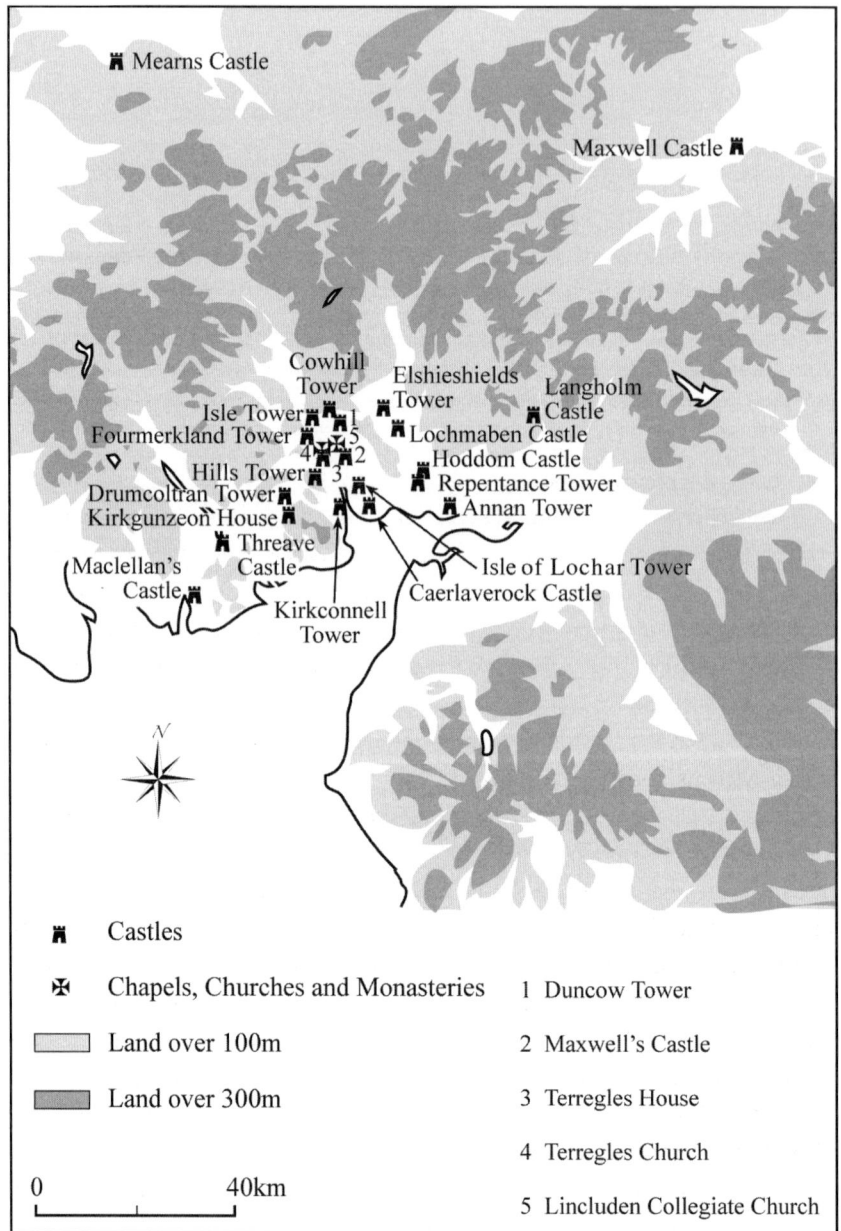

Mearns Castle

Maxwell Castle

Cowhill Tower
Elshieshields Tower
Langholm Castle
Isle Tower 1
Fourmerkland Tower 4 5
Lochmaben Castle
3 2
Hoddom Castle
Hills Tower
Repentance Tower
Drumcoltran Tower
Kirkgunzeon House
Annan Tower
Threave
Maclellan's Castle
Castle
Isle of Lochar Tower
Caerlaverock Castle
Kirkconnell Tower

N

Castles

Chapels, Churches and Monasteries

Land over 100m

Land over 300m

0   40km

1 Duncow Tower

2 Maxwell's Castle

3 Terregles House

4 Terregles Church

5 Lincluden Collegiate Church

Figure 10.1
Maxwell properties
mentioned in the text

Chapter 10

ও

THE MAXWELLS OF CAERLAVEROCK

Alastair M. T. Maxwell-Irving

The following account is designed to give an outline of how the Maxwells' fortunes fared during their first 500 years in Scotland, and of the architecture that they produced during that period. It was an age when one's wealth was very much dependent upon one's position in society and the offices one held. But whilst there are certain characteristic styles of architecture which can be attributed to the church and certain other families (as shown elsewhere in this work), there was no characteristic 'Maxwell' style: instead, each building was typical of its period and of the constraints imposed by the materials available locally.

The Maxwells are descended from Maccus, son of Undweyn, a Saxon lord who is said to have taken refuge in Scotland some time after the Norman Conquest.[1] There is no contemporary record of Undweyn, other than as Maccus's father, but Maccus himself soon achieved a position of considerable importance during the reigns of Alexander I and David I, and as early as *c.*1119 was witness to a charter by Earl David founding a monastery at Selkirk. This was the first of many royal charters concerning the church to which Maccus and his immediate descendants were witnesses. He was also a witness to the foundation charter granted to the monks of Melrose *c.*1143.

It was apparently from David I that Maccus received an important grant of lands on the south bank of the Tweed, opposite Kelso (where the monks of Selkirk had moved *c.*1128); and it was from these lands, which subsequently took their name from Maccus' 'wiel', a distinctive pool in the River Tweed, that his descendants took their designation 'de Maccus-well', later 'Maxwell'. Here Maccus built his castle. This became the family's principal residence and stronghold, and so it remained until it was finally eclipsed by Caerlaverock, in Dumfriesshire. Thereafter, the lands and castle of Maxwell were only retained as a minor residence, until they were finally sold by the 1st Earl of Nithsdale in 1631. Today, nothing is known about the castle itself, and not even the site is certain.

LORDSHIP AND
ARCHITECTURE
IN MEDIEVAL
AND
RENAISSANCE
SCOTLAND

❧

*Figure 10.2
Caerlaverock Castle,
Dumfriesshire: view
from north-west.
A.M.T. Maxwell-
Irving*

Maccus was succeeded by his son Herbert de Maccuswell, who, like his father, was devoted to the church. In 1159 he gave the church of Maxwell to the monks of Kelso, and later he added an oratory dedicated to St Thomas the Martyr. Both Herbert and his eldest son, Sir John de Maccuswell, were successively sheriffs of Teviotdale and regular attenders at court. Sir John was especially high in favour; he was twice sent as ambassador to England, and in 1220 was one of the guarantors for Alexander II's marriage. Ten years later he was appointed chamberlain of Scotland, being one of the first to hold that office. He acquired extensive additions to the barony of Maxwell.

It was Sir John who first acquired the lands of Caerlaverock, presumably from Alexander II, after they had been ceded by the abbey of Holm Cultram in Cumbria,[2] and there built himself a new stronghold. Timber recently recovered from the site has given a date for its construction *c.* 1225.

The castle stood on the edge of the Solway, some 200m south-east of the present castle. It was surrounded by an elaborate arrangement of earthworks and enclosures, which cannot be explained in terms of mediaeval defence, but which it is believed started life as a major Roman port for supplying the legions in south-west Scotland.[3] Sir John was thus taking advantage of the existing works for his defences, as well as having a ready-made harbour for trade with Skinburness, on the other side of the Solway, where the monks of Holm Cultram also had a harbour and grange. The castle, which comprised a quadrilateral enclosure measuring some 30m by 26m, with a wide moat 3m deep, appears to have had a close affinity with other early thirteenth-century enceinte castles such as Auchencass in Annandale and Kinclaven in Perthshire. Little of this structure survives above ground level apart from the outline, but a splayed freestone plinth was exposed during excavations in the nineteenth century.[4]

Sir John was succeeded by his brother Aymer de Maxwell, who was one of the Guardians of the kingdom during the minority of Alexander III, and was later sheriff of Dumfries and Peebles, justiciar of Galloway and chamberlain of Scotland. It was during his time that the lands and castle of Maxwell became increasingly subordinated to the family's new base in the south-west. Aymer also acquired the lands of Mearns, in the sheriffdom of Renfrew, through his wife, the heiress of Mearns. It was from one of their younger sons that the Maxwells of Pollok were descended, though the lands of Mearns were retained by the Maxwells of Caerlaverock, and it was there that the 1st Lord Maxwell built Mearns Castle in, or soon after, 1449,[5] of which more presently.

Aymer was succeeded in 1266 by his eldest son, Sir Herbert de Maxwell, who, in a charter of the lands of Maccuswell and Wester Pencaitland (East Lothian) ten years later, is designated 'of Carlaverock'. It was evidently around this time that he started to build the great new castle of Caerlaverock, a short distance to the north-west of the earlier one and on a firmer foundation.[6] It was a massive undertaking, and the fact that it was to become one of the most impressive castles in the kingdom shows the power and wealth that Sir Herbert had at his command. At the same time, one has to bear in mind that the immensely impressive façade seen today, with its massive keep-gatehouse and corner towers with their heavily corbelled-out parapets, owes more to several phases of fifteenth- and sixteenth-century reconstruction and embellishments than to the original structure. And while there can be no doubt that the builder was acquainted with the castles being built south of the Border by Edward I, the shield-shaped plan at Caerlaverock was a unique example of economy, a significantly smaller version of the fortress being laid out by the Moray family at Bothwell around the same time. In essence, it comprised just

Figure 10.3
Caerlaverock Castle,
Dumfriesshire:
Nithsdale Apartments.
A.M.T. Maxwell-
Irving

three stretches of curtain wall, with a round tower at two of the corners and a strongly defended gateway, flanked by two massive drum towers, at the third. Immediately behind the gateway, and integral with it, was the accommodation block for the lord: any other buildings at this time were probably of timber, abutting the curtain walls. Outer defences were provided by a double moat and earthworks.[7]

Sir Herbert sat in Alexander III's parliament of 1283/4, and in 1291 he was one of the auditors named by John de Balliol for deciding the succession to the Crown. The report bore his seal (a saltire). In 1296 he granted some lands at Mearns to the abbey of Paisley. It was not until

Figure 10.4
Mearns Castle,
Renfrewshire: view
from south-east.
A.M.T. Maxwell-
Irving

October 1299, however, during the subsequent Wars of Independence, that the new castle first comes on record, when it was reported that 'a castle near them called Carlaverok ... has done and does great damages every day to the King's castle [Lochmaben] and people'.[8] Caerlaverock was at the time held by a Scots garrison under the command of Robert de Cunningham, 'vallet' to the Steward of Scotland. The Maxwells, who had sided with the Balliols, were evidently absent.

The following July saw the famous siege of Caerlaverock, when a garrison of only about a hundred men took on the might of Edward's army. In fact, the siege lasted less than two days, but the graphic and meticulous detail with which it was recorded in *Le Siège de Karlaverock*, a metrical history written by an eye-witness at the time, has ensured it lasting fame. According to this account, 'Karlaverok was a castle so strong that it did not fear a siege'.[9] However, with siege engines brought from as far afield as Carlisle, Roxburgh and Jedburgh, as well as by sea from Skinburness, and a force of some 3,000 men-at-arms under the personal command of King Edward I, the defenders were hopelessly outnumbered, and on the second morning surrendered. When the English saw how few men had held it against them, 'of different sorts and ranks sixty men', they were 'beheld with much astonishment'.

LORDSHIP AND
ARCHITECTURE
IN MEDIEVAL
AND
RENAISSANCE
SCOTLAND

⁂

During the next sixty years, Caerlaverock had a chequered history as the allegiances of its Maxwell lords fluctuated between the two kingdoms. At first, the Maxwells were compelled to acknowledge the sovereignty of England, while England put the castle under the command of its own constable. Later the Maxwells resumed command. Then in 1312, soon after being granted a remission of £22 by Edward II, Sir Eustace de Maxwell, 5th of Caerlaverock, changed sides and joined Bruce. The English promptly laid siege, but were forced to withdraw. Lest it might again fall into English hands, and in accordance with Bruce's 'scorched earth' policy of rendering all strongholds unusable by the enemy, Caerlaverock was dismantled. This evidently entailed the partial destruction of the towers and curtain walls. Later, Sir Eustace was compensated by Bruce 'for demolishing the castle of Caerlaverock'.[10]

After Bruce's death, Sir Eustace supported the claims of Edward Balliol, and in 1332 he attended his coronation. It was probably around this time that the castle was repaired. Work dating from this period includes parts of the east gatehouse tower (which fell again later), much of the south-east and south-west corner towers (though the former was demolished again in 1640), some of the curtain walling adjacent to the gatehouse, and perhaps the south curtain (now almost entirely missing). Three years later Sir Eustace received a grant of £20 from the English Exchequer towards the cost of maintaining twenty men-at-arms and twenty light horsemen. Although he subsequently abandoned the English cause, he submitted to Edward again in 1339.

The next laird, Sir John de Maxwell, 6th of Caerlaverock, granted the patronage of Pencaitland Church to the abbey of Dryburgh. He was a supporter of David II, and was taken prisoner with him at the battle of Neville's Cross in 1346. He died the next year, after which his eldest son, Herbert, submitted to Edward, and surrendered Caerlaverock in return for his protection. Then, in 1356, Roger Kirkpatrick of Closeburn recovered the castle for the Scots, but the following year he was murdered there by Sir James de Lindsay. After this, the castle is said to have been 'levelled with the ground',[11] though this was clearly an exaggeration, as the only known damage was to the top of the west gatehouse tower and parts of the south-west corner tower and the west curtain wall. It is not certain when these were repaired, but timber from the bridge shows that it, at least, was rebuilt by Sir John Maxwell, 8th of Caerlaverock, c. 1370.

Despite the vicissitudes to which it had been subjected, Caerlaverock was the symbol of the Maxwells' power in the Borders. It had shown throughout the Wars of Independence how much importance the English attached to its possession as the bastion controlling south-west Scotland, and it was the power-base from which the Maxwells' fortunes, and thus their influence on local and national affairs, were to continue to ebb and flow for the next three centuries.

Early in the fifteenth century, Sir Herbert Maxwell, 10th of Caerlaverock, received the lands of Carnsalloch as security for his wife's dowry. By this time the earls of Douglas had control of south-west Scotland, both as lords of Galloway and, after 1409, as lords of Annandale, and the Maxwells had become their close allies. Indeed, Sir Herbert is repeatedly described as 'beloved cousin'.[12] He had twice been a hostage for the 4th Earl in England, and in return the earl made him steward of Annandale, and later granted him lands in Galloway. This gave Sir Herbert tremendous power, and this was further consolidated by his son, who succeeded him in 1420.

It was during the time of the son, also Sir Herbert, that the Regent Albany was sent to prison at Caerlaverock before his trial and execution in 1425. The tower where he is reputed to have been held, the south-west tower, has ever since been known as 'Murdoch's Tower'. For a while, Sir Herbert also fell under the suspicion of James I, but later he returned to favour and subsequently served as a commissioner for conserving the truce with England, admiral of the sea and warden of the West March under both James I and James II. It was James II who raised him to the peerage as Lord Maxwell, although the exact date is not known.[13] Lord Maxwell is said to have made various repairs to Caerlaverock, including the restoration of the curtain walls and rebuilding work on the gatehouse towers, though in truth there is no general agreement as to exactly when this work was carried out. His younger sons were ancestors of the Maxwells of Tinwald, Carnsalloch and Southbar (Renfrewshire).

As already related, it was the 1st Lord Maxwell who built Mearns Castle, seven miles south-west of Glasgow, c. 1449. It is a solid, oblong keep of four storeys, two of which are vaulted, with mural stairs and a corbelled-out parapet on all sides. It was originally entered at first-floor level, where the round-headed doorway may still be seen; but at some later date a new entrance was formed at ground level. Although now missing its roof and parapet, it is still complete to the level of the wall-head, 13.7m above the ground.

Soon after the 2nd Lord Maxwell succeeded his father, the Douglases finally overreached themselves in flaunting their power, and challenged the authority of the Crown itself. This led to a series of campaigns against them and their dramatic downfall in 1455. No longer could the Douglases count on the support of the Maxwells, who fought for the Crown at both the battle of Arkinholm and the siege of Threave in that year. As a result Lord Maxwell recovered the family's former lands in Eskdale, while, without the Douglases, the way was clear for the Maxwells to become the dominant power in the West March.

LORDSHIP AND
ARCHITECTURE
IN MEDIEVAL
AND
RENAISSANCE
SCOTLAND

🪶

According to a family historian in the seventeenth century, it was the 2nd Lord Maxwell who 'compleated the bartisan of Caerlaverock' and was responsible for the castle's present, impressive, outward appearance.[14] He evidently built the front and rear additions to the gatehouse, raised the height of the gatehouse towers, and added the bold machicolated parapets on the gatehouse and the south-east and south-west corner towers. He also added the accommodation block along the west curtain wall, with its seven or eight rooms, each with its own fireplace, some of which were of handsome proportions with finely moulded pillars and caps.

Lord Maxwell's son and heir, John, Master of Maxwell,[15] was killed at the battle of the Kirtle in 1484, whilst pursuing the Duke of Albany and a force of Douglases who had tried to raise a rebellion at Lochmaben. The fine Merkland Cross, near Kirtlebridge, is said to have been erected by Lord Maxwell in his memory. From the Master of Maxwell's sons were descended the Maxwells of Cowhill, Cavens, Portrack and Glenesslin, while another son became abbot of Holywood. An illegitimate son, Herbert, was ancestor of the Maxwells of Hills and Drumcoltran. The acquisition of all these lands and offices around the turn of the sixteenth century increased the Maxwells' power in Nithsdale considerably, while further influence, and eventually wealth, was to accrue from their patronage of the church.

The monasteries and other religious communities were by this time in serious decline, and suffering from an acute shortage of manpower to manage their estates. Accordingly, in 1495, the abbot of Holywood appointed his brother, Lord Maxwell, and his two eldest sons bailies of all the abbey's lands for 19 years. This office was later confirmed in liferent, and eventually outright possession was obtained by grants of the feus. But it was not just the abbey of Holywood that looked to the Maxwells to manage their lands. In 1503 Lord Maxwell was given bailiery jurisdiction over the lands belonging to Sweetheart Abbey, while his son Robert, 4th Lord Maxwell, later added the bailieries of the abbeys of Dundrennan [16] and Tongland, the provostry of Lincluden and the preceptory of Trailtrow.

After their devastating defeat at Flodden in 1513, the Scots were in fear of an imminent invasion by the English. Lord Maxwell and three of his brothers had fallen in the battle, but his eldest son, Robert, had been absent at sea at the time as admiral of a fleet passing to France. Driven back by a storm, he returned home as soon as he heard the news, and took possession of Threave. Queen Margaret then appointed him captain and keeper of Threave and steward of the Stewartry of Kirkcudbright. He also took command of Lochmaben Castle. Two years later he was made warden of the West March. His keepership of Lochmaben and Threave and of the Stewartry of Kirkcudbright was again confirmed in 1524. It is

*Figure 10.5
Hills Tower,
Stewartry of
Kirkcudbright: view
from north.
A.M.T. Maxwell-
Irving*

212

LORDSHIP AND
ARCHITECTURE
IN MEDIEVAL
AND
RENAISSANCE
SCOTLAND

✿

generally believed that it was this Lord Maxwell who built Langholm Castle for the Crown, though the date is not known. Langholm, of which only fragments of the tower house now remain, played an important role in maintaining law and order in Eskdale. Although the Maxwells coveted it as their own, and maintained a garrison there for much of the time, it was officially regarded as the local base for whoever held the office of warden of the West March. Lord Maxwell also built 'Maxwell's Castle', as it became known, in Dumfries. This was a strong townhouse with battlements, described in an English report *c.* 1563 as 'a fare howse, battaled within this towne, but not tentable nor strong aganis any battry or gownes [guns]'.[17] It was demolished by the Earl of Sussex in 1570. In 1528, Maxwell was also granted the lands and castle of Crawfordmuir, in Strathclyde, which had been forfeited by the Earl of Angus.

It was during the time of the 4th Lord Maxwell that his kinsman Edward Maxwell built Hills Tower. Edward had purchased the 18 merklands of Lochrutton and Hills from James Douglas of Drumlanrig in 1527, and Hills must have been built soon after. Hills is a solid, rectangular tower with a vaulted basement, three upper storeys and an attic. It has a corbelled-out parapet-walk with crenellations on all sides, but, unlike later towers, it has no provision for the use of firearms. There are few mouldings, but there is an unusually elaborate panel over the entrance which bears the arms and initials of Edward Maxwell and his wife, Janet Corsane, beneath the arms of Lord Maxwell. A feature of special interest, although much restored, is the two-storeyed gatehouse and associated barmkin wall.

Lord Maxwell had a distinguished career. Among the various offices he held were comptroller of the royal household, privy councillor, chief carver to the king, provost of Edinburgh, extraordinary lord of session and warden of the West March. He was also one of the regents of Scotland during James V's absence in France in 1536 and 1537. In 1542 he was commanded to raise a new army in the West March to invade England, but due to a last-minute change of command by the king, and the resulting disaffection of the troops, the whole enterprise resulted in the disgraceful rout of Solway Moss. Lord Maxwell was taken prisoner, and it was not until 1545 that he was finally released on a promise to hand over the castles of Caerlaverock and Threave to the English. The English also wanted Lochmaben, but it was held by his second son, Sir John Maxwell, later 4th Lord Herries, who successfully held out. The English did not, however, enjoy Caerlaverock and Threave for long, as they were almost immediately retaken by the Regent Arran, who also took possession of Lochmaben.

Lord Maxwell was succeeded in 1546 by his eldest son, Robert, 5th Lord Maxwell. Robert had also been a prisoner of the English for a while, as a hostage for the release of his father, but he was released on a promise to further the plans of Henry VIII. In 1544 he was made warden of the West March. The following year he was commanded to keep the castles of Caerlaverock, Lochmaben and Threave for the queen, while the Crown agreed to provide artillery for their defence. But in 1545 he was again taken prisoner, and so he remained for the next four years. This left the Maxwells without a chief after the death of the 4th Lord. They were, however, anything but leaderless, for Lord Maxwell's younger brother, Sir John, Master of Maxwell, proved more than equal to the task. By this time the Maxwells were by far the strongest clan in the West March, an English report of 1547 crediting the Master of Maxwell with '1000 and moe' fighting men, while the Maxwells of Tinwald, Cowhill and Breckonside could provide a further 513, out of a reported total of 7,241 for the whole of Dumfriesshire and Galloway.[18]

Prior to this period, relations between the Maxwells and Johnstons had been perfectly amicable. Since the twelfth century, the Johnstons had held lands in Upper Annandale, where their stronghold of Lochwood Castle had grown steadily in size and importance; but, despite the high offices held by some of the family over the centuries, both the clan's numbers and territorial possessions remained relatively small before 1484. It was the final defeat of the Douglases at the battle of the Kirtle, and the forfeiture of their allies, notably the Corries of that Ilk, in that year that was to transform their fortunes. By one means or another they soon acquired many of the forfeited lands, and thereafter their power and influence increased dramatically, until they became the dominant power in all Annandale. The battle of the Kirtle also brought them powerful new allies in the Irvings of Kirtledale, whose prosperity was also to benefit from the conflict. By 1547 the various branches of the Johnston clan could put 1,000 men in the field, and the Irvings, their feuars, almost 500. Rivalries began to develop between the clans.

By 1545 Sir Thomas Wharton, now Lord Wharton, was reporting that John Johnston of that Ilk and Sir James Gordon of Lochinvar were Maxwell's greatest enemies, as each sought to supplant his power and influence, the one in Annandale, the other in Galloway. Wharton believed that he could turn this rivalry to his advantage. If he could stir up feuds between the clans, it would destabilise the whole of the Scottish West March, making England's task of annexation that much easier. He certainly tried. By February the following year he was boasting of his efforts to stir up discord between the Maxwells and Johnstons, and reported that a feud had broken out. At first it was not too serious, but with the passage of time it was to develop into one of the fiercest feuds that Scotland had ever known, involving the whole of the West March and lasting into the

The Maxwells
of Caerlaverock

215

LORDSHIP AND
ARCHITECTURE
IN MEDIEVAL
AND
RENAISSANCE
SCOTLAND

❧

Figure 10.6
Kirkconnell House
and Tower, Stewartry
of Kirkcudbright: view
from east.
A.M.T. Maxwell-
Irving

next century. Indeed, it was to dominate every facet of life, from rivalry over official appointments to local pillaging, fire-raising and murder.

After the truce concluded between Scotland and England in 1550, Lord Maxwell was one of the commissioners appointed to settle Border disputes, and also to agree on the partition of the Debateable Land between the two countries. And shortly before his death in 1552, he entered into a bond with various other chiefs for mutual defence against the Grahams on the English side of the Border, whose raids were causing him much trouble.

It was around this time, or not long afterwards, that the Maxwells of Kirkconnell, near Dumfries, built the present Kirkconnell Tower. They were a scion of the Caerlaverock family. Kirkconnell is an L-plan building with three stories and an attic in the main block and a stair in the wing. The basement of the main block is vaulted, and there is a parapet walk around the wall-head. Of special interest are the crosslet-shaped shot-holes in the walls of the main block and wing at ground level, the only known examples of this rare feature in the south of Scotland.[19]

With the death of the 5th Lord Maxwell in 1552, leaving an only son – his second son was born posthumously – aged only about two, it fell to the lot of the young lord's uncle, Sir John Maxwell, Master of Maxwell, to be both the boy's guardian and leader of the clan. It would have been

BASEMENT

KIRKCONNELL HOUSE

hard to find anyone better suited to the task. In a distinguished career lasting nearly forty years, Sir John proved to be one of the greatest statesmen the Borders had known. Born *c.* 1512, he was educated at Sweetheart Abbey, an experience he always remembered with gratitude;[20] and later the abbey was to reward him for loyal service with a grant of the Isle of Lochkinderloch. Sir John's first appointment was in 1546, when he was made warden of the West March in succession to his late father.

The following year, when the English were making great inroads into the West March and Sir John was supporting the cause of the banished Earl of Lennox and his English allies, the Regent Arran entreated him to change sides with a promise of the hand in marriage of Agnes, Baroness Herries, the eldest daughter and co-heiress of the 3rd Lord Herries of Terregles, whom he had courted but whom Arran had intended for one of his own sons. Sir John accepted the offer, and thereafter was zealous in his pursuit of the campaign against the English, successfully holding Lochmaben Castle against them, and playing an active part in ultimately driving them out altogether. Sir John was well rewarded. By his marriage he acquired a third of all the vast Herries estates of Terregles, Kirkgunzeon, Moffatdale, Evandale, Lockerbie, Hutton, Hoddom, Urr, etc., and in 1561

Figure 10.7
Kirkconnell House and Tower, Stewartry of Kirkcudbright: ground-floor plan. A.M.T. Maxwell-Irving

217

LORDSHIP AND
ARCHITECTURE
IN MEDIEVAL
AND
RENAISSANCE
SCOTLAND

ᘒ

he purchased the other two-thirds from John Hamilton, Arran's younger son, who had acquired them from Lady Agnes's younger sisters. This greatly increased Sir John's power and influence in the West March. It was not, however, until December 1566 that Sir John was able to purchase from Hamilton his right of redemption. Only then was he recognised in his own, and his wife's, right as 4th Lord Herries, appearing as such for the first time at the baptism of Prince James, on 17 December, 1566. He was then granted his own coat of arms as 'Johnne Lord Maxwell of Hereiss'.[21]

In 1553, Sir John was appointed a Commissioner for the Borders, and the following year he was again made warden. He was subsequently re-appointed warden many times, holding the office during a total of some 21 years before he finally resigned in 1579. Throughout his life he was dedicated to maintaining law and order in the Borders, and was tireless to that end. In 1560 he complained that Lord Dacre, the English warden, was being dilatory in seeking redress, and three years later, at his behest, Queen Mary wrote to Elizabeth on the same subject. As a result, he and Sir Thomas Bellenden, justice-clerk, were appointed to represent Scotland in reaching an agreement with England concerning the keeping of the peace on the Borders. In 1566 even Queen Elizabeth bore testimony to his work, though a compliment from her ambassador, Sir Nicholas Throckmorton, four months later was more backhanded: 'The Lord Herryes ys the connynge horseleache and the wysest of the whole faction'.[22]

It was around this time that Sir John embarked upon an extensive programme of building towers and other defensive works, both to help in the maintenance of order locally and also for protection against any future English incursions, the memory of which was still fresh in his mind. In, or shortly before, 1565 he built a tower in Annan to replace the steeple that had been destroyed by the English in 1547, and in 1565 he built the new stronghold of Hoddom and the nearby watch tower of 'Repentance', on the top of Trailtrow Hill.[23] He also added a strong tower, 'Mosstroops' Tower, to his principal residence at Terregles, and built a new 'house' at Kirkgunzeon, as well as raising 'warden dykes', or defensive ramparts, at Annan and Dumfries. Only Hoddom and Repentance have survived, although there are two contemporary sketches showing how Mosstroops Tower looked before it was finally demolished in 1789.

Hoddom was the strongest and, with the exception of the new Thirlestane castle, near Lauder, the largest castle or tower house to be built in the Borders in the sixteenth century. It is of massive construction, L-plan in shape, with walls almost 3m thick rising some 17m to the top of the main block and more than 20m to the top of the wing. Rather than being a conventional residence, it was designed to be held by a

Figure 10.8
Hoddom Castle,
Dumfriesshire: view
from south.
A.M.T. Maxwell-
Irving

218

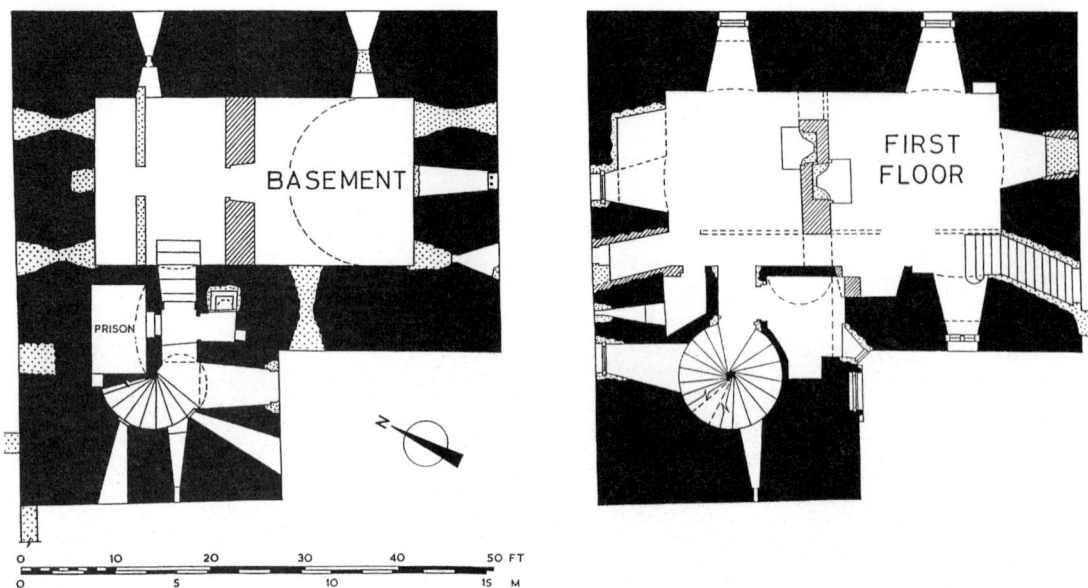

BASEMENT

FIRST FLOOR

PRISON

| 0 | 10 | 20 | 30 | 40 | 50 FT |
| 0 | 5 | 10 | 15 | M |

*Figure 10.9
Hoddom Castle,
Dumfriesshire:
ground- and first-floor
plans.
A.M.T. Maxwell-
Irving*

garrison. In addition to a generous array of splayed gun-loops at ground level and shot-holes in the parapet, the main block was also provided with no fewer than seven more gun-loops at third-floor level, which could fire over the barmkin, while the barmkin itself had corner towers, two storeys in height, which were also provided with gun-loops. The castle was built on land acquired from the preceptory of Trailtrow, and used stones from the Herries' old castle of Hoddom, on the other side of the river, hence its popular name of 'Hoddomstanes'.[24]

Lord Herries' influence is also seen in the design of the tower built on the Maxwells' lands at Isle of Lochar *c.*1568. Indeed, he probably ordered its construction, for it guarded the ford leading across the southern end of the vast Lochar Moss to Caerlaverock. Low in stature, and with no vaulting and walls only 1m thick because of the soft nature of the ground, its predominant feature was the generous array of splayed gun-loops covering all sides at both ground- and second-floor levels.[25]

Another Maxwell stronghold that apparently dates from the same period is Drumcoltran, eight miles south-west of Dumfries. Built by Edward Maxwell, the younger son of the builder of Hills, it is an L-plan tower of three storeys and a garret, with a vaulted basement, a corbelled-out parapet around the main block and a look-out chamber at the top of the wing. In its layout, it clearly drew upon the design of Kirkconnell, but, because it is built almost entirely of the local greywacke, its construction is much more rugged, with the simplest of mouldings, the use of rounded and canted corners instead of quoins, and single corbels to support the

*Figure 10.10
Terregles 'Queir',
Stewartry of
Kirkcudbright: view
from south-east.
A.M.T. Maxwell-
Irving*

parapet. However, unlike Kirkconnell, it was liberally provided with the new, splayed gun-loops.

As well as being concerned with law and order, Lord Herries – as he had now become – had a strong sense of national duty, being an ardent supporter and close confidant first of Queen Mary, and later of King James VI. He fought for Mary at Langside, entertained her at Terregles during her flight south, and accompanied her to England. It was during his absence that the Regent Moray marched through the West March and attacked Lochmaben, Hoddom and Annan, which all surrendered, though not before Hoddom had put up a spirited defence. Terregles was also spared in the belief that Herries intended to rebuild it anyway, which suggests that Mosstroops Tower was built after this time.

The English invaded Dumfriesshire again in 1570, in the spring under Lord Scrope, and four months later under the Earl of Sussex. Scrope was resisted in Nithsdale and Galloway by Herries and in Annandale by Johnston, but on his way home he attacked and badly damaged the castles of Dumfries, Hoddom and Annan, while Sussex again 'threw down the castles of Annand and Hodoun belonging to Lord Herris, the castles of Domefrese and Carlaverock belonging to Lord Maxwell,

LORDSHIP AND
ARCHITECTURE
IN MEDIEVAL
AND
RENAISSANCE
SCOTLAND

✺

the castles of Tynhill and Cohill belonging to the lairds [Maxwells] of Tynhill and Coohill',[26] and others. As usual, such reports were greatly exaggerated for political effect, but the Scots still protested most strongly. It is thought that the main damage caused to Caerlaverock on the latter occasion was the destruction of the east gatehouse tower. There is no evidence of any serious damage to Hoddom.

In 1572/3 peace was agreed between the supporters of Mary and James VI, after which Herries and the young Lord Maxwell, who had previously supported Mary's cause, submitted to the king's government, and as soon as James assumed power, Herries was appointed one of his council of twelve. Six years later, in 1578/9, Herries submitted to the privy council his proposals for keeping peace and good order in the Borders. These included the recommendation that (a) the warden should reside at Lochmaben and have a deputy there (b) a captain and 24 horsed men should lie at Annan, and (c) the deputy warden and a captain should be based at Langholm. The proposals were vehemently challenged by the young Lord Maxwell, who claimed Lochmaben as his hereditary residence as Steward of Annandale, and who also looked upon Langholm as his own; but Maxwell's protests were overruled, and Herries was made warden and justiciar. Maxwell's tenure of Lochmaben was revoked, and the keepership given to Herries. Later that year, however, Herries resigned and went into retirement. He died four years later, and was interred in the 'queir' (choir) of Terregles Church, which he is said to have had rebuilt especially for the purpose.[27] It is an unusual, post-Reformation building in a late Gothic style, and of pre-Reformation layout. On the outside, it is adorned with one of the Maxwell crests [28] and a shield bearing the plain Herries arms (three hurcheons, or hedgehogs) with the initials 'J', 'H' and 'A', for John, Lord Herries, and his wife Agnes.

It was in 1569/70 that the 7th Lord Maxwell first took to the field with his clan, when he attacked an English force under Lord Scrope. His enthusiasm, however, was greater than his judgement, and he was forced to flee. Later in 1570, he was accused by the English of supporting the rebellion of Leonard Dacre; there is no evidence that he did so, although they did have some correspondence.

The Earl of Sussex's destruction of his castle in Dumfries in August of that year was presumably fairly extensive, for in 1572 he decided to rebuild it on a larger scale. The new castle was much stronger than its predecessor, with 'four large vaults with small wickers of light, and the whole windows of this Castle were barred strongly with iron, being of 3 large stories with Turnpike and Bartisan covered with lead'.[29] In addition, it is known to have had a parapet walk projecting boldly on three-stage corbels. Lord Maxwell also restored the tower at Annan in 1579.

Maxwell was made warden of the West March in 1573, and, to assist him in his duties he was also made captain and keeper of Lochmaben castle. This again brought the Maxwells into conflict with the Johnstons, not only because it was the warden's duty to pursue and seek redress from all malefactors – and the Johnstons were as guilty as any – but also because the Johnstons looked upon Annandale as their territory and resented Lord Maxwell having a foothold there. Indeed, the appointment of either Lord Maxwell or Johnston of that Ilk as warden was a certain recipe for trouble in the West March throughout the rest of the century, with first one side and then the other, especially the Johnstons, taking the opportunity to settle old scores. Yet, as often as not, the government felt compelled to appoint one or other of them, as being the only persons who had the resources to back up their office.

In general, Lord Maxwell proved a good warden, but the office was never free from politics. Lord Scrope attested to his efficiency in 1576, and two years later the privy council reported that there was none more able, because of his knowledge and understanding of the affairs of the country. But in 1578/9 he was accused of neglecting his duties, and removed from office in favour of his uncle, Lord Herries. A year later Johnston was made warden. He promptly complained about Maxwell to the privy council, and had Maxwell put to the horn; but in 1581 Maxwell was again made warden. Later that year, Maxwell and Herries were again asked for their advice concerning good order in the West March. And so the pendulum of power continued to swing as first Maxwell and then Johnston became warden.

In 1581 another event occurred which was to be a source of contention for the next forty years. It was the forfeiture and execution of the Regent Morton. Both Maxwell and the Earl of Angus now laid claim to the vacant earldom, which Maxwell, who was high in favour at court at this time, won.[30] In June he was granted the earldom and regality of Morton, and in October the dignity of Earl of Morton.

Then, in 1584/5, the all-powerful Earl of Arran, having unsuccessfully tried to persuade Maxwell to part with some of his lands, sought revenge by having Maxwell ordered to deliver up his castles of Caerlaverock and Threave and his houses of Dumfries, Mearns and Goatgellis.[31] Arran added fuel to the fire by inciting the Johnstons, whose chief had meanwhile become warden, to step up their attacks on the Maxwells. This they did with a vengeance, attacking and burning Maxwell houses and lands, including Cowhill and Duncow. The Maxwells retaliated, burning Lochwood, and driving Johnston to seek refuge at Bonshaw,[32] whither the Maxwells brought up cannon. Further bloodshed was only spared by the mediation of Lord Scrope, who reported that Maxwell had 'gotten alredy into his handes and at his commandement all the cheife ston howses which ar of

LORDSHIP AND
ARCHITECTURE
IN MEDIEVAL
AND
RENAISSANCE
SCOTLAND

2̶

strength in that countrey – savinge the howse of Loughmabell and one other'.[33] Scrope also reported that Maxwell 'myndeth to plante some forces of footemen in Carlaverocke, the Treive, Loughmaban, Langholm, and Tortarrell [Torthorwald]', and had at his disposal 200 horse and 300 'shotte' (footsoldiers) besides 'the whole force of the country at his devotion'. Johnston was taken a prisoner to Caerlaverock, and Lochmaben finally surrendered.

At the same time as the Johnstons were pillaging the Maxwells' lands, in April, James VI revoked the grant of the earldom and regality of Morton to Lord Maxwell, and granted them instead to the next heir, the earl of Angus. The peerage, however, was not revoked; although the title ceased in everyday usage – to avoid the confusion of two earls bearing the same name – it was still used in certain official documents, until, in 1620, the 9th Lord Maxwell had the earldom of Morton exchanged for that of Nithsdale, with the precedence of the original grant.

While Queen Mary was still a prisoner in England, her cause remained a focus in both countries for the outlawed Catholic faith. Among the nobles of that persuasion were the Lords Maxwell and Herries. When, therefore, Lord Scrope learned that the two lords had been attending mass at both Lincluden and Maxwell's house in Dumfries at the end of 1585, the English were very disturbed. So too was James VI, who promptly had Maxwell arrested. He was, however, soon free again, and after the execution of Queen Mary in February 1586/7, Maxwell arranged a visit to Spain for consultation with Philip II, who was by then planning an invasion of England. He returned the following April, and prepared his castles, intending to join the Spanish forces when they landed; but Lord Herries, who did not support such a course of action, warned James of the danger. Maxwell was declared a rebel, and soon thereafter he was taken prisoner, while the castles of Lochmaben, Langholm, Threave and Caerlaverock were ordered to surrender, and taken. With the subsequent failure of the Spanish Armada, the danger subsided, and Maxwell was released. But the Catholic threat did not totally disappear, for in 1590 both Maxwell and Herries were arranging to levy horsemen to assist the rebellion against Elizabeth in Ireland.

It was in the same year that one Robert Maxwell [34] built Fourmerkland Tower, a few miles north-west of Dumfries. This perfectly preserved little keep, of three storeys and a garret, has no parapet, just two corbelled turrets at diametrically opposite corners. The dormer windows are a later addition, although such features had already appeared in a few tower houses in the West March by this time, examples being found at 'The Isle' Tower, a little further up Nithsdale, Elshieshields, near Lochmaben, and Maclellan's Castle, in Kirkcudbright.

*Figure 10.11
Fourmerkland Tower,
Dumfriesshire: view
from south.
A.M.T. Maxwell-
Irving*

LORDSHIP AND
ARCHITECTURE
IN MEDIEVAL
AND
RENAISSANCE
SCOTLAND

Two years later, Lord Maxwell was made hereditary keeper of Lochmaben, with unusually extensive judicial powers in Dumfriesshire and Galloway. This only served to inflame the enmity between Maxwell and Johnston, as Johnston now looked upon Lochmaben more than ever as his own preserve. But Maxwell took his duties as warden seriously, and to make his position more secure decided, in 1593, to further strengthen his strongholds, especially Caerlaverock. In June that year Lord Scrope reported on Maxwell's 'presente fortifyeinge at Carlaverock, where (as I am informed) he setteth 200 men on worke dailie',[35] and John Carey likewise reported that 'Lord Maxwell makes great fortification, and has many men working at his house'.[36] It is thought that it was at this time that the gun-loops were inserted into Caerlaverock's gatehouse. Maxwell's motives were, however, thought to have political overtones. Scrope expressed a general distrust in Maxwell, whom he described as 'an unmeete man for that office or a comune commander of many men so neare us',[37] while Carey suspected him of being 'the king of Spain's treasurer for Scotland'.

Meanwhile, the Johnstons' aggression found another target. Turning their attention northwards, they raided the lands of Lord Crichton of Sanquhar, and in so doing slew a number of hapless Crichtons who fell in their path. This caused such general revulsion that Douglas of Drumlanrig and other nobles subscribed to an agreement to assist Lord Maxwell, in his capacity as warden, in apprehending Sir James Johnston of that Ilk, while James VI gave Maxwell a special warrant to do just that. Six weeks later, Maxwell marched into Annandale; but Johnston was ready, and just north of Lockerbie their forces met at Dryfesands. The ensuing battle, the last clan battle ever fought in the Borders, was a disaster for Maxwell; he was outmanoeuvred, his forces were routed with heavy loss, and he himself was slain. Thus fell the chief whom the contemporary historian Spottiswood described as 'humane, courteous, and more learned than Noblemen commonly are'.[38]

Lord Maxwell was succeeded by his eldest son, John, 8th Lord Maxwell and titular 2nd Earl of Morton (though he was never so designated by the Crown). Like his father, he continued to hear mass contrary to the law, and for this was twice declared a rebel and imprisoned. During 1606, he also came into dispute with the 'other' Earl of Morton over who had the right of jurisdiction in Eskdale, both claiming authority as Earl of Morton. The matter came to the attention of the privy council, who ordered them to disband their forces. Maxwell refused, and in 1607 was again imprisoned. He later escaped and fled to Caerlaverock, whereupon James VI ordered that all his castles and houses, including the castle of Lochmaben, should be rendered up and garrisoned for the Crown.

Meanwhile, in 1605, an attempt was made to reconcile the differences between the Maxwells and Johnstons, and three years later another meeting was arranged through the mediation of Lord Herries; but at the second meeting the arrangements went disastrously wrong. Their servants fell out, shots were exchanged, and Maxwell killed Johnston. Maxwell was charged with treason, and had to flee to France, while his lands and honours were forfeited. In 1610, the lands of Caerlaverock and Maxwell (Roxburghshire), with all their castles, were granted to Sir Robert Ker, while Maxwell's lands in Eskdale were granted to Lord Cranstoun. Two years later, Maxwell returned to Scotland; but he was never forgiven, and was eventually captured and executed.

Lord Maxwell was succeeded by his younger brother, Robert, 9th Lord Maxwell. At first, Robert was left with nothing, apart from certain lands that he had acquired in his own right; but he soon set about restoring the family's fortunes. By an Act of Parliament in 1617, it was declared that he could hold all the lands and heritages formerly held by his brother, except all titles and honours and the offices of steward of Annandale and Nithsdale, and shortly afterwards he recovered the family's former lands in Eskdale from Lord Cranstoun. During the next two years, James VI progressively restored his other lands and offices. In 1619 he was made a privy councillor, and the following year he was created Earl of Nithsdale, in place of the former earldom of Morton and with the original precedence. This was confirmed by parliament in 1621. In the same year he was also made a lord of articles.

After Charles I came to the throne, the Earl of Nithsdale was put in command of the forces promised to Christian IV of Denmark, by whom he was appointed a general. He served in Germany for a while in 1627–8, but later returned home, and in 1630 was made a Justiciar for 'the Middle Shires'.[39] Again in 1636, he was one of the commissioners appointed to punish and prevent disorders in the Borders.

Ever since the Earl of Sussex had attacked Caerlaverock in 1570, the castle had been in a poor state, despite the repairs and alterations carried out in 1593. In 1607 Camden, in his Annals, had described Caerlaverock as 'a weak house of the Barons of Maxwell'.[40] The Earl of Nithsdale now sought to upgrade Caerlaverock to a modern house worthy of his station, and to this end he built a fine new palace block, the 'Nithsdale Apartments', along the east and south sides of the courtyard, though the full extent of the latter portion is not known because it was later almost totally destroyed. What remains on the east side, however, is, as MacGibbon and Ross described it in 1887, 'one of the finest and richest specimens of early Renaissance in Scotland'.[41] It comprised an accommodation block of three storeys and an attic, symmetrically disposed about a central doorway from

LORDSHIP AND
ARCHITECTURE
IN MEDIEVAL
AND
RENAISSANCE
SCOTLAND

🦌

the courtyard. On the east side the windows were quite plain, but on the courtyard side they were framed within beautifully moulded, Renaissance surrounds, with elaborately carved triangular or segmental pediments, which at the lowest level bear the various arms of the earl's family, his lady and the date 1634, while on the upper floors they bear mythical scenes taken from the early sixteenth century *Emblemata Andreae Alciati* and Francis Quarles' *Emblemes* of 1635.[42] At the south end of this building was a fine scale-and-platt stair, which also connected with the magnificent, new, great hall in the south range.

Sadly, though, the earl was not able to enjoy his new mansion for long, before the troubles of Charles I also became those of Caerlaverock. In 1638, the earl had to take steps to stengthen the defences of the castle, and two years later the Covenanters laid siege. For thirteen weeks the garrison of 200 held out against a fierce onslaught, but in the end King Charles, being powerless to help, instructed the earl to deliver the castle up on the best terms he could get. The castle surrendered, and was promptly ransacked, Colonel Home protesting that he was only carrying out the instructions of the committee of estates to demolish the castle. It was never rebuilt.

Thus the Maxwell family, who for so long had wielded immense power and held the highest offices of state, were again reduced to poverty, with little land and no money. They had zealously adhered to the Roman Catholic faith at a time when most of their fellow countrymen were turning away from it, and had paid dearly for the privilege. They had loyally supported their king, even after his cause was lost, and for so doing had lost their home. They struggled on, but by now their estates had been decimated; and after backing the wrong side in the Jacobite Rebellion of 1715, they forfeited their earldom too. It was a tragic story. The Maxwells had tried to serve their country, their sovereign, and their faith, with honour and dedication, but at the end of the day it had cost them almost everything they possessed.

NOTES

1. There is no record of Undweyn in Scotland, so it may be that it was not Undweyn, but Maccus, who was the first of the family to come north, in the train of Prince David.

2. The lands of Karlaveroc had been granted to the monks of Holm Cultram by Ranulf, son of Dunegal of Stranith (Nithsdale), and confirmed by Malcolm IV c. 1153–65. This subsequently led to a dispute with the monks of Dundrennan, and it appears to have been as a result of this that they gave them up (F. Grainger and W. G. Collingwood, *The Register and Records of Holm Cultram*, (Kendal, 1929), 52–3).

3. Research has established that the level of the Solway was higher in Roman times,

and that the elaborate earthworks of the supposed port would have corresponded with this level. See R. C. Reid, 'The Old Castle Site at Caerlaverock', *TDGNHAS*, 3rd series, xxiii (1940–4), 66–71.

4. More recent excavations, carried out in 1998–9, have now revealed details of the castle's entire layout, including four corner towers, which have the rare distinction of being set at 45 degrees to the main walls (*DES*, 1998, 25; *DES*, 1999, 22–3).

5. The licence was granted in 1449. As the Lords Maxwell were rarely there, the castle was put in the charge of a constable.

6. Timber from the earliest bridge has been tentatively dated by dendrochronology to c. 1277, but this is currently being re-assessed.

7. The extent of the original earthworks is not clear, as they were later extended, and some only date from the Civil War of 1640.

8. *CDS*, ii, no. 1101.

9. N. H. Nicolas, *The Siege of Carlaverock* (London, 1828), 60.

10. W. Robertson, *An Index of Records of Charters granted by the different Sovereigns of Scotland between the years 1309 and 1413* (Edinburgh, 1798), 12, no. 75; 15, no. 13.

11. Fraser, *Caerlaverock*, i, 55.

12. Ibid., 122–3. The relationship – assuming there was one – has not been established.

13. It was sometime between January 1440/1 and July 1445.

14. Fraser, op. cit., I, 56.

15. Sometimes wrongly called 3rd Lord Maxwell. Although his father resigned the barony of Maxwell in his favour in 1478, his father did in fact survive him (See G. E. Cokayne, *The Complete Peerage* (London, 1910–59), viii, 590–1n, and *Scots Peerage*, vi, 477).

16. His brother John was for a time abbot of Dundrennan.

17. R. B. Armstrong, *The History of Liddesdale, Eskdale, Ewesdale, Wauchopedale and the Debateable Land* (Edinburgh, 1883), cx.

18. Ibid., lxxiii.

19. All the other known examples are in Aberdeenshire. See A. M. T. Maxwell-Irving, 'Early Firearms and their Influence on the Military and Domestic Architecture of the Borders', in *PSAS*, 103 (1970–1), 215–6.

20. When the Lords of Congregation later ordered him to demolish the abbey, he refused.

21. Fraser, op. cit., i, 514–15.

22. Ibid., i, 518.

23. The English agent Thomas Randolph made a special journey to Dumfriesshire in the spring of 1565 to 'see the works he [Lord Herries] has in hand'. He reported that 'In Annan town he has builded a fair tower ... within two miles of it he byldethe two other forts – the one [Hoddom] great – the other [Repentance] a watch tower of great height; in that he has a bell to warn the country at need, and beside the same a "become"' (*CSP Scot.*, ii, no. 174).

24. *RMS*, iv, no. 2311.

25. Originally it was oblong in plan, but in 1622 it underwent major alterations when a large stair-wing and new entrance were added on the north-west side by Edward Maxwell of Isle.

26. *CSP Scot.*, iii, no. 436.

27. The 'Queir' is dated 1583, and so presumably was not completed until the year after his death.

28. A stag couchant before a holly bush. The same crest appears on the armorial panel over the entrance at Caerlaverock.

LORDSHIP AND
ARCHITECTURE
IN MEDIEVAL
AND
RENAISSANCE
SCOTLAND

🏵

29. *An Introduction to the History of Dumfries, by Robert Edgar (1746)*, ed. R. C. Reid (Dumfries, 1915), 35.

30. Maxwell claimed the title through his mother, Beatrix Douglas, second daughter of the 3rd earl of Morton.

31. Goatgellis has not been identified.

32. Described by Lord Scrope at this time as 'one of the strongest howses of that border' (*Cal. Border Papers*, i, no. 321).

33. *Cal. Border Papers*, i, no. 334.

34. His relationship to the Maxwells of Caerlaverock has not been established.

35. *Cal. Border Papers*, i, no. 845.

36. Ibid., no. 852.

37. Ibid., no. 845. A report by Edward Aglionby in 1592 stated that the Lords Maxwell and Herries had 1,000 Maxwells at their command (Ibid., i, 394).

38. *Scots Peerage*, vi, 483.

39. As the Border counties became known after the Union of the Crowns in 1603.

40. F. Grose, *The Antiquities of Scotland* (London, 1797), i, 163.

41. MacGibbon and Ross, *Castellated and Domestic Architecture*, i, 133.

42. J. Hunwicke, 'Robert Maxwell of Caerlaverock and his Fashionable Windows', *TDGNHAS*, 3rd series, lxviii (1993), 107–21.

Chapter 11

ॐ

THE HOMES AND
THE EAST MARCH

Maureen M. Meikle

The Anglo-Scottish Borders witnessed repeated turmoil from the fourteenth to the sixteenth centuries. Nevertheless, international warfare and cross-border raiding have perhaps received too much attention from historians. Some Border families were very successful during these times and the Homes are a case in point. Although they had existed since the twelfth century, their collective rise to power and influence began in the mid-fifteenth century. This was as a result of a power vacuum in the region created by the fall of the Black Douglases. Sir Alexander Home of Home and Dunglass had been 'loved squire and ally' to Archibald, 4th Earl of Douglas, but he was happy to subvert the interests of his lord to further his own family's fortunes. His son and heir Alexander would become the 1st Lord Home in 1473. Other Home laird families were formed from the lords' younger sons or grandsons such as Home of Ayton and Duns, Home of Cowdenknowes, Home of Fast Castle, Home of Huttonhall, Home of Manderston, Home of Polwarth and Home of Wedderburn.[1] By 1600 the Homes dominated the East March, both socially and politically. They held all the important offices, owned much of the land and had impressive kinship networks. They celebrated their rise with new buildings and the rebuilding of substantial castles and monasteries. As their prestige grew, so too did the elaboration of their houses. Whilst these structures were not unique to Scotland as a whole, their juxta-position to the volatile Anglo-Scottish frontier makes this house-building significant.

The structures built and rebuilt by the Lords Home, and the various greater Home lairds, include Cowdenknowes, Coldingham Priory, Duns Castle, Home Castle and Huttonhall, Manderston, Redbraes (Polwarth) and Wedderburn in Berwickshire. Their power and influence extended into East Lothian and Roxburghshire as well. Sadly, very few of these buildings or their builders' families have survived into modern times. Those

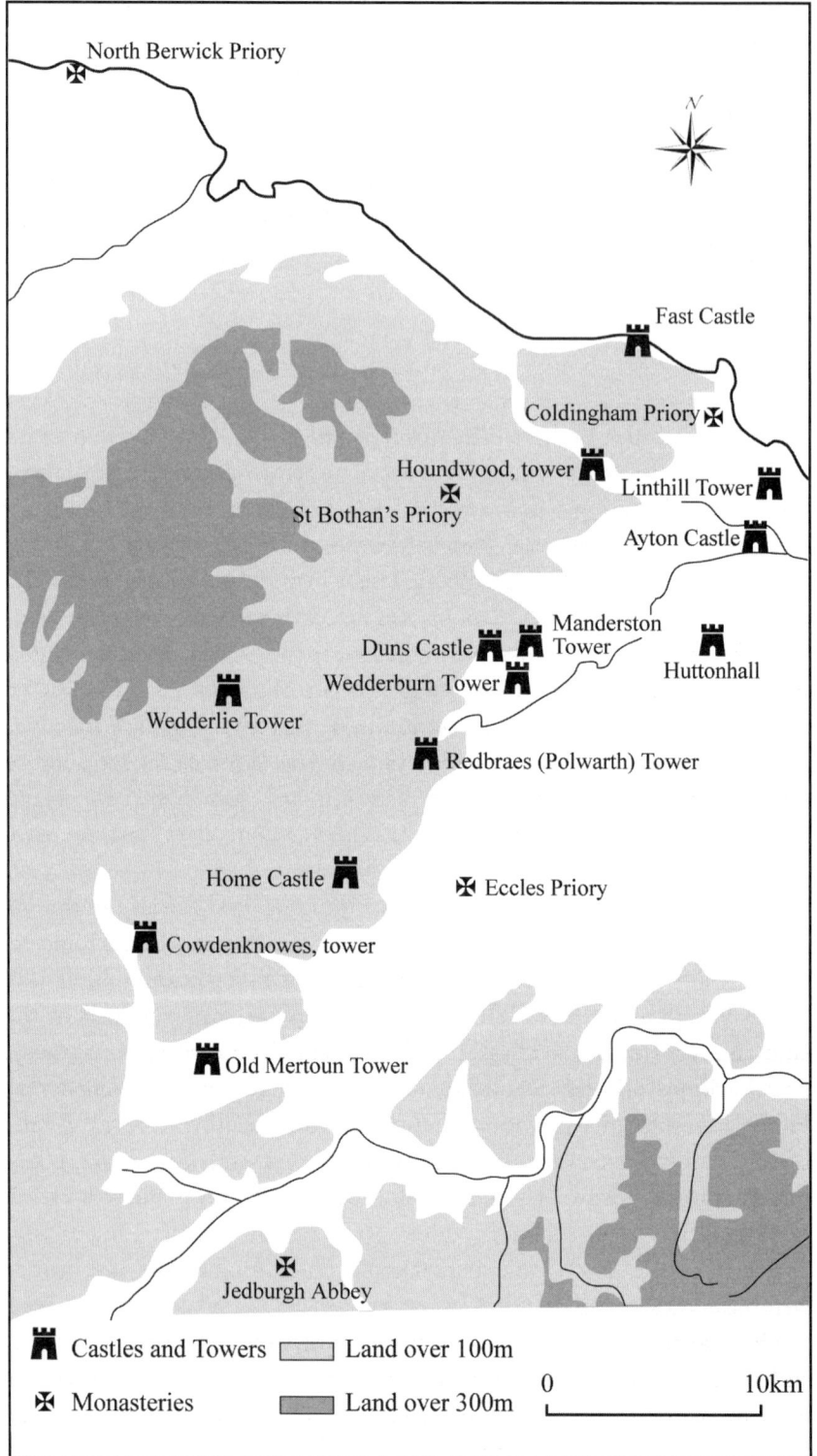

LORDSHIP AND
ARCHITECTURE
IN MEDIEVAL
AND
RENAISSANCE
SCOTLAND

❧

North Berwick Priory

Fast Castle

Coldingham Priory

Houndwood, tower

Linthill Tower

St Bothan's Priory

Ayton Castle

Manderston
Tower

Duns Castle

Huttonhall

Wedderburn Tower

Wedderlie Tower

Redbraes (Polwarth) Tower

Home Castle

Eccles Priory

Cowdenknowes, tower

Old Mertoun Tower

Jedburgh Abbey

Castles and Towers   Land over 100m

Monasteries   Land over 300m

0   10km

Figure 11.1
Home properties
mentioned in the text.

232

that did survive the ravages of time have been altered many times, or transformed into architectural follies as Home Castle was in the 1780s.

Families who built towers, castles and houses in the East March were exclusively from the laird classes. Those just below them in the social scale built bastles, such as George Ramsay's bastle in Foulden. This laird stratum of Border society did not include some of the notorious thieves who were mostly from the Middle and West Marches and were arguably unrepresentative of Border lairds anyway. East March lairds usually derived their income from legitimate sources and they seem to have indulged in widespread house-building in the later sixteenth century to prove this legitimate affluence.

In the sixteenth-century East March there were large numbers of lairds, with the Homes dominating.[2] They ranged from a humble bonnet laird like Home of Middlethird, who owned and farmed as little as 52 acres (two husbandlands), to the great surname chief Lord Home. The Lords Home owned vast acres and commanded a huge kinship following. Greater lairds were next in the social scale. They were above farming their own land and usually leased their farms to kinsmen and other tenants, reserving only a home farm for their own household requirements. These lairds were the most obvious builders and improvers of East March houses. The majority of the East March lairds were categorised as lesser lairds and they are not renowned for building ostentatious structures. They were not as impoverished as bonnet lairds, but they lacked the wealth and political power of the greater lairds. Families could naturally rise and fall within these landed circles, though most of these lairds were more fortunate than their ancestors.[3]

The sixteenth century witnessed dramatic changes in the land market that opened up new opportunities for many lairds and their sons. Principal amongst these benefits was the feuing (or leasing) of Crown, Church and monastic land to laymen. The East March was particularly rich in monastic land, having Coldingham Priory, Coldstream Priory, Dryburgh Abbey, Eccles Priory, St Bothans Priory and St John's Chapel within its boundaries. Home lairds feued from them and from other religious houses further afield. By the end of the sixteenth century Home lairds had a controlling interest in the lands of Coldingham, Eccles and St Bothans, plus North Berwick Priory and Jedburgh Abbey beyond their March. Church land and teinds were eagerly exploited by the Homes as well, especially if they were near their existing lands.

Those fortunate enough to gain these new leases were known as feuars, and though they were not exclusively lairds, the larger grants inevitably went to landed men, wealthy merchants or substantial office holders. The Homes of Ayton, for example, feued land from Coldingham Priory and

LORDSHIP AND
ARCHITECTURE
IN MEDIEVAL
AND
RENAISSANCE
SCOTLAND

☙

Restalrig Collegiate Church, whilst the Homes of Bassendean feued Gordon Moss from Kelso Abbey and part of Redpath from Coldingham.[4] The lucrative Crown lands in Ettrick Forest were feued by the Lords Home and the Homes of Wedderburn, amongst others.[5]

Feuing accounted for much of the new wealth in the Borders, as elsewhere in sixteenth-century Scotland. This was sometimes the explanation for conspicuous consumption by the lairds, but there were other factors to be considered. Many of the greater Home lairds and their sons were successful at court, gaining offices and gifts from the Crown. There was also the possibility of serving in the Border administration with its resultant prestige and remuneration.

Many of the sixteenth-century Home buildings have been lost, though there are a few examples left to demonstrate the remarkable variety of fortified buildings in the Borders. These include the more civilised country-house type,[6] as well as the more familiar Border tower house. The best examples are at Cowdenknowes and Huttonhall (Hutton Castle). Duns Castle, in spite of rebuilding, still has its tower, whilst the situation of Home (Hume) Castle is undeniably important even if its mock castle walls bear no resemblance to its former grandeur.

The Homes' income from agriculture was dependent upon good harvests and adaptable leases, but land in itself was a useful source from which to raise credit. Many lairds borrowed money to build new houses or to adapt older buildings. Their income did not necessarily come from property in the countryside, as some lairds owned land in burghs. The acquisition of a monastic house and its lands was also lucrative, as the Homes of Cowdenknowes discovered when they eventually gained control of Eccles Priory.[7]

The Homes of Cowdenknowes lived in the heart of Lauderdale. They were descendants of the first Lord Home and had been granted Cowdenknowes by James IV in 1506. By quirk of fate they became the earls of Home when the 2nd Earl died without children in 1633,[8] yet for much of the sixteenth century they were greater lairds who gathered their rents and served their country in time of war. They intermarried with other Border laird families, though they eventually broke into the ranks of the nobility in the later sixteenth century when Sir John Home married a half-sister of the earl of Bothwell and his younger brother, James, married a daughter of Lord Home. The Homes of Cowdenknowes were ascendant at the Scottish court by this time and were very much at the centre of political intrigue. Sir James Home had managed to join the most powerful political faction of the 1570s and as a result he was made warden of the Scottish East March, bailie of the earldom of March, a privy councillor, a gentleman of the bedchamber to James VI, a commissioner for both wappinshaws (musters) and against Jesuits in Berwickshire, and finally the captain of Edinburgh Castle.[9] He was undeniably successful, and to show off his newly acquired status he began to alter his home at Cowdenknowes. This house came into his possession after his father's death in 1573.

The original tower at Cowdenknowes was built before the 1540s. It was evidently still standing in 1574, despite an attempt by the English to blow up the tower in 1546.[10] Sir James decided to extend the property by adding a mansion house in 1574 and a further tower beside the River Leader in 1581. All three buildings were connected by a curtain wall that enclosed a considerable courtyard. A door lintel in the mansion has the initials and date, S.J.H.V.K.H. 1574, representing Sir James and his wife, Katherine Home of Blackadder. There is also a panel with the motto 'Feir God. Flee From Sin. And Mak For The Lyfe Everlasting', reflecting the Homes' adherence to the reformed church. Panels like this are not uncommon as there is a similar one at, for example, Holydean, near Melrose.[11] The present house has extensive Victorian additions that rather take away the impact of the sixteenth-century building. Fortunately, a sketch was made of the house in 1845, before the changes. Local historian James Tait described this as a mansion belonging to the sixteenth century 'in the baronial style of the Elizabethan period', which should have been more correctly called Jacobean.[12]

The additions made to Cowdenknowes in the sixteenth century were probably funded by loans from friends that were subsequently paid back

*Figure 11.2
Cowdenknowes,
Berwickshire: view
c.1845 (from
H. Drummond,
British Noble
Families (1846))*

LORDSHIP AND
ARCHITECTURE
IN MEDIEVAL
AND
RENAISSANCE
SCOTLAND

❧

from the fruits of office. For instance, Sir James borrowed 200 merks [13] from his deceased brother-in-law, Robert Cairncross of Colmslie, in 1574, but received £20 [14] per annum as bailie of March, £100 expenses for forfeiting Walter Davidson in Raperlaw during 1577 and £700 per annum as captain of Edinburgh Castle. [15] When he died on 16 April, 1596, Sir James left an inventory of moveable goods totalling £7,545-3-4, including £2000 worth of personal effects, but he owed £11,844 and thus died in debt. Some of these debts may have related to his captaincy of Edinburgh Castle as he owed James Purves, a flesher, £1,440, but they could equally be accounted for through good living. These arrears were only for Sir James's household, for it is known that his eldest son John kept a separate household after he married in 1587. It should be remembered that inventories reflected only the moveable wealth of the deceased and did not take account of lands and properties that could be worth far more. [16]

The Homes of Huttonhall were similar to the Cowdenknowes branch in that they were descendants of a Lord Home, although in their case they were illegitimate descendants of the 3rd Lord. Illegitimacy does not appear to have barred these Homes from inheriting or acquiring some property from their father. John Home was first granted Huttonhall in 1534 by his sister Elizabeth. She had procured the lands from the Kers of Samuelston in 1532, but it was likely that her father bought the lands on her behalf. The Homes feued the land thereafter from Lord Home, for £20 per annum. John's legitimated son Alexander inherited Huttonhall in 1557, and when he died in 1594 the estate passed to the first Home of Huttonhall to be born within wedlock, his eldest son John. [17]

The Homes of Huttonhall feued Crown land in other parts of Berwickshire, such as Greenlaw, Leitholm and Birgham. They also managed to gain monastic leases of land at Stitchill from Jedburgh Abbey, Coldstream Mains from Coldstream Priory and various lands belonging to St Bothans. Both Jedburgh and St Bothans were in the hands of Lord Home and his kindred. The prioress of Coldstream was a Pringle, but she yielded to the local power of the Homes. [18] There is little doubt that their close kinship to Lord Home enabled them to accumulate property from the 1530s onwards, but the consolidation and expansion of these lands in future decades would be dependent on their own survival and success at court in addition. As with the Homes at Cowdenknowes, it was a later generation that achieved most. Alexander Home made considerable sums from his feued lands as his rent remained static in a period of inflation. He would have been able to increase the rents he demanded from his own tenants, thus profiting from the deal. Alexander also acquired much monastic property and rights to teinds such as those of Over and Nether Nisbet near Jedburgh. [19] In fact he was prosperous enough to help the debt-laden

Figure 11.3
Huttonhall,
Berwickshire: general
view.

6th Lord Home in 1591 when he purchased Ladykirk, Framepath, Hardiesmill and Quixwood, as well as lands near Abbey St Bathans, Kelloe, Reedyloch and Chirnside, including the patronage of Chirnside Parish Church, for 6,000 merks. Lord Home returned the favour in 1600 when he had control of Coldingham Priory in addition to Jedburgh. He granted Alexander's son John the profitable 'first fruits' of Coldingham and Jedburgh.[20]

Alexander was a friend and counsellor to the young Lord Home, but he was also a highly respected Borderer. He served as a Border commissioner in 1585, 1588 and 1591, was deputy warden of the East March from 1582 until his death, a commissioner against Jesuits and deputy bailiff of Coldingham Priory for Lord Home. His son, John, continued two of his East March offices after his death as deputy warden and commissioner against Jesuits. John, however, managed to go further in 1601 by becoming appointed a gentleman of the bedchamber to James VI.[21] The Homes were a dominant force in the Scottish court during the 1590s, so this appointment was probably gained through the preferment of his kinsmen. As with Cowdenknowes' appointment there in earlier years, the

LORDSHIP AND
ARCHITECTURE
IN MEDIEVAL
AND
RENAISSANCE
SCOTLAND

❧

rewards for a competent gentleman of the bedchamber could have been substantial.

Alexander had married Isobel Home of Carolside, a remote cousin of lesser laird ranking. They had six surviving sons and five daughters, who were well provided for in Alexander's will. He left future tochers (dowries) totalling 9,000 merks, being 3,000 merks to Jane and 2,000 merks each to Barbara, Isobel and Alison. Elizabeth, who had already married John Seton of Touch, had the rest of her tocher paid. His heir, John, had also married in 1590. His bride was a friend of the Homes, Elizabeth Carmichael, of the greater gentry family of Carmichael of that Ilk, of the West March. Her tocher amounted to 10,000 merks.[22] John was executor to his father and honoured all these financial agreements, as well as providing for his mother. This was unusual amongst the Border lairds who were often hard pressed to meet their predecessors' legacies. Alexander also left an impressive inventory totalling £4,651, though he owed his creditors £4,501. However, he had many debtors and they were due to pay his estate £5,361. He apparently did not hound friends and kinsmen for repayment[23] and had been generous to his kinsmen in time of need. For example, he lent 800 merks to James Home of the Style in 1589.[24]

Huttonhall, or Hutton Castle as it is known today, is another interesting example of a Border laird extending a small tower into a country house to show off his newly acquired wealth and status. The tower was besieged and burned by English raiders in 1542 and again in 1544.[25] This damage was presumably repaired, although it was not until the time of Alexander that expansion took place. MacGibbon and Ross have dated his L-shaped extension of the hall to 1573, possibly as a result of Huttonhall being confirmed to him by the privy council in 1567, though an English ransom of £1,500 (£300 sterling) must have helped as well.[26] As with Cowden-knowes, there was a large enclosed courtyard for the new house. In 1585 Huttonhall was described as 'a maist godlie and comfortable house'.[27] There were impressive fireplaces by Border standards, but the panelled dining room of the new house with its beautiful plasterwork ceiling was outstanding. This room was used by many distinguished visitors in the later sixteenth century, perhaps most notably in 1597 when a cross-Border meeting at Norham Ford went disastrously wrong. The Homes of Ayton, Huttonhall and Wedderburn had escorted the English Border commissioners, including Sir William Bowes, to Huttonhall for their own protection after bullets had flown around their meeting place. It is recorded that they dined at Huttonhall before safely returning to Berwick-upon-Tweed.[28] This meal must have taken place in the dining room. This room survived intact until 1915 when the estate was sold to Sir William Burrell. Being a wealthy antiques collector, he found the ceiling and panelling too plain for his acquired taste. Burrell therefore ordered their destruction in an act that can only be described as architectural vandalism.[29] Burrell also dismantled the vaulted ground floor and added huge rooms to the west wing which took the heart out of the sixteenth-century design.

Huttonhall, however, has been altered many times since the sixteenth century. The original tower had a steep roof with gables in 1845, yet by the early 1880s [30] it was ruinous. This tower was then rebuilt, for Mac-Gibbon and Ross reported that the tower had 'lately been built up and covered with a platform roof' when they surveyed the castle in the late 1880s. In the eighteenth century the whole building had been semi-ruinous, but it was certainly inhabited in the mid-nineteenth century. It was modernised by Lord Tweedmouth after he purchased the estate in 1876, which was noted during a RCAHMS visit in 1908.[31] The heraldic panel over the original front door is slightly puzzling as it is undated. The letters AH and EH were incorporated into the panel, though it is now weathered. Alexander Home was married to Isobel Home, so this is either a mistake or it may refer to another Alexander Home and his wife Elizabeth Home of the mid-seventeenth century.[32]

There are, of course, many sixteenth-century lairds' houses that have

Figure 11.4 Huttonhall, Berwickshire: general view showing ruinous tower, c. 1880. RCAHMS, BW/147

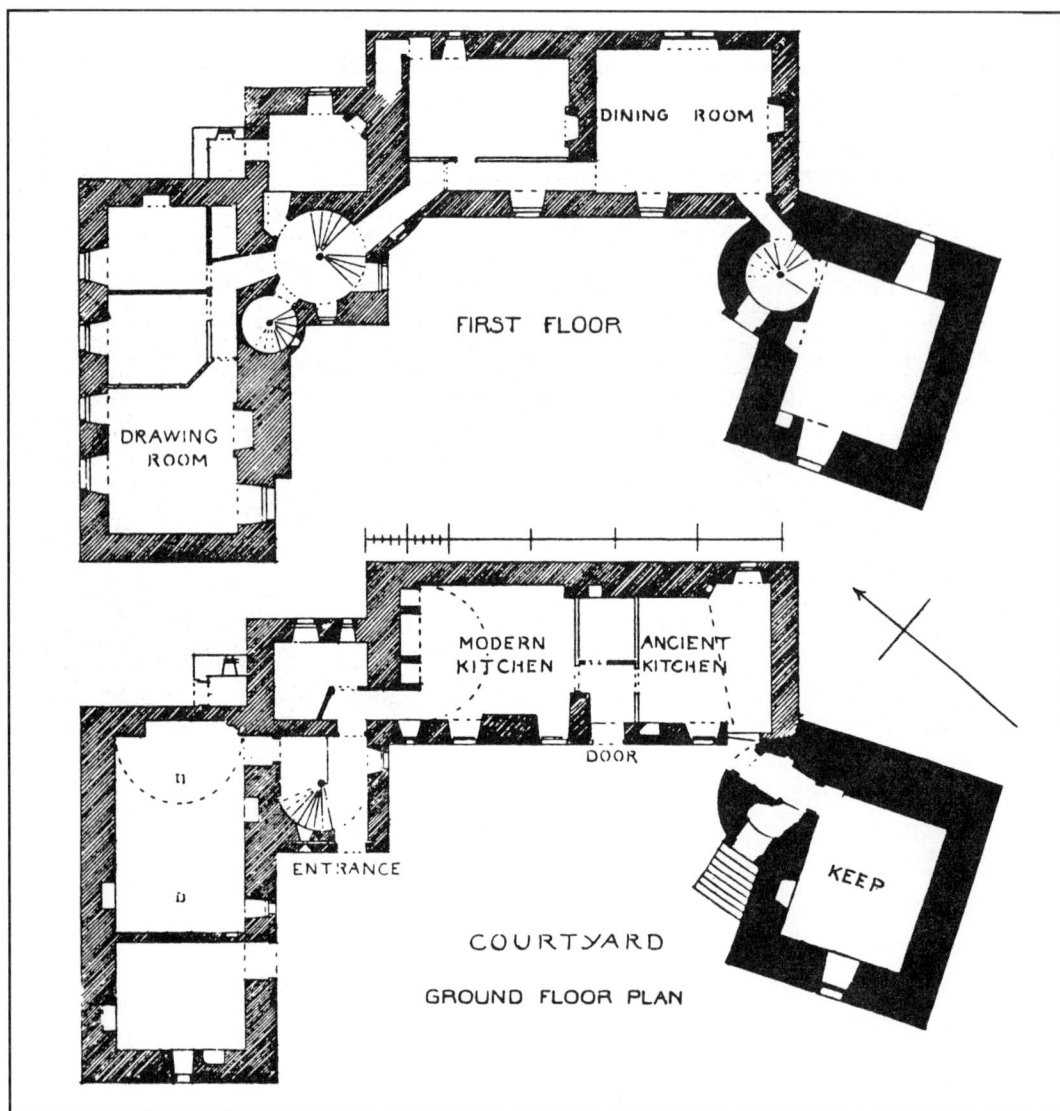

FIRST FLOOR

DINING ROOM

DRAWING ROOM

MODERN KITCHEN

ANCIENT KITCHEN

DOOR

ENTRANCE

KEEP

COURTYARD

GROUND FLOOR PLAN

Figure 11.5 Huttonhall, Berwickshire: ground- and first-floor plans, c.1892 (from Cast. and Dom. Arch., *vol. iv, p.193)*

completely disappeared or have been left in a far more ruinous state than Huttonhall. Home Castle and Fast Castle had the most important positions in the East March, yet they are now much decayed. Home's natural vantage point made it the target of English forces on many occasions during medieval and early modern times. Whoever had possession of Home could dominate the Merse and the north of the English East March. It was no coincidence that Saxton's 1570 map of Northumberland shows Home Castle very prominently across the frontier. Unfortunately, no illustration of the original castle has survived, so its strength and grandeur can only be guessed at.

Home Castle was indicative of the political and financial upheavals of

Figure 11.6
Huttonhall,
Berwickshire: dining
room, 1915.

the Lords Home. Every time it was taken by English troops and garrisoned, the Lords Home lost their goods and gear, furnishings and crops from the nearby fields. It was therefore not surprising that Dunglass in East Lothian became a more usual dwelling for them in the sixteenth century. During 1543 Lord Home was paid 900 crowns to fortify the castle against the English, and again in 1547 he received £1,845 to garrison the place. Unfortunately, Home Castle then fell into English hands, though it was recaptured in 1548. In 1549 Lord Home was ordered to resign the castle to Mary of Guise and Regent Arran so that a garrison could be established. Lord Home and his son, the Master of Home, were allowed to remain in the west or the north quarter of the castle, but it is unclear if they did so.[33] When a similarly tense situation occurred in 1559, Lord Home was licensed to garrison the castle himself. With a £75 allowance he was to have twelve hagbutters, two cannoners and a captain.[34] By siding with the rebellious supporters of Mary, Queen of Scots, in 1569, Lord Home again endangered his property. An English army took the castle without a fight in 1570 and garrisoned it for three years.[35] It was then garrisoned by twelve Scotsmen for a further five years as the 5th Lord Home had been forfeited for treason. After this the castle must have been made habitable again by the 6th Lord Home. He would have needed the castle for Border business, and his first wife is noted as writing her will there in 1604.[36] The quieter

LORDSHIP AND
ARCHITECTURE
IN MEDIEVAL
AND
RENAISSANCE
SCOTLAND

❧

times that ensued after the Union of the Crowns in 1603 may have lulled the newly created earls of Home into a false sense of security. The Home family fortunes were never in much danger, despite remaining Catholic and failing in the direct male line, when a tailzie of 1604 was invoked giving the descent to the Homes of Cowdenknowes.[37] Nevertheless, as far as Home Castle was concerned its days were numbered. Siding with the defeated royalists at the battle of Dunbar against the republican forces of Oliver Cromwell put the 3rd Earl of Home in a predicament. Cromwell ordered Colonel Fenwick to destroy the castle as it posed a threat to his

line of communication. In 1651 this army succeeded in reducing the medieval castle to rubble for the last time. What remained gradually decayed over the next century, although its commanding position remained of crucial importance in the Jacobite risings, the Napoleonic era and both World Wars.[38]

Another important stronghold that appears to have belonged to the Lords Home was Fast Castle on the Berwickshire coast. The absolute title is unclear before the later fifteenth century when a younger son, Sir Patrick Home of Fast Castle, appears in documentation. It changed hands many times during the Anglo-Scottish wars of that century. The strategic importance of Fast Castle lay in its guardianship of important shipping routes in that part of the North Sea off the Berwickshire and East Lothian coastline. In 1503 Margaret Tudor rested here on her way to marry King James IV, signifying the castle's completeness at this time. Sir Patrick's son and heir, Cuthbert, later died at the battle of Flodden, after which the keepership of the castle passed to the 3rd Lord Home. Cuthbert had left heiresses, who were probably in the care of Home. They later married the lairds Logan of Restalrig and Ogilvy of Dunlugus, but the Lords Home maintained their interest in the castle. During the troubled 1540s their men recaptured it from English occupation in both 1547 and 1549. The 5th Lord Home reoccupied the castle in 1567 when he married the widow of Logan of Restalrig, but he died in disgrace and her son inherited it in

Figure 11.8
Home Castle,
Berwickshire: detail of
Saxton's map of
Northumberland,
1570, showing the
castle (left).

Figure 11.7
Home Castle,
Berwickshire: aerial
view.
RCAHMS, A 56686

243

LORDSHIP AND
ARCHITECTURE
IN MEDIEVAL
AND
RENAISSANCE
SCOTLAND

1576. Until 1606 Fast Castle was Logan of Restalrig's domain. However, he chose to live at his comfortable home at Gunsgreen on the Eye Water instead of putting up with the rigours of living in a cold and windswept castle. The castle returned to the Homes in the seventeenth century for a number of years. This was after the Logans were disgraced by their alleged involvement in the notorious Gowrie Conspiracy against King James VI. The castle was not ruinous, but neither was it a commodious dwelling for the laird classes, so it was not lived in very much. Serious decay set in during the eighteenth century and there is now very little left of the castle.[39]

Duns Castle, unlike Home or Fast Castle, has probably been occupied by Homes since the fourteenth or early fifteenth centuries. The Homes of Ayton and Duns were descendants of the first Lord Home. They held the tower and mains of Duns, Duns Law and other lands near Duns that constituted the £20 land there. They also had a 'pyle' at Ayton with surrounding lands, and held Houndwood and Reedyloch as well.[40] Like other greater Home lairds in the sixteenth century, they were accumulating land and prestige as opportunities arose, culminating in the creation of Duns as a burgh of barony in 1605, with all its trading privileges. They had previously persuaded the privy council to change the market day of Duns from Wednesday to Monday.[41] Today, neither Duns nor Ayton castle bears much resemblance to its predecessor. The tower built into later extensions of Duns Castle possibly dates from c.1320. It is only visible from the north side of the castle and is much altered. However, it is likely that the original tower was extended in the sixteenth century to form an L-shaped dwelling. A plan of the ground floor made by MacGibbon and Ross in the 1880s indicates an early extension, though they perhaps erroneously state that the 1320 tower was L-shaped.[42]

The Homes' acquisition of feued land from Coldingham Priory has already been noted. They eagerly sought kirklands as well and succeeded

*Figure 11.9
Duns Castle,
Berwickshire: 1790s
(from* Country Life,
28 December 1989)

in gaining those of Ellem and Blackhill.[43] The teinds of Ayton were acquired on a 19-year tack in 1558 and those of Duns were leased from the Homes of Wedderburn. In 1593 Patrick Home gained a tack of the teinds of Yetholm in Roxburghshire, probably through court favour as they were outside his family's usual sphere of influence. They also leased Cheeklaw near Duns from the heirs of Home of Fast Castle and purchased Duns Park and Caldside in 1539, with Fairnieside following in 1559. In 1599 lands held in Ayton by Home of Wedderburn were resigned to William Home of Ayton.[44] They imposed their will on tenants who were recalcitrant and defended their property interests against interlopers. William Home complained that the tenants of Eyemouth were not using his mill there in 1568 and 1583.[45] He took action to ensure that his miller did not lose out. He also feuded with laird neighbours over minor property matters, including his kinsman Home of West Reston.[46] His son, Patrick, was equally quarrelsome when it came to property rights. He had a serious argument with Home of Tynnes over Duns teinds in 1591. Tynnes had land in Ettrick Forest, but was really a younger son of the neighbouring Homes of Manderston. They were rivals with the Homes of Ayton in the Duns area and at court.[47] Kinship affection amongst the Homes could easily be stretched beyond repair when it came to local avarice. Where this occurred, each branch of the Homes was clearly out for its own family fortune, in disregard of collective kinship.

The Homes of Ayton and Duns funded their land purchases from advantageous manoeuvres within the sixteenth-century economy and at court. For fighting off the English occupiers, George Home of Ayton was awarded his own ward and marriage in 1549. This meant that no guardian could access and plunder his family wealth. In the 1560s a £200 per annum pension from Kelso Abbey was granted to a younger son Alexander Home, again for service to the Crown. George Home's post as a deputy warden of the East March in the 1540s should not be forgotten, but a court office was undoubtedly more lucrative. The Homes' greatest achievement at court was therefore in the 1590s when William was made a gentleman of the bedchamber, like his Cowdenknowes and Huttonhall kinsmen. The royal bedchamber was known to be a good source of patronage and a few land deals were definitely the result of having the king's ear.[48] If the laird of Ayton borrowed money, he repaid the loan on time, usually avoiding the need to wadset land to extend a loan. George Home borrowed 500 merks from John Sinclair, Dean of Restalrig, in 1552 and had repaid him by 1554. In 1579 George Home felt affluent enough to lend his step-nephew, Alexander Home of Dens, £1,500. Surprisingly, these Homes did not give excessive tochers for their daughters, thus avoiding the fashion to over-extend one's finances to impress the bridegroom's family. Elspeth Home

LORDSHIP AND
ARCHITECTURE
IN MEDIEVAL
AND
RENAISSANCE
SCOTLAND

❧

received only 300 merks in 1563, yet Patrick Home received a 10,000 merk tocher from George Douglas of Parkhead in 1587.[49] When the 'honourbale man George Home laird of Aitton in the Merse' died in 1585, his inventory was worth £5,469. He was owed £1,062 and had 40 ounces of gold worth £960. In turn he owed his creditors a mere £396. His resources were not strained by family commitments, as he appears to have had no wife or children. His heir was his brother, William, father of Patrick.[50] This family's fortunes continued to be stable into the seventeenth century. Nonetheless, by the end of this century the castle became the property

of the Hays of Drummelzier, ending the Homes' connection with the
building.

The Home branches of Manderston, Polwarth and Wedderburn were
generally more successful than the Homes of Ayton or Huttonhall in the
sixteenth century. However, these other Home lairds have left no visible
signs of their power and influence in the East March. Later aggrandisement
of Manderston, Polwarth (Marchmont) and Wedderburn has wiped out
the architecture that was undoubtedly there in the sixteenth century. Some
of the post-1603 houses in the East March have survived to give the
impression that there were few buildings of note before the Union of the
Crowns because of the proximity of the frontier. They are the Hirsel,
Houndwood, Linthill, Old Mertoun, Nisbet and Wedderlie. The impressive
house-building and extensions of Cowdenknowes and Huttonhall prove,
though, that some lairds were not afraid to display their wealth and status
in the East March. They were not alone in defying the unsettled nature
of the pre-Union Borderland, as there were other lairds who adapted
existing towers or monasteries rather than building anew, such as the
Douglases at Melrose, the Haigs at Bemersyde and the Kers of Cessford
at Holydean and Friars.[51] However, the Home kindred's expansion and
financial success in the sixteenth-century East March was certainly remarkable. The overall impression is that their good family fortunes were once
visible in a landscape now sadly depleted of their building works.

NOTES

1. *Scots Peerage*, iv, 439–84.
2. M. M. Meikle, Lairds and Gentlemen: a study of the landed families of the
   Anglo-Scottish Borders, c. 1540–1603, (PhD thesis, University of Edinburgh,
   1989), 28–40. Hereafter Meikle, Lairds and Gentlemen, and now published as *A
   British Frontier? Lairds and Gentlemen in the Eastern Borders, 1540–1603* (East
   Linton, 2004).
3. There were at least 49 Home laird families in the sixteenth-century Borders.
   They are recorded being of Ayton, Bassendean, Bellitaw, Blackadder (East and
   West), Blacksmill, Broomhouse, Carolside, Cheeklaw, Chirnside East Mains,
   Cowdenknowes, Cranshaws, Crossrig, Crumiecruke, Crumstane, Eccles, Edrom,
   Fairnieside, Fans, Fishwick, Fleurs of Coldingham, Framepath, Godscroft,
   Hardiesmill, Hilton, Hutton, Huttonhall, Hutton Bell, Jedburgh (as abbot and
   commendator), Lauder, The Law, Manderston, Middlethird, Ninewells, Polwarth,
   Prenderguest, Reidheuch, Renton, West Renton, Rollandstoun, Simprim, Slegden,
   Spott, Timnis, Wedderburn, Whitchester and Whiterig.
4. *HMC*, Fifth Report, 63, 68–9; *RMS*, v, no. 2108; *RMS*, vi, no. 123; *RSS*, viii, no.
   1093.
5. NAS,GD 267/27/67; *HMC*, Twelfth Report, no. 277; *RMS*, iii, no. 1593.
6. C. McKean, 'Castle-wise Country Houses', in *The Architecture of Renaissance
   Scotland*, ed. D. Howard (Edinburgh, 1990), 17–18.
7. NAS, Register of Deeds RD1/13 fo. 359; *RSS*, v, no. 3041; *RSS*, vi, nos. 1042, 2816.

*Figure 11.10
Fast Castle,
Berwickshire: aerial
view of headland and
castle.
RCAHMS, BW/3060*

LORDSHIP AND
ARCHITECTURE
IN MEDIEVAL
AND
RENAISSANCE
SCOTLAND

❧

8. *Scots Peerage*, iv, 467–79.

9. Meikle, *Lairds and Gentlemen*, 502–3.

10. *L. & P., Hen. VIII*, xxi, part 1, 1279.

11. RCAHMS, *Berwickshire*, 68, 71–2.

12. *HBNC*, v (1868), 268–9.

13. A merk was 13s 4d.

14. All amounts are in £Scots unless otherwise indicated. The exchange rate of Scots pounds to sterling was £4 to £1 in 1560, falling to £12 to £1 in 1603.

15. NAS, Edinburgh Commissary Courts: Testaments CC8/8/3 fo. 405r; *APS*, iii, 404; *RSS*, vi, no. 2381; *TA*, xiii, 165.

16. NAS, CC8/8/31 fos. 381r–382v; NAS, RD1/36 fo. 271.

17. NAS, CC8/8/26 fos. 179–81; *RMS*, iii, nos. 1111, 1302, 2416; *RMS*, iv, no. 2929; *RSS*, v, no. 3506.

18. NAS, CH6/6/1 fos. 29–30; GD158/454; *RMS*, iii, 1302, 1481, 2011; *RMS*, iv, no. 2255; *RMS*, v, nos. 1264–5.

19. NAS, E48/1/1 fo. 200; GD40/3/389/1 and 2.

20. NAS, GD242/45; NRAS, 859/1/2, 859/134/1; *RMS*, v, nos. 1962–3.

21. Meikle, *Lairds and Gentlemen*, 507.

22. NAS, CC8/8/26 fo. 181; RD1/48 fos. 199–201; RD1/50 fo. 814.

23. NAS, CC8/8/26 fos. 179r–181v.

24. NAS, RD1/34 fo. 398.

25. *L & P Hen VIII*, xvii, 1197; *Hamilton Papers*, ii, 465.

26. NAS, CS7/42 ff. 59–60; *RSS*, v, no. 3506; MacGibbon and Ross, *Castellated and Domestic Architecture*, iv, 193–9. There are some inaccuracies about the family's history in MacGibbon and Ross.

27. *The Diary of Mr James Melvill, 1556–1601*, (Wodrow Society, 1842), 219.

28. *Cal. Border Papers*, ii, no. 784.

29. He replaced Alexander Hume's panelling with some from Harrington Hall in Lincolnshire and it is this room which is now on display at the Burrell Collection in Glasgow (*The Burrell Collection*, ed. R. Marks and others, (Glasgow, 1988), 19).

30. MacGibbon and Ross, *Castellated and Domestic Architecture*, iv, 194.

31. Hutton was extensively altered by Sir William Burrell and his various architects and again received poor treatment after Burrell gifted his collection to Glasgow City Council in 1944. They eventually stripped everything of value from the building (RCAHMS, *Berwickshire*, 98).

32. NAS, GD158/51.

33. NAS, CS6/26 fo. 66; *ADCP*, 568; *Hamilton Papers*, i, 556; J. Lesley, *The Historie of Scotland* (Scottish Text Society, 1988–95), 222–3; Pitscottie, *Historie*, 105.

34. NRAS, 859/134/4.

35. *Calendar of State Papers, relating to English Affairs, preserved principally at Rome, 1558–78*, ed. J. M. Rigg (London, 1916–26) i, no. 709.

36. NAS, CC8/8/44 fo. 74; RD1/13 fo. 13; *RSS*, vi, nos. 2007, 2381.

37. The 6th Lord Home became 1st Earl of Home in 1605. NRAS, 859/14/4; *RMS*, vi, no. 1721.

38. RCAHMS, *Berwickshire*, 97.

39. *PSAS*, lv (1921), 56–83.

40. NAS, CC8/8/22 fos. 119–120; *ER*, xxi, 513; *Hamilton Papers*, i, 69, 91; *RMS*, iv, no. 49.

41. NAS, CC8/8/22 fo. 119; NRAS, 778/6; *RMS*, iii, no. 1948; *RMS*, vi, no. 1628; *RPC*, iv, 206.

42. MacGibbon and Ross, *Castellated and Domestic Architecture*, v, 265.

43. NRAS, 2720/245, 338.

44. NAS, GD247/94/1; RD1/28 fo. 304; NRAS, 778/1; NRAS, 2720/259; *RMS*, iii, no.
1948.
45. NAS, GD267/27/78.
46. *RPC*, iv, 395, 396, 554, 612.
47. Ibid., iv, 613, 677, 689–93.
48. NAS, E48/1/1 fo. 228; RD1/29 fo. 20; RD1/47 fo. 16; *Hamilton Papers*, i, 69; *RSS*,
iv, no. 151; *RSS*, v, no. 962.
49. NAS, CC8/8/22 fo. 121; CS6/27 fo. 130; CS7/10 fo. 165; RD1/27 fo. 276;
RH15/16/4/1.
50. NAS, CC8/8/22 fos. 119–22.
51. RCAHMS, *Berwickshire*, passim; RCAHMS, *Roxburghshire*, passim; Meikle, Lairds
and Gentlemen, 261–2, 267–9, 451.

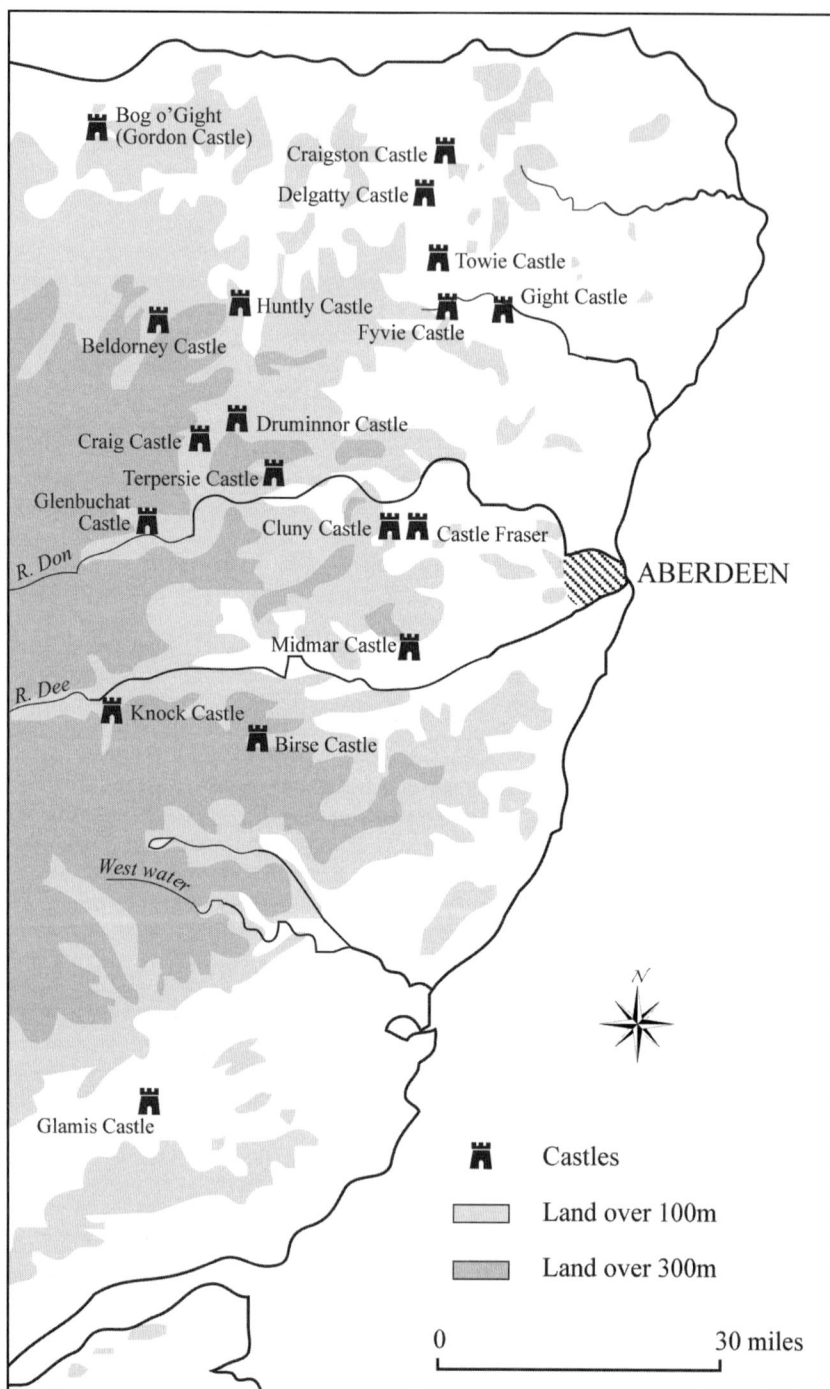

LORDSHIP AND
ARCHITECTURE
IN MEDIEVAL
AND
RENAISSANCE
SCOTLAND

Bog o'Gight
(Gordon Castle)

Craigston Castle

Delgatty Castle

Towie Castle

Gight Castle

Huntly Castle

Fyvie Castle

Beldorney Castle

Druminnor Castle

Craig Castle

Terpersie Castle

Glenbuchat
Castle

Cluny Castle

Castle Fraser

R. Don

ABERDEEN

Midmar Castle

R. Dee

Knock Castle

Birse Castle

West water

N

Glamis Castle

Castles

Land over 100m

Land over 300m

0   30 miles

Figure 12.1
Gordon properties
mentioned in the text

250

Chapter 12

꙳

THE GORDONS AND THE NORTH-EAST, 1452–1640

Harry Gordon Slade

Amongst the great and the grand families of the north-east of Scotland none stood higher in its own estimation than the House of Gordon, a view not always shared by its neighbours. In the course of its history the family, with its 156 cadet branches,[1] was to boast one dukedom, one marquisate, three earldoms, one viscounty and ten baronetcies; and the expression 'Gay' or more properly 'Gey Gordons' suggested that in the eyes of many they were altogether too much of a good thing.

By the conservative standards of the north-east the Gordons were new people, a branch of a Border family, only arriving in Aberdeenshire in 1319, when the lands of Strathbogie were granted to Sir Adam of Gordon by Robert I, a grant finally confirmed in 1351. The direct male line lasted for only four generations. On the death of Sir John Gordon, who left two illegitimate sons, in 1394, the Strathbogie lands passed to his younger brother, Sir Adam Gordon, killed in 1402 at the battle of Homildon Hill. He was succeeded by his daughter, Elizabeth, wife of Sir Alexander Seton, and the legitimate male line came to an end. Although the descendants of this couple have always been known as 'Gordon', Lord Byron's mother, Catherine Gordon of Gight, always referred to them slightly contemptuously as the 'Seton Gordons' – after all she was one herself. It is this line that has attracted the attention of historians, rather than the more numerous descendants of the twenty grandsons of Sir John Gordon from whom the male line descends.

After all it was the Huntly or Seton Gordons who married daughters, legitimate and illegitimate, of kings, held great offices of state, boasted of giving a daughter as wife to a pretender to the English throne and numbered a Tuscan Grand Duke amongst their sponsors.[2] They supported and betrayed the Crown, and contributed, with the enthusiastic support of their cousins, to spreading bloodshed and warfare across the north-east in the years between 1560 and 1660, when King's Men fought Queen's Men,

LORDSHIP AND
ARCHITECTURE
IN MEDIEVAL
AND
RENAISSANCE
SCOTLAND

⪫⪪

Reformers fought Catholics, Covenanters fought Episcopalians, Scots fought the English and always the Gordons fought the Forbes. Yet in this pattern of mayhem there were periods of peace when men enjoyed prosperity and when there was time to build. This was particularly true in the years between 1590 and 1630, and in those years there were no finer buildings than those found in the north-east of Scotland, many of them associated with the House of Gordon, and with the Huntly line in particular.

It must always be a point of debate whether the development of style or detail in a group of associated buildings owes more to the taste of designers than to that of the patrons: whether the mason or architect has certain features that he likes to peddle; whether a family will like certain elements which, like the family face, will appear in future generations; or whether a particularly dominant member of a family will force his or her views and taste on the next generation.[3] Human nature being what it is, all these considerations will probably play a part, but in the end the most important element must be the influence of the mason/architect. Beyond a certain level of building a trained mind must come into play, a mind which will have a professional knowledge of, and interest in, what others are doing in the same field.

Nowhere is this more true than in the buildings of Aberdeenshire and Banffshire erected in the last four decades of the sixteenth and the first three decades of the seventeenth centuries. The names of three families of architect/masons, Con, Leiper and Bell, are known; it is becoming increasingly possible to identify groups of buildings, however tentatively, as the work of one or other of these families. Mostly this has to be done through the comparison of plans or architectural detail; sometimes it can be done through the study of family connections; sometimes, but much more rarely, through documentary evidence. Castle Fraser and Craigston both bear, carved in the stonework, the sign manual of their designer, John Bell; and James Leiper is known to have failed to complete a decorative pavement at Castle Fraser, for which failure he was put to the horn.[4] Unfortunately, among the mass of family papers which survive in north-east Scotland, there is a dearth of material relating to private building work prior to the middle of the seventeenth century, and, although one day papers and drawings may be found which will throw light on this very important period, which saw the culmination and termination of medieval and Renaissance architecture in Scotland, the time has not yet come.

It would be reasonable to suppose that any family as wealthy, powerful and widespread as the Gordons would make a strong imprint on the houses built for them. At first sight this is so, but on closer examination every group of Gordon castles which share strong common characteristics,

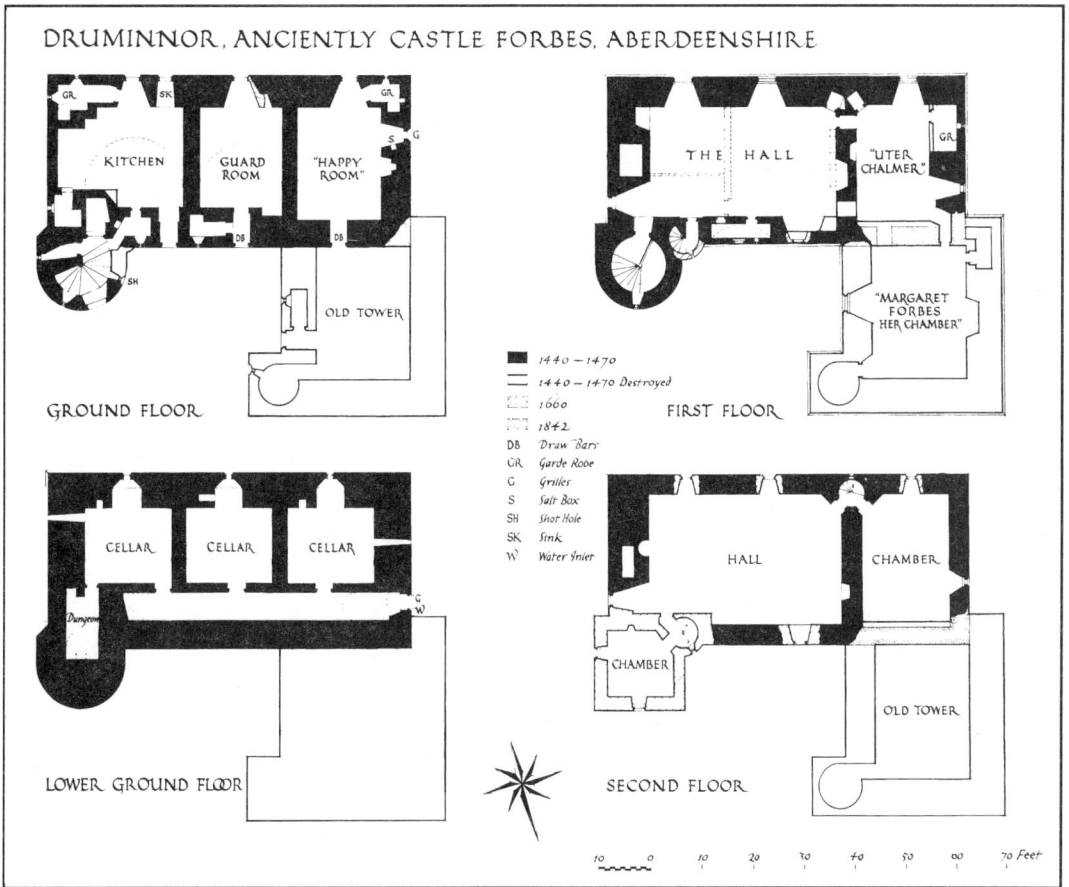

DRUMINNOR, ANCIENTLY CASTLE FORBES, ABERDEENSHIRE

KITCHEN
GUARD ROOM
"HAPPY ROOM"
OLD TOWER
GROUND FLOOR

THE HALL
"UTER CHALMER"
"MARGARET FORBES HER CHAMBER"
FIRST FLOOR

1440 – 1470
1440 – 1470 Destroyed
1660
1842
DB   Draw Bars
GR   Garde Robe
G   Grilles
S   Salt Box
SH   Shot Hole
SK   Sink
W   Water Ynlet

CELLAR   CELLAR   CELLAR
Dungeon
LOWER GROUND FLOOR

HALL   CHAMBER
CHAMBER
OLD TOWER
SECOND FLOOR

10   0   10   20   30   40   50   60   70 Feet

*Figure 12.2
Druminnor (Castle
Forbes),
Aberdeenshire:
floor-plans.*

share these characteristics with castles not built for Gordons; castles with which there are no close family links, or indeed any links at all. This raises yet again the question of architect versus patron: whose influence was the stronger? Increasingly the thought intrudes that some mason/architects were more fashionable than others; that some would be more likely to be employed by families of a similar social background or financial standing, and that family, political and even religious bonds were of less importance than has often been supposed.

The Gordon castles considered here are those, large or small, which have either some intrinsic architectural importance or have a part in the developing history of building in the north-east. Small and simple towers or lairds' houses are not part of the story. They are thirteen in number, nine associated with the Seton-Gordon line, four with the male line. They embrace the splendours of Huntly and the now-vanished Bog of Gight, and the small tower houses of Forest of Birse and Knock. Six are still inhabited, but only one, Cluny, is still occupied by a family of the name and descent of Gordon.

Figure 12.3
Huntly Castle,
Aberdeenshire: south
front by R.W. Billings.

The story starts not with Huntly, but with the Forbes stronghold of Druminnor,[5] built according to a bond in the Forbes charter chest between 1440 and 1460 for Lord Forbes by John of Kemlock, a mason who had previously worked at Kildrummy. The building of Druminnor was licensed in 1456, a legal fiction which was usually retrospective. Built as a palace house with a single corner tower, its plans, although much altered, bear an uncanny resemblance to Huntly, the principal seat of Lord Huntly, some five miles distant. Huntly, or Strathbogie as it was then known, was largely destroyed in 1452. A Sir John Kemlock was in the service of Lord Huntly as a chaplain at Strathbogie in 1474, and Huntly's third daughter, Christian, had married the Master of Forbes, Lord Forbes' eldest son. More has been built on less.

Figure 12.4
Huntly Castle,
Aberdeenshire:
principal doorway by
R.W. Billings.

Druminnor and Huntly are unusual in that both were built on sloping ground, giving a lower floor or half-cellar with three vaulted rooms and a long passage along one side. Three vaulted rooms are provided on the ground floor and the two upper floors each contained a sequence of hall, outer chamber and inner chamber. This sequence survives at Huntly, and

254

IN DEFENS

I R   A R
6   S

LORDSHIP AND
ARCHITECTURE
IN MEDIEVAL
AND
RENAISSANCE
SCOTLAND

❧

is known from a sixteenth-century bill of divorce to have existed at Druminnor.[6] In both castles the inner or bed-chamber was situated in a large angle tower. The principal difference was that at Druminnor both the stair tower and the chamber tower were on the same side of the main body of the palace, whereas at Huntly they were placed diagonally. Both buildings, particularly Huntly, have been greatly altered subsequently, but these alterations have hidden and confused, rather than displaced, the original structures.

The understanding of Huntly has been confused by the discovery early in the twentieth century, of the foundations of a massive L-tower hard by the palace block. Such a tower is typical of late fifteenth-century building and it has tempted some writers to assume that the palace block must therefore date from the next century. This need not be so: at Glamis in the fifteenth century a palace house and an even more massive L-tower were being built at virtually the same time in much closer proximity.[7]

The most complete study of Huntly castle was written by W. Douglas Simpson when the work of consolidation was commencing at the hands of the old Office of Works.[8] Simpson had the advantage of visiting the structure before the archaeological evidence disappeared under the all-purpose Ancient Monuments pointing that was to spread from Orkney

Figure 12.5
Huntly Castle,
Aberdeenshire: from
north-east.
Historic Scotland,
A.690-8

to Cornwall, and was thus able to see much that was subsequently hidden. His conclusions were that the original castle was a timbered motte-and-bailey castle dating from the thirteenth century and known as the *Peel of Strathbogie*. At some time after the 1319 grant, probably late in the same century, a massive stone L-tower was built in the bailey. This survived the 1452 burning, but was replaced as the principal building by the palace house, or new wark, which forms the core of the present build. The new wark consisted of a rectangular block with a large round tower at one corner. The two lower floors were vaulted, the upper floor a great hall and chambers. When he took on this view Simpson was not aware of the parallels between Huntly, Druminnor and Glamis. At this stage Huntly would have differed only in detail from other palatial blocks built for owners of a similar social standing to that of the earl.

The remodelling of the castle in the years 1553 to 1560 by the 4th Earl of Huntly may not have been as drastic as Simpson believed, although it almost certainly led to an additional floor being added. It was far-reaching in one respect: a staircase was added to the palace diagonally opposite the round chamber tower, which seems to be the genesis of the Z-plan, so distinctive a mark of castles of the second half of the sixteenth century. It seems to have been adopted almost at once at two other Gordon castles – Beldorney c.1554–61 and Terpersie 1561 – and its popularity spread. Its advantages for both domestic convenience and defensive utility were quickly realised, and, although the type can be found throughout Scotland, there is an unusually large and early concentration in the area between the Dee and the Spey, an area particularly susceptible to Gordon influence. The Z-plan survived its first appearance in the north-east for over a hundred years, being used at the Cromwellian citadel at Aberdeen, and the 1719 Board of Ordnance forts and barracks along the Highland line.

Beldorney shows the plan at its least developed, with the staircase occupying the two lower floors of one tower – a pattern followed at Glenbuchat and Midmar – which allowed for only two rooms, hall and chamber, on the principal floor. The same criticism did not apply at Huntly, where there was ample space for three rooms in sequence: hall, inner chamber and bed-chamber, as an account of the death of the 5th earl shows.[9] This of course may have been the original medieval plan, as it seems to have been at Druminnor. Terpersie, although much smaller, is more sophisticated in its planning; a mural stair in the gable wall allows for a hall and two chambers, one in each of the diagonally opposed towers.

A non-Gordon house, Carnousie,[10] built for the Ogilvies c.1577, a fully-developed Z-house, has affinities with Beldorney and Midmar, and the later Glenbuchat, in that the principal staircase fills the two lower floors of one of the towers. It appears, however, to have been designed

*Figure 12.6
Terpersie Castle,
Aberdeenshire: view
from south-west by
R.W. Billings.*

by a mason, or family of masons, responsible for a group of castles in the north-east, two of which, Gight and Craig, belonged to branches of the Gordons; the others in the group were Towie Barclay and Delgatty.

The link with Carnousie lies in the planning of the lower end of the Hall. Both the main stair and the service stair give onto the hall by way of doorways into the window embrasure at the lower end, conveniently set behind the screens. This arrangement pertains at Craig, Gight and Towie Barclay, but not apparently at Delgatty. At Towie Barclay and at Craig, where the halls are vaulted, there is a gallery or oratory in the wall above the embrasure, a feature which probably existed at Gight. A feature which all four castles have in common is that the lobby immediately inside the entrance is covered by a small ribbed vault. As far as dating can be established, Craig, Gight and Delgatty appear to have been built, probably in that order, between 1573 and 1579, with Towie Barclay dating from *c.* 1593. There is also a religious connection: the south-west corbel-cap at Craig bears the Five Wounds of Christ, the keystone at Gight depicts the Arma Christi, and at Towie Barclay the vault in the oratory displays the symbols of the Evangelists on the corbel-caps and the Arma Christi on the central boss. There is no very obvious religiosity at Delgatty.

In the fascinating web of family connections the first laird of Craig had married a Barclay of Towie, and the families of Craig, Delgatty and Towie remained interconnected and staunchly Roman Catholic in their sympathies. The two earliest in date, Craig and Gight, are Gordon houses, so the vocabulary of these four houses is initially Gordon, though whether because of the patrons' predilections or the designers' is not clear; presumably, as is generally the case, the client looked for a sympathetic mason.

There is a curious footnote to this: along the Kirtle Water in Dumfriesshire, and as far removed from Aberdeen as Orkney, are four Irving towers in various stages of preservation.[11] In three of these the entrance lobby is covered by a small ribbed vault, one of which – Bonshaw – has its boss carved with the sacred monogram IHS; two other towers in the neighbourhood, both connected by marriage to the Irvings, show similar features. The building of these towers follows the destructive raid of Lord Suffolk into the Borders in 1570. This puts them as contemporary with the Aberdeen group with which there seems to be no family connection. The religious link cannot be overlooked, and one must speculate as to the existence of a school of actively Roman Catholic masons working within a Catholic freemasonry – if such a term is permissible – whose influence was country-wide.

Between the Gight-Craig group of the 1570s [12] and the post-1600 Huntly castles there are two important buildings, Midmar (*c.* 1579) and Glenbuchat (1590), which have certain similarities. Midmar, however, was greatly enlarged *c.* 1609 after it had been burned by the army of King James VI in 1594. Both were Z-houses, consisting of two principal living floors with cellarage and attics, with the stair largely filling the lower two floors of one of the towers. The designer of Midmar has not been happy in the proportions of the central block, which is almost square, nor with the junction between it and the round tower, but the staircase, a scale-and-plat, is handled with more authority than at Glenbuchat. Here, a half-round stair is fitted, almost as an afterthought, into a square tower.

Glenbuchat, Simpson suggests,[13] was the work of an Angus mason, a view he derived from Dr Kelly, both likening it to Hatton Castle, except in its use of corner rounds and square caps. John Gordon, the building laird, had married Helen Carnegie from south of the Mounth, and the argument is that it was her influence that imported the mason who built her husband's castle – the speculation becomes fascinating. Was Glenbuchat based on an Angus model which in turn had been imported from Aberdeen? And were the *trompes* which rather clumsily support the round stair turrets a French importation by way of Dame Helen's deceased father, Sir Robert Carnegie, who at one time had been ambassador to France? These *trompes* reappear after 1600 in the building of the upper stage of Midmar,[14] but here they are handled much more successfully. If Glenbuchat's plan is

LORDSHIP AND
ARCHITECTURE
IN MEDIEVAL
AND
RENAISSANCE
SCOTLAND

❧

from Angus, and this is by no means certain, its roofline, with square and rounded turrets, double corbel courses, moulded courses to the rounds and finely coped chimneys is pure Aberdeen, and the presence of rounded door jambs, far from arguing an Angus provenance, can argue the presence of a mason of the Bell family.

Glenbuchat seems to be the last major Gordon house to be built before the overthrow of Huntly's power in 1594 and the destruction of parts of Huntly Castle. With so many branches of the family being involved in this breach with the Crown, it appears that very little building work was undertaken until the return of the marquis of Huntly in 1602.

The traditional story of the destruction of the castle and palace of Huntly in 1594 tells of how the building, which took fourteen years to build, was destroyed by the combined use of unlimited gunpowder and the muscles of 5,000 men. This seems to be a dangerous departure from reality: the logistical problems alone, conjured up by the presence of 5,000 bodies on a very restricted site, are mind-boggling. It is almost certainly due to a misreading of the *Calendar of State Papers*, whose ambiguity is compounded by the tergiversation of the king himself, torn as usual between a personal liking for the marquis, a reluctance to proceed to extreme measures, a disinclination to accept responsibility, and a general tendency to haver.

The account of total destruction hinges on a passage in the *Calendar of State Papers* which states that '... nothing was left unhocked save the greate olde tower which shall be blown up with powder ...' and mentions the loan from the Town Council of Aberdeen of '20 stone weight of powder' – presumably to be returned after use – together with 'certane mattokis, gavillokis and other werklumes and matteriallis for dimolishing and casting doun of houssis and fortalices' without specifying which ones these were to be.

'The Act anent the demolishing of the Earl of Huntley's house and fortalice of Strathbogie' of 1594 is not helpful either. It begins with the instruction '... that the place and fortalice of Strathbogie sall remaine in the estate that it is presently undemoliseit and cassin doun, in respect that it may serve for a ressut and refuge to sic garrisonis of horsemen and futemen as sall be appointit ...', which would be ambiguous enough were it not followed by a bad case of royal swithering between two evils as the king ordered '... the works new and old to be cast down by William Schaw, Master of Works ... His Majesty always protesting before the Lords of His Secret Council that whatsoever inconvenience should proceed from this action was not to be imputed to His Majesty'.

Faced with this, the Lords of the Council saw that any blame for this policy, should Huntly return to power, would be visited on their heads, and so settled for a less drastic course of action. The Great Tower was

demolished, almost certainly by explosives, though whether at the hands of William Schaw or the town council is not certain. The rest of the castle, having been thoroughly plundered, suffered the demolition of part of the north range, and possibly the stair tower of the new wark. How effective the structural plundering of such a place could be is shown in the later destruction wrought at Gight by the Covenanters.[15]

Lord Huntly returned to his plundered estates in 1596, and rebuilding began at Huntly and, presumably, at his other great house, The Bog, in 1602. Building on this scale was to set an example for his adherents to follow. He had been educated in France as a young man, and had just returned from exile in the same country. He was fully imbued with French

Figure 12.7
Midmar Castle,
Aberdeenshire:
reconstruction of south
front as in c.1609
(from PSAS, cxiii,
1983). H.G. Slade;
Society of Antiquaries
of Scotland

LORDSHIP AND
ARCHITECTURE
IN MEDIEVAL
AND
RENAISSANCE
SCOTLAND

❧

ideas. Exactly the same could be said of half the nobility of Scotland, who set about building, in the fashionable jargon of today, not castles but *chateaux*. French influence has long been an article of faith of certain Scottish architectural historians, and nowhere is the doctrine more ruthlessly applied than to the wonderful burst of building that took place in the north-east in the first quarter of the seventeenth century. It is tempting to see Aberdeenshire as a Scottish Touraine, with the Dee, the Don, the Deveron and the Spey taking the place of the Loire, the Indre, the Vienne and the Sarthe, but this is pure romance – or at least it is romance. It is almost equally ludicrous to see this outburst of building as some sort of Renaissance; more properly it should be described as a swansong or an Indian summer. The buildings themselves remained obstinately medieval, and the fantastical decorations which covered them had only the slightest acquaintance with the fashions current in polite architecture in the south. They were further from the Renaissance spirit than the royal works of one hundred years earlier had been, and if any French influence can be detected, it is the style of Francis I rather than of Henry IV. Aberdeen masons were either conscious antiquaries, which is doubtful; imitators of out-of-date pattern books, which is possible but unlikely; or working, as so often happens in art and science, towards a goal which others are reaching by different means or at different speeds. If their patrons had seen the latest architectural fashions in England and France, they had kept that dangerous knowledge to themselves. Even Drum, much vaunted as the new style, outward-looking country house, is nothing more exciting when stripped to its essentials than an old-style palace or laird's house attached to an earlier medieval tower, and garnished to taste. It was to this distinctive but indigenous school of building enriched with some outside influences, already long past their sell-by date, that the exiled marquis returned.

It is worth rehearsing the number of first-rate examples of the Aberdeen style that were building, not all of them associated with the Gordons, in the first quarter of the seventeenth century: the frontispiece at Fyvie for Lord Dunfermline *c.*1600; Huntly 1602–; Cluny 1604–; Midmar 1609; Craigston for John Urquhart, 1604; Castle Fraser for Lord Fraser, 1617; Glamis for Lord Strathmore, 1606–; and The Bog, which presumably dates from this period, together with a host of other castles and towers, some of almost equal quality. Those specifically mentioned are all, it has been suggested, associated with the Bell family,[16] and represented a considerable degree of organisation in the building industry. Skilled craftsmen would have been at a premium, and it is hardly surprising that although Lord Huntly returned to Scotland in 1595–6, work did not start at the castle until 1602. Demand for labour was outstripping supply.

How badly Huntly was damaged in 1594 is not certain, but it gave a

The Castle of Inverero

perfect excuse for the remodelling of the palace block in the most elaborate taste, and the embellishment of the courtyard buildings. The whole of the upper works was redesigned to provide two new floors, one a part-attic. The intention – and this is certainly the external architectural suggestion – seems to have been to provide two long galleries, as was later done at Glamis and Craigston. If so, it did not come to fruition, and the palace block remained obstinately medieval in plan. New taste, however, was evidenced in the elaborate series of two-floored hanging oriels on the upper work in the south front.

Hanging oriels are rare in Scotland, but they occur, amongst other places, at Glamis and the Earl's Palace, Kirkwall, and there was one at Cluny. New fashions could also be seen in the symmetrical treatment of the gatehouse wall, where the central opening is flanked by pilaster-like projections and two towers, and by the piazza which extends from the southern gable of the palace block, and of which only the footings of the piers of the arcade remain. There was access to the roof over this piazza from the hall, and from a description in the *Old Statistical Account* this seems to have been a loggia.[17]

LORDSHIP AND
ARCHITECTURE
IN MEDIEVAL
AND
RENAISSANCE
SCOTLAND

❧

Little remains of the marquis's other great house, Bog of Gight, later
to be transmogrified by John Baxter into Gordon Castle, which was largely
demolished in the second half of the twentieth century. Said to have been
built originally by the second earl of Huntly, it was sometimes described
as 'New Werk on Spey', a description confirmed in a charter of 1493 given
'Apud palacium nostram de Newark'. The plans made for proposed alterations by both John Adam and John Baxter show how extensive were the
remains incorporated into the later house, probably because they were too
massive to demolish, and Slezer's drawing of the castle from the south-west
makes it possible to reconstruct its original form. Slezer's illustration is
captioned *The Castle of Inverero*, and his published drawing entitled *Bogen-
geigt, the Seat of His Grace the Duke of Gordon*, is in fact Heriot's Hospital,
but Pennant, whilst on his tour of Scotland, was told by members of the
Gordon family that *Inverero* was The Bog; the building shown by Slezer
is certainly elaborate enough to justify the claim.[18]

The Bog of Gight was a massive, almost Z-plan castle, its principal
rooms facing south and west as was so often the case, and seems to have
reached the form shown by Slezer as the result of a number of alterations.
The core of the building appears to be the 'New Werk' of the 2nd Earl,
a massive L-tower with cellars and a mezzanine below a large second-floor
hall, measuring 13.7 metres by 7.6 metres. To the east of this the plans
suggest that there was an earlier and smaller tower, which would not be
seen from the viewpoint of Slezer's drawing. The jamb of the L-tower
was at its south-east corner, and the principal floor was at the same level
as the hall. At this period the low end, judging by the number of doors
and stairs opening in the east wall, may have been at the east end. Both
Adam and Baxter show a timber partition across this end of the hall,
which may in fact incorporate the original low end screen. This large
L-tower with the hall on the second floor is typical of the late fifteenth
century; it can be paralleled at Glamis and Cromarty, and would agree
with a date of *c.*1480–90.

The north-west tower, which converted the L into an irregular Z, appears
to date from the second half of the sixteenth century at the earliest,
although its upper stages may be later. The floors are not at the same
level as those in the L-tower, and this shows that its chambers were not
designed to be used with those in the L until the third stage was reached.
In appearance it closely resembles the square towers at Midmar and Castle
Fraser. The resemblance to the latter is enhanced by the two-floored
rounds, so peculiar to the Aberdeen school. This could mark a building
programme started *c.*1588–90, before Lord Huntly went into exile in 1594.
At this stage the principal stair and main entrance appear to have been
moved to the re-entrant between the L and the new tower. This provided

Figure 12.9
The Bog (Gordon
Castle), Moray: sketch
reconstruction of
first-floor plan.

10   0   10   20   30 feet

46 x 25 x 18

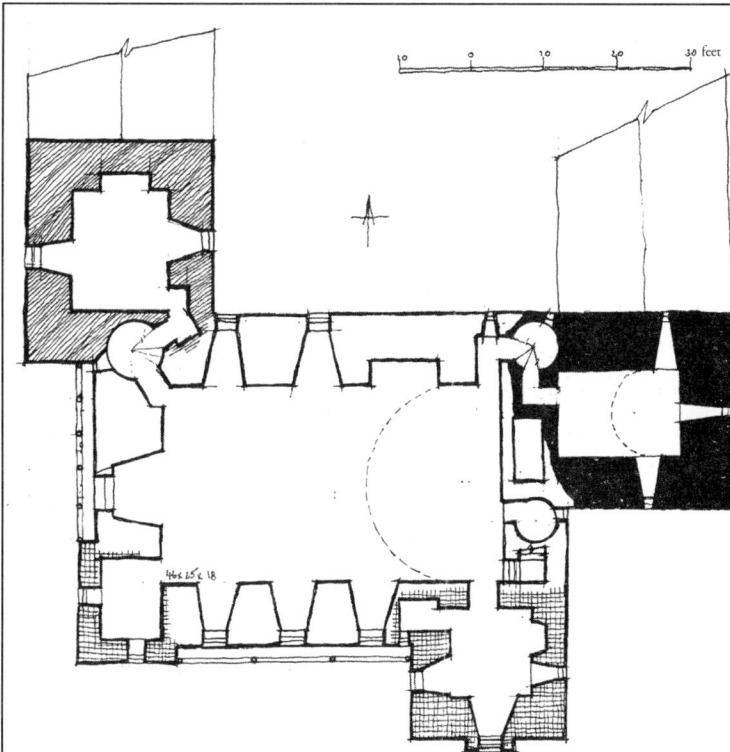

First Period
Second Period
Third Period
Fourth Period

THE BOG

A. Main stairs from entry
B. Hall 45 x 25 feet
C. Closet or pantry
X. Line of screen
D. Kitchen lum – formed into closet 18th century
E. Earlier tower
F. Fireplace
G. Secondary stairs
H. Service stairs

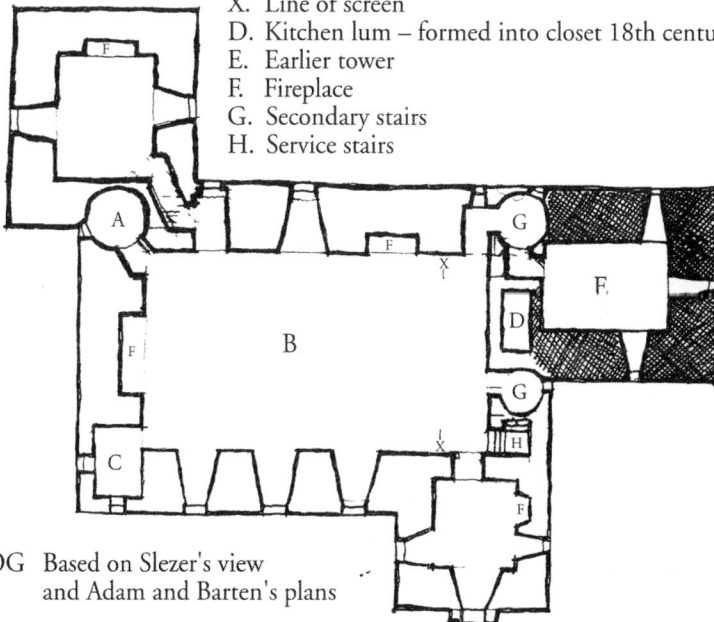

THE BOG   Based on Slezer's view
and Adam and Barten's plans

LORDSHIP AND
ARCHITECTURE
IN MEDIEVAL
AND
RENAISSANCE
SCOTLAND

❧

a more conventional access to the upper floors, but may have led to a re-arrangement of the hall, since the entry would now be at the original high end.

It certainly introduced another variation in planning. In the earlier palace-plans, as at Druminnor and Huntly, the sequence had been stair – hall – outer chamber – inner chamber, or stair – hall – withdrawing room – bedroom. Smaller houses and the early Z-plans reduced this to stair – hall – chamber, as at Beldorney, Midmar and Carnousie. The introduction of the stair in the re-entrant provided a room accessible from the stair, but not accessible from the hall: a room which could serve as a waiting room, or business room for the reception of those who neither merited nor warranted admission to the hall. At The Bog, as at Castle Fraser, the tower and stair had been additions to earlier structures, but an early attempt to achieve the same purpose can be seen in the very clumsy handling of the chamber off the stair at Glenbuchat. By the early seventeenth century this arrangement was handled with much more confidence at Cluny, and even more so at Craigston and Drum, where it is separated by a spacious square landing from the hall. That such a feature should occur so widely is another indication of the predominance of the experience of the architect over the taste of the patron.

The development of The Bog was completed by the building of two low gabled wings at right angles to the north face of the main block, as was to be done at Beldorney, Midmar and Castle Fraser, probably *c.* 1630 and by the provision of a magnificent top-hamper and a great deal of architectural elaboration of the sort described as *Fandangling*. It is doubtful if many of the turrets shown, as suggested by Slezer, could have been built if the hall had not been covered by a massive stone vault.

Together with the upper works there are a number of *Fandanglings* which are peculiar to The Bog and which may show that in these the architect had to give way to the marquis's whims. These are largely to be seen in the elevational treatment of the central block and the south-east tower – unless of course Slezer is wildly out in his drawing. At the point where the principal floor level would normally be marked by a chamfered in-set of the wall face, the reverse is adopted at The Bog. Here the wall faces of both the hall and the south-east tower are carried on a moulded string or corbel course in advance of the walls of the cellar and mezzanine. The south-east tower is distinguished by a great bay or oriel on the south face which rises the full height of the tower. Even the corner rounds on this tower are eccentric, in that they are crowned by square bartisans set on the diagonal, a feature reminiscent of the corner towers at Cluny.

By far the most unusual features are the two loggias on the west and south faces of the main block, opening off the hall. A more unsuitable

Figure 12.10
Cluny Castle,
Aberdeenshire:
reconstruction of view
from south-west.

feature in the face of the usual weather in the north-east would be hard to conceive. Given that they are outwith the architectural canon of the district, and that something similar appeared at Huntly, the beholder is left with the distinct impression that they are imperfectly understood attempts by the masons of the district to translate into the local idiom something that had struck Lord Huntly as a very desirable addition to his house; one which would cry out to every visitor that here lived a cultivated and travelled man of taste. The larger of the loggias is of three bays, with rounded arches carried on what may be classical columns; the smaller, on the west, of four bays, with trefoil arches.[19] If the external treatment of the building went well beyond the normal designs of the day, the internal arrangements, as far as can be judged, show little advance on medieval practice.

Although quite as fantastical a building as Glamis, The Bog never seems to have captured the imagination of travellers or artists in the same way. Consequently, its importance as a source of ideas has never been recognised. It must be a matter of regret that when Baxter's monstrous great barrack

LORDSHIP AND
ARCHITECTURE
IN MEDIEVAL
AND
RENAISSANCE
SCOTLAND

❧

was demolished in the 1950s, no attempt was made to record the earlier remains.

After The Bog the two most important Gordon castles to be completed were Cluny and Midmar. Cluny [20] was probably built *c.* 1604 by Sir Thomas Gordon, grandson of the 3rd Earl of Huntly. A conventional Z-plan castle, Cluny would not have excited comment had it not been for its unusually elaborate upper floors recorded by Hullmandel, and, in a simplified form, by William Adam, which have made its reconstruction possible. At the lower level both towers were circular, but at the third floor level one was crowned by a five-sided cap house with a remarkably fine oriel in its gable wall. The other continued as a round and was probably given a balustraded parapet similar to the great tower at Castle Fraser. The circular principal stair was crowned by a lofty square tower with a small circular stair turret clinging to its side. Instead of rounds, small square caps were set diagonally on the two free corners of the central block. Cluny was not destroyed but engulfed in the later enormous house, designed by John Smith for Colonel John Gordon in 1818–40. Smith took the original castle, matching it exactly with another wing and linking them both with a staircase, halls, corridors and library. The richness was removed, replaced by granite austerity; and by lowering the roof-line and both emphasising and heightening the square cap to the older stair Smith managed to make the whole effect slightly ridiculous.

The alterations to Midmar, which had been plundered – certainly – and burned – possibly – in 1594, were probably the work of William Gordon, 6th laird of Midmar and Abergeldie, between 1601 and 1609. The Gordons of Midmar and Abergeldie descended from the 1st Earl, and shared the taste of the main line for fine building. The design of Midmar is frequently attributed to George Bell, a mason buried in the old kirkyard at Midmar in 1575. If this is so, then he would have been responsible for the early Z-plan castle, of three floors, on the Carnousie and Glenbuchat plan, but the date of his death makes it impossible for him to have been the author of the upper works, which are in the fully developed mid-Mar style also associated with the Bell family. The transition between the two periods, especially in the handling of *trompes* where the round tower and central block are joined, is masterly, and the enrichment of the worked stone is particularly fine. Well worth noticing are the triple courses of fretted label mouldings. These appear, but only as double course, at two small towers, Knock and Forest of Birse, associated with the Cluny and Abergeldie families, a type of decoration well above the station of the buildings on which it is found.

Is there a common ground which points to the branches of the Gordons imposing a family face on the buildings which they erected? Two of the castles discussed hardly fall into such a category: Gight and Craig were certainly built for Gordons and are so alike as to be by the same mason. But the two branches of the family were not closely connected; the two castles are not in the same locality, and with other castles – three in Aberdeenshire and several in Dumfriesshire – share identical characteristics which may have religious connotations and are more likely to derive from those, or from the vocabulary of the masons, than from any other cause.

Is the Z-plan an example of Gordon taste and influence? Again, this is very difficult to say. Huntly is certainly early, probably fifteenth century, and the same can be said of the genesis of The Bog. Terpersie in 1561, and Beldorney and Midmar, are early examples, but the Z-plan is a logical solution to a particular defensive problem, the provision of the most effective and economical defensive field of fire. The problem is not unique to Scotland, nor apparently is the solution, towards which many military engineers in many different parts of the world had been moving; it would be rash to suggest anything more definite than that the Gordons may have been first amongst many in the north-east to use it.

By the beginning of the seventeenth century a pattern of building, or at least of enrichment of building, was beginning to emerge, inspired to a greater or lesser extent by the work being done for the 1st Marquis at Huntly and The Bog, although nothing quite comes up to the splendid outburst of the frontispiece of the former. However, apart from certain strange features like the piazzas and loggias, both buildings, which appear to be the reworking of earlier structures, remain firmly rooted in the medieval building traditions of the north-east.

Apart from these certain individual features, there is nothing to set either Huntly or The Bog apart from Glamis or Castle Fraser, both the seats of magnates, other than the particular grandeur of the marquis, which drove him to need, and enabled him to afford, two such piles, in which display of taste and splendour he was followed by his kinsmen, as far as their means allowed. It may be coincidental but this taste for grandeur seems to have been largely confined to the Seton-Gordon line, the line that suffered most in the post-1594 destruction and needed to repair or rebuild their homes at the beginning of the seventeenth century. Fortunately, this need arose at just the time when the north-east school of design and masonry work had reached its peak in a glorious flowering, but it was the autumnal flowering of the Middle Ages, not the spring flowering of the Renaissance.

Huntly and The Bog, together with Glamis, Castle Fraser and Fyvie, are the equivalent of the Elizabethan prodigy houses, for truly they are prodigious, but they remain medieval in essence and in inspiration. Whatever influences may have come the way of the master-masons, and no

LORDSHIP AND
ARCHITECTURE
IN MEDIEVAL
AND
RENAISSANCE
SCOTLAND

❧

man, not even an Aberdonian, is an island, those influences were largely from pattern-books of Germanic or Netherlandish provenance and seem to have been confined to sculptural or carved details.[21] What French and Italian influence there is, if any, has been greatly diminished by time and distance.

These castles, towers and palaces – for *chateaux* and *villas* they are not – exemplify one great architectural principle: they are decorated constructions, not constructed decorations.[22]

APPENDIX

The earliest account of non-building activities on the part of the 4th Earl of Huntly was a discharge of 1532[23] which relieved him of the obligation to '... build at his own expense upon the castlehill at Inverness a Hall upon vaults of stone and lime 100 feet of length and 30 feet of breadth and 30 feet high of the wall, theikit with slate or skailzie,[24] and a Kitchen in the said hall with a chapel of competent length beside the said hall with a wall about the castle hill foresaid including the tower and houses foresaid therein ... because he was not of age, in the king's ward and must pay to us, our dearest mother the Queen and others great sums of money for his ward and marriage'.

The discharge was for five years, from 16 February 1532. Lord Huntly, who had inherited from his grandfather in 1525, was still a minor. Through his mother, Margaret Stewart, an illegitimate daughter of James IV, he was a cousin of James V.

From its size this hall, which may never have been built, seems to have been intended for public rather than private use.

NOTES

1. This was in the north-east alone. It is believed there are 34 cadet branches in the Borders.
2. George Gordon, 2nd Earl of Huntly, married Annabella (or Arabella) Countess of Geneva, daughter of James I. Both had been married and divorced previously, and were to be divorced themselves. Catherine Gordon, daughter of the 3rd earl, married Perkin Warbeck, pretender to the English throne. John, Lord Huntly, son of the 3rd earl and father of the 4th earl, married Margaret Stewart, illegitimate daughter of James IV. Cosimo de Medici, 3rd Grand Duke of Tuscany, is supposed to have stood as sponsor to the third duke, bringing the name *Cosmo* into the family.
3. This was certainly true of the 1st Lady Cowdray, who was quite ruthless in settling her children in suitable houses.
4. There are the remains of a similar pavement at Tolquhon Castle, and these may have existed in other castles of the first quarter of the seventeenth century.
5. H. G. Slade, 'Druminnor, formerly Castle Forbes: an investigation into the

original building of mid-fifteenth-century palace house', *PSAS*, xcix (1966–7) 148–66.

6. This account is not only useful for its description of the plan of the principal floor of Druminnor, but also shows that its was perfectly habitable at the time when most historians claim it was totally destroyed.

    Extract from the process of divorce between John, Master of Forbes, and his wife, Margaret Gordon, second daughter of the 4th Earl of Huntly, Edinburgh, 24 June, 1573:

    ... In placis of Druminnor and Rannallock within the Sherifdom of Aberdein and sumtymes being sa convoyit that no persoun knew of him but the said Margrat and her serving womane familiar unto her in thair unlauchfull doings as they supposit ... Lykas for the better accomplishment thairof the said Margrat having lytill or na regard to her schame and at all tymis and nytis quhar the said umquhill Patrick was separit lyid and harberit in Druminnor, he lay in the uttir chalmer within the hall nixt to the said Margratis chalmer quherin he myt hav enterit at his plesir he beand soletar within the said utter chalmer and the hall dour steikit upone hime within and the said Margrat havand na persoun with her bot her servand womane pertesepant and beand upon the cunsall of the said filthie crym, for the accomplischment quherof sche left her awin chalmer quherin sche was accostomit to remain befoir ...

7. The Palace House *c.* 1427 and the Great Tower c. 1435 are barely 12 feet (3.6m) apart.

8. W. D. Simpson, 'Further notes on Huntly Castle', *PSAS*, lxvii (1932–3), 137–60.

9. Richard Bannatyne's Memorials, 'The Maner of the Erle of Huntlies Death' describes how, after he was seized by an apoplectic fit when he was playing football, the 5th earl was carried by his servants to 'his owin chalmer and laid him in his bed, quhilk chalmer was ane round within the grit chalmer of the Newe Warke of Strathbogie'. The great chamber, which is also described as the 'chalmer of daice', had a chamber door – to the bed chamber – and an outer chamber door – leading from the hall.

10. H. G. Slade, 'Carnousie, Banffshire', *The Archaeological Journal*, cxxxvi (1979), 229–39.

11. H. G. Slade, 'Buildings Survey', in *Kirkpatrick Fleming, Dumfriesshire, An Anatomy of a Parish in South West Scotland*, ed. R. J. Mercer (Dumfriesshire and Galloway Natural History and Antiquarian Society, Dumfries, 1997), 82–225 (at 'Towers', 91–103).

12. W. D. Simpson, 'Craig Castle and the Kirk of Auchindoir, Aberdeenshire', *PSAS*, lxiv (1929–30), 48–96.

13. W. D. Simpson, *The Book of Glenbuchat* (The Third Spalding Club, Aberdeen, 1942).

14. H. G. Slade, 'Midmar Castle, Aberdeenshire', *PSAS*, cxiii (1983), 594–619.

15. An account from Spalding's *Memorials* (J. Spalding, *Memorials of the Troubles in Scotland and England* (The Spalding Club, Aberdeen, 1850–1)) describing the spoiling of Gight by the Covenanters shows how destructive men could be, even without the aid of gunpowder:

    ... places they sat not idill, bot plunderit them both. And, first, thay tuke out the staitlie insicht and plenishing, sic as bedding, naiprie, veschell cauldrouns, chandleris, fyre veschell, quhairof thair wes plenty; kistis, cofferis, cabinetis, trvnkis, and all vther plenishing and armour (quhairof thair wes plentie in both thir houssis) quhilk they could get careit on horss or foot, bot wes takin away south; togidder withthe haill oxin, nolt, ky, horss, meiris, and scheip, quhilkis war vpone the saidis Maynes of Haddoche and Geight,

LORDSHIP AND
ARCHITECTURE
IN MEDIEVAL
AND
RENAISSANCE
SCOTLAND

❧

and not ane four footed best left that they could get. When thir commodeteis wes plunderit and spolzeit, then thay began to wirk vpone the tymber wark quhilkis war fixt, and thair thay cruellie brak doun the wanescot burdes, bedis, capalmreis, tymber wallis, sylring, toome girnellis, and the lyk, and maid fyre of all. Thay took out the iron yettis, iron stancheouns of windois, brak doun the glassin windois, and left nather yett, dur, nor wyndo onbrokin doun; and, in effect, left thame desolat befoir thay removit.

16. John Bell signed Castle Fraser with his name and his badge – a heart. The same badge appears on the great frontispiece of Craigston.

17. The description (*OSA*, xi (1794), 477, note) is as follows:

Many people, still in life, remember to have seen a range of pillars, supporting an arched roof, which seemed to have been intended as a cover for such as inclined to take the air, or a view of the garden which lay before the Castle: there being a door that led to it, from the upper hall, on a level with it.

This feature had vanished before 1792 when this account was written.

18. This useful piece of information is confirmed in K. Cavers, *A Vision of Scotland, The Nation Observed by John Slezer 1671 to 1717* (Edinburgh, 1993), 86.

19. This curious trefoil is repeated on the overmantel of the fireplace of the upper hall at Huntly, dated 1606.

20. H. G. Slade, 'Cluny Castle, Aberdeenshire', *PSAS*, cxi (1981), 454–92.

21. The Craigston panels (which may have come from Cromarty) and the 'Old Kings', formerly at Castle Fraser, are almost certainly based on continental models. At Edzell in 1604 Sir David Lindsay decorated his garden with sculptured panels including ones depicting the planetary deities. These are based on copperplate engravings originally made by Meister J. B. of Nuremburg, and first published in 1528.

22. Anthony Trollope's description of Mrs Stanhope's manner of dressing in *Barchester Towers* (London, 1857).

23. Spalding, *Memorials of the Troubles.*

24. Scailzie (Scots), slate and/or scale, and in this context, something more elaborate than a slate, but cut to resemble fish scales. It could have been a glazed tile.

Chapter 13

๙

THE MACKENZIES

Jean Munro

The Mackenzies were late in coming to a position of power and influence, and their development before 1680 can be divided into three stages: before 1476 living in the shadow of the Lordship of the Isles; up to 1594 (the death of Colin Cam Mackenzie of Kintail), amassing land and building up power locally in Ross; and finally, the impact of the chiefs on the national scene and of the cadets at home.

It has generally been accepted that the Mackenzies built up their power from west to east, but this is probably to over-simplify. To understand the background requires some knowledge of their Gaelic origins. They shared a common ancestor with the Mathesons, tracing themselves back to one Gilleoin of the Aird, the fertile lands round Beauly to the west of Inverness. To explain their move to the west coast, one suggestion is that they were some of the rebellious men of Moray moved by Malcolm IV or William the Lion to make way for the Bisset family. What is clear is that the Mackenzie-Matheson connection came to be based in the west, and that well before the beginning of the fourteenth century a representative was in charge, possibly as constable, of the earl of Ross's castle of Eilean Donan in Kintail. It is also clear that they lost this position, and it has been suggested that this was the consequence of not following the earl of Ross into the Bruce camp in 1308. The expedition in 1331 by Thomas Randolph, Earl of Moray, and the execution of 'misdoers' at Eilean Donan seem to support this, and the continued unrest in the west during the next 20 or 30 years points to uncertain loyalty.[1]

During this time the Mackenzies must have lost their foothold in Kintail, and it is not known where they settled. It is not for another 50 years that any firm evidence of their history can be found, and then the Mackenzies emerge as a separate unit from the Mathesons under a recognisable chief – Alastair Ionraic (Alexander the Upright). He appears as an opponent of the Lord of the Isles (soon to become earl of Ross) and a supporter of the Crown. It has been claimed that his predecessor fought for the earl of Mar at Harlaw, and he was certainly rewarded in 1414 with a grant

LORDSHIP AND
ARCHITECTURE
IN MEDIEVAL
AND
RENAISSANCE
SCOTLAND

❧

from the Exchequer 'pro laboranti in partibus Rossie pro quiete regni'.[2] In 1463 the Lord of the Isles as earl of Ross gave Alastair a charter of lands near Garve in Brae Ross, and family tradition, recorded two centuries later, says that the lands were given to defray expenses in making peace between the king and the Lord of the Isles.[3] Indeed, the Mackenzies may already have been established in the area, for Achilty (with a crannog in the loch) is said to have been their first possession in the area, and Alastair Ionraic is reported to have been the first of the family to live on another

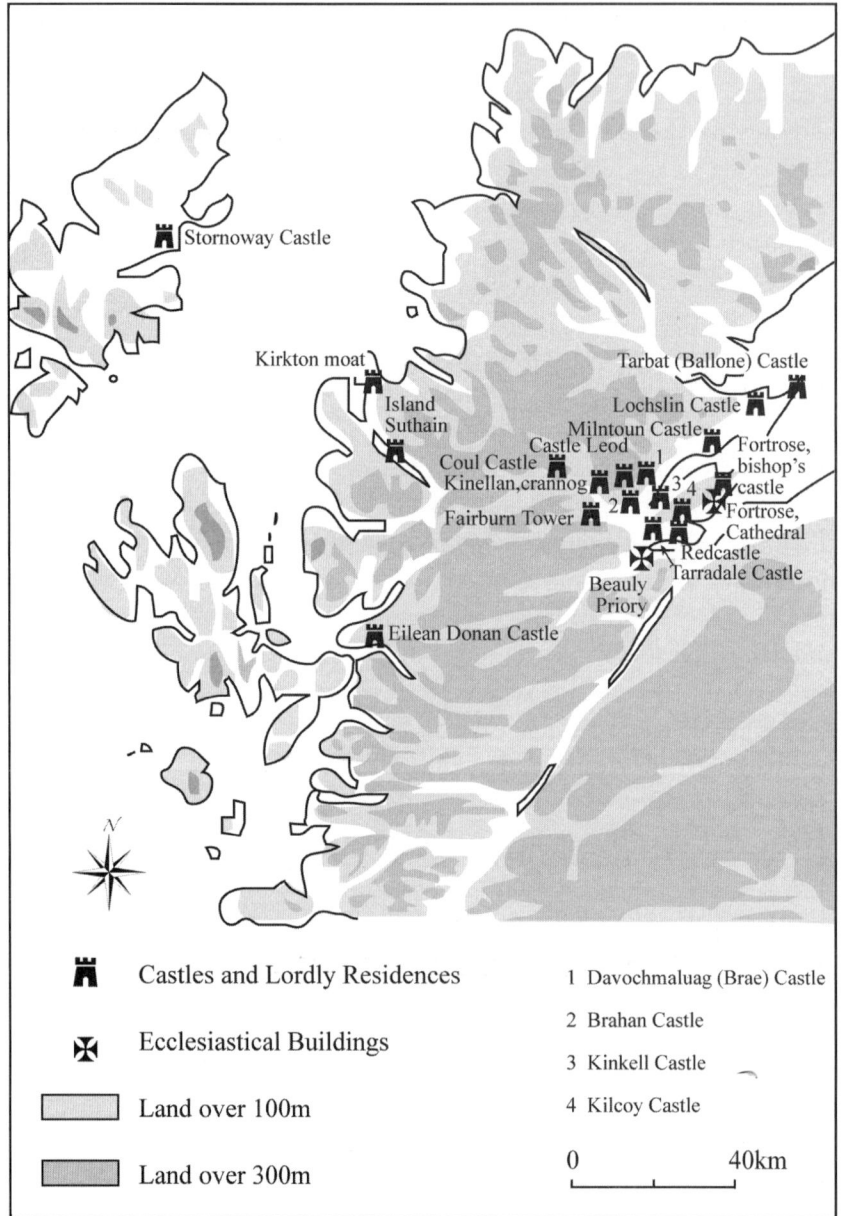

Figure 13.1
Mackenzie properties.

crannog at Kinellan, near the modern Strathpeffer: 'being ane ile in ane loch, Alexander did ordinarily reside in it for security'.[4] Perhaps, as William Matheson suggests, the earl of Ross had granted them this land as being within his reach and for Mackenzie to be 'in some sort a hostage for the good behaviour of his kinsmen towards the west'.[5]

But what of Kintail? No official document records Mackenzie ownership of Kintail until 1509 when John Mackenzie, Alastair's grandson, was confirmed there in a charter which combined his lands in the west and Brae Ross into a barony of Eilean Donan.[6] A family annalist maintains that Kintail was included in an unrecorded royal charter of confirmation in 1477 and also in a precept of clare constat by the duke of Ross in 1500.[7] Nor is it easy to discover exactly when the head of the family first used the designation 'of Kintail'. Alastair is apparently described in this

Figure 13.2
Mackenzie of Kintail:
genealogical table,
identifying builders.

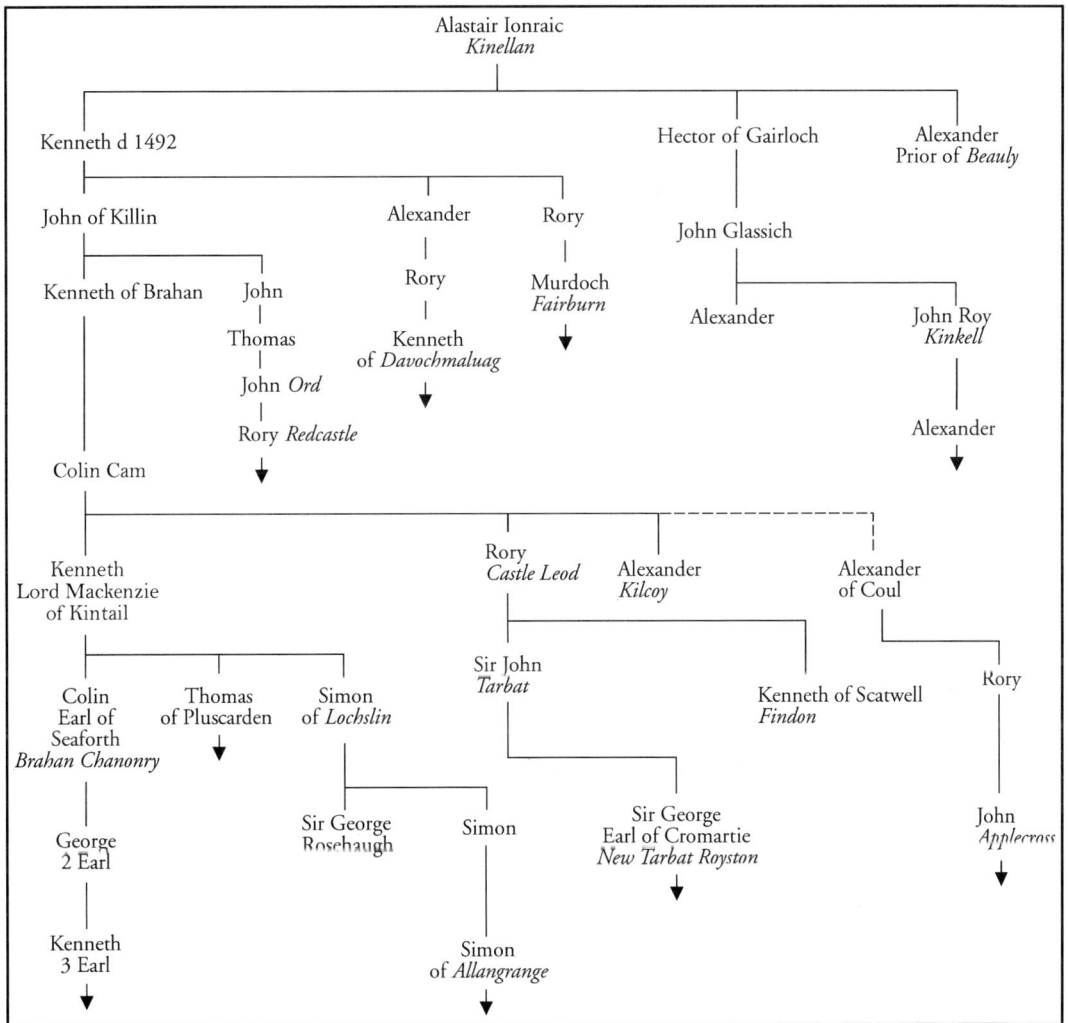

Alastair Ionraic
Kinellan

Kenneth d 1492 — Hector of Gairloch — Alexander Prior of *Beauly*

John of Killin — Alexander — Rory

Kenneth of Brahan — John — Rory — Murdoch *Fairburn* ↓

John Glassich — Alexander — John Roy *Kinkell*

Thomas — Kenneth of *Davochmaluag* ↓

John *Ord*

Rory *Redcastle* ↓

Alexander ↓

Colin Cam

Kenneth Lord Mackenzie of Kintail — Rory *Castle Leod* — Alexander *Kilcoy* — Alexander of Coul

Colin Earl of Seaforth *Brahan Chanonry* — Thomas of Pluscarden ↓ — Simon of *Lochslin*

Sir John *Tarbat* — Kenneth of Scatwell *Findon* — Rory

Sir George *Rosehaugh* — Simon — Sir George Earl of Cromartie *New Tarbat Royston* ↓ — John *Applecross* ↓

George 2 Earl

Kenneth 3 Earl ↓

Simon of *Allangrange* ↓

LORDSHIP AND
ARCHITECTURE
IN MEDIEVAL
AND
RENAISSANCE
SCOTLAND

☙

way as a witness in 1471,[8] but the original of this charter has not been found and it is possible that later readers may have mistaken Killin or Kinellan for Kintail. In 1479 Kenneth is mentioned in the Exchequer Rolls and the editors have given him the designation 'of Kintail' both in the preface and in the index, but he is not so described in the text.[9] Perhaps the first or certainly an early example of the designation was on the tomb of Kenneth who died in 1492 and who was buried at Beauly where the inscription read 'Hic iacet Kenitus MKinyth dns de Kintail'.[10] This was the first of several burials of Mackenzie chiefs at Beauly over the next century and may be explained by the fact that the former prior, who died in 1479, was a natural son of Alastair Ionraic and is said to have repaired the priory at his own expense. So at present it is not possible to know whether the Mackenzies ever held Kintail from the Lords of the Isles, but clearly they held it very soon after, and regarded it as their main stronghold, though probably not their chief residence. In spite of the marriage of Alastair's son, Kenneth, to a daughter of Celestine of the Isles,[11] the Mackenzies do not seem to have made any great progress towards power during the time of the Lordship.

The fall of the Lordship certainly opened the way for the Mackenzies but their rise was not immediate. The 1509 charter did consolidate their lands but it was not followed up at once by further royal grants, though they did make additions in Brae Ross, at Scatwell in 1528 and Fodderty in 1532.[12] They did not support the various risings by claimants to the Lordship of the Isles and fought against the first, Alexander of Lochalsh, in 1492, and the fourth, Donald of Sleat, in 1539. For the latter in December 1540 John Mackenzie (called John of Killin in family histories) received a charter of Glengarry's lands 'pro bono servitio in insularum partibus'.[13] Though he did not keep these long, it was the start of serious expansion. In 1541 he got a charter of the lands of Meikle Brahan in Strathconon and the following year one of the 'terras vastas' of Monar and Ned (the latter placed by Watson in the modern Fannich Forest).

The real breakthrough in the west began in 1543 when John exchanged the lands of Fodderty near Dingwall for half the lands of Lochbroom which then included the modern Dundonnell, Gruinard and Inverewe.[14] The west coast north of Kintail – Lochalsh, Lochcarron and Lochbroom – had belonged to Celestine of the Isles and descended to his son, Alexander, and grandson, Donald. The latter died without male heirs in 1519 and the lands were divided between his two sisters, Margaret, wife of Alexander MacDonald of Glengarry, and Janet, wife of William Dingwall of Kildun. Each sister got half of the three estates, a recipe for trouble if ever there was one. Gradually, throughout the sixteenth century, the Mackenzies acquired all these lands – peacefully by exchange and purchase from the

Dingwall family, Lochbroom in 1543, Lochalsh in 1554, and Lochcarron, following a wadset, in 1579.[15] The Glengarry half of the lands was not acquired so easily or so peacefully, and led to a long feud. The first to fall to the Mackenzies was Lochbroom. This, with the rest, had been given to Grant of Freuchie as compensation for the devastation caused by Glengarry in a raid on Castle Urquhart in 1546,[16] but it was never effectively possessed by him and was sold by Grant to Colin Mackenzie of Kintail and Barbara Grant, who married in 1572.[17] In 1571 Grant had married another daughter to Glengarry's son and given back the lands of Lochalsh and Lochcarron.[18] But this was not the end of the story, and according to a seventeenth-century family history 'Ther were manie more skirmishes betwixt Glengarrie and McKenzie but to conclude Glengarrie was necessitat to take his peace with the loss and qwiting of his part of Lochalsh and Lochcarron'.[19] This followed the destruction of Strome Castle in 1602 and much bloodshed on both sides, and completed the Mackenzie ownership of the west coast of Ross and much of the rough bounds inland.[20]

Meanwhile the family was expanding in the east, first by means of feus and wadsets and then by purchase. Further lands in upper Strathconon, Cultaloid (later Castle Leod near Strathpeffer), Fodderty again, Tarradale, Redcastle and Allangrange in the Black Isle were theirs by the end of the sixteenth century.[21] Church lands in the Black Isle and in the west at Applecross followed the Reformation, and this expansion led to another feud, this time mainly with the Munros over property at Chanonry (the modern Fortrose). The bishop of Ross had given the castle and lands there to his cousin, Leslie of Balquhain, who sold them to Colin Mackenzie of Kintail, but the Regent Moray had given them just before his death to Andrew Munro of Newmore who refused Mackenzie access to the castle.[22] After much turmoil over several years the two sides agreed to arbitration, and a 26-page decreet in March 1574 decided in favour of Mackenzie,[23] and marked the start of their influence in what was to become an important legal centre. It was said that Kintail's brother Rory, later of Redcastle, had occupied the steeple, and was even said to have built it, to terrorise the burgh and countryside,[24] but it is more probable that he merely strengthened it. More than a century later a family historian wrote that 'He put upwards of 30 men in the steeple which stood in the cathedral of Chanonry very magnificent untill it was cast doun by the English in 1652'.[25] On the death of Bishop Hepburn in 1578, Mackenzie of Kintail took over the bishop's palace, and later the Mackenzies became hereditary constables of the palace and castle,[26] living in the castle themselves.

For a time there appeared a new rival in the bid for power in east Ross when the earldom was formally dissolved in 1587. Andrew Keith (an illegitimate member of the Earl Marischal's family) was created Lord

LORDSHIP AND
ARCHITECTURE
IN MEDIEVAL
AND
RENAISSANCE
SCOTLAND

꙳

Dingwall by James VI in 1584 and his lands erected into a barony of Dingwall in 1587.[27] At the same time Sir William Keith, brother of Keith of Ravenscraig near Peterhead, and master of the king's wardrobe (almost certainly a relative of Andrew), got feu charters of extensive lands in Ross erected into a barony of Delny.[28] It would appear that the Keiths were concerned with the profits rather than the lands themselves, but William, or his deputes, John Vass of Lochslin and John Keith, apparent of Ravenscraig, ran into trouble at the hands of some four hundred people when attempting to hold a baron court in March 1588. The crowd, complete with 'jakkis, steilbonnettis, pistollis, bowis, darlochs' and other weapons, forced the bailies to leave the scene by a mixture of 'maist insolent behavior and sindrie contumelious speichis'.[29] Perhaps deterred by such displays, Sir William Keith began to divest himself of his feus and granted charters to Mackenzies and Munros from 1589.[30] William became a privy councillor in 1593, ironically in place of Colin Mackenzie of Kintail who did not respond to the invitation. In the following year he apparently conveyed his rights in the barony of Delny to his brother Ravenscraig, and much of it eventually came to Mackenzie of Tarbat in 1656.[31] In 1595 a large part of the Black Isle lordship of Ardmannoch was sold by Keith to Kenneth Mackenzie of Kintail.[32] So a possible Keith takeover was averted and the intervention probably had little impact in Ross.

Meanwhile another feud was drawing in the Mackenzies – ultimately to their considerable advantage. The Macleods of Lewis were involved in a family quarrel which stemmed from the marriage and divorce of Roderick MacLeod and his first wife Janet, daughter of John Mackenzie of Kintail, and the disowning of their son, Torquil, known as Cononach from being brought up among his mother's people in Strathconon. This happened in 1541, but with the death in 1566 of Roderick's heir by his second wife, also called Torquil, the quarrel between Cononach, several bastard brothers and their father became heated.[33] In the course of a very long-drawn-out affair lasting beyond the death of Roderick in 1595, Torquil Cononach made over Assynt and Coigach and even his rights in Lewis to Colin Mackenzie,[34] who was confirmed in Assynt in 1592 and in Coigach before January 1608 when Kenneth his son sold it to his brother Rory and his wife Margaret, daughter of Torquil Cononach.[35] In Lewis the trouble went on rather longer, for James VI was anxious to colonise part of the island and gave the land first to the Fife Adventurers and after their withdrawal to three individuals. The phrase 'fishers in drumlie waters' used of the Campbells applies equally well to the Mackenzies' dealings over Lewis. Kenneth set about turning each side against the other, using local opposition to the Fife men while appearing to help the colonists.[36] At length, after trying to exploit Torquil's grant to gain himself a charter in 1607,

Kenneth did obtain a royal charter of the lands and barony of Lewis with the castle of Stornoway in July 1610.[37] Possession was not immediate in spite of invasion in force by the Mackenzies, but did follow the death of the last of the MacLeods of Lewis in 1613.

So Mackenzie lands, by the turn of the century, stretched from sea to sea and even across the Minch, but landed wealth for the chief was not the only source of power for a clan. There was landed wealth for junior members of his family – the cadets. In the seventeenth century the Mackenzies were to become an outstanding example of the value of cadets, rivalling the Campbells in this essential ingredient of power, but not many were well established before 1600. The earliest, and for a time a potential danger to Kintail, were the Mackenzies of Gairloch, who were descended from Hector, a younger son of Alastair Ionraic. They held Gairloch before 1494 when they had royal letters of confirmation[38] but had uneasy possession for at least a century.[39] Hector threatened to withhold land and power from his nephew, John of Killin, to whom he was tutor.[40] But after Hector's death about 1528 his successors did not present the same menace. In the next generation Rory, brother of John of Killin, made his mark at court and in 1520 was made gentleman and squire of the king's house for life.[41] He had a royal charter of Achilty in 1529 and his son Murdoch, legitimated in 1530, obtained Fairburn 'pro ejus bono servitio' in 1542,[42] on which he proceeded to build a tower. The only other cadet prominent before 1600 was Rory, brother of Colin Cam, whom we have met occupying the steeple at Chanonry in the 1570s. He acquired lands at Artafallie and Redcastle mill in the Black Isle and in 1589 had a charter from Keith of Delny of the lands of Redcastle and others with the old royal castle.[43] It was said that Colin Cam was a 'tender feeblie man but wise and judicious and had much trouble in his tyme with the feud of neighbours, against whom he had always the lawes of the country and his brother Rorie Moire still acted in the fields and put the law in execution'.[44] Whether Rory was always on the side of the law is not certain, and Colin had to give bond at least once for his brother's good behaviour, but he was clearly a useful ally. Several other cadet families were established before 1600 on lands held by charter from the king in Kintail, but they had not yet made their mark.

In addition to cadets, alliances were a source of power. These included marriages, and by the mid-sixteenth century the Mackenzies of Kintail were exploiting these to the full. John of Killin married Elizabeth Grant, probably a daughter of Freuchie, his son, Kenneth of Brahan, married a daughter of John, Earl of Atholl, and his son, Colin, married Barbara Grant, and, as we have seen, this brought him part of Lochbroom. Kenneth's daughters married well – Glengarry and Chisholm, Mackintosh,

LORDSHIP AND
ARCHITECTURE
IN MEDIEVAL
AND
RENAISSANCE
SCOTLAND

ॐ

Innes of Inverbreakie, Ross of Balnagown and a son of Urquhart of Cromarty. Colin's daughters married Lovat, MacLean of Duart and Macdonald of Sleat, thus in two generations setting up a network of relationships.[45] The Mackintosh marriage is interesting. The bridegroom's father was murdered by Huntly in 1550 and his seven-year-old son sent off to Strathnaver to be out of the way of further bloodshed. But on the way he was intercepted by Kenneth Mackenzie and kindly brought up for some years at Brahan until sent to Edinburgh for his education.[46] In 1567 he married Kenneth's daughter, Agnes.

Marriage was not always a sure way to lasting alliance, and many families entered into more specific bonds. Only a few such bonds concerning the Mackenzies are known, and most seem to be the outcome of their connection with the Grants which began with the marriage of John of Killin. The earliest bonds belong to the period of great unrest in the Highlands in 1545 when John and Kenneth his son bound themselves to other northern lords 'because of the blood, alliance, friendship and neighbourhood between them and their desire for unity and concord and the common weal of the country'.[47] More bonds were given in the 1570s and 1580s, again involving the Grants and Huntly.[48] In May 1606 Kenneth Mackenzie and John Grant of Freuchie agreed that, in future, disputes between them should be settled by arbiters – six Grants and six Mackenzies, the latter all cadets of Kintail.[49]

So by the mid-1590s the Mackenzies of Kintail were established as a considerable power in the northern Highlands with property from west to east Ross and alliances or connections with most of their neighbours. They were emerging as rivals to Huntly, whose supremacy in the Highlands was undermined by his own political and religious actions which led amongst other things to the great feud with Moray and on 20 January, 1591, to exemption from Huntly's commission of justiciary and lieutenancy granted to a group including the Mackenzies of Kintail and Redcastle, in which Grant and Mackintosh, both related to Kintail by marriage, were among the leaders.[50]

The pattern of residence is less easy to determine. Fairburn had built his tower on a hill above Strathconon. Gairloch probably had his *tighe dige* moat or stankhouse at Kirkton on the west coast, and island retreats on Loch Maree mentioned in the following century were probably already in use.[51] In 1581 John Mackenzie of Gairloch bought the lands of Kinkell-Clarsach, including the manor place, from Fraser of Guisachan[52] and, as we shall see later, built a castle which would become the principal messuage of the barony of Gairloch. This pattern of eastern residence seems to have been followed by Kintail himself. Alastair Ionraic certainly used the isle of Kinellan, and his son's widow was apparently living there in 1494.[53]

His grandson, John, took, or was given, a bye-name from Killin at the western end of Loch Garve where he was born about 1480.[54] No trace of a building has been located there, and confusion may have arisen with Kinellan not far away. Indeed, one reference to the widow of 1494 says she was living at Kynlyn, which seems like a mixture of the two, but the lands of Killin are clearly included in the early charters.[55] Perhaps the fact that John had the bye-name may suggest that it was unusual for the chief to be born or to live there, but John's son, Kenneth, died there in 1568,[56] though he seems to have lived at Brahan; and in the next century Colin, 1st Earl of Seaforth, was recorded in the course of a journey around the estates with several young clansmen as staying 'several days at Killin whither he called his people of Strathconon, Strathbran, Strathgarve and Brae Ross, and did keep courts upon them and saw all things rectified'.[57] Brahan, later to be the principal eastern home of the family, was feued from the early sixteenth century and used 'for a mains' for Kinellan.[58] There must have been a dwelling house, as the marriage contract of Agnes Mackenzie and young Mackintosh was signed there in 1567,[59] and Lovat's marriage to Katherine Mackenzie in 1589 was celebrated at Dingwall and Brahan when expense was 'truly noble and generous but not extravagant.'[60] Eilean Donan does not seem to have been the chief's home but even in the following century was regarded as a very strong point and focus for the military face of the clan – Tullochard, the rallying cry of the Mackenzies, is a hill above the castle in Kintail.[61]

The pattern of Mackenzie development in the seventeenth century differed in several respects from what went before. The chiefs themselves ceased to acquire land on a grand scale but increased power in other ways on the national scene, while the cadets, rapidly multiplying at this time, received grants of land from their chief or directly from the king.

In 1593, just before he died, Colin Cam accepted a seat on the privy council. His son Kenneth was chosen in February 1595[62] and this opened the way to a wider stage for Mackenzie power. From that time on he was given commissions for keeping order in Lewis and elsewhere in the Highlands, and came under the influence of Alexander Seton, soon (1604) to become chancellor and earl of Dunfermline. Their first known contact seems to have been when Seton sold Pluscarden to Kenneth in 1593.[63] This was important politically, and opponents of Kintail ascribed his progress (especially in Lewis) to the patronage of the chancellor. It was also, as we shall see, important architecturally. Kenneth, created Lord Mackenzie of Kintail in 1610, died in 1611 having married, as his second wife, Isobel Ogilvy of Powrie, the first bride to come from beyond the Highlands.[64] As a widow she married Sir John Seton of Barnes, providing a further link with the Seton family.

LORDSHIP AND
ARCHITECTURE
IN MEDIEVAL
AND
RENAISSANCE
SCOTLAND

❧

Kenneth's son, Colin, was clearly part of the establishment, a privy councillor, son-in-law of the chancellor (he married Margaret Seton in 1614) and from 1623 earl of Seaforth.[65] He held commissions of justiciary at various times but seems more remote from the Highlands than his predecessors. By tradition and perhaps under Seton influence he was a builder. Dunfermline's father, Lord Seton, was 'one of the greatest builders in that age',[66] and his son added the Seton tower at Fyvie and the painted gallery, among other work, at Pinkie,[67] both of which would presumably have been familiar to Colin and his wife. The castle at Chanonry became home to Colin, and he evidently improved the 'stately well contrived commodious house'[68] built nearly a century before by Bishop John Fraser.'[69] One family manuscript says that Colin 'caused Build … the Easter half of the Castle of Chanonry'.[70] Colin was said to live there 'in great state and very magnificently'.[71] Certainly the contents and furnishings sold by Smythe of Methven in the 1650s bear out this statement – silver and silver gilt, velvet curtains with gold thread, arras hangings and petit poynt are among the items calculated at Chanonry to the total of £5,594.11.7 and transported to Edinburgh at a cost of £108.12.0.[72] Stornoway castle was also apparently rebuilt from a ruined state, only to be broken down again by an English garrison during the 1650s.[73] Nor was this all, for Colin wanted to build himself a castle from scratch. He seems to have intended this to be at or near Dingwall, the traditional centre of the earldom of Ross. But he was dissuaded by Rory Mackenzie of Coigach, his uncle and former tutor, who had his own house at nearby Castle Leod and got Dunfermline 'to prevail upon him to build his castle on his own ancient inheritance' which he subsequently did, and which became 'one of the most stately houses in Scotland'.[74] This was Brahan in Strathconon which became the clan centre in the east, while Eilean Donan remained the symbol of their west-coast power.

Colin was succeeded in 1633 by his brother, George, to whom he left an estate deeply in debt. During almost all his time as chief of the Mackenzies, George was involved with the civil war and the politics of religion. He was basically loyal to the Crown but was not decisive and at times, such as the spring of 1645, actually opposed Montrose before the battle of Inverlochy and was present with his clan supporting the Covenanters at the battle of Auldearn.[75] From 1647 he was a confirmed royalist but it seems surprising, in view of his hesitancy, that in 1648, when Hamilton was raising men for the Engagers' invasion of England, twenty-four Mackenzies and other followers, though anxious to fight, agreed to serve only under Seaforth himself, who was not acceptable to many of the leaders.[76] Soon after this George joined Charles II in Holland, where he died in 1651. It was left to his brother, Thomas Mackenzie of Pluscarden, to raise rebellion in the north in February 1649 when, with some 700 horsemen, mainly Mackenzies, he seized Inverness. The rising flickered on and off, but in April he and other leaders submitted.[77] The Mackenzies failed to join Montrose in 1650 but were part of Glencairn's rising three years later under young Kenneth, 3rd Earl of Seaforth.[78] On the failure of this rising Seaforth made his peace in a treaty made on his behalf between General Monck and Thomas of Pluscarden in January 1655, by which he gave security for his own and his clan's good behaviour.[79] They were deprived of their horses and arms but his estate was not apparently forfeited as Monck had already decided that, if Seaforth agreed to give up Eilean Donan and some lands about it, the estate otherwise was not worth much as it was deep in debt.[80] He had recorded earlier that the lands of Lochbroom, Strathgarve, Strathconon and Strathbran were all burnt and destroyed. Now garrisons were placed in the castle of Chanonry, and at Brahan, as one writer had it, 'uppon Seafort's nose'.[81] All were returned at the Restoration and Seaforth himself was made hereditary sheriff of Ross, but his energies were mainly directed at trying to wipe out his debts – the result of his forbears' lifestyle and building, the ravages of war, neglect of agriculture and the expense of keeping troops in the field. Here the cadets came to his aid, and the pattern of wadsets traced in Lochbroom was probably followed elsewhere on the estate.[82] Some building seems to have been undertaken at Chanonry, for a dormer pediment survives showing the initials CBS, thought to be those of Barbara, Countess of Seaforth,[83] George's widow, who was visited there by Lovat in 1667.[84]

During all this time it was the cadet families who were expanding and building. The foremost now and later were the descendants of Rory Mackenzie of Coigach. We have seen that he married the daughter of Torquil Cononach MacLeod of Lewis, and in 1609 they had a charter which included Coigach and Cultaloid[85] – the latter being the site of the castle they built and called Castle Leod, where Rory died in 1626. Three years before his death he had bought from George Munro of Meikle Tarrell the lands of Easter Aird, Easter Tarbat and Meikle Tarrell, rich agricultural land on the Tarbat peninsula, with the castle of Tarbat.[86] This castle, on record in 1593, was formerly the seat of the Dunbars.[87] It was added to by Rory's son, John, who used Tarbat as his designation instead of Coigach. He was made a baronet in 1628 and used his influence in the clan for the benefit of the church party who became the Covenanters. After opposing Montrose, Sir John, along with Seaforth and the northern lairds, supported the Engagement in 1648[88] but his estates do not seem to have suffered as badly as his cousin's. He died at Tarbat in 1654 but three years earlier Dingwall presbytery recorded that Sir John 'hes ordinarie residence in the paroch of Fodertie'[89] – presumably at Castle Leod.

*Figure 13.3
Tarbat House (Old),
Ross and Cromarty:
from Fraser, William,
The Earls of
Cromartie (1876), i,
opp. p. clxxii.*

There is considerable confusion over the name of Tarbat Castle. In 1656 Sir John's son, Sir George, bought the lands of Meddat, including the sixteenth-century Munro castle of Milntoun.[90] This was situated on the sheltered north shore of the Cromarty Firth, and Sir George saw that it would make a better centre for his estates than Tarbat. The castle was said to be in ruin, for in 1642 it was recorded that 'the hous of Milltoun was brint negligentlie be ane keais nest',[91] but Spalding, who calls it a 'staitlie hous', says that it was 'rekleslie brynt (except the tour) with mekill good insicht and plenishing'.[92] It was thus not completely destroyed and in 1658 Sir George's mother was living there, while in the following year the Wardlaw Manuscript records that 'Sir Georg M'Kenzie of Tarbat comes north and solemnised the marriage betuixt his sister and Lovat at Miltoun of Ross, his own dwelling house'.[93] Evidently this marriage was considered by the Fraser writer to have been 'so privat that none of his friends knew of it till it was consumat', so perhaps Milntoun was not yet his principal residence. Having been a supporter of Glencairn and a leader of his rising, Sir George was promoted at the Restoration and became a lord of session and a considerable politician. But his politics caused him to be out of favour from 1664 until 1678 and he spent much of his time adding to and improving his estate, before returning to even greater political power as lord justice general.[94] In 1685 he was created viscount of Tarbat and in 1703 he became earl of Cromartie.[95] During the period of his eclipse he undertook to build a completely new house at Milntoun which he called New Tarbat, and it is possible that old Tarbat Castle was thereafter called Ballone from a place nearby on the peninsula.[96] To create even more confusion, Alexander, the fourth son of Sir Rory of Coigach, held a wadset of lands in Lochbroom, formerly called Auchlunachan, to which he gave the name Ballone, traditionally from the name of his brother's castle,[97] but the name, meaning 'town of the damp meadow', may have been local and certainly occurs in several other places in Ross.[98] At any rate, the family of Mackenzie of Ballone were not directly associated with the castle.

New Tarbat was perhaps designed by Sir George himself and probably influenced by his marriage connection with Sir William Bruce and by his residence in Bruce's new additions to the palace of Holyroodhouse. Sir George's house was demolished the following century when another new one was built on the site, but he also built himself a town house in Edinburgh which he called Royston and which was later known as Caroline Park.[99]

The Mackenzies

*Figure 13.4
Castle Leod, Ross and Cromarty: view from south-east.
RCAHMS, RC/209*

LORDSHIP AND
ARCHITECTURE
IN MEDIEVAL
AND
RENAISSANCE
SCOTLAND

Sir George was by no means the only Mackenzie cadet to be building castles and houses in the seventeenth century. The lands of Davochmaluag, later called Brae, near Fodderty, were granted to Kenneth Mackenzie, great-grandson of Kenneth of Kintail, in 1607.[100] It is not known when the castle was built – a bond was signed 'at Daochmolowak' in Strathpeffer in 1570[101] – but the present ruin of a three-storeyed tower house has a date stone of 1687[102] and Alexander Mackenzie states (without reference) that Davochmaluag was garrisoned by Cromwell's troops;[103] certainly the Mackenzie of the day was forced to find caution in 1647 as a follower of Montrose, so there may have been an earlier castle on the site.

Fairburn, who as we have seen was established in his hilltop tower by the mid-sixteenth century, apparently added a stair tower to the original block early in the following century.[104] Gairloch, having bought lands at Kinkell in the 1680s, proceeded to build his new tower house on another hilltop. Tradition has it that John Roy Mackenzie of Gairloch built the first three storeys with the date stone 1594, but that building was completed by his son, Alexander, about 1614,[105] although John was certainly still alive in 1619 when Kinkell became the principal messuage of the barony of Gairloch.[106] At this time the manor place and gardens of Kirkton at Gairloch (probably the original moat or stankhouse called *tighe dige*) were mentioned, as were the manor place and gardens on Ilanrorie in Loch Maree on which there was a good house.[107] Alexander apparently died at Island Suthain, also in Loch Maree, in 1638; no house or manor place is recorded there, although Alexander Mackenzie, writing in the late nineteenth century, says that 'traces of his house still remain'.

We have seen that Rory, brother of Colin Cam, was occupying the steeple at Chanonry in the 1570s.[108] He had a charter from Sir William Keith of Delny in 1589 of the lands of Redcastle with the castle and fortalice. This was an old royal castle from the time of William the Lion, already much rebuilt, and the Mackenzies continued the process. The Wardlaw Manuscript records that in 1646 Redcastle was 'fit enough for a flying army',[109] but after the defeat of Pluscarden's rising 'Rory Reedcastell's own new strong house at Redcastle' was evidently besieged and 'brunt to ashes with all the good furnitur'.[110] Redcastle was evidently not garrisoned in the 1650s and it would appear that the core of the present castle dates from the second half of the seventeenth century, though destruction may not have been so complete as the Fraser minister feared.

Alexander, a younger brother of Sir Rory of Coigach, also built himself a castle. This was Kilcoy, which lands he had acquired in 1611 on his marriage with Janet Fraser, widow of Sir James Stewart of Muren.[111] The castle was probably built very soon after this, although the stone chimney-piece dates from 1679.[112] Another brother, this time illegitimate, was

Figure 13.5
Beauly Priory,
Inverness-shire: view
from south-west.
Historic Scotland,
A.1343-2

another Alexander, founder of the important family of Mackenzie of Coul and prominent supporter of his father and brothers. He made good sums of money which he left to his sons Roderick of Applecross and Kenneth of Coul who was made a baronet in 1673 and whose money helped rescue the Seaforth family from their debts. It is not certain where the family lived, although it is thought that a ruined castle depicted on a tomb at Fortrose may represent what stood in ruins on the site of the later Coul House in 1746.[113] The Applecross part of the family, whose house in the west appears to have been built about 1730 (although a datestone of 1675 suggests an earlier building),[114] also lived at Tarradale [115] in the Black Isle where an 'old castell' is mentioned in notes possibly by Timothy Pont.[116]

A seventeenth-century datestone suggests an early building at Ord, the home of another Mackenzie cadet. It bears the date 1637 and the arms and initials of John Mackenzie [117] who received the lands from Seaforth in the same year, though he had formerly held a tack of them.[118] Finally, in the catalogue of Mackenzie castles comes Lochslin, near Fearn, now only a pile of stones. The Mackenzies came into possession of this castle in 1624,[119] and there is reference to the castle in 1589,[120] but its style,

EILAN DONAN CASTLE, LOCH-ALSH. 815. G.W.W.

showing links with Ballone and Castle Leod, suggests that John or Simon, sons of Kenneth, Lord Kintail, who owned it successively, may have altered or enlarged it. Simon of Lochslin was the father of Sir George Mackenzie of Rosehaugh, the lawyer who shared with his cousin Sir George of Tarbat much of the power of the Mackenzies in the later seventeenth century. Rosehaugh was possibly born at Lochslin in 1636, though there is some confusion on the subject.[121] He later acquired an estate on the Black Isle near Avoch, where in 1673 he was building on an unidentified site, as testified by his agreement with Alexander Chisholm of Comer over timber for a roof for which he ordered 73 joists and 19 spars, paying for them in January 1678.[122]

So Mackenzie cadets took over castles with the lands they acquired and in many cases extended or rebuilt them. Brahan and New Tarbat seem to be the only sites selected from a wide choice. It has been claimed that the hilltop sites at Fairburn, Kilcoy and Kinkell were specially placed for mutual defence, but the acquisition of lands does not seem to have followed any obvious pattern, although the immediate sites of the castles were probably chosen with defence in mind. The pattern of land ownership in the west but residence on smaller and richer estates in the east does seem to have persisted and was reinforced when so many cadet families took wadsets of west coast lands to help Seaforth with his debts. The web of cadet inter-relationship was made more extensive by frequent marriages, and the close links can be seen through their correspondence and the use they made of each other. Certainly they played a very important part in the development of the clan, and in the castles and houses built in the period of Mackenzie power in Ross.

NOTES

1. W. Matheson, 'Traditions of the Mackenzies', *TGSI*, xxxix–xl (1963), 200–5.
2. *ER*, iv, 211.
3. *Acts of the Lords of the Isles*, 129.
4. Fraser, *Cromartie*, ii, 474.
5. Matheson, 'Mackenzies', 211.
6. *RMS*, ii, no. 3313.
7. Fraser, *Cromartie*, ii, 474, 484.
8. *Acts of the Lords of the Isles*, 161.
9. *ER*, x, 26, 93, 95.
10. E. C. Batten, *History of Beauly Priory* (Edinburgh, 1877), frontispiece, 105.
11. *Acts of the Lords of the Isles*, 244, 261.
12. *RMS*, iii, nos. 690, 1176.
13. Ibid. iii, nos. 2238, 2449, 2817.
14. Ibid., iii, no. 2957.
15. Ibid., iv, nos. 969, 1579; v, no. 665.
16. Ibid., iv, no. 204.
17. Ibid., iv, no. 2273; Fraser, *Grant*, iii, 150.
18. Fraser, *Grant*, iii, 143.
19. *Highland Papers*, ii, 49.
20. A. Mackenzie, *History of the Macleods* (Inverness, 1889), 327; *RMS*, vi, no. 1879.
21. *RMS*, vi, no. 229; iv, nos. 1091, 2272; v, no. 2042.
22. A. M. Mackintosh, *The Mackintoshes and Clan Chattan* (Edinburgh, 1903), 156.
23. NAS, RD1/13/459; *RPC*, ii, 276.
24. *RPC*, ii, 276 7.
25. Glasgow Mitchell Library, MS 591703.
26. *RMS*, vi, no. 265.
27. Ibid., v, no. 1337.
28. Ibid., v, nos. 1331, 1625.
29. *RPC*, iv, 254–6.
30. D. Warrand, *Some Mackenzie Pedigrees* (Inverness, 1965), 68.
31. NAS, GD305/1/25/5.
32. *RMS*, vi, no. 229.
33. I. F. Grant, *The Macleods: the History of a Clan* (London, 1959), 127–30.
34. Grant, *Macleods*, 186.
35. *RMS*, v, no. 2024; vii, no. 52.

LORDSHIP AND
ARCHITECTURE
IN MEDIEVAL
AND
RENAISSANCE
SCOTLAND

❧

36. D. Gregory, *History of the Western Highlands and Islands* (Edinburgh, 1836), 278ff.
37. *RMS*, vii, no. 341.
38. A. Mackenzie, *History of the Mackenzies* (Inverness, 1894), 388.
39. Gregory, *History*, 341.
40. *ADC*, ii, 484.
41. *RSS*, ii, 562.
42. *RMS*, iii, nos. 731, 1987, 2632.
43. Ibid., v, no. 707; Warrand, *Pedigrees*, 68.
44. *Highland Papers*, ii, 36.
45. Warrand, *Pedigrees*, 9–12.
46. Macfarlane, *Genealogical Coll.*, i, 234–5.
47. J. Wormald, *Lords and Men: Bonds of Manrent 1442–1603* (Edinburgh, 1985), 286, 300, 386: Fraser, *Grant*, iii, 102.
48. Wormald, *Lords and Men*, 389, 390, 290, 292, 369.
49. Fraser, *Grant*, iii, 201–2.
50. Ibid., iii, 176–9.
51. Mackenzie, *Mackenzies*, 425, 429.
52. *RMS*, v, no. 508.
53. *ADC*, i, 327.
54. Warrand, *Pedigrees*, 7.
55. *Acts of the Lords of the Isles*, 129.
56. Macfarlane, *Genealogical Coll.*, i, 63.
57. Mackenzie, *Mackenzies*, 243.
58. Fraser, *Cromartie*, ii, 474–5.
59. NAS, GD176/83.
60. W. Mackay, *Chronicle of the Frasers: the Wardlaw Manuscript* (Edinburgh, 1905), 218.
61. W. J. Watson, *Place-Names of Ross and Cromarty* (Inverness, 1904), 178.
62. *RPC*, v, 90.
63. *RMS*, vi, no. 410.
64. Warrand, *Pedigrees*, 14–15; R. Gordon, *Genealogical History of the Earldom of Sutherland* (Edinburgh, 1813), 248.
65. Warrand, *Pedigrees*, 15–16.
66. G. Seton, *The History of the Family of Seton* (Edinburgh, 1896), i, 195.
67. J. G. Dunbar, *The Historic Architecture of Scotland* (London, 1966), 54; J. G. Dunbar, *The Architecture of Scotland* (London, 1978), 71.
68. Mackay, *Wardlaw Manuscript*, 115–16.
69. Glasgow Mitchell Library, MS 591703, p. 74.
70. Edinburgh Public Library, RBR QX DA7583MK 37, p. 78.
71. Mackenzie, *Mackenzies*, 243.
72. NAS, GD190/2/210.
73. E. P. D. Torrie and R. Coleman, *Historic Stornoway* (Edinburgh, 1997), 24–7.
74. Mackenzie, *Mackenzies*, 244.
75. D. Stevenson, *Alasdair MacColla and the Highland Problem in the 17th century* (Edinburgh,1980), 162, 166, 177–8.
76. D. Stevenson, *Revolution and Counter Revolution in Scotland, 1644–51* (London, 1977), 110.
77. Stevenson, *Revolution*, 145–7.
78. F. Dow, *Cromwellian Scotland* (Edinburgh, 1977), part ii passim.
79. *Scotland and the Potectorate*, ed. C. H. Firth (Edinburgh, 1899), 234.
80. Ibid., 186.
81. Mackay, *Wardlaw Manuscript*, 332.

82. M. Bangor-Jones, 'Mackenzie families in the barony of Lochbroom', in *People and Settlement in North West Ross*, ed. J. R. Baldwin (Edinburgh, 1994), 86–7.

83. E. Meldrum, *The Black Isle* (Inverness, 1979), 21.

84. Mackay, *Wardlaw Manuscript*, 471.

85. *RMS*, vii, no. 52.

86. Ibid., viii, no. 509.

87. NAS, GD305/1/166/2.

88. Fraser, *Cromartie*, i, pp. lx–lxii.

89. W. Mackay, *Inverness and Dingwall Presbytery Records 1643–1688* (Edinburgh, 1896), 214.

90. NAS, GD305/1/25/5.

91. R. J. Adam, *Calendar of Fearn, 1471–1667* (Edinburgh, Scottish History Society, 1991), 205–6.

92. J. Spalding, *Memorialls of the Troubles in Scotland and England* (Aberdeen, 1850–1), ii, 142.

93. Mackay, *Wardlaw Manuscript*, 422.

94. Fraser, *Cromartie*, ii, 431.

95. *Scots Peerage*, iii, 73–5.

96. M. Clough, *Two Houses* (Aberdeen, 1990), 71–81.

97. Bangor-Jones, 'Mackenzie families', 92.

98. Watson, *Place-Names of Ross and Cromarty*, 251.

99. Clough, *Two Houses*, 71–81, 125–137.

100. Warrand, *Pedigrees*, 98.

101. Fraser, *Grant*, iii, 141–2.

102. Drawing by Sir J. D. Mackenzie, dated 1870, in the possession of the author (copy in NMRS).

103. Mackenzie, *Mackenzies*, 500.

104. E. Beaton, *Ross and Cromarty* (Edinburgh, 1995), 43.

105. G. Laing, *Kinkell: the Reconstruction of a Scottish Castle* (London, 1974), 65–6.

106. *RMS*, vii, no. 2078.

107. Macfarlane, *Geographical Coll.*, ii, 539; Mackenzie, *Mackenzies*, 423–4.

108. Warrand, *Pedigrees*, 68.

109. Mackay, *Wardlaw Manuscript*, 317.

110. Ibid., 341.

111. *RMS*, vii, no. 1764.

112. Beaton, *Ross and Cromarty*, 11.

113. Ibid., 19, 45.

114. Ibid., 101.

115. NLS, MS 1316.

116. Macfarlane, *Geographical Coll.*, ii, 555.

117. J. Gifford, *The Buildings of Scotland: Highland and Islands* (Harmondsworth, 1992), 443.

118. Warrand, *Pedigrees*, 98.

119. *RMS*, viii, no. 691.

120. NAS, GD305/1/166/12 no. 91.

121. Fraser, *Cromartie*, i, lxvii–lxviii.

122. J. Munro, *Inventory of Chisholm Writs 1456–1810* (Edinburgh, 1992), 177, 189.

Fort Charlotte

Dornoch, bishop's castle

Huntly Castle ■   ■ Fyvie Castle

Aberdeen,
King's College Chapel ✠

Melgund Castle ■

Balloch
(Taymouth)
Castle   Glamis Castle ■

Barcaldine Castle   ■ Panmure House

Finlarig Castle   Elcho
Castle

Scone Palace   Dairsie ✠   ■ St Andrews Castle

Carnasserie
Castle   Falkland Palace
Cambuskenneth   n   d
Kilmartin Castle   Abbey   m   ■ Balcaskie House
Stirling Castle ✠   s   Ravencraig Castle
Airth, royal dockyard   o   1 g j   a 2   Newhaven

Newark Castle   b   3
Linlithgow Palace   p   ✠ 2   ■ Dirleton, Archerfield Aisle
Glasgow,   Inchgarvie, fort ✠   k   4.5   t   Dunbar Castle
Skipness Castle   Tolbooth ▲   Midcalder   q   Haddington, Lauderdale Aisle
Rothesay   Church   e   Winton House   Eyemouth, fort
Castle   h   f
Glasgow, Shawfield House   ■ Drochil Castle
Hamilton Palace   Cadzow Craignethan
Castle   Castle   Ladykirk ✠

Saddell Castle

Kilkerran Castle

Durisdeer, Queensbury Aisle

Drumlanrig Castle ■

0   50km   Lincluden
Collegiate Church
Terregles
Church ✠
Threave Castle ■

Land over 100m

❖ Royal Docks
▲ Public Building
♦ Military Architecture

Royal Castles & Palaces
● 1 Dunfermline Palace
● 2 Edinburgh Castle
● 3 Holyroodhouse

Ecclesiastical Buildings
✠ Burntisland Church
✠ Dairsie Church
✠ Dalgety Bay, St Bridget's Church
✠ Edinburgh, Trinity College Chapel
✠ Restalrig, St Triduana's Chapel

■ a Aberdour Castle
■ b Airth Castle
■ c Alloa Tower
■ d Balgonie Castle
■ e Borthwick Castle
■ f Crichton Castle
■ g Culross Abbey House
■ h Dalkeith Palace
■ i Edinburgh, Moray House
■ j Fordell Castle
■ k Kilbaberton House
■ l Kinneil House
■ m Kinross House
■ n Leslie House
■ o Mar's Wark
■ p Niddrie Castle
■ q Pinkie House
■ r Pitreavie House
■ s Sauchie Tower
■ t Whitehill (Newhailes) House

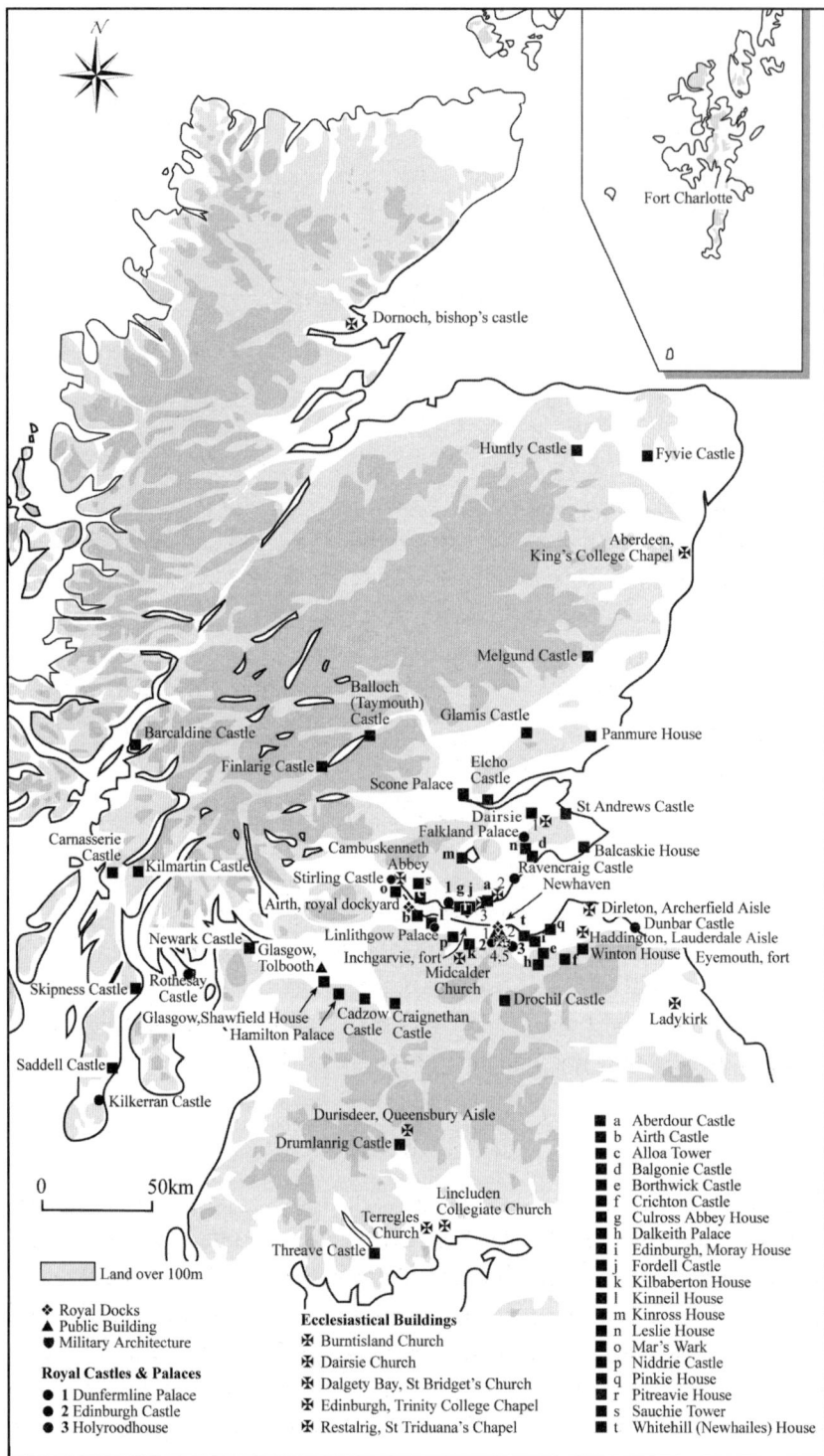

Figure 14.1
Properties mentioned
in the text.

292

Chapter 14

❦

COURT AND COURTIER ARCHITECTURE, 1424–1660

Aonghus McKechnie

Preparations by the Privy Council for King Charles I's coronation, 1633:[1]

> Forsameekle as the King's Majestie has resolved that his coronatioun sall, God willing, be in the Abbey Kirk of Halyrudhous, and whereas it is verie requisite both for the credite of the countrie and for the solemnitie of this important actioun that the said kirk be repaired and ordered in suche a decent and comelie maner as is most fitting for suche ane great and honnourable actioun, thairfoir the Lords of Secreit Counsell ordains and commands James Murray and Antony Alexander, Maisters of his Majesteis Workes, to enter with all possible diligence to the repairing and ordering of the said kirk ...

King Charles I, following his coronation, 1633:[2]

> Seing the Abbey Church of Halyruidhius that had bene so dark befoir was by the course takin by yow becum so lightsome that it gave ws a great deall of contentment at our being ther: To the effect that it may continew so still, it is our pleasur that yow have a speciall care that no seatts nor lofts be built therein unless it be such places as may nather impair the beautie nor light of the said church ...

INTRODUCTION

This final chapter focuses highly selectively upon architectural patronage from the close of the Middle Ages, when the culture responded to the momentous transformations brought about by the coming of the Renaissance. Unlike the foregoing chapters, this account necessarily goes beyond straightforward private aristocratic patronage to include royal or 'state' patronage. The first, and the key, innovations date from James I's return from captivity in 1424, when he began the process of developing the image

LORDSHIP AND
ARCHITECTURE
IN MEDIEVAL
AND
RENAISSANCE
SCOTLAND

𝕒

and ideology of the Crown which demanded appropriate architectural settings. Royal patronage was wide-ranging and highly culture-focused, embracing intellectualism and the arts, while more widely, architectural patronage and design were shaped by successive political and religious changes. Following the re-defining innovations which first climaxed during the reign of James IV (1488–1513), Scotland's developing role as a cosmopolitan European power entered a period of abrupt reversal with military defeat in 1513. Thereafter, while continuing to maintain external diplomatic contacts, notably with France and the papacy, politically and perhaps culturally she relied more heavily upon France until the protestant Reformation of 1560. Religious tensions between reformers and Catholics then pushed her in the direction of political alignment with protestant northern Europe, and at last with neighbouring England, with whom cultural interchange increased significantly, especially after regnal union in 1603.

Within Scotland, internal polarisations moved from international politics, via the Reformation, to Episcopacy versus Presbyterianism, leading to dynastic change from 1689, and to Jacobitism versus the new monarchical settlement. In 1707, Scotland entered into political union with England; and by the latter third of the eighteenth century, imperial Scotland had emerged as a vigorous partner in what had become a more stable British union. External cultural links with mainland Europe, Ireland and England continued throughout our period; the British period after 1707 brought a new set of contacts, and a new militarism, through the actions of imperialism. The emigration of the court in 1603 bestowed upon the nobility a new status as leaders of fashion and consequently an enhanced role as patrons, together with – to a lesser extent – the municipalities. A new, more explicit classicism based on the architectural Orders was introduced in the 1670s, but by the end of the 1715 Rising the old, largely Jacobite, grouping of architects was becoming eclipsed by a new order committed to Hanoverian unionism.

1406–88

We have seen how the great families of mediaeval Scotland were empowered to build, and seen also the characterisation of their architecture: Gothic, and from c. 1400, combined with neo-Romanesque, in the case of ecclesiastical; and castellated, in the case of rural domestic, which style had by 1424 been described as 'usual in the manner of the kingdom of Scotland'.[3] Less evidence exists regarding urban domestic, but it seems likely that the narrrow gable-fronted streetscapes typical of northern Europe were seen also in this country, though little more than their burgage plots survive to-day. Land-holding, commercial activity and even service abroad might

*Figure 14.2
Linlithgow Palace,
West Lothian: general
view of east front.
Historic Scotland,
A 567-12*

all generate wealth. In the *Gaidhlig* west, the sometimes ambitious building enterprises may have been funded in great part by mercenary hire, as the gauge of wealth moved from terms of fighting men, to cattle, and finally to money. In the lowland east, on the other hand, commercial contacts with mainland Europe funded patronage more straightforwardly, while diplomatic bargaining sometimes brought in money, notably from France.

Our period opens when architectural patronage was still in the hands of an elite few within a highly-structured hierarchical society, in which the intellectual class was still the clergy. After 1424, a massive programme of royal palace-building began, foremost being James I's reconstruction of Linlithgow as a 'palatium ad modum castri', an appropriately high-status setting – referred to as a 'palace' from 1429 – for his re-defined kingship.[4] By 1542, a series of six magnificent palaces had been constructed within the east-central part of the country, where the court was now centred. The innovations of these palaces possibly struck a chord elsewhere in Europe, as Scotland shared a place at the cutting edge of the northern European counterpart of, or response to, the Italian Renaissance.[5] At home, their primary effect was to underline an ever-less bridgeable gulf in status between nobility and the Crown. Royal patronage had a powerful political agenda, and the propaganda value of architecture was exploited by the Crown. Visual images of security, stability, power, wealth, artistic or cultural

LORDSHIP AND
ARCHITECTURE
IN MEDIEVAL
AND
RENAISSANCE
SCOTLAND

༜

refinement and perhaps even of 'national' pride were conveyed, while allegorical references expressed scholarship. Within a culture which tended to favour minimising exterior decoration, all these images were perhaps broadcast most loudly by the wealth of exterior sculpture on James V's palace at Stirling Castle, set above and in contrast to James IV's monumental, multi-turreted forework – grandeur without parallel among contemporary secular work anywhere in the country.

Driving these innovations was the crown's own all-consuming ideology; introduced with James I's kingship, and reaching a new level of accomplishment in the age of James IV, when his forfeiture of the lordship of the Isles and follow-up campaign laid the ground for the crown's achieving de facto supreme status at home. Dynastic, political/ constitutional, religious and personal aspects of kingship all found representation in royal patronage, often drawing on carefully chosen precedent or allusion. For instance, the antique, classical past provided two areas of inspiration, or categories of ideas: firstly, concepts such as 'imperial Rome' – and so by implication, the king's 'imperial' status – were recalled by *imagery* appropriated for political use; secondly, and more straightforwardly, there was use of revived 'antique' *ornament*, more ready evidence of artistic sophistication. Paradoxically, the comparatively recent, but national, mediaeval past also provided inspiration for a new chivalric monarchy. This was evidenced most clearly by James IV, not only by elaborate tournaments, but by actions such as his granting of free pardon to the humiliated English bounty-hunter, Stephen Bull, and (ironically) dying a chivalric death at the head of his army, employing – characteristically, but unsuccessfully – the latest scientific military techniques.[6] The dynastic and constitutional aspects of the 'national' past was referred to, in architecture, by the use of castellation.

Although replaced by a propaganda 'war' of national origin-myths and imagery, the thirteenth- and fourteenth-century wars with England were successfully over, effectively confirming the status of the independent nation. At home, successive offences taken against the stronger factions incrementally enhanced the status of the crown. It was primarily the dual issues of national 'fredome' and escalated royal status which inspired the 1469 claim that James III had 'ful jurisdictioune and fre impire within his realm', an ideology which then became translated into visual terms.[7] From *c.* 1485, imperial crowns appear on coinage, an idea translated into architecture, with crown spires built or planned at several urban centres including Edinburgh which was increasingly taking the role of capital. The spire of King's College Chapel, Aberdeen (*c.* 1500), was described by Boece as being 'a stone arch in the shape of an imperial crown'.[8] Similar imagery was conveyed by triumphal arches, with temporary arches constructed for state entries of both James IV's and James V's queens, while the first stone-built version was contained within James IV's castellated, perhaps neo-chivalric, forework gateway at Stirling (1500–10).[9] Interpretation of these palaces is limited, as all have to a greater or lesser degree been spoiled, their rich furnishings near-totally lost or dispersed, the consequence of absentee, subsequently of changed, monarchy; Edinburgh and Stirling were converted to military barracks, Linlithgow was burned by Hanoverian troops and Dunfermline and Falkland left to ruin. Holyrood, as we will see, was rebuilt for Charles II in the 1670s.

Besides his investment in Linlithgow and other palaces, including Dunfermline, James I began a new palace at Leith (1434), established a Carthusian priory at Perth (begun 1429, Scotland's first monastic house since the thirteenth century), and in the nearby Blackfriars monastery, built or occupied an unfortified house, all in line with the images of internal peace and royal invincibility which he promoted.[10] Thin documentary evidence makes James II's contribution more enigmatic. Perhaps he was responsible for the dramatic and early artillery works at his queen's jointure house at Ravenscraig – unless these were built for William Sinclair, Earl of Caithness, who acquired it in 1470.[11] Massive artillery fortifications of *c.* 1447 at Threave have been interpreted as symbolising the attitude one nobleman (8th Earl of Douglas) to crown authority (built in the decade following the defeat of a royal army by another magnate), while at another extreme, the massive, near-symmetrical Borthwick (begun *c.* 1430 for William, Lord of Borthwick, veteran of the 1429 royal campaign in the Highlands) represents the grandeur available to a nobleman loyal to the crown.[12]

As regards monuments, neglect, wars and iconoclasm have resulted in the tomb at Lincluden of James I's sister, Princess Margaret (d. *c.* 1450), Duchess of Touraine, Countess of Douglas and Lady of Galloway, being the closest visual indication of what royal funereal work of the period might have looked like, though crown patronage would surely have produced grander.[13] The role of royal women as patrons has yet to be assessed, but besides continuing the newly-begun work at Ravenscraig, James II's queen, Mary of Gueldres (d. 1463) built, or continued building, a gallery at Falkland (1461) and was responsible for the foundation (1462) in his memory of Trinity College Chapel on the outskirts of Edinburgh.[14] Although only its choir, transepts and crow-stepped steeple were built, it was a lofty structure with extensive decorative stone sculpture. The quality of the Flemish-made Hugo Van der Goes altarpiece made for it by James III and his queen suggests that the interior was stunningly beautiful.

James III's works included substantial additions to Linlithgow Palace, work at Stirling Castle and also the foundation of a royal chapel, the 'capella regis' at Restalrig, dedicated to St Triduana. It comprised a choir

with an attached, hexagonal two-level chapel, the upper level being roofed without a central pillar. Should it thus be interpreted in the context of contemporary centrally-planned Italian Renaissance chapels? However, given the royal fascination with crusading and the Eastern Mediterranean, possibly the more direct source was Phileremos, Rhodes, where near-contemporary hexagonal chapels were built. Because the destruction of St Triduana's was explicitly ordered by parliament at the Reformation, its interior was possibly uniquely elaborate. James's friendship with the builber of the Jerusalem Church in Bruges, Anselm Adornes, who with his son travelled the Mediterranean (including Rhodes) as James's proxy, is perhaps vitally important to the architecture of this time, for his mission required him to report back what he saw. Consequently, James III and, later, James IV came to know much about architecture in the Mediterranean region, including that of the Italian Renaissance.[15] Conceivably, James's friendship with the 'mason' Thomas Cochrane (supposed builder of Auchindoun) could indicate the name of his architect.[16]

1488–1513

Documentation is richer for the reign of James IV when the royal building programme reached a climax. The cosmopolitan court and patronage of this extraordinary, multi-lingual king, and of his multi-faceted kingship, was impressive: Italian trumpeters and dancers, Irish (presumably Highland) clarsairs (harpists), Moorish tabrouners (drummers), French, English, Flemish, German and other nationalities of craftsmen, French shipwrights for the royal navy and armourers. Nephews of both the Danish king and his chancellor came to the court to be educated; other Danes included a gunner, quickly sent to the siege of Cairnburgh.[17] Court literature, music and architecture all flourished, and in 1511–12 there was even an Italian mason (named 'Cressent') engaged in the royal works.[18] The Italian links are particularly intriguing: besides numerous craftsmen/artists retained by the court, they ranged from James's receipt of papal gifts, to having two sons taught in Padua by Erasmus, and to a less exalted level of Jerome Frescobaldi, merchant in Florence and Bruges, and 'a very good friend' of the king of Scots.[19]

James commissioned work at all the palaces, and this contribution has recently been evaluated.[20] At Stirling, besides the above-mentioned fore-work, he built or completed the massive great hall and a new palace block and chapel royal. A Scots and a French gardener oversaw creation of a huge pleasure garden beneath the castle rock with a vast numbers of trees, including fruits, vines, fish-stocked ponds and possibly embracing the now-drained Rap Loch. There was also a small garden, possibly at the

Figure 14.3 Restalrig, St Triduana's Chapel, Edinburgh: interior. RCAHMS, ED/2641

LORDSHIP AND
ARCHITECTURE
IN MEDIEVAL
AND
RENAISSANCE
SCOTLAND

⊱

higher level. He perhaps modified the structure now known as the 'King's Knot' (then called 'Arthur's Seat'), probably as a ceremonial symbol of his pan-British political ambitions, which countered English claims of overlordship. He completed Linlithgow as a symmetrical corner-towered quadrangle, a formula reproduced in high-status/royal works in other countries, and the courtyard-facing gallery of the south (chapel) quarter was given a seemingly English-inspired façade. It is unclear whether this reflected straightforward friendship with England, whether it was part of his 'British' political agenda, or whether it simply referred to the English origins of his queen, one of whose dowry houses this was. Reconstruction of James IV's summer palace of Falkland was continued, and in 1504 a loch built, stocked with pike, probably a different water feature from the 'aqueduct' to the palace referred to later.[21] He seems to have invested less at Dunfermline, while at Edinburgh Castle work included the great hall, reconstruction of the palace and a new chapel. The gardens nearby were reconstructed by Sir John Sharp. At the palace of Holyrood he built a new gatehouse and a forework and chapel in 1502 (by Walter Merlzioun); work at the gallery was undertaken by William Turnbull, and a new 'hie altar in the chapell' was created in 1507–8.[22] Work in the gardens included draining a loch in 1507.[23] A *lione house* was built in 1511, to accommodate a living heraldic device.[24] From the narrower, art-historical perspective there was also an important and precocious innovation. His great hall at Edinburgh bears monogrammed cyma consoles of Italianate type, while a

*Figure 14.4
Stirling Castle:
Forework.
RCAHMS, E 82918*

Figure 14.5
Stirling Castle, Palace:
sculpture on north
quarter.
Historic Scotland,
A 369-4

Renaissance roundel installed at Holyrood in 1512 further demonstrates that his court employed the latest trends in contemporary European artistic fashion. His approval of scholarship, evidenced in the 1496 Education Act and in creation of colleges at Aberdeen and St Andrews, was also in the spirit of the Renaissance.[25]

From 1424, the church was presented as decidedly safe in royal hands, and James IV's kingship included church patronage. Ladykirk was a token for his having been saved from drowning nearby. He also built a royal tomb, 'the Kingis sepultur', at Cambuskenneth, where his parents lay buried and where masons worked with David Pratt, an English painter.[26] In his role as imperial monarch he built military architecture to guard against both internal and external aggression. His strongest assertion of crown authority at home was his forfeiture of the lordship of the Isles (1493), followed up by a campaign of royal castle-building along or near the east flank of Kintyre. This included a completely new fortification at Kilkerran (*Ceann Loch Cille Chiarain*), subsequently Campbeltown, while crown supporters, including Duncan Forrester at Skipness and David Hamilton at Saddell (1508), reinforced this process.

LORDSHIP AND
ARCHITECTURE
IN MEDIEVAL
AND
RENAISSANCE
SCOTLAND

༉

Partly to check potential external aggression via the usual eastern routes, Dunbar Castle was massively reconstructed between 1496 and 1501.[27] Taking the idea perhaps from his uncle, King Hans, or from the maritime exploits of King Manuel in Portugal, he built an impressive navy which included one of the greatest ships of the age, the *Michael*. James safeguarded the Forth from external aggression by building defences on either side of the Queensferry and an intermediate fortification begun or built on Inchgarvie Island.[28] Having previously built docks at Leith and Newhaven, where also a bulwark was created in 1504, a rope-walk (still visible in the eighteenth century), and new chapel, James built three docks at Airth in 1511 and a stable for 50 horses.[29] Royal docks in the west included Glasgow, Dumbarton and Ayr. He had, allegedly, 50 ships ready for action in 1512–13.[30] A vast armoury employed French armourers, while guns were cast within the castles of Edinburgh and Stirling by Robert Borthwick. More broadly, James contributed generously to architecture elsewhere, often making gifts while on his travels. These included work at the royal castle at Inverness, his father's Restalrig, Darnaway, where Janet Kennedy stayed, and St John's Church of Dunbar, built by Sir Andrew Wood. Further contributions to works or workmen at Pluscarden, Coupar Angus, Scone, Paisley, Whithorn and many other places are also recorded.

1513–42

The country entered a stage of transition after James IV's death. His nephew, Albany, was recalled from France, and was present as governor from 1515–17 and 1521–4, James V then being a child. New palace construction came to a temporary halt, though maintenance and modifications continued. Holyrood, for instance, was altered for Albany (who spent much time both here and at Dunbar Castle): a new turnpike stair was built in 1516, while James IV's one-time glazier Thomas Peebles provided 'ane gret lantern of glass' in 1515, and 'i payntit rownd' for a reconstructed window in 1516.[31] The French presence was reinforced due to the new need for military protection (see below), and more singularly French ideas fed into the culture. Yet much of the old court culture lived on, for instance, with 140 'payntit armyis' made in 1515 by Alexander Chalmers, 'paynteour' for St Giles, for the 'obsequijes' of James III.[32] Yet James V was to continue the work of his predecessors, building more and sometimes grander palaces.

Official and other communications with Italy remained extensive, and the young Catherine de Medici, Duchess of Urbino, featured as a possiblity in James's list of potential consorts.[33] But perhaps it was more towards France that James V's court looked as a cultural resource, and in adulthood, James continued Albany's greater political reliance upon France, making a personal visit there, still in search of a queen. Falkland was included in the marriage negotiations as – in the event, both his queens' – dowry house, and it was possibly because of this intended new use that it was reconstructed with French-style courtyard façades, with French masons brought to help in its construction.[34] The east quarter was remodelled in 1537, its courtyard façade given characteristically French full-height bay divisions detailed in a manner reminiscent of Francis I's Villers Cotterets (1533), which James had seen. Roundels on that wall date from either his or (less probably) James IV's time. The south or chapel, quarter by contrast was entirely re-fronted in pure French style by addition of a Linlithgow-type gallery range, the façade, dated 1539, a homogenous one and a more easily-read signal of cultural alignment than its Linlithgow predecessor. It seems likely that the twin-turreted gatehouse was a James IV project completed by his son, who also completed the south front. His Stirling Palace was a miniaturised quadrangle, differing from Linlithgow (and possibly Falkland) in that it comprised essentially twinned (as against superimposed) royal apartments on the same floor, entered at ground level, and exploiting James IV's forework as a high terrace in the manner of Francis I's St Germain-en-Laye (1539–42). Its classicising courtyard was seemingly used for the royal menagerie, which again, included a lion.

LORDSHIP AND
ARCHITECTURE
IN MEDIEVAL
AND
RENAISSANCE
SCOTLAND

❧

Linlithgow was altered, its south front regularised by partial re-facing and made into the main entrance, with a new gatehouse built. Holyrood was rebuilt, with an approximately double-square plan new tower (1529–32), a forework and chapel (1535–6), all possibly designed by Sir John Scrymgeour of Myres. Payment was made in 1535 'to Alexander Mure for ane patrown of ane dowbill turngrece', evidently a double spiral stair, perhaps on the form of the innovative Chambord stair, but otherwise unknown in accounts of Holyrood and probably therefore unbuilt.[35] Architectural ideas validated at these palaces, such as Scottish castellation combined with decorative motifs from abroad, came to enter the wider architectural mainstream.

Military architecture post-1513

The militarism of James IV's reign was not repeated in the same way by his Stewart successors, but unexpected vulnerability to attack after 1513 resulted, as we have seen, in protective works being built for the Crown, notably the blockhouse at Dunbar (*c.* 1515–20s), which an English spy portrayed as impregnable, while from 1515 Inchgarvie was reinforced or completed.[36] Docks were built at Dumbarton for the *James* and the *Margaret*,[37] and the gun foundry at Edinburgh Castle continued production, still under Robert Borthwick, though that at Stirling seems not to have continued. But no major invasion followed then, though internal unrest in the Highlands and Borders necessitated fortification of strategic castles. After James attained freedom from the control of the Earl of Angus in 1528, he continued the process of asserting Crown rule; Rothesay Castle, for instance, was re-fortified, the gatehouse completed, while the reconstruction of Blackness for artillery could be regarded as a precaution against either internal or external attack. James V's death in 1542, though, foreshadowed a new phase of wars of independence, when architectural patronage, naturally, gave new focus to military works. Wedge-shaped and polygonal forts of up-to-date European pattern were built in mostly the southern and eastern parts of the country. Scots built the Italian-designed spur at Edinburgh Castle (1547–50), and the French, lending assistance, fortified Leith and built a series of forts such as Luffness, while the English built invader footholds at, for example, Eyemouth (1547) and Lauder.

By the time of James VI's long reign (1567–1625), the Platonic idea had developed elsewhere of the philosopher king, who ruled less by might than by learning, and at home, the related idea promoted by George Buchanan of a 'rex stoicus', who cared little for riches and honour was aimed at James; perhaps to effect, as his reign was characterised by a 'Solomonic' peace and friendship with England.[38] Mid-seventeenth-century wars again resulted in construction of sophisticated military works by the English (for example, Ayr and Leith). Seventeenth-century crown, state or municipal-sponsored Scottish fortifications are now best seen at John Mylne's fort at Lerwick, later known as Fort Charlotte, or Robert Mylne's eastern ravelin at Edinburgh Castle, upon which the present forework is built. Eighteenth-century fortifications were mostly post-1707, funded by the new British state, and aimed at countering militarised Jacobitism. These comprised, most notably, massive 1708 artillery works at Edinburgh and Stirling Castles, and a series of garrison-posts and forts in the Highlands linked to a road-building programme, culminating ultimately in the stupendous Fort George, Ardersier.

Houses of courtiers and nobility: late 15th century–1542

Throughout Europe, the response to the Italian Renaissance included grafting on to existing cultures ideas which were bound up with issues of patriotism or nationhood. Manueline architecture in Portugal, for instance, used seafaring imagery, reflecting national accomplishments; in France, a 'French Order' was devised, and in Spain, use of the baluster was linked to ideas of nationhood.[39] In Scotland, high status architecture, royal and non-royal, remained – perhaps patriotically – castellated, despite application of imported ideas such as triumphal arches, balusters or roundels. Even churches were castellated; the chancel of Stirling's Holy Rude Kirk (1507), for example, had a crow-stepped gable set within crenellated parapets. Castellation may have been partly derived from old images of a 'nation at arms', of national antiquity and of neo-Arthurian and neo-crusader chivalry.[40]

The role of the royal master of works appears to have been developing during James V's time, a process which continued into the next century.[41] John Scrymgeour of Myres, for instance, witnessed a document guaranteeing completion of Midcalder Church (1540), implying a possible architectural role outwith the royal works, while Sir James Hamilton of Finnart is believed to have been both patron and designer of his own Craignethan (1530s), a 'fortified' palace of the type then and afterwards common in France, at for example Maules-en-Tonnerrois (1566).[42]

The several decades up to and including James IV's reign witnessed construction of a vast number of castellated, stone-built towers with severely plain exteriors, many with straightforward rectangular plans. Their ground floors were vaulted, with principal rooms above. Examples include Airth, rebuilt from 1488 for Robert Bruce. Others, such as Niddrie, built *c* 1500 for George, 4th Lord Seton, have an L-plan form, on the model, apparently, of David II's tower at Edinburgh. Typically, such buildings were harled, with ashlar highlights, though wealthier houses, such as Sauchie, were faced entirely in ashlar. But even these were vastly inferior to contemporary royal works.

LORDSHIP AND
ARCHITECTURE
IN MEDIEVAL
AND
RENAISSANCE
SCOTLAND

❧

1542–1603

After 1542, the dominance of the crown as patron was challenged. Spurred on by the projects of successive regents, a changing emphasis of patronage was already beginning which led after 1603 to the nobility again, as before 1424, sometimes overshadowing the crown. The post-Reformation trans-formation in requirements made of churches resulted in a far less ornate ecclesiastical architecture.

Mary's presence in Scotland as queen (1561–7) – when her principal work seems to have been at Edinburgh's palace, including the French or Italian-inspired rusticated 1566 doorway and associated straight stair – lay between two periods of governorship, or regencies. The 2nd Earl of Arran was governor between 1542 and 1554. He had already begun Cadzow *c.* 1530, completed during his governorship when he also undertook work on behalf of the state at Edinburgh Castle. He built a new house or palace for himself at Hamilton (1538), and another in the east at Kinneil. Kinneil's pre-existing tower (*c.* 1553) was given massive gunholes like those of Cadzow and Craignethan, and then a larger palace block adjoining (begun 1553), more horizontally-proportioned and with asymmetrically-placed jamb, in the new fashion.[43] The subsequent governorship of Mary of Guise (1554–60) witnessed military constructions (such as the French spur at Stirling) in response to the invasions, but Mary also built a house at Leith, of which only one James V-type roundel survives, dated 1560; she was also possibly, or at least partly, responsible for the ornamentation of the 'Queen Mary apartment' ceilings in Holyroodhouse.

In 1567, the infant James VI was crowned, and the Earl of Moray became regent until 1570. Better-known for civil war destruction – notably of the Hamilton properties in the west – than for building, the best-known work with which he is associated is his memorial in St Giles (reconstructed in the nineteenth century), possibly the prototype of the end-pilastered, flat-arched type. The Earl of Mar's regency followed, 1571–2. Mar probably added to the family seat at Alloa, and in Stirling, from the late 1560s, he built a town house, 'Mar's Wark', which bears 1570 and 1572 datestones. It was prominently placed overlooking the market square, beside the Holy Rude Kirk and on the route to the castle. Formulae from the castle and palace were reproduced here, such as the twin-towered entrance (popular elsewhere, as for example at Tolquhon, Aberdeenshire), used in the James IV manner and combined with an explicit triumphal arch. The style, characterised by shafts with mouldings, shows clear artistic links between this building, Carnasserie Castle, Argyll, and the Regent Morton gateway at Edinburgh Castle.

The 4th Earl of Morton succeeded Mar as regent from 1572 to 1578.

Figure 14.7
Mar's Wark, Stirling:
principal façade.
RCAHMS, ST/1078

Morton's substantial patronage was twofold. For the Crown, he reconstructed the eastern defences of Edinburgh Castle, shattered in the 1573 bombardment which ended the Marian War, built the portcullis, or Regent Morton gateway, ornamented with distinctive shafted detail, and the half-moon battery, partially enfolding the palace.[44] A new Holyrood gallery was also created for him, doubling the depth of the palace north quarter. On his own behalf, he added to Aberdour Castle, and built the massive, spine-walled Drochil Castle, conceivably taking advice from the royal master of works, Sir William MacDowall, whose involvement in the Crown works from Mary's time onwards is documented.

Houses of courtiers and nobility: 1542–1603

Following the Reformation, resources previously given the church helped to sponsor a vast building drive, not by the crown but by the nobility. Greater perhaps than that of the decades up to 1513, this was carried through especially after 1560 in a long period of (mostly) peace, modernisation, improvement and development of industries such as coal and salt. The *Black Book of Taymouth* provides informative documentation of the extensive patronage of one family, the Glenorchy Campbells, at Balloch (later Taymouth), Barcaldine, Finlarig and elsewhere, including the creation of parkland, and

LORDSHIP AND
ARCHITECTURE
IN MEDIEVAL
AND
RENAISSANCE
SCOTLAND

the commissioning of paintings, including a family tree by George Jamieson.[45] In the wake of the settlement in 1560 when foreign soldiers withdrew and peace was re-established, a new trend of house-building with more developed planning and in a distinctive 'neo-castellated' style was developing or begun (for example, Fordell, 1567), and this phase continued into the seventeenth century (for example, Huntly, 1602). These houses were, *typically*, asymmetrical and tower-like – albeit usually with a much increased ratio of length:depth – with castellation (but far less 'fortification' than Craignethan) in the form of bartizans, parapets, machicolations and gunholes. Their ground floors were vaulted, the main door and a scale-and-platt staircase typically contained in a vertically-emphatic, separately-roofed jamb (a subordinate though high wing at one end of the front of the body of the house, cf. French 'jambe', a leg), ascending to the 'piano nobile' above, leading immediately into the largest room. At the far end of this room, there would be a 'parpan', or cross-wall, with a near-square room beyond, a secondary stair at the axis providing main access to the floor(s) above. Scores of these houses were built throughout the country, from Kilmartin in the *Gaidhlig* west to Elcho in the lowland east. The primary differences between them were in terms of scale and of ornamental style rather than fundamentals of provision, the greater houses obviously possessing more than the minimum described above. The idea of a taller tower – a badge of high status – remaining the dominant compositional element is seen either by retention of an old tower in later work (for example, at Airth), or – more rarely – by intergrating a tower within a new composition, almost like a miniaturised version of the royal apartment in Linlithgow's east quarter. New building on such a scale was possible only for wealthier clients. The prototype was probably Cardinal Beaton's Melgund (1543–6), but more elaborate was Carnasserie, built for Bishop John Carsewell, Dean of the Chapel Royal. Both houses date from periods during which clerics could still challenge the nobility in terms of patronage, and the design of Carnassarie may have been a conscious reference to the pre-Reformation status of bishops. Other examples of clerical patronage in this period include Archbishop John Hamilton's 1550s reconstruction of St Andrews Castle, and the archbishops' summer palace in Monimail, mostly demolished except for a 1578 tower named after Cardinal Beaton (d. 1546).

Towards the close of the century came a new series of courtier/nobility-led innovations incorporating wider references to classicism. For instance, Crichton, reconstructed in 1581–91 for the earl of Bothwell, incorporated an Italianate piazza at ground level, and a diamond-faceted façade above in Mediterranean-inspired style. This courtyard front introduced a new formula, that of ashlar-faced symmetry in composition, the symmetrical logic of the façade extending into its planning, while a scale-and-platt staircase lit by paired intermediate-level windows interrupts façade rhythm at one end in a way that was to be repeated into the eighteenth century.

Façade and 'footprint' symmetry conditioned work at a group of houses including Newark (1597), but more massively at Fyvie (1596–9), rebuilt for Alexander Seton. Scone House, gifted in 1600 to Sir David Murray of Gospetrie (subsequently Lord Scone and Viscount Stormont) from the forfeited Gowrie lands, was likewise rebuilt. Like Fyvie, its main front had centre and end emphasis, created here by crowstep- gabled jambs. Unusually, it had only two storeys, its long façades fashioning a more horizontal emphasis, though small ground-floor openings were more familiar.

Crown patronage 1567–1603

James VI's cultural interests tended more towards literature, and perhaps music, rather than towards architecture. His court inherited a series of modern palaces, but before 1603 he built comparatively little, focusing his cultural energies on literature. However, his queen, Anne, required a suitable jointure house, and Dunfermline Palace was rebuilt in the 1590s for her by the master of works, William Schaw (d. 1602). Yet James shared the sense of regal status developed from the time of James I, even setting himself up as the Apollo of his 'Castalian Band' long before the greatest 'sun-king' of all, Louis XIV, though without what appears to us as the excessive formality associated with French or English monarchy. When in

Figure 14.8 Eyemouth Fort, Berwickshire: aerial view. RCAHMS, BW/3069

LORDSHIP AND
ARCHITECTURE
IN MEDIEVAL
AND
RENAISSANCE
SCOTLAND

ℛ

1594 a prince was born, it was already anticipated that he might rule a united 'Britain'. His baptism demanded a sensational Renaissance pageant, with the chapel royal in Stirling rebuilt for the event. Necessarily small by some European standards, partly for reasons of economy and speed of building, this chapel sought to impress less by its scale, more by its proportions, which were those of the Biblical Soloman's Temple, and by its classical sophistication – an almost secular-looking Florentine composition, with (subsequently, much-simplified) couple-columned triumphal-arch entrance.[46]

1603–60

Regnal union in 1603 was followed by James's quest for political union. Loss of a royal presence, of a resident and, more gradually, a distinctively Scottish court culture, and of straighforward royal patronage – James even having taken his master of works to England – created a cultural vacuum. This brought a new, enhanced role for the nobility, for municipal patrons, as well as for the increasingly prosperous merchant community (for example, the Primroses at Dalmeny) which was now joining the landed class.[47] The royal masters of work, however, were still in the vanguard of architectural innovation. Besides royal palaces, one of the most prestigious buildings of the age was Heriot's Hospital, begun 1628, and likely – as visual evidence strongly suggests – to have involved them, as was the case at Parliament House, begun 1632. Charles I's reign was effectively an absolute monarchy, which triggered a counter-movement to his autocratic promotion of episcopacy, leading to civil unrest and ultimately war; by which time the last highlight of this phase of royal patronage was past and the effectiveness of the mastership was in decline, following the death of Sir James Murray of Kilbaberton in 1634, and that of his partner, Sir Anthony Alexander, in 1637.

Besides Alexander Seton, the earls of Dunbar and Kinloss were James's foremost 'politicians' in the early post-union years, and each built houses which can be linked to James's ideas of regal unionism or 'Britishness'. After 1603, Edward Bruce, Lord Kinloss, became an English privy councillor, master of the rolls, and a naturalised Englishman.[48] Yet he invested in Scotland, building Culross Abbey House in 1608. Whatever the original conception – possibly a symmetrical quadrangle, like Fyvie, – its south quarter incorporated two show fronts; that to south was set above a garden terrace and with square end pavilions, strictly regular fenestration with different window detailing at either level, it was a remarkably classical composition. It conformed to the style James had required of his Chapel Royal (1594) and which he was to promote subsequently for his chosen image of new 'British' monarchy in England. Like Scone, it had two storeys and long, uniform façades, but was more horizontally-proportioned and with an unbroken façade creating an impression of more rigid uniformity. Its ground floor, unusually, was unvaulted and contained important rooms, while it had evidently a parapeted, probably flat, roof originally (possibly inspired by work of the Smythsons in England), and a spine wall topped by a rank of stacks – all features which would be reproduced in the royal works, notably Linlithgow's north quarter. At principal floor level, a full-length gallery had stone-panelling. The overall conception can be related to, for example, Courances (1606) in France, or, given its sloping site, to the much bigger Villa d'Este at Tivoli.

The earl of Dunbar – appointed English chancellor in 1603 – promoted construction of a permanent, stone-built bridge over the Tweed at Berwick, where the practical requirements of absentee rule simultaneously symbolised James's idea of union. His 'sumptuous and glorious palace', designed by the master of works, James Murray, was evidently colossal, its gallery alone reportedly of a scale without contemporary parallel on either side of Tweed.[49] It was symbolically placed within the militarily redundant Berwick Castle, on territory which had for centuries represented Scoto-English warfare and which was now a symbol of peace and of union. Like Culross, it was evidently flat-roofed and probably had square end pavilions, but it remained incomplete after Dunbar's death in 1611. Dunbar's monument in Dunbar Kirk introduced English artistic links, being designed by Maximilian Colt, sculptor at the English court, and possibly the first major instance of architectural patronage from England since James IV's time.

The patronage of the Setons stands apart as remarkable, especially that of Alexander Seton, Earl of Dunfermline and, latterly, chancellor. Seton, a godson of Queen Mary, was widely travelled and highly educated, having received a Catholic education in Rome and studied law in France. At court, outwardly conforming Catholics could make a career, and Seton gave loyal service to James. His Fyvie – conceived, probably, as a symmetrical corner-towered composition – adopted a massive castellated style of enormous vigour and self-proclamatory swagger, with a multi-turreted gate tower of almost James IV-like vitality. At St Bride's, Dalgety, he built a new family aisle *c.* 1610. Domestic in character, with skews, an 'L-plan' south front and a polygonal staircase, its stone-panelled interior represents an extraordinary lavishness. He had also, or built, a house at Dalgety – easily accessible from Pinkie – about which little is known.

This aisle at Delgaty heralded a massive change in Seton's architectural endeavours, seen in maturity at his suburban villa at Pinkie which was dated 1613, incorporating a pre-existing house. The garden front is flat and plain (the Scottish norm in the period), regular window bays ornamented

LORDSHIP AND
ARCHITECTURE
IN MEDIEVAL
AND
RENAISSANCE
SCOTLAND

⚘

originally only with string courses. Square bartizans of the type shortly thereafter used at Edinburgh are on the north gable, a big bay window suggestive of Danish or English influence is on the south gable opposite. Alterations to the courtyard front and the evident incompleteness of the composition means that, once again, Seton's original concept remains unclear. In sharp contrast to the swagger of Fyvie, Pinkie is the product of a new stage in his thinking, and perhaps also of a new age, its design bound up with anti-war images of a reticent stoic modesty and of peace. An inscription (now in the garden wall) emphasises the house's peace-loving dedication to Renaissance ideals of 'humanitas' and 'urbanitas'. It tells that Seton:

> … a man of high culture and urbanity, has laid out and ornamented this villa and gardens near the city, for his own pleasure and the pleasure of his noble descendants, and of everyone of culture and urbanity. This is no place of warfare, designed to repel enemies. Instead, there is a welcoming and kindly fountain of pure water, a grove, pools, and other amenities – everything that could afford decent pleasures of heart and spirit.

Some garden structures survive, including the elaborate well-head, and some piers with sophisticated Italianate Mannerist rustication. 'Near the city' ('suburbanus') in classical Latin meant close to, specifically, Rome;[50] and the parallel image of the two cities was to continue into the eighteenth century, with villas or houses aligned upon Edinburgh in the same way villas were aligned upon the dome of St Peter's. As already noted, George Buchanan had propogated the ideal of the 'rex stoicus',[51] while stoic imagery was central to the classical iconography of Seton's painted gallery. One reference from Horace (*Epist.* 1.10.41) praises the simplicity of country life, for which the town is left behind. Vigilance, for instance, was also represented, and besides suppression of his – technically, illegal – Catholicism, perhaps much of the imagery relates to what has been termed Seton's 'public self-fashioning'.[52] Seton was described in his epitaph as having, among many virtues and gifts, skill in architecture; furthermore, he had previously written William Schaw's epitaph, in which he described himself as Schaw's 'true-hearted friend'. He presumably exerted an influence upon court and courtier architecture, in possibly the same way as, later, Bruce, Mar and Clerk were to do as arbiters of taste, and Seton's patronage deserves much fuller study. The patronage of his successor as chancellor, the more business-orientated Hay of Kinfauns, has by contrast left much less behind.

By the 1610s, a new fashion was emerging, under the leadership of (later Sir) James Murray of Kilbaberton, who seems also to have been a friend of Seton. The palaces had mostly been overhauled for James's 1617 visit, that at Edinburgh Castle rebuilt in the flat-roofed fashion introduced at Culross. The Linlithgow north quarter was rebuilt from 1618 in an almost tenemental manner, but with the expected sophistications of royalty including classical chimneypieces (those in the gallery being remarkably classical for their date) and a gilded, painted façade with part-engaged stair-turret of the type used at Edinburgh, an idea possibly introduced by Schaw at Dunfermline (and also used, for example, in Frederik II's Kronborg, the exemplar being Francis I's at Blois).

Little can yet be said of the patronage of another of James's greatest politicians, Sir Thomas Hope ('Tam o the Cowgate' / 'Auld Melrose'), latterly Earl of Haddington. He appears to have owned Binning/Binnie House, of which only one Murray-type pediment survives re-set in the present house. The 1616 doorway salvaged from his house in the Cowgate is re-set within Edinburgh Public Library, showing by its detailing that it belonged to, or was influenced by, the Murray group of buildings. Tyninghame House appears to have been built for him.

Three important rural houses of this period are Kilbaberton, Pitreavie and Winton, all probably dating from the 1620s-early 1630s, and all evidently designed by Murray or by those in his circle – as can also be said of two contemporary town houses, Argyll Lodging, Stirling, and Moray House, Edinburgh.

Both Kilbaberton, now called Baberton, and Pitreavie were given a symmetrical U-plan with stair turrets in the internal angles, and perhaps both were intended to be regarded as suburban villas. Baberton, which

*Figure 14.9
Culross Abbey House,
Fife: general view.
RCAHMS, F/3316/3*

LORDSHIP AND
ARCHITECTURE
IN MEDIEVAL
AND
RENAISSANCE
SCOTLAND

❧

has 1622–3 datestones, was built for Murray and Dame Katherine Weir, then his spouse. Its east flank – and drawing room window – is aligned upon Edinburgh Castle in the manner discussed above. Pitreavie was built for Schaw's successor as chamberlain to Queen Anne, Sir Henry Wardlaw, another courtier friend of Murray, and a colleague in the royal works. His house was an enlarged version of Kilbaberton, and was, externally, even plainer. Its curvilinear south wall-head gable, a flattened, two-dimensional version of contemporary domes (such as those at Edinburgh Castle palace) was possibly the prototype of what was by the century's end a very popular detail. One of Wardlaw's daughters married Sir Anthony Alexander, who, 'by his learning and travellis abroad haveing acquired skill in architectorie' was in 1628 conjoined with Murray in the mastership.[53] On the other hand, the sculpted panel set in Wardlaw's family aisle at Dunfermline Abbey (acquired from Queen Anne) betrays no suggestion of involvement by the masters of works.

The client at Winton, 8th Lord Seton and 3rd Earl of Winton (a nephew of Chancellor Seton), was a thrusting businessman, promoter of the coal and salt industries, and builder of a harbour at Port Seton. Despite compelling artistic similarities between it and the other two houses in this group, it is by contrast wilfully asymmetrical, richly-ornamented outside and in, and castellated. The elaborate hall overmantel containing the 'British' royal arms and other unionist/loyalist symbolism represents a formula popular in other houses built or remodelled in this period, such as Craigievar.

Artistically, Moray House also relates to this group. It was built for the dowager Countess of Home in *c*. 1625. It was at first small with a narrow gable to the street (a pre-existing east wing may have been retained for bedrooms), a two-room, richly-decorated apartment, with a stone-bracketted balcony in each gable, and alongside a gateway with spiked finials. Once-elaborate gardens still contain a decorative gateway and a summer-house. Acheson House nearby sports a screen-wall to the street and a gateway of 1633, the year of Charles I's visit, for which event the Argyll Lodging in Stirling was also rebuilt. The Lodging lies on the route up to the castle, and the patron was another English-based Scot, Sir William Alexander, one-time poet at James's court, and by then Charles I's secretary for Scotland. Best-known for the Nova Scotia scheme and as one-time owner of Manhattan Island, Alexander was father of the junior master of works, who evidently (and presumably with Murray) designed the work, as its porch replicates the design of Murray's Kilbaberton doorcase, while features of the royal works such as the Linlithgow gallery chimneypieces were reproduced here in variant form. There was even a terraced garden, in the manner of contemporary rural houses, while the

Figure 14.10
Barcaldine Castle,
Argyll: general view.
RCAHMS, AG/3749

unvaulted ground-floor hall looked back to Culross, and forward to a new generation which began with Panmure.

King Charles's visit in 1633 prompted the reconstruction by the masters of works of Holyrood Abbey Kirk for his coronation, and of the palace alongside. Surviving work from this time includes the great east window, as well as the reconstruction of the west façade, which was given new windows with cusp-ornamented tops, possibly a reference to Stirling Palace and to royal lineage. The north-west steeple was modified and topped with a (now-gone) distinctive cupola, of a pattern subsequently popular on civic architecture. Lesser works elsewhere made for the visit included the repainting of the Stirling Chapel Royal by Valentine Jenkin. Payments for the royal works were made both by the treasury and the comptrollery. Under Sir Gideon Murray, treasurer-depute, over £100,000 was spent on the royal houses for James VI's visit of 1617 when a rich chapel, partly prefabricated in the English royal workshops, was installed at Holy-rood.[54] Sometimes other sources were used, and debts incurred, as in 1631–3 when the masters of work used personal funds to maintain building works. At his death, Murray was still owed a fortune by the Crown.

Figure 14.11
Argyll Lodging,
Stirling: general view
RCAHMS, ST/1018

Private or family investment in pre-Reformation chapels (for example, at Melrose) or religious buildings had their counterparts after 1560 in the form of family aisles. The Dunfermline aisle has already been noted. Other sophisticated examples include the Archerfield aisle at Dirleton (1664), where revived Gothic tracery is set within an otherwise classical structure. At St Mary's, Haddington, the sacristy became the Maitland/Lauderdale family aisle, where the monument to the 1st Earl and his spouse was installed *c.* 1638, probably again an English work. In the decades around 1600 burial monuments often had horizontally proportioned tomb recesses with paired pilasters, while by the 1620s a more upright aedicular formula was favoured, with Murray-style examples at Greyfriars, Edinburgh, involving the King's master mason, Willam Wallace, and another mason, William Ayton. Ayton's monument commemorates George Foulis of Ravelstoun, whose house had ornamental work of the same type.

Regarding churches, the town council of Burntisland commissioned in *c.* 1589 a remarkable centralised plan-type of a form soon to be popularised in the Protestant Netherlands, from where in turn came the inspiration for Edinburgh town council's Tron Kirk of 1636, contracted for by John Mylne. At Terregles, by contrast, a pre-Reformation Gothic informed the design of the semi-polygonal-ended 1573 aisle or 'queir', whose traditionalist design might represent the Catholicism of the patron, Agnes, Lady Herries. More typically, a straightforward centralised form of planning was adopted, within either a rectangular two- or three-winged, or, more rarely, a cruciform plan, as at Fenwick, 1644. Openings were typically flat-lintelled, as at, for example, in the original work at Weem (1602), or more rarely round-arched, that is, not Gothic.

But Gothic also survived as a secondary design option, often within more provincial work, until it was explicitly reinvigorated for iconographic reasons. Here, the key building is Dairsie, Fife. Built as a follow-up to the ecclesiastical innovations known as the Five Articles of Perth in 1618, its 1621 datestone coincides with the year in which the Articles were ratified by parliament. The innovations were James's, and were advocated on his behalf by Archbishop Spottiswoode. Dairsie was Spottiswoode's own model church, built beside his own house and intended as an exemplar for episcopal worship. It was given an emphatically antique-looking form of Gothic tracery. Windows in subsequent prestige works including Heriot's chapel (1628-) and Murray and Alexander's 1633 window at Holyrood, reconstructed at King Charles' instruction, similarly employed Gothic.

Patronage abroad

While the emphasis of this study is upon Scotland, there was also Scottish architectural patronage abroad, especially from the sixteenth century onwards, when vast numbers of Scots travelled or settled elsewhere. Perhaps the best known of these are the buildings of early seventeenth-century settlers in 'Plantation' Ulster, such as Bishop Knox's various works at Raphoe. Other colonial developments included the plans, albeit only partially followed through, for Nova Scotia, following Sir William Alexander's project, while the Scottish highlands and islands were viewed as an internal colony, with the creation of Stornoway following soon after the 'Fife Adventurers' first enterprise of 1597, and Campbeltown resulting from a similarly commercial project begun by the 7th Earl of Argyll after 1609. Scots were also numerous throughout much of northern Europe. In Denmark, for instance, David Hansen was responsible for the 1579 Renaissance façade of 72, 74 Stengade, Elsinore, while in France Sir John Stuart of Darnley, one of the victors at Baugé, was given the château of La Verrerie by Charles VII, to which the family – which long afterwards kept close contact with Scotland – added.[55] Above all, until the age of the British Empire, Scots patronage in England (Dunbar's Berwick house has been

LORDSHIP AND
ARCHITECTURE
IN MEDIEVAL
AND
RENAISSANCE
SCOTLAND

褝

noted above) became more commonplace after 1707, and examples are included in Colen Campbell and others' three-volume *Vitrivius Britannicus* (1715–25).

POSTSCRIPT: 1660–1715

A greater number of surviving buildings and associated documents permits wider discussion of patronage within this period. The aristocratic classical country house emerged at last from the role it had been developing since the 1560s, as the dominant building type. Stoicism was left behind and the client was now more likely to be a virtuoso, albeit still an aristocrat steeped in classical learning, and, for the last time until Balmoral in the nineteenth century, the Crown re-emerged briefly in the 1670s and 1680s as an important patron.

In this necessarily brief account, attention is focused on the patronage of only one aristocratic family, the Queensberrys, and on the houses of two premier architects, Sir William Bruce's Kinross and Mr James Smith's Whitehill. Both houses represent something of an architectural ideal, and thus help to extend the social and architectural coverage, embracing the 'reforming' of ancient houses (a standard approach of the third quarter of the century), as well as construction of the new, an option promoted in Bruce's and, later, Smith's work, as characterised by houses such as Yester and Hopetoun. How far there was overlap between political align-ment and building patronage has yet to be researched, but current evidence suggests that, like William Schaw a century earlier, Smith's Catholicism presented few problems until 1689, while Bruce's Episcopalianism became more a political than a patronage issue. Another area awaiting exploration within this period is the patronage of aristocratic women, who were highly influential in works carried out in the names of Lauderdale and Rothes, and dominant at Kinneil, Hamilton Palace and Dalkeith, all 'reformed' houses.

The restoration of Crown rule came in 1660. John Mylne was first established as the premier builder of country houses, and soon he was operating with Bruce (1645–1710), who, as an aristocrat and politician turned amateur architect, was to emerge as the most fashionable arbiter of taste, a role seemingly in abeyance since Murray and Alexander's time. Mylne was patronised by the earl of Panmure at Panmure House, and more significantly, for the earl of Rothes at Leslie and Balgonie, with Bruce involved in possibly all three projects.

Within this period crucial changes were under way. As the Atlantic trade developed, the financial supremacy of the east was, correspondingly, challenged. With her tolbooth (begun 1626) and college (1632–1660s), not only did Glasgow come to possess the two tallest secular steeples in the country, but also the most architecturally up-to-date college. Her acquisition of land at Newark (Port Glasgow) in 1668 provided a springboard to vast wealth in the years ahead. Correspondingly, the merchant community in the west found readier access to landownership. Daniel Campbell of Shawfield was one who underwent the transition from merchant to landed aristocrat. His enlightened patronage is exemplified by his Glasgow town house alone, a classical pedimented composition designed by a kinsman, Colen Campbell. His country seat at Woodhall (undated, possibly by Campbell or Smith) seems to have been no less sophisticated, employing studied references from Roman Renaissance palaces.

Bruce was appointed royal architect for the reconstruction of Holyrood, with Robert Mylne as king's master mason. This was Charles II's only significant instance of Scottish architectural patronage, and the idea of recreating the palace was a logical statement of restored royal power, as well as of a lineal antiquity traced through Scotland. At the rebuilt palace all old work was concealed, except for the James V tower, the most prominent element of the old palace, which was instead highlighted in the new design both by its relationship to lower ranges as well as by being duplicated. Messages of lineal antiquity were continued inside, with specially commissioned portraits of the entire line of kings, and a depiction of Scota. For James VI's Holyrood chapel reconstruction of 1617 and James VII's chapel, craftsmen were sent from the royal works in England.

The second instance of royal patronage in this period was James Smith's 1688 reconstruction of Holyrood Abbey Kirk as James VII's chapel royal, complete with a Baroque interior including aedicular classical benches and a throne. A new church, the Canongate Kirk, was also built nearby, incorporating references from Italy and the Netherlands in its design, and a plan designed for Episcopal, or counter-Reformation, worship, although never used for such, being completed at the point when Presbyterianism finally came into the ascendancy as the established church.

Besides his work for the Crown, Bruce produced designs primarily for himself and his fellow-aristocrats, and for municipal projects, including Edinburgh Exchange and Stirling Tolbooth. His own houses, firstly, Balcaskie and, secondly, Kinross (1686) were innovative; the former established a common formula for creating through duplication a symmetrical house from an L-plan front, a principle also used at Holyrood.

Bruce's most prestigious non-royal patron was the virtual 'viceroy' of Scotland, King Charles II's secretary, John Maitland of Thirlestane, Duke of Lauderdale, whose patronage has been researched elsewhere.[56] Another high status source of patronage was the Queensberry family who proved themselves to be agile, occasionally chameleon-like, politicians. The mid-century

LORDSHIP AND
ARCHITECTURE
IN MEDIEVAL
AND
RENAISSANCE
SCOTLAND

❧

English wars had almost ruined them. Largely through the influence of Lord Chancellor Rothes, noted above in connection with Bruce at Leslie, William, 3rd Earl, who inherited in 1671, was appointed Lord Justice General in 1680. He was created marquis and was appointed Lord High Treasurer in 1682, and then created Duke of Queensberry in 1684. Apparently an Episcopalian, he fitted in well with the policies of both Charles II and James VII, having opposed the Covenanters. Yet, following the departure of James, he served in the new administration.

Queensberry had promoted Smith's career, and in 1683 secured for him the premier architectural post, that of surveyor or overseer of the royal works. He had also patronised Smith, at Queensberry House, extending the duke's recently-bought huge town house in fashionable Canongate, near Holyrood. More spectacular still is Drumlanrig, which was massively rebuilt 1675–90s and, together with the earl of Strathmore's rebuilt Glamis, represents Scotland's most spectacular example of castellar Baroque. The old and – by the seventeenth century – widely popular idea of adorning steeples with crown spires had been used at the Holyrood entrance front and was exemplified elsewhere in Denmark and France. At Drumlanrig, whose formula owed much to Holyrood, as well as to Heriot's and Fyvie, a ducal coronet was placed in a corresponding position.

Smith was responsible for ongoing works at or near Drumlanrig, including the gardens. The 1st Duke died in 1695, shortly after contracting with Smith for a new burial aisle at Durisdeer. The project stalled, and in 1707 a second contract was signed with the 2nd Duke (d. 1711), one of the most influential politicians of the age. He was, as one political opponent put it, 'the first Scotsman that deserted over to the Prince of Orange',[57] and his key role in the union treaty brought him the English dukedom of Dover. At Durisdeer, his completed aisle was given Scotland's earliest post-Reformation baldacchino, a version of that at St Peter's in Rome, while his Gothic-traceried window which comprised '*Nyn hearts great and small*', proclaimed lineal antiquity.[58] A second, sculptural marble, by Jan Van Nost, was thereafter installed within the aisle as his own memorial.

The 3rd Duke (b. 1698) succeeded as a minor, but his curators continued investment in the estate, both in revenue-earning improvements and in embellishments, redesigning the gardens at Drumlanrig, and creating in 1714 a new town at Thornhill. A new church at Durisdeer, begun 1716, was also part of this programme. Largely stylistic evidence suggests that Smith was again employed, and the result is one of Scotland's most extraordinary church designs of the age, with an enormous ducal wing wrapped round the steeple. The suggestion is, though evidence is scanty, that despite a mixture of sometimes diametrically-opposing political

*Figure 14.12
Dunbar Monument,
Dunbar Parish
Church, East Lothian.
RCAHMS,
D 46554/CN*

320

LORDSHIP AND
ARCHITECTURE
IN MEDIEVAL
AND
RENAISSANCE
SCOTLAND

🙰

loyalties, including Smith's Catholicism, an attachment to the architect who had served three generations of the family so well remained unaffected. Only after Smith's death in 1731, and that of his partner, Alexander MacGill in 1734, did the Queensberry family eventually turn to William Adam (as at Sanquhar town-house, 1735).

Kinross, where he had a completely free hand in his carefully crafted synthesis of planning, architecture and landscape, represents Bruce's ideal. It was intended to be a new seat representative of his status, but his declining fortunes resulted in slow progress, with the apartment of state remaining incomplete. While the house was a classical design, the site had historical resonances which he exploited, by focusing the entire composition upon the castle in which Queen Mary had been detained. The dramatic story of Mary's escape from Lochleven Castle, combined with her status as the 'Martyr Queen' or (until James VII in Bruce's own time) the last Catholic monarch, suggests the possibility of Bruce combining interests in what came to be called 'Romanticism' with those of national history. Whether there was any latent Roman Catholic image seems unlikely, but Bruce had validated the use of the classical co-existing with or complementing the national 'antique'.

Kinross was the most decisive visual development of the compact, yet monumental house, and exemplified the ashlar-faced classicism of country house architecture that followed. English houses such as Coleshill (c. 1650) informed elements of the plan, but for the exterior, Bruce created an image of monumental, almost palazzo-like grandeur, with comparatively small and widely-spaced openings, the relatively unadorned exterior contrasting with what was intended to become a lavish interior.[59]

Unlike Bruce, Smith's background was non-aristocratic. His father was a mason. But Smith had benefited from a liberal education at home and abroad, and from extensive foreign travel. Following the precedent set by Murray, Smith had been appointed to the premier government role whilst having a background as an operative. He had studied in Rome, almost becoming a priest, and maintained a reputation as an intellectual. Also like Murray before him, and William Adam after, he had business interests which assisted his acquisition of a small estate, and in 1686 he acquired Whitehill, near Musselburgh. In those years his involvement at several major projects, besides his crown salary, made him wealthy, and his country house was a badge of new-found status. Whitehill was the prototype of Smith's compact, shallow-plan classical formula, with unadorned elevations and pedimented centrepieces, and a suite of rooms fitted ingeniously in a spiral plan. It was given identical opposing elevations, but a dropped level on the garden front enabled him to create, as at Drumlanrig, a double staircase, covering a summer-house. Smith was representative of the still-emerging class of educated specialist professionals who were now joining the successful merchant class as new landowners and architectural patrons. Similarly, Robert Mylne, king's master mason and Smith's father-in-law, acquired Balfarg in Fife, and had a villa at Inveresk. However, business failures lost Smith Whitehill. The new owners were the Williamite Dalrymples, brother of the master of Stair who carried forward the king's wishes at Glencoe, and who re-named the house Newhailes, and added to it the wings seen to-day. Like the great aristocrat houses, and Bruce's Kinross, Newhailes was influential in its own way, Shawfield Mansion in Glasgow being but one derivative. The spiral-plan was long popular, though by the mid-eighteenth-century paired, equal-sized and shared-aspect public rooms, symmetrically placed on plan had become the norm. But perhaps longest-lasting was its formula of a basically flat, uniform façade with advanced, pedimented centrepiece, typically three bays on a five-bay front, the basis of countless designs into the nineteenth century.

An apparently new category of investor in architecture emerged in this period, the speculative builder, whose activities went hand in hand with a new class of urban domestic residence, that is, the monumental stone-built tenement.[60] In Edinburgh and Leith the formula was worked through principally by three figures: Robert Mylne, James Smith, and, probably firstly, Thomas Robertson (d. 1686). Robertson's works in this area began in 1671, and he was responsible 'for all the statelie buildings ... on both sides of the Kirkheugh, the Exchange and the whole Parliament Closs except the Treasury House ...', which were destroyed by fire in 1700.[61] Robertson, a town councillor, was a brewer and merchant whose interests led him into speculative building. He was associated with James Smith, for example on the Exchange project, but while Smith too was involved in speculative tenement building (at, for example, Smith's Land, or Paisley's Close), Mylne's role was perhaps more significant. His first project was on land reclaimed by him at Leith, where he built Mylne's Land. Thereafter, major projects were Mylne's Square and Mylne's Court (1690), faced to the street in dressed ashlar, and built as quarters around an open square, a distinctively Scottish arrangement, subsequently developed as the pattern in all the cities, as was the role of the speculative builder.

On 13 September 1715, John Erskine, Earl of Mar, politician and gentleman architect, led an army in open battle against the infant British state which – ironically – he had helped to build, though he had failed to shape. The failure of this uprising led to Mar's flight into exile. Bruce had died five years earlier, his fellow Episcopalian Alexander Edward in 1708, and since 1689 the Roman Catholic James Smith was progressively losing state support until he was eventually sacked from his government post in 1719. The

LORDSHIP AND
ARCHITECTURE
IN MEDIEVAL
AND
RENAISSANCE
SCOTLAND

status of the old generation of architects ended with the courts they had served. The way thus opened for a new chapter in architectural patronage, with a vacancy for a Presbyterian, pro-union and pro-Hanoverian Whig to serve the newly British aristocracy of Scotland. This is the point at which the story of William Adam and Mar's successor as the new 'Maecenas', Sir John Clerk of Penicuik, takes over.

୬६

NOTES

Except where otherwise stated, descriptions of buildings referred to in this chapter will be found in M. Glendinning, R MacInnes and A. MacKechnie, *A History of Scottish Architecture* (Edinburgh, 1996), R. Fawcett, *Scottish Architecture from the Accession of the Stewarts to the Reformation 1371–1560* (Edinburgh, 1994) and D. Howard, *Scottish Architecture: Reformation to Restoration 1560–1660* (Edinburgh, 1995).

1. *RPC*, ii, 12–13.
2. C. Rogers, *The Earl of Stirling's Register of Royal Letters relative to the affairs of Scotland and Nova Scotia* (Edinburgh, 1885, Abbotsford Club), ii, 707.
3. *RMS*, ii, no. 1, discussed by W. M. Mackenzie, *The Medieval Castle in Scotland* (Edinburgh, 1927), 182, 223–4, and cited by S. Cruden, *The Scottish Castle* (Edinburgh, 3rd edition, 1981), 141.
4. I. Campbell, 'A Romanesque revival and the early Renaissance in Scotland c. 1380–1513', *Journal of the Society of Architectural Historians*, 54/3 (September 1995), 314; M. Brown, *James I* (Edinburgh, 1994), 114.
5. Campbell, 'Romanesque revival', 319.
6. N. Macdougall, *James IV* (Edinburgh, 1989), 276. Perhaps even the battle could be regarded as almost neo-chivalric, for according to one account, James instructed his gunners not to fire (see discussion in *ER*, xiii, clxxiv).
7. N. Macdougall, *James III, A Political Study* (Edinburgh, 1982), 98.
8. Boece, *Vitae*, 95.
9. I. Campbell, 'James IV and Edinburgh's First Triumphal Arches', in *Architecture of Scottish Cities: Essays in honour of David Walker*, ed. D. Mays (East Linton, 1997), 26–33.
10. Brown, *James I*, 114, 116.
11. J. Gifford, *Buildings of Scotland: Fife* (Harmondsworth, 1988), 295.
12. C. J. Tabraham, *Threave Castle* (Edinburgh, 1993), 8; C. McWilliam, *Buildings of Scotland: Lothian* (Harmondsworth, 1978), 118.
13. A recent study identifies an effigy at Arbroath as that of William the Lion (see G. S. Gimson, 'Lion hunt: a royal tomb-effigy at Arbroath Abbey', in *PSAS*, cxxv (1995), 901–16).
14. I. Campbell, 'Linlithgow's "Princely Palace"', *Architectural Heritage* (Edinburgh, 1995), v, 2.
15. The Adornes journals are being researched by Ian Campbell.
16. N. Macdougall, ' "It is I, the Erle of Mar": In search of Thomas Cochrane', in *People and Power in Scotland: Essays in honour of T. C. Smout*, eds., R. Mason and N. Macdougall (Edinburgh, 1992), 28–49.
17. T. Riis, *Should Auld Acquaintance be Forgot ...: Scottish-Danish relations c. 1450–1707* (Odense, 1988), i, 257–62; *James IV Letters*, lxii; *TA*, ii, 94.
18. *TA*, ii, 271.
19. *James IV Letters*, 97.
20. J. G. Dunbar, *Scottish Royal Palaces* (East Linton, 1999).

21. *TA*, ii, 448, 461; *ER*, xiv, cxlix. Sir Andrew Wood, one of James IV's famous naval commanders, is said to have built an ornamental canal at Largo, to convey himself from house to church.
22. *TA*, ii, 344; iv, 100.
23. Ibid., iv, 44.
24. Ibid., iv, 275. The idea was used elsewhere, and perhaps derived ultimately and symbolically from the she-wolf kept at Rome, which had reared Romulus and Remus.
25. Elements of James's character seem mirrored in that of another great architectural patron of the age, France's Francis I, of whom it was said in an epitaph (1547) that he 'applied all his spirit ... to the liberal arts and sciences, wishing to acquire knowledge of the nature and properties of many things' (see *European Monarchy*, eds. H. Duchhardt, et al. (Stuttgart, 1992), 134–5).
26. *TA*, ii, 140,289.
27. Fawcett, *Scottish Architecture 1371–1560*, 289.
28. *James IV Letters*, 294.
29. *TA*, iv, 280; ii, 449; W. Maitland, *The History of Edinburgh* (Edinburgh, 1753), 500.
30. *James IV Letters*, 294.
31. *TA*, v, 41, 78, 96. 'Rownd' = roundel, a coin-like motif favoured in antique Roman and Renaissance architecture.
32. Ibid., v, . 26.
33. *James V Letters*, 143, 172–3.
34. Ibid., 325; 340–1.
35. *Accounts of the Masters of Works for Building and Repairing Royal Palaces and Castles*, i, 1529–1615, ed. H. M. Paton and others (Edinburgh, 1957), 191.
36. Fawcett, *Scottish Architecture 1371–1560*, 290; *TA*, v, 23.
37. *TA*, v, 17.
38. *European Monarchy*, eds. Duchhardt et al, 135; R Mason, '*Rex Stoicus*: George Buchanan, James VI and the Scottish Polity', in *New perspectives on the Politics and Culture of Early Modern Scotland*, eds. J. A. Dwyer, R. A. Mason and A. Murdoch (Edinburgh, 1982), 9–33.
39. H-W. Kruft, *A History of Architectural Theory* (Princeton, 1994), 219–20.
40. Ideas of military accomplishment are reflected in, for example, the lion as the royal symbol, the national motto, and the choice of the thistle as national emblem, which in coronation ceremonies would contrast with the surrounding finery.
41. *Reign of James VI*, eds., J. Goodare, M. Lynch (East Linton, 2000). The term 'master/maister' ('magister') was used elsewhere in the period for perhaps a comparable role (see, for instance, R. Ivancevic, *Art Treasures of Croatia* (1993), 112.
42. Ideas of castellation being linked to status were to persist, for example, in France, notably at Vaux-le-Vicomte with its wet moat of 1652. The moat idea used at Leslie, Aberdeenshire, presumably forms part of the new building of 1661.
43. Dates are taken from Historic Scotland's most recent leaflet, *Kinneil House* (Edinburgh, 1983).
44. This arrangement of a palace set above a curved fortification is reminiscent of Castel St Angelo in Rome.
45. *Taymouth Bk.*
46. Though palace chapels, for example, Sainte Chapelle, Kronborg and Frederiksborg, were, typically, comparatively small.
47. For municipal architecture see RCAHMS, *Tolbooths and Town Houses: civic architecture in Scotland to 1833* (Edinburgh, 1996). The merchants, particularly the wealthiest 310 'elite' in and around Edinburgh, were by the early-mid seventeenth

LORDSHIP AND
ARCHITECTURE
IN MEDIEVAL
AND
RENAISSANCE
SCOTLAND

࿐

century the linchpin of the national economy. The master of works, Sir James
Murray, was included in their number, but probably the wealthiest was his
friend, Sir William Dick of Braid, who was later to personally finance the
Covenanters. Nothing of Dick's Braid survives, but his Edinburgh town house of
c. 1630, now 'Adam Bothwell's House', partly survives. It has a narrow plan and
a three-sided north gable, evidently built for the purpose of enjoying the view.
Like Pinkie, pedimented dormer heads bear classical quotations, in this case from
Horace and Ovid.

48. *Accounts of the Masters of Works for Building and Repairing Royal Palaces and
Castles*, ii, 1616–1649, eds. J. Imrie and J. G. Dunbar (Edinburgh, 1982), lxviii.
49. Ibid., lxix.
50. M. Bath, 'Alexander Seton's Painted Gallery', in *Albion's Classicism : the Visual
Arts in Britain 1550–1660*, ed. L. Ghent (New Haven and London, 1995), 103.
51. Ibid., 98.
52. Ibid., 96.
53. *Accounts of the Masters of Works*, ii, lix.
54. Ibid., ii, xxxviii–xxxix.
55. Riis, *Scottish-Danish relations*, I, 171; *Architectures en Région Centre: Val de Loire,
Beauce, Sologne, Berry, Touraine*, eds. A. Blanc and J-M. Pérouse de Montclos
(Orléans, 1988), 661–2.
56. J. G. Dunbar, 'The building activities of the Duke and Duchess of Lauderdale',
Archaeological Journal, cxxxii (1975).
57. *Dictionary of National Biography*, eds. L. Stephen and S. Lee (London, 1885–1904
and later editions), v, 1229.
58. A. MacKechnie, 'Durisdeer Church', *PSAS*, cxv (1985), 429–442.
59. Bruce's (influential) idea of a suppressed attic storey, possibly derived from Italian
models, has north European parallels, such as Skokloster, in Sweden, 1654–76
(see *Castles around the Baltic* T. Kjaergaard, ed. (Malbork, 1994), 29).
60. Though the existence in 1635 of a 'Master of Works Close' in Edinburgh raises
the possibility of the business-focused Murray having set a precedent (see *The
Book of the Old Edinburgh Club*, xiii (1924), 135.
61. *The Book of the Old Edinburgh Club*, xxiv (1942), 151. Robertson's headstone at
Greyfriars is of the Mylne family type, by Robert Mylne, and also dates from
1674.

INDEX
of PERSONS and PLACES

Abbey St Bathans, 237

Abercorn Castle, 160, 170, 174, 181, 182, 184, 185

Aberdeen, Aberdeenshire, 80, 177, 178, 229, 250, 251, 252, 257, 259, 260, 262, 264, 269, 292, 296, 301

Aberdour, 292, 307

Aberdour (New), 71, 73

Abergeldie Castle, 268

Abertarff, 74

Achadun Castle, 84, 88, 90, 100

Achilty, 274, 279

Adam, John, 264

Adam, William, 268, 321, 322, 324

Aden, 60, 72

Adornes, Anselm, 299, 324

Aglionby, Edward, 231

Aignish Church, 96, 102

Aird, 273, 283

Airth, 292, 302, 305, 308

Albany, duke of, regent, 131, 132, 144, 145, 152, 153, 168, 169, 170, 171, 211, 212, 302
James, son of, 132
Finlay, son of, 152, 153
Marjory, daughter of, 131

Albany, Finlay de, bishop of Argyll, 132, 133, 145

Alexander I, king of Scots, 205

Alexander II, king of Scots, 4, 63, 74, 85, 87, 89, 90, 206

Alexander III, king of Scots, 35, 37, 67, 71, 73, 75, 79, 80, 81, 189, 207, 208

Alexander, Anthony, 293, 310, 314

Alexander, William, 314, 317

Allangrange, 277

Alloa, 292, 306

Altani, Anthony, bishop of Urbino, 137

Anecol, 38

Angus, 28, 259, 260

Angus, earl of, 161, 169, 172, 174, 175, 185, 214, 223, 224, 304

Annan, Annandale, 44, 45, 48, 49, 50, 51, 52, 53, 54, 55, 56, 57, 58, 168, 169, 170, 172, 176, 204, 207, 211, 215, 218, 221, 222, 223, 226, 227, 229

Anne, queen, 314

Antrim, 104

Appin, 149

Appin of Dull, 127

Applecross, 277, 287

Applegarth, 44, 46, 51

Arbroath Abbey, xxii, 11, 12, 15, 16, 17, 21

Arbroath, Declaration of, 190

Archerfield, 316

Ard, Alexander de, 192

Ardchattan Priory, 84, 87, 92, 104

Ardgowan, 144, 157, 158

Ardmaddy, 89

Ardmannoch, 278

Ardnamurchan, 91, 95, 104, 115

Ardtornish Castle, 84, 103, 104, 105, 113, 114, 117, 118, 119

'Argadus', 143

Argyll, 28, 80, 85, 87, 90, 91, 92, 93, 123, 124, 127, 128, 129, 130, 131, 132, 133, 134, 135, 136, 137, 138, 139, 141, 142, 143, 144, 145, 147, 148, 149, 317

Arisaig, 95

Arkinholm, battle of, 185, 211

Aros Castle, 84, 90, 91, 96, 101, 103, 107, 113, 114, 115, 117, 118, 119, 120, 121

Arran, 100, 104, 106, 124, 125, 126, 136, 150

LORDSHIP AND
ARCHITECTURE
IN MEDIEVAL
AND
RENAISSANCE
SCOTLAND

Arran, earl of, regent, 124, 130, 184, 214,
    217, 218, 223, 241, 306
Artafallie, 279
'Aschebi', 57
Assynt, 278
Atholl, 63, 74, 77, 78
Atholl, John, earl of, 279
Auchen Castle, 44, 52, 54, 207
Auchindoun, 299
Auchinleck, chronicle, 19, 155, 175, 181, 184
Auchlunachan, 285
Augustinian, order, 86, 87
Auldearn, 3, 282
Auldton, 44, 46, 50, 51
Avandale, earl of, 175, 176
Avenel, Robert, 45
Avoch, 288
Awe, Loch, Lochawe, 85, 88, 89, 93, 94,
    105, 117 123, 124, 128, 129, 130, 131, 132,
    134, 136, 137, 138, 143, 145, 150, 151, 152,
    153, 154, 156, 157
Ayr, Ayrshire, 144, 147, 152, 155, 159, 302,
    304
Ayton, 231, 232, 233, 238, 244, 245, 247
Ayton, William, 316

Baberton, 313
Badenoch, 2, 3, 61–81 passim, 93
Balliol, family, 64, 79, 81, 208, 209, 210
    Edward, 124, 150, 184, 210
    John, 208
Balcaskie, 292, 319
Balfarg, 323
Balgonie, 292, 318
Balloch, 292, 307
Ballone Castle, 274, 285, 288
Ballygrant, Loch, 109
Balmerino Abbey, 14
Balmoral, 318
Balnagown Castle, 280
Balquhain, 277
Balquhidder, 26, 32
    Duncan of, 32
    James, parson of, 32
Balvenie Castle, 60, 64, 65, 66, 74, 79, 80,
    160, 170, 171, 174, 175, 176, 178, 185
Banff, Banffshire, 63, 64, 65, 74, 80, 170,
    178, 252
Bannockburn, battle of, 190
Barbour, John, 93, 128, 150

Barcaldine Castle, 292, 307, 315
Barclay, family, of Towie, 259
Barnes, 281
Barra, 103, 107, 111, 116
Basle, Council of, 177
Bass, The, 172
Bassendean, 234, 247
Baugé, battle of, 317
Baxter, John, 155, 264
Bayeux Tapestry, 45
Beaton, Cardinal David, 8, 10, 308
Beauly, Beauly Priory, 14, 87, 273, 274,
    276, 287
Beaumont, Robert III de, 4
Beaumont, Roger de, bishop of St
    Andrews, 4, 5
Bedfordshire, 65
Bedrule, 60, 62, 63, 66, 67, 69, 78, 80
Beldorney Castle, 250, 257, 266, 269
Belhelvie, 64
Bell family, 252, 260, 262, 268, 272
    George, 268
    John, 252, 272
Bellenden, Sir Thomas, 218
Bellitaw, 247
Bemersyde, 247
Benbecula, 114
Benderloch, 124, 150
Benedict of Peterborough, 48
Benedictine, order, 86, 87
Bergen, 202
Berkshire, 65
Berwick-upon-Tweed, 195, 238, 311, 317
Berwickshire, 138, 170, 231, 235, 236, 243, 248
Bethoc, daughter of Donald III Ban, 62
Bethoc, prioress of Iona, 86, 87
'Biarnaborg', 90
Biggar, 176
Binning/Binnie House, 313
Birgham, 236
Birse Castle, 250, 253, 268
Bisset, family, 75, 273
Black Douglases, 161–87 passim
Black Isle, 178, 277, 278, 279, 287, 288
Blackadder, 247
Blackfriars, order, 133, 175, 297
Blackhill, 244
Blackness Castle, 174, 304
Blacksmill, 247
Blackwood, 56

Blair Atholl, 70, 74, 77, 78
Blind Hary, 141, 142, 143, 144
Blois, 313
Boece, Hector, 140, 141, 143, 144, 296, 324
Bog of Gight (Gordon Castle), The, 250, 253, 261, 262, 264, 266, 267, 268, 269
Bois, Walter del, 55
Bondington, William de, bishop of Glasgow, 4
Bonshaw Tower, 223, 259
Borthwick Castle, 292, 297
Borthwick, family, 155, 297, 302, 304
    Robert, 302, 304
    William, 297
Borve Castle, 96, 114, 118, 121
Bothwell Castle, 8, 160, 161, 162, 163, 164, 166, 168, 169, 170, 174, 176, 207
Bothwell, earl of, 234, 308
Bower, Walter, 61, 78, 93, 95, 130, 133, 140, 141, 148, 164, 168, 195
Bowes, Sir William, 238
Boyd, family, 198
Braal Castle, 188, 202, 203
Brae, Brae Ross, 274, 275, 276, 281, 286
Brahan Castle, 274, 279, 280, 281, 282, 283, 288
Brander, Pass of, 93
Breachacha Castle, 96, 99, 103, 107, 111, 116, 117, 118
Brechin, xxii, 16
Breckonside Tower, 215
Brice, parson of Crieff, 32
Brideburgh, 80
Bristol, 92, 146
Britán Máel, 144
Broomhouse, 247
Bruce, Brus (de), family, 45–58 passim, 61, 69, 71, 72, 74, 80, 81, 93, 124, 128, 150
    see Robert (Bruce) I, king of Scots
    Edward, 15
    Edward, Lord Kinloss, 310
    Robert, 45–58 passim
    Robert, of Airth, 305
    William, 55
    Sir William, 285, 312, 318, 319, 322, 323, 326
Bruges, 299
Bryan, 157, 158
Buchan, earl of, 36, 40, 61–81 passim, 171, 196
Buchanan, George, 176, 304, 312

Buchollie (Lambaborg), 202
Buckinghamshire, 65
Bull, Stephen, 296
Burgundy, 87, 179, 185
Burntisland, 292, 316
Burrell, Sir William, 238, 239, 248
Bury St Edmunds, 15
Bute, 124

Cadzow Castle, 292, 306
Caerlaverock Castle, 204–30 passim
Cailean Mór, 154
Cairnbulg Castle, 60, 72, 79
Cairnburgh Castles, 84, 88, 90, 91, 92, 96, 99, 299
Cairncross, Robert, 236
Caithness, 2, 10, 297
Caithness, earl of, 190, 192, 193, 194, 196, 199, 201, 202
    Malise, 190, 192, 193, 194, 196
Caldside, 245
Callendar, 171
Cambridgeshire, 65
Cambuskenneth, 292, 301
Cameron, family, 9, 112, 177
Cameron, John, bishop of Glasgow, 9, 177
Campbell, family, 85, 88, 93, 94, 117, 123–60 passim, 278, 279, 307
    Archibald, 2nd earl of Argyll, 154, 157
    Arthur, 93, 94, 124, 149, 152
    Colen, 318, 319
    Colin, 1st earl of Argyll, 123, 128, 131, 134, 135, 136, 139, 140, 141, 142, 145, 146, 147, 148, 149, 150, 151, 152, 153, 154, 156, 157, 158
    Colin, of Glenorchy, 134
    Colin, of Lochawe, 150
    Daniel, of Shawfield, 319
    Donald, brother of Neil, 124
    Dugald, 137, 150, 154
    Duncan, 123, 130, 132, 133, 134, 136, 137, 138, 140, 144, 145, 149, 152, 153, 154, 155, 156, 157, 158
    Duncan, 'Johannis Beg', 155
    Gill-easbuig, 124, 125, 126, 127, 128, 130, 131, 134, 136, 150, 151, 154, 157
    James, 133
    John, 152
    John, earl of Atholl, 124

LORDSHIP AND
ARCHITECTURE
IN MEDIEVAL
AND
RENAISSANCE
SCOTLAND

❧

John Gallda, 124, 127, 128, 150
John, son of Neil, 124
John, of Lundie, 141
Margaret, daughter of Sir Duncan,
      158
Mariota, 152
Neil, 123, 124, 137, 150
Neil, archdeacon of Argyll, 152, 155
Neil, of Lochawe, 123
Campbeltown, Campbeltown Loch, 104,
      301, 317
Canonbie Priory, 58
Canville, William de, 146, 157
Cardeny, Robert de, bishop of Dunkeld, 8,
      9
Carey, John, 226
Carlisle, 209
Carlyle, Adam de, 55
Carmelite, order, 145, 157
Carmichael, Elizabeth, 238
Carn Drome, 151
Carnassarie Castle, xxii, 10, 22, 292, 306,
      308
Carnegie, Helen, 259
      Robert, 259
Carnousie, 257, 258, 266, 268, 271
Carnsalloch, 211
Carnwath, 144
Caroline Park, 285
Carolside, 238, 247
Carrick, 155, 168, 174
Carrick Castle, 129, 130, 152
Carruthers, 55
Carsaig, 101, 104, 105, 106
Carsewell, John, bishop of the Isles, 10,
      308
Carthusian, order, 297
Castle Campbell (Gloum), 158
Castle Camus, 96, 113, 118
Castle Coeffin, 84, 90
Castle Douglas, 164
Castle Fraser, 250, 252, 262, 264, 266, 268,
      269, 272
Castle Hill, East Kilbride, 67
Castle Knowe, 66
Castle Leod, 274, 277, 282, 283, 285, 288
Castle Maol, 96, 116
Castle Sinclair Girnigoe, 188, 200, 201, 202,
      203
Castle Sinclair (Dùn Mhic Leoid), 96, 116

Castle Sween, 84, 85, 88, 96, 100, 103, 105,
      107, 116, 117, 119, 122, 125
Castle Tioram, 84, 88, 89, 89, 91, 94, 96,
      101, 107, 116
Castle Uisdein, 96, 116
Castle Urquhart, 277
Castlehill, Caithness, 3
Castlemilk, 44, 56, 57
Castleton, 31
Cavens, 212
Cawdor, thane of, 152, 184
Cessford, 247
Chalmers, Alexander, 302
Chambord, 304
Chanonry, 277, 279, 282, 283, 286
Chapelknowe, 55
Charles I, king, 227, 228, 293, 310, 315,
      317
Charles II, king, 282, 297, 319, 320
Charles VII, king of France, 179, 317
Charles the Bold, duke of Burgundy, 179
Cheeklaw, 245, 247
Chirnside, 237, 247
Chisholm, family, 279, 288
      Alexander, of Comer, 288
Christian, king of Denmark, 198, 199, 227,
      320
Christina/Cristina of Mar, 86, 91
Cistercian, order, 86
Clackmannan, 64
Claig Castle, 96, 99, 104, 116
Clanranald, 91, 116
Clary, xxii, 3
Clerk, Sir John, of Penicuik, 312, 324
Cleveland, 45, 55, 58
Closeburn, 210
Cluniac, order, 86
Clunie, 80
Cluny Castle, 250, 253, 262, 263, 266, 268,
      272
Clyde, Clydesdale, 48, 50, 63, 67
Cnoculeran, 57
Coates Hill, 44, 47, 48, 49, 50, 51
Cochrane, Thomas, 299
Coigach, 278, 282, 283, 285, 286
Coldingham, Coldingham Priory, 169, 231,
      232, 233, 234, 237, 244, 247
Coldstream Priory, 233, 236
Coleshill, 322
Colin, abbot of Crossraguel, 14

Coll, 92, 99, 103, 104, 107, 111, 116
Colmslie, 236
Colt, Maximilian, 311
Comer, 288
Compostella, 153
Comrie, 30
Comyn, Cumin, family, 35, 36, 40, 61–81
    passim, 93, 99, 119, 178, 184
    Alexander, 73, 79
    David, 62
    John, of Badenoch, 35, 77, 78, 80, 93
    Osbert, 62
    Richard, 62
    Walter, 63, 75, 77, 78
    William, 36, 62, 63, 67, 69, 80
Con, family, 252
Copenhagen, 199
Cornwall, 257
Corr, Loch, 109
Corrie, family, 54
Corsane, Janet, 214
Coul, Coul House, 274, 287
Coupar Angus, 302
Courances, 311
Courcy, de, John, 86
Cousland, 189
Cowal, 88, 94, 110, 124, 125, 126, 127, 129,
    130, 135, 136, 137, 144, 145, 150, 151, 152,
    155, 157, 158
Cowdenknowes, 231, 232, 234, 235, 236,
    237, 238, 242, 245, 247
Cowdray, Lady, 270
Cowgask, 30
Cowhill, 204, 212, 215, 222, 223
Cowie, 64
Craig Castle (Aberdeenshire), 250, 258, 259,
    269, 271
Craigievar Castle, 314
Craignethan Cstle, 292, 305, 306, 308
Craignish, 151
Craigston Castle, 250, 252, 262, 263, 266, 272
Craik Cross, 50
Cranshaws, 247
Cranston, William, 181
Cranstoun, lord, 227
Crawford, earl of, 153, 175, 180
Crawfordmuir, 214
Cree, River, 161, 179
'Cressent', 299
Crichton Castle, 292, 308

Crichton, family, 174, 175, 176, 177, 178, 226
    George, 174
    James, 177
    William, 174, 176
Crieff, 26, 30, 31, 32
    Malise, parson of, 32
    Nicholas, parson of, 32
Cromartie, earl of, 285
Cromarty, 264, 272, 280, 284
Cromwell, Oliver, 242, 257, 286
Crosby, family, 55, 57, 58
    Robert, 58
Crossraguel Abbey, xxii, 11, 13, 14, 15, 19, 20
Crossrig, 247
Cruden, 73
Cruggleton Castle, 60, 73, 74, 79
Crumiecruke, 247
Crumstane, 247
Cubbie Roo's Castle, 202
Culdees, 18
Cullen, 74
Culross, 155, 292, 310, 311, 313, 315
Cultaloid, 277, 283
Cumbernauld, 176
Cumberland, Cumbria, 48, 65, 206
Cummertrees, 58
Cunningham, 45, 144, 155, 158
Cunningham, family, 157
    Andrew, of Glengarnock, 144, 158
    Robert de, 209
Cushendall, 104

Dacre, Lord, 218
Dairsie, 292, 317
Dalavich, 154
Dalgety, 292, 311
Dalkeith, 292, 318
Dalkeith, Peter of, 136, 137, 153, 155
Dalmally, 136
Dalmeny, 310
Dalry, 128
Dalrymple, family, 323
Dalserf (Machan), 60, 62, 63, 67
Dalswinton Castle, 60, 63, 68, 69, 78, 80
Darnaway Castle, 8, 160, 182, 183, 302
Darnley, 317
David I, king of Scots, 34, 45, 48, 50, 62,
    205, 228
David II, king of Scots, 94, 127, 128, 150,
    151, 161, 170, 182, 210, 305

LORDSHIP AND
ARCHITECTURE
IN MEDIEVAL
AND
RENAISSANCE
SCOTLAND

❦

Davidson, Walter, 236
Davochmaluag, 274, 286
Debateable Land, 216
Dee (Aberdeenshire), River, 250, 257, 262
Dee (Stewartry), River, 164
Deer Abbey, 60, 66, 69, 70, 71, 72, 73
Deeside, 74
Delgatty Castle, 250, 258, 259
Delny, 278, 279, 286
Denmark, 193, 194, 195, 197, 198, 199, 227, 299, 312, 317, 320, 324, 325
Dens, 245
Derbyshire, 65
Derry, 85
Dewar, Alexander, 155
    John, 154
    Robert, 154
Dick, William, of Braid, 325, 326
Dingwall, 80, 99, 281, 282, 283
Dingwall, family, 276, 277, 278
    William, of Kildun, 276
Dinwoodie, 44, 55, 57
    Adam of, 57
    John of, 57
Dirleton, 194, 292, 316
Doide, 105
Dollar, 158
Dolpatrick, 39, 40
Dominican, order, 145, 157
Don, River, 250
Donald III Ban, king of Scots, 62
Donald, 85, 86, see MacDonald
Donald, Clan, see MacDonald
Dornoch, xxii, 10, 292
Dornock, 57, 58
Dorset, 65
Douglas, family, 9, 155, 161–87 passim, 190, 195, 196, 199, 211, 212, 214, 215, 226, 231, 246, 247, 297
    Archibald 'the Grim', 3rd earl, 161, 164, 166, 168, 170, 172, 178
    Archibald, 4th earl, 168, 170, 171, 173, 179, 231
    Archibald, 5th earl, 171, 175, 177
    Archibald earl of Moray, 177, 178, 185
    Archibald, earl of Wigtown, 9, 169, 170
    Beatrice, 185
    David, 176
    George, 161
    George, of Parkhead, 246
    Hugh, earl of Ormond, 178, 185
    James, 2nd earl, 161
    James, 7th earl, 176, 177, 178, 179, 181
    James, 9th earl, 181, 184
    James, of Balvenie, 170, 174, 186
    John, of Balvenie, 178, 185
    Margaret, duchess of Touraine, 168, 172, 179
    Margaret, of Galloway, 176, 178, 182, 185
    Mary, daughter of Archibald, 164
    William, 1st earl, 161
    William, 8th earl, 164, 176, 177, 178, 179, 180
    William, 6th earl, 176
Douglas, Red Douglas, family, 161, 169, 175, 185
    George, earl of Angus, 185
    William, earl of Angus, 169, 175
Douglas Castle, Church, 160, 181
Douglasdale, 155, 161, 169
Dover, duke of, 320
Downpatrick, 86, 94
Dreux, Yolanda de, 189
Drochil Castle, 292, 307
Drum Castle, 262, 266
Drumalban, 27
Drumcoltran Tower, 204, 212, 220
Druminnor Castle, 250, 253, 254, 256, 257, 266, 271
Drumlanrig Castle, 214, 292, 320, 322
Drummelzier, 246
Drummond, John, 126, 127
    Margaret, 127, 151
Drumochter, 74, 77
Dryburgh Abbey, 57, 169, 210, 233
Dryfesands, battle of, 226
Dryfesdale, 50, 55, 56, 57
    Hugh, son of Ingebald of, 56
Duart Castle, 84, 88, 90, 92, 94, 100, 109, 116, 118, 158, 280
Dublin, 110, 120, 157
Dugald, 85, 86, see MacDougall
Dull, 80
Dull, Appin of, 127
Dumbarton, 128, 130, 131, 146, 147, 152, 158, 159, 302, 304
Dumfries, Dumfriesshire, 44, 48, 64, 80, 168, 175, 181, 207, 214, 216, 218, 220, 221, 222, 223, 224, 230, 259, 269, 271

Dùn Ara Castle, 96, 112, 118
Dùn Ban, 109, 118
Dùn Chonaill, 84, 88, 90, 92, 96, 98, 99
Dùn Mhic Leoid (Castle Sinclair), 96, 116
Dunaverty Castle, 96, 104
Dunbar, 189, 242, 292, 302, 304, 310, 317, 319, 320, 321
Dunbar, family, 168, 174, 177, 182, 283, 311
    Elizabeth, 168, 177
    George, earl of March, 168, 174
    James, earl of Moray, 177
    Janet, 177
    John, earl of Moray, 182
    William, 143
Dunbeath, 199
Dunblane, 75
Duncan II, king of Scots, 62
Duncow Tower, 204, 223
Dundarg Castle, 60, 71, 72, 73, 79
Dundonald Castle, 114, 120, 121, 152
Dundonnell, 276
Dundrennan Abbey, 212, 228, 229
Dundurn, 26, 28
Dunegal, 228
Dunfallin, 26, 30, 31
Dunfermline Abbey, xxii, 12, 16, 17, 313, 314, 316
Dunfermline, earl of, 262, 281, 282, 292, 297, 300, 309, 311
Dunglass, 171, 231, 241
Dunivaig Castle, 96, 102, 103, 104, 105, 114, 117, 118, 153
Dunkeld, xxii, 8, 9, 190
Dunkerd, castle, 96, 99
Dunknock, 26, 33, 34
Dunlugas, 243
Dunning, 31, 34, 38, 40
Dunollie Castle, 89, 116
Dunoon Castle, 124, 125, 150
Duns, 231, 232, 234, 244, 245, 247
Dunstaffnage Castle, 80, 84, 85, 87, 88, 89, 90, 91, 93, 94, 158
Dunstaffnage Chapel, 102
Dunure, 20
Dunvegan Castle, 96, 116, 118
Dupplin, 37
Durham, 62, 86
Durisdeer, 292, 320
Durward, family, 63
Dysart (Glenorchy), 136, 154

Eachaig, Strath, 154
Earl's Palace, Kirkwall, 263
Earn, Loch, 28, 30, 32
Earn, River, 28, 30, 31, 32
Easdale, 106, 111
(East) Kilbride, 60, 61, 62, 63, 65, 67, 68, 69, 80
    Isabella, of, 67
East Lothian, 64, 74, 138, 207, 231, 241, 243
East Mains, 247
Easter Aird, 283
Easter Ross, 161
Easter Tarbat, 283
Eccles, Eccles Priory, 232, 233, 234, 247
Edinburgh, 152, 154, 158, 168, 169, 170, 171, 172, 174, 175, 176, 180, 181, 185, 214, 229, 231, 235, 236, 271, 280, 282, 285, 292, 296, 297, 300, 302, 304, 305, 306, 307, 312, 313, 314, 317, 319, 323, 325, 326
Edrom, 247
Edward I, king of England, 35, 66, 73, 74, 77, 80, 81, 184, 189, 209
Edward II, king of England, 93, 94, 210
Edward III, king of England, 190, 210
Edward IV, king of England, 156
Edzell Castle, 272
Egidia, grand-daughter of King Robert II, 195
Eilean da Ghallagain, 109
Eilean Dearg, 122, 130, 152, 158
Eilean Donan Castle, 273, 274, 275, 281, 282, 283, 288
Eilean Mór, MacCormac Isles, 96, 99
Elcho Castle, 292, 308
Elgin, 74
Elizabeth, queen of England, 218, 224
Ellem, 244
Ellon, 60, 71, 72
Elshieshields Tower, 204, 226
Elsinore, 317
Enguerrand (Ingram), bishop of Glasgow, 3
Erasmus, Desiderius, 299
Erik, king of Norway, 196
Erik, king of Pomerania, 193
Erskine, John, 323
Eskdale, 45, 161, 169, 211, 214, 226, 227, 229
Essex, 65
Etive, Loch, 87, 89, 104
Ettrick, 50, 169, 172, 173, 181, 234, 245
Eugenius, pope, 177

LORDSHIP AND
ARCHITECTURE
IN MEDIEVAL
AND
RENAISSANCE
SCOTLAND

🐿

Evan Water, 50
Evandale, 217
Eye Water, 244
Eyemouth, 245, 292, 304, 309

Fairburn Tower, 274, 279, 280, 286, 288
Fairnieside, 245, 247
Falkirk, 65
Falkland, 292, 297, 300, 303, 325
Fannich Forest, 276
Fans, 247
Fast Castle, 231, 232, 240, 243, 244, 245, 246
Fearn, 287
Fedal, 38
Felix, pope, 177
Fenton, Alicia de, 190
Fenwick, 317
Fenwick, colonel, 242
Fiddich, Glen, 74, 178
Fife, 28, 64, 73, 131, 155, 174
Fife Adventurers, 278, 317
Fincharn Castle, 84, 85, 93
Findogask, 63
Finlaggan Castle, 84, 89, 96, 97, 99, 101,
    103, 104, 105, 106, 107, 108, 109, 110, 111,
    112, 113, 117, 118, 119
Finlarig Castle, 292, 307
Finlay, bishop of Argyll, see Albany, Finlay
    de
Finnart, 151, 305
Fishwick, 247
Fithkil, 64
FitzAlan, Walter, 45
Flanders, 195, 297, 299
Fleming, family, 164, 170, 176
    Malcolm, of Biggar and Cumbernauld,
        176
    Robert, 176
    Thomas, 2nd earl of Wigtown, 164
Fleurs, 247
Flint Castle, 78
Flodden, battle of, 154, 212, 243
Florence, 299
Fodderty, 276, 277, 283, 286
Fogo, John, 171
Forbes family, 252, 254, 271
    John, master of, 271
Fordell Castle, 292, 308
Fordun, John of, 78, 90, 95, 99, 120, 140,
    148, 155

Forfar, 63
Formartine, 64
Forres, 75
Forrester, Duncan, 301
Fort Charlotte, 292, 305
Forth, River, 27, 28, 164, 174
Fortriu, 28
Fortrose, xxii, 10, 274, 277, 287
Forvie, 73
Foulden, 233
Foulis, George, of Ravelstoun, 316
Fourmerkland Tower, 204, 224, 225
Fowlis, 30, 31, 39
Fowlis Wester, 26, 31
Framepath, 236, 247
France, 87, 164, 166, 168, 169, 172, 176, 179,
    195, 196, 212, 214, 227, 259, 261, 262,
    270, 294, 295, 299, 302, 303, 304, 305,
    306, 308, 309, 311, 317, 325
Francis I, king of France, 262, 303, 313, 324
Fraoch Eilean Castle, 84, 88, 93
Fraser, family, 262, 280, 286
    Janet, 286
    John, bishop of Ross, 282
Frederik II, king of Denmark, 313
Frederiksborg, 325
French, Roger, son of William, 56
Freuchie, 277, 279
Friars, 247
Friscobaldi, Jerome, 299
Fyvie Castle, 250, 262, 269, 282, 292, 309,
    310, 311, 312, 320
Fyne, Loch, Lochfyne, 117, 130, 133, 135,
    136, 146, 157, 158

Gairloch, 279, 280, 286
Galloway, 45, 49, 64, 73, 75, 79, 80, 151,
    161, 164, 169, 170, 172, 176, 177, 178, 179,
    181, 182, 185, 189, 207, 211, 215, 221, 226,
    229, 297
Garioch, 2, 196
Garmoran, 85, 94, 95, 133, 149
Garpol Water, 44, 47, 48, 51, 52, 54
Garve, 274, 281
Garvellach Isles, 88, 98, 99, 104, 120
Gask, 32
    Malise, parson of, 32
Geneva, Annabella (Arabella), countess of,
    270
Gerald of Wales, 148

Germany, 227, 299

Giffard, William, 172

Gigha, 105

Gight Castle, 250, 251, 253, 258, 259, 261, 264, 269, 271

Gille-Brigte, 87

Gilleoin of the Aird, 273

Gillesbie, 44, 55

Gimmenbie, 55

Girnigoe Castle, see Castle Sinclair Girnigoe

Glamis Castle, 250, 256, 257, 262, 263, 264, 267, 269, 292, 320

Glasgow, xxii, 2, 3, 4, 5, 9, 17, 57, 58 , 62, 145, 155, 157, 159, 177, 211, 248, 292, 302, 318, 319, 323

Glashan, Loch, 109, 120

Glassary, 93, 132, 152, 153, 155

Glenbuchat Castle, 250, 257, 259, 260, 266, 268, 271

Glencairn, 283, 284

Glencoe, 323

Glendinning, Simon, 181

Glenesslin, 212

Glengarnock, 144, 158

Glengarry, 276, 277, 279

Glenlitherne, 38

Glenn, Paul, 151

Glenorchy, 134, 135, 136, 153, 154, 307

Glens, 153

Glensanda Castle, 96, 106, 115, 116, 117

Gloucestershire, 65

Goatgellis, 223, 229

Godscroft, 247

Goes, Hugo Van der, 297

Goil, Loch, 129

Gordon Castle, see Bog of Gight

Gordon, family, 251–72 passim
    see Huntly, earl, marquis of
    Adam, 251
    Catherine, of Gight, 251, 270
    Christian, 254
    George, 270
    George, Lord Byron, 251
    James, of Lochinvar, 215
    John, colonel, 268
    John, 251
    Margaret, 271
    Thomas, 268

Gordon Moss, 234

Gorm, Loch, 110

Gorthy, Henry, son of Tristram of, 39, 40

Gotterbie Moor, 44, 56

Gowrie, 309

Graham, family, 36, 39, 40, 26, 126, 127, 176, 216
    David, 36, 39, 40
    John, 126
    Malise, 176
    Margaret, 126, 127

Granada, 190

Grant , family, of Freuchie, 277, 279, 280
    Barbara, 277, 279
    Elizabeth, 279

Grantown-on-Spey, 75, 184

Great Glen, 75, 79

Greenlaw, 236

Gretna, 58

Gruinard, 276

Gueldres, 179, 196, 297

Guisachan, 280

Guisborough Priory, 58

Guise, 306

Gunsgreen, 244

Gylen Castle, 89

Haddington, 292, 316

Haddington, earl of, 313

Haddo (Kelly), 60, 71, 271

Haig, family, 247

Haakon, king of Norway, 90, 93, 192

Haliburton, Jean, 194
    Walter, 194

Halidon Hill, battle of, 124 , 150

Hamilton, 292, 305, 306, 308, 318

Hamilton, David, 301
    James, 185, 196, 305
    John , 218
    John, archbishop of St Andrews, 8

Hans, king of Denmark, 302

Hansen, David, 317

Hardiesmill, 236, 247

Harlaw, battle of, 273

Harlech Castle, 78

Harrington Hall, 248

Harris, 104

Hatton Castle, 259

Hay, family, of Drummelzier, 246

Hay, family, of Kinfauns, 312
    John de, of Tulibothil, 192
    Richard, Father, 189, 195, 196

LORDSHIP AND
ARCHITECTURE
IN MEDIEVAL
AND
RENAISSANCE
SCOTLAND

᭡

Hebrides, 85, 92
Heneville, Heineville, William de, 55
Henry I, king of England, 45, 48, 62
Henry II, king of England, 29
Henry III, king of England, 78
Henry IV, king of England, 168
Henry VIII, king of England, 215
Henry IV, king of France, 262
Henry, earl, 62
Henshaw, 62
Hepburn, Alexander, bishop of Ross,
    277
    John, prior of St Andrews, 21
    Patrick, bishop of Moray, 9
Herbert, bishop of Glasgow, 3
Herbertshire, 171
Heriot's Hospital, Edinburgh, 310, 317, 320
Herries, family, 55, 214, 217, 218, 220, 221,
    222, 223, 224, 227, 229, 317
    Agnes, 217, 218, 222, 317
    John, 222
Hertford, 65
Hexham, 62
Hills Tower, 204, 212, 213, 214, 216, 220
Hilton, 247
Hirsel, The, 247
Hoddom, family, 55
Hoddom Castle, Hoddomstanes, 204, 218,
    219, 220, 221, 222, 229
Hoddom Church, 57, 58
Holland, 282
Holland, Richard, 182
Holm Cultram Abbey, 206, 207, 228
Holydean, 235, 247
Holyrood, Holyroodhouse, 15, 161, 169, 171,
    285, 292, 293, 297, 300, 301, 302, 304,
    306, 307, 315, 317, 319, 320, 325
Holywood, abbot of, 212
Home, families, 231–49 passim, 314
    Alexander, 231, 236, 239, 245
    Alison, 238
    Barbara, 238
    Cuthbert, 243
    Elizabeth, 236, 238, 239
    Elspeth, 245
    George, 245
    Isobel, 238, 239
    James, 234, 235, 236, 237, 238, 243, 244,
        248
    Jane, 238

John, 228, 234, 236, 237
    Katherine, 235
    Patrick, 243, 245
Home Castle, 231, 232, 240, 241, 242,
    243
Homildon Hill, battle of, 168, 251
Hope, Thomas, 313
Hopetoun House, 174, 318
Houndwood, 232, 244, 247
Houston, 138, 155
Houston, Sir Patrick, 138
Hullmandel, 267
Humbleton, battle of, 195
Hume, Alexander, of Dunglass, 171
Humez, family, 55
Hunter, Andrew, abbot of Melrose, 13
Hunthill, 69
Huntingdonshire, 65
Huntly, Huntly Castle, 74, 99, 250, 251,
    252, 253, 254, 255, 256, 257, 259, 260,
    261, 262, 264, 266, 267, 268, 269, 270,
    271, 272, 292
Huntly, earl, marquis of, 254, 260, 262,
    264, 266, 267, 268, 269, 270, 271, 280,
    see Gordon family
Hutton, 44, 47, 49, 50, 54
    Adam of, 54
    Gilbert of, 54
    Juliana, wife of Gilbert, 54
Hutton Castle, Huttonhall, 218, 231, 232,
    234, 236, 237, 238, 239, 240, 241, 245,
    247, 248

Ilanrorie, 286
Inchaffray Abbey, 26, 30, 31, 39
Inchcolm, abbot of, 140
Inchgarvie, 292, 302, 304
Inchmahome Priory, 60, 65, 68, 75, 77
Inchtalla Castle, 60, 77
Indre, River, 262
Inishail, 152, 154, 158
Innerpeffray, 26, 30, 31, 32
Innes, family, of Inverbreakie, 280
Inninmore, 101, 104
Innis Chonaill Castle, 84, 85, 88, 93, 94,
    122, 129, 152, 158
Inveraray, 117, 122, 130, 135, 145, 146, 147,
    148, 149, 154, 158
Inveravon Castle, 160, 182, 184
Inverbreakie, 280

Inverchapel, 137
'Inverero', 262, 264
Inveresk, 323
Inverewe, 276
Inverie (Knoydart), 80
Inverlochy, battle of, 282
Inverlochy Castle, 60, 65, 74, 75, 77, 78,
    79, 80, 84, 85, 93, 99, 119
Inverness, Inverness-shire, 64, 74, 99, 119,
    133, 178, 192, 273, 283, 302
Inverurie, 2, 3
Iona, 84, 85, 86, 87, 88, 91, 92, 96, 98, 100,
    101, 103, 104, 105, 106, 112, 113, 114
Ireland, 85, 86, 87, 92, 94, 104, 110, 120,
    132, 135, 141, 142, 143, 144, 148, 149, 224,
    294
Irvine, 145, 146, 147, 157, 159
Irving, family, 215, 259
'Iselborg', 90
Island Suthain, 274, 286
Islay, 85, 87, 89, 93, 94, 97, 98, 99, 101, 102,
    103, 104, 105, 106, 109, 110, 113, 114, 116
Isle of Lochar Tower, 204, 220
Isle of Lochkinderloch Tower, 204, 217
Italy, 270, 295, 299, 300, 302, 304, 306,
    308, 312, 319

James I, king of Scots, 9, 130, 131, 132, 133,
    134, 136, 137, 138, 140, 145, 153, 157, 164,
    168, 169, 170, 171, 172, 174, 175, 177, 180,
    182, 195, 196, 211, 270, 293, 294, 295,
    296, 297, 301, 309, 324
    James and Alexander, sons, 133
    Joan, wife, 134 , 174
    Margaret, sister, 169
James II, king of Scots, 15, 19, 133, 134, 153,
    155, 164, 167, 171, 175, 178, 179, 180, 181,
    184, 185, 196, 197, 198, 211, 297
James III, king of Scots, 10, 110, 142, 147,
    148, 158, 198, 199, 294, 296, 297, 299, 302
James IV, king of Scots, 15, 147, 148, 158,
    234, 243, 270, 294, 296, 297, 299, 300,
    301, 302, 303, 304, 305, 306, 311, 324
    Margaret, sister, 297
James V, king of Scots, 14, 214, 270, 296,
    297, 302, 304, 305, 306, 319, 325
James VI, king, 218, 221, 222, 224, 226,
    227, 234, 244, 259, 278, 304, 306, 309,
    313, 315, 317, 319
James VII and II, king, 319, 320, 322

Jamieson, George, 308
J. B., master, of Nuremburg, 272
Jedburgh, Jedburgh Abbey, xxii, 12, 16, 54,
    80, 181, 209, 232, 233, 236, 237, 247
Jenkin, Valentine, 315
Jesuit, order, 235, 237
John (Balliol), king of Scots, 64, 81
John, lord of the Isles, see MacDonald,
    family
Johnston, family, 215, 223, 224, 226, 227
    James, 226
    John, 215
Johnstone, family, 54, 185
Jura, 104, 105, 106

Kather Mothel, 38
Keills Church, 96, 101, 102
Keith, 74
Keith, family, Earl Marischal, 277
    Andrew, 277
Keith, William, of Ravenscraig, 278, 286
Kelloe, 237
Kelly (Haddo), 60, 71, 72, 73
Kelso, Kelso Abbey, 3, 205, 206, 234, 245
Kelvin, River, 67
Kemlock, Sir John, 254
Kenmore, 26, 29, 32
Kennedy, family, 14, 18, 20, 174, 197
    Gilbert, 20
    James, bishop of St Andrews, 18, 197
    Janet, 302
    William, abbot of Crossraguel, 14, 20
Kennoway, 64
Keppoch, 158
Kerr, family, 185
Ker, family, of Cessford, 247
Ker, family, of Samuelston, 236
Kidwelly Castle, 78
Kilbaberton, 292, 310, 312, 313, 314, 315
Kilbrannan Chapel, 84, 87, 91, 96, 100
Kilbride (East), 60, 61, 62, 63, 65, 67, 68,
    69, 80
Kilchrenan, 154
Kilchurn Castle, 96, 117
Kilcoy, 274, 286, 288
Kildalton Church, 96, 101, 104
Kildrummy Castle, 6, 254
Kildun, 276
Kilkerran, 292, 301
Killean Church, 84, 87, 96, 101, 104

LORDSHIP AND
ARCHITECTURE
IN MEDIEVAL
AND
RENAISSANCE
SCOTLAND

Killin, 276, 279, 280, 281
Kilmartin, 292, 308
Kilmelfort, 151
Kilmory Knap, chapel, 96, 101
Kilmun, 122, 126, 127, 130, 135, 136, 137, 138, 139, 145, 147, 148, 149, 151, 152, 153, 154, 155, 156, 157, 158
Kinbuck, 39, 40
Kincardine, Kincardine Castle, 36, 40, 53
Kinclaven Castle, 53, 207
Kinellan, 274, 275, 276, 280, 281
Kingedward Castle, 60, 71, 72, 73, 79
Kinkell, 274, 280, 286, 288
Kinlochaline Castle, 96, 116
Kinlochgoil, 136
Kinlochstriven, 150
Kinloss Abbey, xxii, 11, 13, 14, 69
Kinloss, lord, 310
Kinmount, 55, 56
Kinneddar, xxii, 5
Kinneil, 292, 306, 318, 325
Kinross, Kinross House, 292, 318, 319, 321, 323
Kintail, 273, 275, 276, 277, 278, 279, 280, 281, 286, 288
Kintyre, 85, 86, 87, 98, 100, 101, 104, 106, 125, 150, 301
Kirkconnell Tower, 204, 216, 217, 220, 221
Kirkcudbright, 80, 147, 170, 204, 212, 226
Kirkgunzeon, 204, 218
Kirkham Priory, 15
Kirkintilloch, 60, 62, 63, 67, 68, 69, 78, 80
Kirkpatrick, family, 52, 54, 55, 210
    Stephen, 55
    Roger, 210
Kirkpatrick-Juxta, 57
Kirkpatrick-Fleming, 58
Kirkton, 274, 280, 286
Kirkwall, 100, 188, 192, 193, 196, 202, 263
Kirtle Water, 259, 212, 215
Kirtlebridge, 212
Kirtledale, 215
Kisimul Castle, 96, 103, 107, 111, 116, 118
Knapdale, 85, 93, 94, 100, 101, 105, 106, 109, 124, 125, 126, 128, 150, 151, 155
Knock, 250, 253, 268
Knox, Andrew, bishop of Raphoe, 317
Knoydart, 80, 95
Kronborg, 313, 325

Ladykirk, 236, 292, 301
Lalain, Jacques de, 179
Lambaborg (Buchollie), 202
Lamont, Isobel, 124
Lanark, Lanarkshire, 144, 155, 161, 164, 169, 170, 174, 181, 182
Langholm, 204, 214, 222, 224
Langside, battle of, 221
Largo, 324
Lauder, George, bishop of Argyll, 133, 136, 137, 138
    James, 136, 153
    Robert, 171
Lauder, 218, 247, 304
Lauderdale, duke of, 161, 234, 316, 318, 319, 320
Law, The, 247
Leicester, Leicestershire, 4, 65, 79
Leiper, James, 252
Leith, 297, 302, 304, 306, 323
Leitholm, 236
Lennox, 130, 131, 132, 136, 140, 144
Lennox, earl of, 132, 217
Lenzie, 62, 63, 67
Lerwick, 305
Leslie, 64, 320, 325
Leslie, families, 277, 292, 318
Lethderg, Fergus, 144
Lethendy, 36
Leuchars, 60, 73
Lewis, 102, 103, 120, 278, 279, 281, 283
Liddel Strength, 58
Liddesdale, 45
Limerick, 110
Lincluden Collegiate Church, 9, 160, 167, 168, 204, 212, 224, 292, 297
Lincolnshire, 65, 248
Lindsay, family, 155, 175, 210, 272
    David, earl of Crawford, 175
    David, 272
    Duncan, 155
    James de, 210
Linlithgow, 170, 292, 295, 297, 300, 303, 304, 308, 311, 313, 315, 325
Linnhe, Loch, 63, 90, 104, 106
Linthill, 232, 247
Linton (West), 62, 67
Lismore, Lismore Cathedral, 84, 87, 89, 100, 104, 111
Lithgow, John de, abbot of Paisley, 19

Livingston of Callendar, family, 171, 174, 175, 176, 178
  Alexander, 171, 176
Loch an Eilean, castle, Tiree, 90
Lochaber, 63, 65, 74, 75, 77, 79, 80, 93
Lochaline, 104
Lochalsh, 112, 120, 276, 277
Lochar Moss, 48, 220
Lochawe, see Awe, Loch
Lochbroom, 276, 277, 279, 283, 285
Lochbuie, 116
Lochcarron, 276, 277
Lochfyne, see Fyne, Loch
Lochgilphead, 109, 151
Lochgoilhead, 151, 153
Lochindorb Castle, 60, 64, 65, 74, 77, 78, 80, 160, 182, 184
Lochinvar, 215
Lochleven Castle, 322
Lochmaben, Lochmaben Castle, 44, 46, 48, 49, 51, 54, 55, 58, 160, 170, 172, 180, 181, 204, 209, 212, 214, 215, 217, 221, 222, 223, 224, 226, 227
Lochnaw Castle, 160
Lochranza Castle, 125
Lochrutton, 214
'Lochs', 158
Lochslin, 274, 278, 287, 288
Lochwood, Lochwood Castle, 44, 47, 51, 52, 54, 215
Lockerbie, 55, 218, 226
Logan, Logan Mains, 55
Logan, family, of Restalrig, 243, 244
Loire, River, 262
London, 189
Long, Loch, 130, 151, 152
Lorn, 98, 102, 104, 106, 116, 124, 127, 128, 149, 150, 151, 155
Lothian, 62, 64, 74, 75, 155, 170, 171, 181
Louis XIV, king of France, 309, 320
Lovat, family, 280, 281, 283, 284
'Lowis', 146, 147, 148, 158
Luggie Water, 67
Lull, Ramon, 153
Lundie, 141

McAgrade, Donald, 155
MacArthur, John, 133
MacCormac Isles, 99
Maccus, 205, 206, 228

Maccuswell, 205, 206, 207
  Herbert de, 206
  John de, 206
MacDonald, families, 85, 86, 87, 89, 90, 93, 94, 95, 97, 98, 99, 103, 104, 109, 112, 113, 114, 115, 116, 125, 133, 142, 150, 153, 156, 158, 273–6, 280 see Donald
  Alexander, 86, 93, 276
  Angus Mór, 86
  Angus Óg, 86
  Celestine, of the Isles, 112, 276
  Donald, 276
  Iain Lom, 158
  John, of the Isles, 86, 99, 103, 109, 113, 114, 115, 125, 133, 142, 150, 156
  John Mór, 153
MacDougall, family, of Argyll, 80, 85, 86, 87, 88, 89, 90, 91, 92, 93, 94, 113, 116, 124, 127, 128, 150, 151 see Dugald
  Alan, 86
  Alexander, 86, 92, 93, 127, 150
  Duncan, 86, 87, 93
  Ewen, 85, 86, 89, 93
  John of Lorn, 86
MacDowall, William, 307
MacEwan's Castle, 96, 110
MacFadzan, 142, 143
MacGill, Alexander, 321
Mackenzie, families, 273–91 passim
  Alastair Ionraic, 273, 274, 276, 279, 280
  Alexander, 285, 286
  Agnes, 280, 281
  Colin, 277, 278, 279, 280, 282
  Colin Cam, 273, 279, 281
  George, 282, 284, 288
  Hector, 279
  Janet, 278
  John, 275, 276, 287
  John, of Kintail, 278
  John Roy, 286
  John of Killin, 276, 279, 280
  Katherine, 281
  Kenneth, 276, 278, 279, 280, 281, 282, 283, 286, 287, 288
  Margaret, 278
  Murdoch, 279
  Roderick, 287
  Rory, 277, 278, 279, 282, 285, 286
  Thomas, 282

LORDSHIP AND
ARCHITECTURE
IN MEDIEVAL
AND
RENAISSANCE
SCOTLAND

༄

MacKinnon, family, 112, 116, 118
Mackintosh, family, 279, 280, 281
MacLaine, family, 116
MacLean, family, of Duart, 92, 94, 109, 111, 116, 118, 120, 158, 280
MacLellan's Castle, Kirkcudbright, 204, 226
MacLeod, family, 113, 116, 118, 278, 279, 283
    Roderick, 278
    Torquil Cononach, 278, 283
MacMillan, Duncan, 155
MacNachtan, family, 88, 93
Macneil, family, 111, 116, 118
MacQuarrie, family, 109, 118
MacRuari, family, 86, 91, 92, 93, 94, 95, 133, 149, see Ruari
    Alan, 86
    Alexander, 133
    Amy, 86, 94
    Christina, 149
    Dugald, 86
    Eric, 86
MacSween, family, 85, 93
MacTaggart, Farquhar, earl of Ross, 36
MacWilliam, 63, 74
Machan (Dalserf), 60, 62, 63, 67
Mains Castle, East Kilbride, 67
Maitland, family, of Thirlestane, 316, 320
    John, 319
Malcolm III, king of Scots, 62
Malcolm IV, king of Scots, 3, 29, 228, 273
Maleverer, family, 55
Malise Sperra, 192, 193
Malmesbury, William of, 139
Man(n), Isle of, 74, 86, 100, 120
Manderston, 231, 232, 245, 247
Manhattan, 314
Mantarig, 55
Manuel, king of Portugal, 302
Mar, earl of, 63, 74, 86, 91, 273, 306, 307, 312, 324
    Christina/Cristina of, 86, 91
March, earl of, 168, 169, 170, 172, 174, 177, 178, 181, 184
Marchmont, 247
Maree, Loch, 280, 286
Margaret, daughter of Christian, king of Denmark, 199
Margaret, queen of Norway, 193
Margaret, queen of Scots, 212
Marstrand, 192

Martini, Archibald, 136
Mary, queen of Scots, 218, 221, 222, 224, 229, 241, 306, 307, 311, 322
Mary of Gueldres, 179, 196, 297
Mary of Guise, 241, 306
Matheson, family, 273
Maxwell, family, of Caerlaverock, Lords Maxwell, 185, 204–30 passim
    Aymer, 207
    Edward, 214, 220
    Eustace, 210
    Herbert, 207, 211, 212
    John, 210, 214, 217, 226
    Robert, 212, 215, 227
Maxwell, family, of Hills and Drumcoltran, 212
Maxwell, family, of Pollok, 207
Maxwell, George, 146
Maxwell's Castle, Dumfries, 204, 214
Mearns, Mearns Castle, 63, 204, 207, 208, 209, 211, 223
Meddat, 284
Medici, Catherine de, 302
    Cosimo de, 270
Meikle Brahan, 276
Meikle Tarrell, 283
Meikleour, 36
Melfort, Loch, 151
Melgund Castle, xxii, 10, 292, 308
Mellifont Abbey, Co. Louth, 86
Melrose Abbey, xxii, 12, 13, 14, 15, 70, 160, 168, 169, 171, 172, 186, 205, 235, 247, 313, 316
    Matthew, abbot of, 12, 13
Menstrie, 152
Menteith, earl of, 28, 63, 65, 75, 124, 125, 126, 127, 129, 130, 131, 145, 150, 151, 175, 176, 187
    Helen, 150
    Isabella, heiress of, 63
    John, 124, 125, 126, 150
    Mary, 124, 126, 151
Menteith, Lake of, 75
Menzies, David, of Weem, 195
Merkland Cross, 212
Merlzioun, Walter, 300
Merse, 240, 246
Methven, 282
Midcalder, 292, 305
Midmar Castle, 250, 257, 259, 260, 262, 264, 266, 268, 269, 271

Middlethird, 233, 247

Milntoun, 274, 284, 285

Mingary Castle, 84, 88, 89, 91, 92, 96, 101, 107, 115

Minigaig, 74, 77

Moffat, Moffatdale, 50, 54, 56, 57, 218

Moidart, 95

Moidart, Loch, 91

Monar, 276

Monck, General, 283

Monro, Dean, 99, 119, 120, 122

Montgomerie, family, 157

Montrose, earl of, 282, 283, 286

Morar, 95

Moray, 2, 5, 63, 65, 70, 72, 74

Moray, family, earl of, 161, 162, 177, 178, 179, 182, 184, 185, 207, 273, 277, 280, 306
  Andrew, 162
  Archibald, bishop of, 5
  James Dunbar, earl of, 177
  John Dunbar, earl of, 182
  Joanna, 161, 178
  Walter de, 161

Mor(e)ville, de, family, 29, 45, 57
  Hugh de, 45, 57

Morow, John, 168
  Thomas, 19

Mortlach, 64, 74, 178

Morton, earl of, regent, 223, 224, 226, 227

Morton Castle, 152

Morvern, 91, 92, 95, 101, 104, 114, 115, 116

Mosstroops Tower, 218, 221

Mounth, The, 74, 79, 259

Moy Castle, 96, 103, 106, 116, 117

Mull, 85, 87, 90, 91, 92, 98, 100, 101, 103, 104, 106, 112, 113, 116

Mundeville, John de, 54

Munro, family, 277, 278
  Andrew, of Newmore, 277
  George, of Meikle Tarrell, 283

Muren, 286

Murray, families, 5, 37, 38, 40, 293, 309, 310, 311, 312, 313, 314, 315, 316, 317, 318, 322, 325, 326
  David, bishop of Moray, 5
  David, of Gospetrie, 309
  Gideon, 315
  James, 293, 309, 310, 311, 312, 313, 314, 315, 316, 317, 318, 322, 325, 326
  William, 37, 40

Musselburgh, 322

Muthill, 26, 30, 31, 39

Myln, Mylne, Alexander, 8, 9
  John, 305, 317, 318
  Robert, 305, 319, 323, 326

Myres, 304, 305

Nave Island, chapel, 96, 102

Ned, 276

Nemed, 144

Ness, Loch, 74

Nether Nisbet, 236

Netherlands, 317, 319

Neville's Cross, battle of, 126, 210

New Aberdour, 71, 73

New Tarbat, 285

'New Werk' on Spey, 264

Newark Castle, 8, 172, 173, 174, 175, 181

Newark Castle, Port Glasgow, 292, 309, 319

Newburgh, 60, 73

Newhailes, 292, 322, 323

Newhaven, 292, 302

Newmore, 277

Niddrie, 292, 305

Ninewells, 247

Nisbet, 232, 236, 247

Nith, River, Nithsdale, 48, 49, 63, 66, 68, 78, 80, 161, 168, 171, 195, 196, 212, 221, 224, 226, 227, 228

Nithsdale, earl of, 205, 227

Norfolk, 65

Norham Ford, 238

Normandy, 26

North Berwick Priory, 232, 233

North Kyle, 45

North Tyne, 45

Northallerton, 62

Northamptonshire, 65

Northumberland, 62, 65, 75, 76, 78, 240

Norway, 36, 45, 85, 87, 90, 92, 93, 98, 192, 193, 194, 195, 197, 201, 202

Nost, Jan Van, 320

Nova Scotia, 314, 317

Nuremburg, 272

O'Brolchan, Donald, 98

O'Cuinn, Mael-Sechlainn, 98

Oban, 89

Ochils, 28, 30

Ochtertyre, 63

LORDSHIP AND
ARCHITECTURE
IN MEDIEVAL
AND
RENAISSANCE
SCOTLAND

⅍

Ogilvy, family, 243, 257
    Isobel, of Powrie, 281
Old Mertoun, 232, 247
Old Wick, 202
Olifard, family, 29
Ord, 287
Orkney, 100, 170, 171, 189, 190, 192, 193,
    194, 195, 196, 197, 198, 199, 201, 202,
    256, 259
Ormidule, 152
Ormond, 160, 178, 185
    Hugh, earl of, 178, 185
Oronsay Priory, 84, 87, 96, 98, 103, 104,
    105, 106, 115
Orsay, chapel, 96, 99, 103, 113
Otterburn, battle of, 161
Over Cowal, 130, 151, 152
Over Nisbet, 236
Oxfordshire, 65
Oxnam Water, 69

Padua, 299
Paisley, Paisley Abbey, xxii, 18, 19, 86, 109,
    208, 302, 323
Palestine, 190
Panmure House, 292, 315, 318
Paris, 168, 179, 198
Paris, Matthew, 75
Parkhead, 246
Pearsby, 55
Peebles, Peeblesshire, 62, 65, 66, 67, 207
Peebles, Thomas, 302
Peel of Strathbogie, 257
Pencaitland Church, 210
Penesax, Penresax (Pennersaughs), 55, 56
    John de, 55
    Richard de, 55
Penicuik, 324
Pennant, Thomas, 264
Penninghame, xxii, 3
Percy, family, 168
Perth, Perthshire, 63, 64, 128, 132, 133, 145,
    151, 152, 172, 175, 207, 297, 317
Peterborough, 48
Peterhead, 278
Peterugie, 70
Phileremos, 299
Philip II, king of Spain, 224
Philorth, 60, 72
Picts, 28

Pinkie House, 282, 292, 311, 312, 326
Pitcairn, 31, 34
Pitreavie, 292, 314
Pitscottie, 176
Pittenweem Priory, xxii, 18
Plean, 157
Pleasants Burn, 69
Pluscarden, 87, 161, 281, 282, 283, 286, 302
Pollok, 207
Polwarth, 231, 232, 247
Pont, Timothy, 287
Port Glasgow, 319
Port Seton, 314
Portrack, 212
Portugal, 179, 302, 305
Pow, 30
Powrie, 281
Pratt, David, 301
Prenderguest, 247
Primrose, family, 310
Pringle, family, 236
Purves, James, 236

Quarles, Francis, 228
Queensberry, marquis of, 320, 321
Queensferry, 302
Quincy, de, family, 64, 65, 73, 74, 79
    Roger de, 64, 73
Quixwood, 237

Ramsay, George, 233
    Michael, 170
Randolph, Thomas, earl of Moray, 182,
    184, 273
Rannallock, 271
Ranulf, son of Dunegal, 228
Rap Loch, Stirling, 299
Raperlaw, 236
Raphoe, 317
Rattray, 60, 72, 73, 79
Ravenscraig (Aberdeenshire), 278
Ravenscraig Castle (Fife), 188, 197, 198, 199,
    201, 292, 297
Redbraes (Polwarth), 231, 232
Redcastle, 274, 277, 279, 280, 286
Redkirk, 58
Redpath, 234
Reedyloch, 237, 244
Reginald, 85, 86, 94, see MacDonald,
    MacRuari

Reid, Robert, abbot of Kinloss, 13
Reidheuch, 247
Renfrew, Renfrewshire, 3, 45, 124, 136, 138, 144, 147, 159, 207, 211
Renton, 247
Repentance Tower, 204, 218, 229
Restalrig, Restalrig Collegiate Church, 175, 234, 243, 245, 292, 298, 299, 302
Rhodes, 299
Richard II, king of England, 193
Rickerby, 55
Riddon, Loch, 130
Rinnes, Glen, 74
'Roberdsbi', 55
Robert (Bruce) I, king of Scots, 5, 16, 17, 19, 35, 55, 103, 123, 128, 150, 182, 184, 190, 210, 251, 273, 285
Robert II, king of Scots, 124, 128, 131, 157, 170, 184, 195
Robert III, king of Scots, 4, 18, 19, 164, 168
Robert the Steward, 124, 125, 127, 128, 130, 144, 150 see Albany
    Robert, son of, 126
Robert's Hill, 55
Robertson, Thomas, 323, 326
Rockhall, 44, 47, 49
Rodil Church, 96, 104, 105
Rogermoor, 44, 56
Rollandstoun, 247
Rome, Roman, 31, 32, 50, 51, 67, 68, 179, 296, 311, 312, 320, 322, 324, 325
Rosdale, Turgis de, 57
Rosehaugh, 288
Roslin, 188, 189, 190, 191, 194, 195, 196, 197, 201, 203
Roslin Moor, battle of, 189
Ross, 2, 5, 36, 63, 73, 74, 99, 118, 277, 282
Ross, family, 180, 192, 280
    Hugh, 192
Ross, earls of, 190, 273–91 passim
    William, 190
Rothes, 318, 320
Rothesay, duke of, 164, 168
Rothesay Castle, 84, 88, 292, 304
Roxburgh, Roxburghshire, 62, 63, 66, 68, 69, 78, 80, 133, 170, 209, 227, 231, 245
Royston, 285
Ruari, 85, 86, see MacRuari
Rufus, Geoffrey, bishop of Durham, 62

Rule Water, 66
Rum, 104
Rushen Castle, 100
Ruthven, Ruthven Castle, 39, 60, 74, 77, 78

St Albans, 15
St Andrews, xxii, 4, 6, 7, 16, 18, 20, 21, 172, 187, 193, 292, 301, 308
St Bothans, St. Bothans Priory, 232, 233, 236
Sainte Chapelle, 325
St Connan of Dysart (Diseart), 136
St Fillans, 28, 30, 32
St Fionntáin, 137, 147
St Germain-en-Laye, 303
St Giles, 302, 306
St John's Chapel, 233
St Malachy, 49
St Mary, 157
St Mun, 126, 157
St Oran, 84, 85
St Serf, 34
St Triduana, 299
Saddell, Saddell Abbey, 84, 86, 96, 98, 100, 101, 104, 292, 301
Samuelston, 236
Sanquhar, 226, 321
Sark, River, 55
Sarthe, River, 262
Sauchie, 292, 305
Sauchieburn, battle of, 147
Saxton, Christopher, 240
Scatwell, 276
Schaw, William, 259, 260, 309, 312, 314, 318, 325
Scone, 63, 73, 292, 302, 309, 311
Scone, lord, 309
Scotia, 27, 28, 40, 63, 80
Scott, family, 185
Scrabster, 202
Scraesburgh, 60, 63, 68, 69, 78
Scrymgeour, family, 132, 152, 153, 155, 304, 305
    James, 132, 152, 155
    John, 304, 305
Scrope, lord, 221, 222, 223, 224, 226, 230
Seaforth, earl of, 281, 282, 283, 287, 289
    Barbara, countess, 283
    Colin, 1st earl, 281
Selkirk, 161, 172, 173, 174, 205
Selkirkshire, 173

LORDSHIP AND
ARCHITECTURE
IN MEDIEVAL
AND
RENAISSANCE
SCOTLAND

❦

Seton family, 238, 251, 253, 262, 269, 281, 282, 305, 309, 310, 311, 312, 313, 314
  Alexander, 251, 281, 309, 310, 311, 313
  Elizabeth, 251
  George, 305
  John, of Barnes, 281
  John, of Touch, 238
  Margaret, 282
Sharp, John, 300
Shaw, George, abbot of Paisley, 19
Shawfield, 292, 319, 323
Shepshed, 79
Shetland, 193, 195, 198, 199, 202, 203
Shrewsbury, battle of, 168
Sibbaldbie, 55
Simprim, 247
Sinclair, family, 170, 171, 189–203 passim
  Beatrix, 170
  David, 201, 202
  Earl Henry I, 189, 192, 193, 194, 195
  Earl Henry II, 194
  Henry, 171, 190
  John, 190, 195
  John, dean of Restalrig, 245
  Oliver, 201
  Thomas, 192, 195
  Earl William, 170, 171, 195, 196, 197, 198, 199, 201, 202, 203, 297
  William, 189, 190, 192
  William, bishop of Dunkeld, 190
  William 'the Waster', 199
Skinburness, 207, 209
Skipness Castle, 84, 85, 87, 88, 96, 100, 101, 104, 107, 115, 119, 292, 301
Skye, 103, 104, 113, 116
Slains (Old), 60, 71, 72, 73, 79, 80
Sleat, 276, 280
Slegden, 247
Slezer, John, 262, 264
Smailholm, Adam of, 70
Small Isles, 85
Smith, James, 318, 319, 320, 321, 322, 323
  John, 268
Smythe, family, of Methven, 282
Smythson, family, 311
Solway, 44, 48, 207, 214, 228
Somerled, 85, 86, 87, 127
Somerville, family, of Carnwath, 144, 157
  Elizabeth, 157
  John, 2nd lord, 157

John, lord, 157
  Thomas, 157
Somerville, family, of Plean, 157
Soules, de, family, 29, 45
  Ranulf, 45
Southend Chapel, 96, 104
Southbar, 211
South Queensferry, 174
Spain, 179, 224, 226
Spalding, James, 284
Spean, Glen, 75
Spelve, Loch, 92
Spens, Thomas, 155
Spey, River, 27, 74, 75, 77, 79, 257, 262, 264
Spott, 247
Spottiswood, 226
Spottiswoode, John, archbishop, 317
Spynie Palace, xxii, 5, 7, 8, 9, 10
Staincroft, 62
'The Stank' (Woodhall) 57
Stapleton, 57
Stephen, king of England, 62
Steward, Stewart, family, 2, 3, 5, 9, 10, 18, 75, 88, 93, 124, 125, 126, 127, 128, 129, 130, 131, 132, 134, 137, 144, 145, 150, 152, 153, 155, 157, 161, 169, 170, 171, 184, 202, 209
  Alexander, earl of Mar, 184
  Alexander, lord of Badenoch, 184
  Alexander, 2, 132
  Andrew, 153
  Andrew, bishop of Moray, 10
  Arthur, 153
  David, bishop of Moray, 9, 10
  James, of Muren, 286
  Margaret, countess of Angus, 161
  Margaret, countess of Douglas, 170
  Margaret, 137, 138, 270
  Margaret, daughter of John of Ardgowan, 144
  Marjory, 144
  Robert, 155
  Walter, 75, 132, 153
Steward of Annandale, 211
Stewarton, 182
Stewartry, 19, 212, 214
Stirling, Stirlingshire, 131, 132, 140, 144, 145, 150, 157, 171, 175, 180, 181, 292, 296, 297, 299, 300, 301, 302, 303, 304, 305, 306, 307, 310, 314, 315, 316, 319

Stitchill, 236

Stokloster, 326

Stonehouse, 170

Stormont, 80, 309

Stornoway, 274, 279, 282, 317

Strachur, 133, 151

Strathaven, 170, 175, 182

Strathbran, 281, 283

Strathbogie, 63, 184, 251, 254, 257, 260, 271

Strathconon, 276, 277, 278, 280, 281, 282, 283

Strathearn, earl of, 26–43 passim, 130, 190, 192, 193, 194, 195

   Ferteth, 28, 29

   Gilbert, 30, 31, 32, 35, 36

   Isabella, 190, 192, 193, 194, 195

   Malise, 28, 31, 32, 35, 36, 37, 38, 40

   Robert, 32, 40

   Robert, brother of the steward of, 38

Strathgarve, 281, 283

Strathisla, 63

Strathmore, earl of , 262, 320

Strathnaver, 280

Strathpeffer, 275, 277, 286

Strome Castle, 96, 112, 118, 277

Stronchuillin, 151

Strowan, 30

Stuart, John, of Darnley, 317

Style, 238

Suffolk, 65

Suffolk, Lord, 259

Sumburgh, 201, 202

Sussex, earl of, 214, 221, 222, 227

Sutherland, earl of, 175

Sutherland, Alexander, of Dunbeath, 199

Sutherland, Marjory, 199

Sweden, 326

Sween, Loch, 105

Sweetheart Abbey, xxii, 15, 212, 217

Swinton, family, 171

Tantallon Castle, 161

Tarbat, Tarbat Castle, 274, 278, 283, 284, 285, 288

Tarradale, 3, 80, 274, 277, 287

Tarbert Castle, 96, 98, 103, 109

Tarset Castle, 60, 75, 76, 77, 78

Tarvas, Thomas, abbot of Paisley, 19

Tay, River, 28, 63, 73, 74

Taymouth, 292, 307, 325

Tebas de Ardales, battle of, 190

Templar, order, 56

Terpersie Castle, 250, 257, 269

Terregles, 204, 217, 218, 221, 222, 292, 317

Teviotdale, 45, 206

Thirlestane Castle, 218

Thirlstane, Thomas de, 74

Thornhill, 320

Thornton Priory, 15

Thornton, Tynedale, 62

Threave Castle, 8, 9, 160, 164, 165, 166, 167, 168, 173, 174, 179, 185, 196, 204, 211, 212, 214, 215, 223, 224, 292, 297

Threewater Foot, 50

Throckmorton, Sir Nicholas, 218

Thurso, 3, 202

Tilt, Glen, 74

Tinnis, 247

Tinwald, 44, 49, 51, 53, 54, 211, 215

Tiree, 90, 92, 104

Tivoli, 311

Tolquhon Castle, 270, 306

Tom-a-chaisteal, 26, 30

Tongland, 212

Torbeck, 56

Torthorwald, 44, 46, 49, 50, 51, 52, 54, 224

   David de, 54

Touch, 238

Touraine, duchy of, 168, 171, 176, 262, 297

Tours, 168

Towie Barclay Castle, 250, 258

Traill, Walter, bishop of St Andrews, 7, 8

Trailtrow Hill, 212, 218, 220

Tranent, 74

Tremor, Robert de, 55, 58

Treshnish Isles, 88, 90, 98, 99, 119

Tuikisholm, 55

Tulibothil, 192

Tullibardine, 38

Tulloch, Thomas, bishop of Orkney, 192, 195

   William, bishop of Moray, 9

Tullochard, 281

Turnbull, William, 300

Turmuin, Turmor, 55

Turriff, 60

Tuscany, 251, 271

Tweed, River, Tweeddale, 50, 205

Tweedmouth, lord, 239

Tyndrum, 151

LORDSHIP AND
ARCHITECTURE
IN MEDIEVAL
AND
RENAISSANCE
SCOTLAND

❧

Tynedale, 62, 65, 75, 78, 79
   Uhtred of, 62
   Hextilda, daughter of Uhtred, 62
Tynhill, 222
Tyninghame House, 313
Tynnes, 245

Ugie, River, 69
Ulster, 85, 86, 88, 94, 104, 106, 317
Ulva, 109
Undweyn, 205, 228
Urbino, 137, 302
Urquhart, 80
Urquhart, family, 262, 280
   John, 262
Urr, Water of, 218

Valliscaulian, order, 87
Valognes, Isabella de, 62
Van der Goes, Hugo, 297
Van Nost, Jan, 320
Vass, family, of Lochslin, 278, 288
   John, 278
   Simon, 288
Vatican, 325
Vaus, George, bishop of Whithorn, 15
Vaux-le-Vicomte, 325
Verneuil, battle of, 171
Verrerie, La, 317
Versailles, 320
Vienne, River, 262
Villers Cotterets, 303

Wales, 78, 88
Wallace, William, 316
Walwick, Tynedale, 62
Wamphray, 44, 47, 50, 52, 54
Warbeck, Perkin, 270

Wardlaw, 284, 286, 314
Warmanbie, 55, 56
Warwickshire, 65
Waterford, 110
Wedderburn, 231, 232, 234, 238, 245, 247
Wedderlie, 232, 247
Weem, 195, 317
Weir, Katherine, 314
West Linton, 62, 67
West Lothian, 170, 174
West Renton, 247
West Reston, 245
'Westland', 155
Wester Pencaitland, 207
Wharton, Sir Thomas, 215
Whitchester, 247
Whitehill, 292, 318, 322, 323
Whiterig, 247
Whithorn, xxii, 3, 15, 16, 302
Whitwick, 79
Wigtown, Wigtownshire, 3, 9, 80, 147, 164,
   169, 170, 172, 179, 180, 182
Willamby, 55, 56
William I (the Lion), king of Scots, 4, 16,
   35, 36, 48, 62, 63, 67, 273, 286
Wilson, Peter, 155
Wiltshire, 65
Winton, 292, 313, 314
Wood, Andrew, 302, 324
Woodhall, 44, 56, 57, 319
Wyntoun, Andrew of, 4, 150
Wyre, 202
Wyseby, 55

Yarrow, 50, 173
Yester, 318
Yetholm, 245
Yorkshire, 62, 65